Contributions to Management Science

More information about this series at http://www.springer.com/series/1505

Ann-Kathrin Veenendaal

Toward a Better Understanding of Rule-Breaking Market Behavior

Insights from Performance Breakthroughs in Sports

 Springer

Ann-Kathrin Veenendaal
Steinbeis University Berlin
Berlin, Germany

Dissertation Steinbeis University Berlin, 2018
All illustrations except Figure 2.7 by Christiane Haas, Leipzig

ISSN 1431-1941   ISSN 2197-716X   (electronic)
Contributions to Management Science
ISBN 978-3-030-16106-4   ISBN 978-3-030-16107-1   (eBook)
https://doi.org/10.1007/978-3-030-16107-1

This Springer imprint is published by the registered company Springer Nature Switzerland AG.
The registered company address is: Gewerbestrasse 11, 6330 Cham, Switzerland

Foreword

This is an extraordinary dissertation.

To begin, the value of the work is exceptional. Although business innovation is widely desired, the reality is that many more organizations aspire to it than achieve it. This book provides a deep analysis of the most radical innovations, those that can both create practical novelty and overcome market resistance. The underappreciated challenge of succeeding despite habit-driven resistance is what makes these rule-breaking innovations. The dissertation draws general characteristics from actual cases of rule-breaking innovations. It then turns these into recommendations for specific actions that a firm's employees can use to facilitate rule-breaking innovations.

The methodological approach of the work is equally extraordinary. The author wisely chose the domain of sports where the success of rule-breaking innovations is made transparent through direct competition. At the same time, the market resistance in a sport can be intense as coaches and rule-makers fight change in the status quo. The cases under study are carefully chosen, systematically enriched with data, and subjected to an exemplary analysis.

Finally, the quality of the work is extraordinary. To extract useful guidelines for business managers from a different domain, rule-breaking innovations in sports, is a rare achievement. Further, unlike nearly all doctoral theses in marketing science, the work is not theory-testing but theory-building. Thus, besides its substantive contribution to greater innovation in business, the work provides a model of how a data-based, comprehensive theory can be constructed where none existed before.

I wish the work widespread visibility in both business and science. It can inspire every reader interested in disruptive behavioral innovations and encourage the scientifically minded to pursue unusual ways of understanding complex phenomena.

Berlin   Helmut Schneider
November 2018

Contents

List of Abbreviations

3M	Minnesota Mining and Manufacturing Company
AAU	Amateur Athletic Union
APA	American Psychological Association
BBC	British Broadcasting Corporation
CAIB	Columbia Accident Investigation Board
CEO	Chief Executive Officer
DNA	Deoxyribonucleic acid
e.g.	example given
et al.	et alii, et aliae, et alia ("and others")
etc.	et cetera ("and the rest")
FAZ	Frankfurter Allgemeine Zeitung (German newspaper)
FIN	Finland
FINA	Fédération Internationale de Natation (International Swimming Federation)
FIS	Fédération Internationale de Ski (International Ski Federation)
i.e.	id est ("that is")
IAAF	International Association of Athletics Federations
ibid.	ibīdem ("in the same place")
IBM	International Business Machines Corporation
IOC	International Olympic Committee
IQ	Intelligence quotient
ISHOF	International Swimming Hall of Fame
IT	Italy
Jr.	junior
LA	Los Angeles
MIT	Massachusetts Institute of Technology
n.d.	no date
NAAU	National Amateur Athletic Union
NASA	National Aeronautics and Space Administration
NBA	National Basketball Association

NCAA	National Collegiate Athletic Association
Newark AC	Newark Athletic Club
OECD	Organisation for Economic Co-operation and Development
p.	page
para.	paragraph
PE	Physical education
POL	Poland
pp.	pages
QWERTY	keyboard layout for most keyboards in the U.S.
R&D	Research and Development
resist.	resistance
Sr.	senior
SWE	Sweden
U.S.	United States
USATF	USA Track & Field
USC	University of Southern California
USMS	United States Masters Swimming
viz.	videlicet ("namely")
vs.	versus ("against, turned")

List of Figures

List of Tables

Chapter 1
Relevance and Current Perspectives

Abstract This chapter introduces the research on rule-breaking market behavior. It includes the relevance of the phenomenon; the objectives and research questions; and an outline of the methodological approach.

1.1 A Non-technological Perspective on Breakthrough Innovations

The twenty-first-century business landscape, especially regarding but not limited to the 35-member countries of the Organization for Economic Co-operation and Development (OECD), is characterized by rapid change, fierce global competition, and an increasingly complex and demanding environment. Some minor local difficulties notwithstanding, Europe, from 1945 to the present day, is witnessing its longest period of peace ever. In this context, at the societal level, innovation is a vital requirement for continuing economic growth and social progress (e.g. OECD 2015; The World Bank and OECD 2009). By delivering important benefits to an increasingly wide range of the population, innovation significantly improves people's lives (Ahlstrom 2010). Should the stream of innovation dry up, the economy will settle into a "stationary state" with little or no growth (Metcalfe 1998, as quoted in Fagerberg 2006, p. 20). At the organizational level, too, it is a commonplace to assert that innovation is crucial to a firm's competitive advantage (e.g. Ireland and Hitt 1999; Porter 1990). The growing importance of innovation as a source of organizational performance, success, and long-term survival has been increasingly highlighted in the conceptual and empirical literature (Amabile and Pratt 2016; Anderson et al. 2014; Shalley and Zhou 2008). In fact, innovation is considered one of the major topics of interest across management, economics, business research, sociology and social psychology (Hauser et al. 2006; Martin 2012; Salter and Alexy 2014). However, gaining competitive advantage from innovation is becoming more and more difficult to maintain for extended periods of time. Thus, companies are increasingly looking for novel impactful ways to operate in the market.

© Springer Nature Switzerland AG 2019
A.-K. Veenendaal, *Toward a Better Understanding of Rule-Breaking Market Behavior*, Contributions to Management Science,
https://doi.org/10.1007/978-3-030-16107-1_1

Starting with Schumpeter's (1911) seminal work on the central role of innovation, research in this area has continuously grown. Especially over recent decades, scholars from various disciplines including sociology, psychology, history, philosophy and business administration have devoted attention to innovation to an increasing degree, leading to a plethora of different innovation ontologies and research dimensions (Fagerberg 2006; Fagerberg and Verspagen 2009). To address the challenging breadth of innovation research, scholars typically focus on certain facets of innovation such as specific innovation types (product, process, service, business model, technological, organizational, etc.), stages in the innovation process (generation, diffusion, adoption, implementation), and innovations' consequences (for the firm, industry, community, economy), mostly at one level of analysis (individual, team, organization, industry, economy) (Damanpour and Aravind 2012). Typically, innovation is primarily associated with the domains of technology and the natural, medical and life sciences. The breadth of innovation reaches far beyond the more technical domains, however. As the pace of innovation accelerates, human insight and behavior continues to gain decisive importance in the context of innovation (Sluiter 2017).

Often, innovation takes place within a set of widely accepted rules that are clearly understood, and companies try to innovate by doing what they do better (Tidd 2006). For instance, these accepted rules relate to "industry recipes" that form and influence the commonsense understanding of a particular industry or market. The notion of *doing things better* is typically related to a firm's efficiency and productivity efforts. Abernathy (1978) was the first to suggest that the focus on productivity gains contributes positively to performance outcomes but at the same time often inhibits a company's flexibility and ability to innovate. He coined this the productivity dilemma (Benner and Tushman 2003; see Backhaus and Schneider forthcoming, for an elaborate description in the context of strategic marketing). Apart from these rather incremental efficiency-related efforts, occasionally something happens that fundamentally redefines the common framework of widely accepted rules and causes basic conditions, such as technology, markets, social, and regulatory mechanisms, to shift dramatically.[1] Usually, such dramatic breakthrough shifts are the result of *doing things differently*. Illustrated in a David vs. Goliath-fashion,[2] doing things differently would mean to not fight the competition with the same slightly sharper weapon but to use a completely different approach to succeed. While research on innovation has predominantly followed a technological imperative with many theories and models of innovation based on technologically induced change (Černe et al. 2016; Crossan

---

[1]In his original theory of innovation, Schumpeter (1942) refers to this fundamental reframing process as a process of creative destruction (see Chap. VII "The Process of Creative Destruction").

[2]The story of David and Goliath can be found in First Samuel 17 of the Bible. It tells that Goliath, a nine-foot soldier heavily armed, was defeated by a small shepherd, David, with just a sling and a stone. Focusing on the fact that power does not necessarily have to be physical might but can come in other forms. David substituted speed and surprise for strength. While the story about David and Goliath is primarily used to refer to situations of improbable victory, as when an underdog surprisingly defeats a giant, it also nicely illustrates the potential success resulting from a—seemingly simple—change of behavioral standards (Gladwell 2013).

and Apaydin 2010; Damanpour 2014; Damanpour and Aravind 2012; Keupp et al. 2012), this work focuses on a non-technological perspective. That is, to perpetuate the above-stated example, just like David approached his challenge without focusing on heavy or novel technological equipment, the focus lies on deviating from fundamental assumptions and changing how one would usually behave. In short, this work is focusing on behavioral innovations that primarily pay attention to effectiveness parameters, involving rather high degrees of change, by solving existing problems in a previously unknown form. The ability to create revolutionary innovations can represent a sustainable competitive advantage for firms. Despite its strategic importance, however, little is known about the process by which innovators achieve these valuable breakthroughs (Mascitelli 2000).

Given its widely acknowledged importance, one might expect the context of innovation to have a clear meaning, a rich tradition of theoretical development, and a clear related body of empirical findings. Quite the contrary, conceptual and theoretical work on innovation has been relatively sparse and research is fragmented (e.g. Anderson et al. 2014; Klausen 2017). According to Klausen (2017), Schumpeter's (1934) fundamental work still remains unique in its scope and depth. Carlile and Christensen (2004, p. 1) also allude to the concerns regarding the "paucity of theory that is intellectually rigorous, practically useful, and able to stand the tests of time and changing circumstances" that some of the most respected members of our research profession, such as Simon (1976) and Solow (1985), have long been expressing. Calls for more organic, genuine theory-building contributions are not limited to literature on creativity and innovation but seem to pertain to scholars across a wide variety of disciplines. In marketing in particular, MacInnis (2011) and Yadav (2010, 2014) prominently highlight the critical but neglected role of conceptual contributions for the vitality of knowledge development in the field.

The fundamental question for innovation research is to explain how innovations occur (Fagerberg 2006). However, in his comprehensive review of the field, Fagerberg (2006, p. 3) points out that the innovation process has been treated more or less like a "black box". Hennessey and Amabile (2010, p. 569) add that a more detailed understanding of the creative process is vital if strides are to be made in the sciences and humanities. A further challenge in the context of creativity and innovation arises from so-called lay theories, which are everyday informal theories and often implicit beliefs that lay people hold about a phenomenon and its causes or consequences (Ritter and Rietzschel 2017, p. 95). Lay beliefs may partly be informed by research but also often take the shape of stereotypes and "everybody knows that . . ." discussions that are encountered in daily conversations and popular publications (Ritter and Rietzschel 2017). While lay beliefs can certainly be encountered in several areas (for further examples see Zedelius et al. 2017), creativity seems particularly receptive because it is of such great appeal and relevance to people that they strive to make sense of the phenomenon (Ritter and Rietzschel 2017). Baas et al. (2015) demonstrated that people have strong beliefs about creativity that are often incomplete and not in line with science. In the underlying context, this can become problematic when such lay beliefs wrongly inform the choices that managers and other corporate deciders make.

The starting point for this work is a real-world phenomenon. Thus, the focal perspective has been motivated by "informed curiosity" (Rozin 2001) emerging from the observation of several organizational examples, some of which are outlined subsequently for illustrative purposes.

Ryanair re-invented the European airline industry by deviating from existing structures and conventions: Provincial instead of major airports, direct flights instead of complex route systems, focus on short distance instead of long distance, just one model of aircraft instead of a float consisting of several aircraft types, no business class, no airport lounge, no check in terminals, no complimentary service on board, no gratis inflight entertainment, and advertisements on the back of the seats. By acting this way, CEO Michael O'Leary did not just cut cost dramatically but also focused on different income sources, envisioning that, in the end, tickets may come at no charge. Although the ideas were not completely new (Southwest Airlines), these changes not only kept Ryanair financially viable but also lead to unprecedented consequences for the whole European transportation industry (Day and Schoemaker 2004; Meffert 2009). The energy drink Red Bull created an entirely new category in the global beverage market. Other than existing soft drinks, Red Bull focused on effect (being physically and mentally fit, wide awake) instead of taste. The original working-class drink from Thailand conquered the broad masses and became a top selling world brand (Spindler 2016). The QWERTY myth reportedly states that our dominant keyboard deliberately neglects the most important criteria of keyboard design: When certain combinations of keys on early typewriters (which were designed according to research on efficient typing) were struck quickly, the type bars often jammed. Instead of solving this mechanical problem by improving technical features, the inventors simply redesigned the keyboard in order to make people type slower (Jánszky and Jenzowsky 2010). Cirque du Soleil little by little reinvented the circus: No animals, more intellectual wit, more comfortable tents with high quality sound and lights, introduction of new circus arts, integrative performances following a leading theme, and multiple productions in several locations. Hence, Guy Laliberté established a new kind of entertainment by linking elements from circus and theatre, growing into the largest theatrical producer in the world (Spindler 2016). IKEA revolutionized the furniture industry by highly integrating the customer into the purchasing process. Overall, around 80% of the process steps are outsourced this way. The shopper chooses the piece of furniture, picks it up from the warehouse shelf, ships and assembles it themselves, to name just a few (Jungbluth 2006). In 1937, trucker Malcom McLean initiated a transformation of the global economy by questioning the way cargo is handled at shipping docks. At that time, all the shippers assumed that the only way to get more productive at transferring cargo across the ocean was to build faster ships. However, McLane suggested that instead of building faster boats, build faster docks, unloading whole trailers, not unloading and reloading every single piece. It took him 20 more years to convince anyone else that his idea was right, but he finally cut shipping costs significantly and transformed not only the shipping economy but also the way the whole global economy works (Duhigg et al. n.d.).

This list could potentially go on and on: Think of self-check-out at the supermarket instead of cashiers, Amazon helping people save time instead of Wal-Mart helping them save money (The Economist 2016), and making prices dynamic rather than fixed (as, for example, commonly practiced by hotels and airlines).

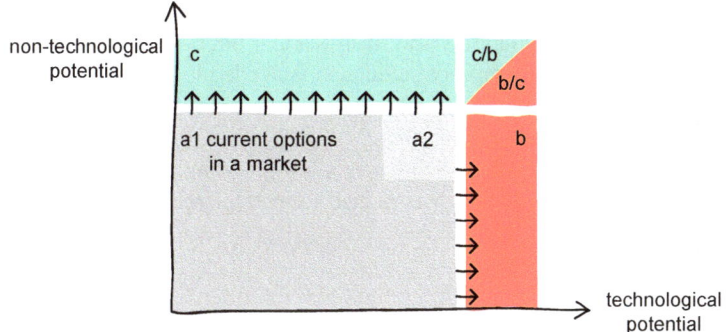

Note: b,c = ways to expand the current options in a market, b indicates technological innovations, c indicates non-technological innovations; see textual description for further explication

Fig. 1.1   Schematic conceptualization of the focal perspective, variant 1 (source: author)

To more specifically depict the above-explained and explicated phenomenon that builds the foundation of this work, the focal perspective is conceptualized in Fig. 1.1.

The large grey field *a* symbolizes all current options in a given market, where a_1 are used options and a_2 are idle options. The options are modeled as a function of the technological potential on the x-axis and the non-technological, behavioral potential on the y-axis. Under the assumption that a firm has exploited all existing options in field a $(a_1 + a_2)$, there are three analytical ways to expand the field, namely, to be innovative. First, companies can develop novel technologies or adapt existing technologies from other areas. In the picture, this option is displayed with field *b*. The red color symbolizes that this option is not part of the underlying work. For instance, this would be innovation resulting from or closely related with digitalization. Second, companies can develop novel non-technological ways of thinking and behaving in the market. In the picture, this option is displayed with field *c*. The green color indicates that this option is part of the underlying work. According to this conceptualization, a third way to extend the options of a company in a market is a combination of the two aforementioned parameters. The determining factor of whether the option is considered as part of this work or not is the order of occurrence. That is, when new ways of behaving lead to the development of a new technology (*c/b*), the new option is considered part of this work, but when the development of new technologies is the major trigger for a novel non-technological way of behaving in the market (*b/c*), it is not considered part of this work. In other words, the red fields basically stand for what is currently impossible from a technological perspective, and green stands for those options that simply have not been done before. The latter is exactly what this work is concerned with.

In short, there is a pivotal and growing need for novel and impactful ways to create a competitive advantage. Moving from that assumption, this work draws on and analyzes a real-world phenomenon that is considered relevant and worthy of inquiry: The pursuit of innovative paths above and beyond technological solutions. Anecdotal evidence from a long list of corporate examples tells compelling success stories of how companies addressed the challenge of expanding the alleged space of opportunities, evidently leading to a change in the dominant market logics. While the importance of gaining perspective and questioning what one knows has likely increased, such instances of seeing things in a different light and changing prevailing assumptions remains a challenging and insufficiently understood endeavor. Thus, a systematic investigation of empirical evidence is needed to recognize patterns that help us to better understand the process of how novel insight with breakthrough character comes into play. Based on the phenomenon's unique focal characteristics and inspired by Backhaus and Schneider (2009), such purpose and impactful deviation from behavioral standards is related to as rule-breaking market behavior.

1.2 Rule-Breaking Market Behavior and Related Constructs

In order to get a systematic understanding of the underlying phenomenon's specifics, a first look is taken at the literal meaning of the two fundamental components *rule* and *breaking*. In line with the Oxford English Dictionary, rule is interpreted as *the normal or customary state of things* and break as *an interruption of continuity or uniformity*, the suffix -ing denoting the action, an instance of this, or its result.

In other words, rules here refer to behavioral standards, to established routines, to the way things are usually done, for instance how tasks are fulfilled, how problems are solved, and how knowledge is learned. Breaking these rules then denotes a purposeful departure from behavioral standards in the sense of doing things differently. Under the fundamental assumption that rule-based behavior incurs the risk of mindless application, it may lead to inertial tendencies and a possible neglect of potential ways to achieve competitive advantage.

The term *market* in rule-breaking market behavior, in a broad sense, refers to the business management and strategic marketing context of this work. In marketing, the market is viewed either as a locus of exchange or as an aggregation of consumers (Kotler and Keller 2014, p. 30). In the traditional, company-centric conception of value creation, the market's role is value exchange and extraction; it is considered the "target" for a company's offerings (Prahalad and Ramaswamy 2004, p. 6).

Deviations from existing behavioral standards in a particular market are likely to open up new business opportunities by going beyond conventionalities, but at the same time challenge existing market players to reframe what they are doing in the light of new conditions. In a figurative sense, what is termed rule-breaking market behavior is also often referred to as changing the "rules of the game" (e.g. Tidd 2006, p. 4).

Apart from this more general introductory description, to fully capture the distinctive dimensions of the phenomenon, existing concepts in the domain of innovation research and a thorough analysis of real-life phenomena are drawn on. A detailed outline of this analytical process deriving the conceptual features will be given in Sect. 2.1. The result of what has been distilled can be summarized in the following core operational definition:

> Rule-breaking market behavior denotes a legal, non-technological innovation that radically changes the dominant logic of a market.

This definition entails four distinct characteristics that must necessarily apply in order for a phenomenon to qualify as rule-breaking. The first two features are related to the input, as in the roots of the innovation, and the other two to the output, as in the impact of the innovation. First of all, rule-breaking market behavior refers to innovations that are of the non-technological kind, as in new ways of thinking and behaving instead of technological progress. Put differently, rule-breaking market behavior can also be thought of as insight innovation. Second, the new way to think and behave must comply with formal rules: it must be legal. If the innovative attempt were illegal (i.e. could be judicially sanctioned), it does not qualify as rule-breaking market behavior. In other words, the new way to behave does not deviate from exogenous regulations that govern a particular market but from endogenous behavioral standards that simply exist and guide behaviors without being further reflected on. Third, such new ways of thinking and behaving are conceptualized as typically leading to changes that are closer to the radical (than the incremental) end of the innovation-degree of the newness-continuum. Thus, rule-breaking market behavior is considered to be both fundamentally different and substantially better than prior approaches. Fourth, such new ways of thinking and behaving must be collectively adopted in order to meet the requirements for being a pure version of rule-breaking market behavior. Put differently, rule-breaking market behavior is not considered to be a rather idiosyncratic style that is just embraced by a small number of agents and not relevant to the majority of the market but thought of as eventually becoming (one of) the dominant approaches in a market (e.g. a new product resulting from rule-breaking behavior that holds a substantial market share). As mentioned above, all features will be discussed more comprehensively at the beginning of Chap. 2.

The term rule-breaking market behavior has not been chosen for the sake of introducing yet another name for an already existing construct[3] but to account for the unique specificities of the underlying phenomenon, which, in this particular combination, to the best knowledge of the author, do not find systematic consideration in the literature. Though researchers have long been interested in the development of breakthrough innovation in a broader sense (i.e. under several different theoretical umbrellas and labels), it is believed that rule-breaking market behavior adds value to existing discussions because it captures an important but systematically understudied way to create competitive advantage. Studying rule-breaking market behavior, with its emphasis on purposeful behavioral deviation from entrenched standards helps understand any individual's possibilities in the important quest for profitable change from a novel and useful perspective.

Suddaby (2010) points out that "constructs are rarely created de novo. Rather, they are usually the result of creative building upon pre-existing constructs, which themselves refer to other extant constructs, in an ongoing web of referential relationships" (p. 350). Therefore, what is conceptualized as rule-breaking market behavior is, to

---

[3]Larsen and How Bong (2016) give insight into how management and other fields suffer from construct fallacies such as jingle (two constructs with identical names referring to two different phenomena) and jangle (two labels referring to the same phenomena).

varying degrees, related to but different from a number of other scholarly discussions. Thus, associated phenomena will be outlined and briefly compared in terms of their similarities and differences with the conceptualization of rule-breaking market behavior.

It is nearly impossible to review all existing constructs that are broadly related to behavioral breakthrough change. To further the understanding of this work's focus, those phenomena that occurred in the course of the research process but which will not be covered in later parts of this work (i.e. areas that are directly related to innovation research such as business model innovation and ambidexterity theory) are briefly discussed in Table 1.1. The review comprises routines (routine dynamics), habits (habit breaking), normality (positive deviance), endogenous growth theory, technology life cycles, path dependency (path breaking), disruption research, opportunity recognition, divergent thinking and lateral thinking. The gist of the subsequent discussion will be summarized thereafter.

In summary, three main aspects become evident after having briefly reviewed the various research areas above. First of all, it stands out that bottom-up empirical approaches, even though considered desirable, are the exception rather than the norm. Second, it can be stated that it seems that the constructs are typically more concerned with describing problems rather than offering solutions. Many resources are spent on construct definition and single effect studies rather than gaining a systematic procedural understanding of the phenomena's basic underlying mechanisms. Especially, the individual processes at the root of the phenomena seem to be poorly understood. For instance, there is a larger focus on the study of norms or path dependency than on the potentially positive effects when deviating from norms or breaking existing paths. And third, regarding the content-related distance to rule-breaking market behavior, it can be summarized that all constructs are somehow related, but none of the concepts go along with all four features that are characteristic of rule-breaking market behavior. The perspectives are either embedded in technological instead of behavioral literature, focus more on evolutionary than revolutionary changes, or are concerned with another level of analysis. Moreover, links to the creativity and innovation literature, as part of what the underlying work classifies, are frequently missing. All in all, some of the discussions may give helpful guidance at later points in this work, but basically, it can be concluded that existing research does not satisfactorily solve the underlying puzzle by answering the focal research questions. Therefore, a contribution shall be made with the help of the following research design.

1.3 Research Design

1.3.1 Research Objectives

In phenomenon-driven exploratory research questions, it is most critical to frame the research regarding the importance of the phenomenon and the lack of plausible existing theory. The research questions are then typically more "*broadly* scoped to give the researcher more flexibility" (Eisenhardt and Graebner 2007, p. 26). Gerring

Table 1.1 Brief review of related discussions

Related construct	Brief description and differentiation from rule-breaking market behavior	Exemplary literature
Routines as a source of change/ routine dynamics	Routines can be defined as a "pattern of behaviour that is followed repeatedly, but is subject to change if conditions change" (Winter 1964, pp. 263–264). Building on theories of structuration, works on routines are primarily focusing on persistence and stability. In the context of routine dynamics, internal dynamics of routines that contribute to both stability and change in organizations are studied (Feldman et al. 2016, p. 505). This latter perspective postulates a recursive relation between routine participants' behavior and the rules, principles and concepts that guide them in doing so, explaining how routines evolve continuously as current performances are adapted to ongoing circumstances (Bucher and Langley 2016). Routine dynamics are distinct from the idea of rule-breaking market behavior because discussions about routine dynamics are embedded in an evolutionary change (continuous improvement) or adaptation to exogenous shocks context rather than a revolutionary framework. Some more recent studies are trying to go beyond local variations of routines: that puzzle has not yet been solved sufficiently, however (Bucher and Langley 2016).	Becker (2004), Feldman and Pentland (2003), Feldman et al. (2016), Nelson and Winter (1982), and Pentland Brian et al. (2012)
Disrupting or breaking habits	Also referred to as the basis and individual analogue of organizational routines (e.g. Hodgson 2008; Nelson and Winter 1982), habits can be interpreted as "... learned sequences of acts that have become automatic responses to specific cues, and are functional in obtaining certain goals or end states" (Verplanken and Aarts 1999, p. 104). More specifically, the defining quality of habit is "the automaticity and efficiency of behavior occurring in stable contexts" (Verplanken 2006, pp. 639–640). Habits require no thought and in consequence people tend to repeat well-practiced actions regardless of their intentions or normative beliefs. Research on habits is mostly concerned with understanding habits and habit formation rather than the quest of how to break habits (e.g. Wood and Rünger 2016). Bottom-up research on how to change habits in the context of innovations is sparse. When comparing habits with the underlying idea of rules, habits are more focused on individual behaviors rather than universally accepted behavioral standards in a market. However, habits will be further addressed later in this work.	Aarts and Dijksterhuis (2000), Aarts et al. (1998), Glăveanu (2012), Labrecque et al. (2017), Neal et al. (2012), Verplanken and Wood (2006), Wendy and Neal (2009), Wood et al. (2002, 2005), Wood and Rünger (2016)

(continued)

Table 1.1 (continued)

Related construct	Brief description and differentiation from rule-breaking market behavior	Exemplary literature
Norm(ality)/constructive or positive deviance	A social norm is a social construction reflecting collectively shared behavioral rules and regulations that govern how people ought to behave in particular situations (e.g. Bicchieri 2006). Individuals usually conform to norms because they experience utility from complying with what is collectively judged to be appropriate (Krupka et al. 2017). Even for those wanting to be different, norms serve as a guide. What is viewed as normal can evolve, dependent on both timeframe and environment going along with changing societal standards and norms. Any violation of or departure from norms is regarded as deviance (Dodge 1985). Deviance is one of the most studied topics in sociology and has traditionally focused on negative social phenomena such as morally objectionable, forbidden, and disvalued behaviors (Spreitzer and Sonenshein 2004). It, therefore, continues to be negatively connoted and is typically associated with criminals, sexual predators and other harmful behaviors at the margins of society (Herington and van de Fliert 2018). In organizational research, too, it has been primarily argued that deviating from norms is harmful, e.g. fraud or theft (Robinson and Bennett 1995). More recently it has been acknowledged, however, that certain kinds of deviance can also positively contribute to organizational effectiveness (Vadera et al. 2013). Termed constructive or positive workplace deviance, these behaviors are defined to violate organizational norms with the intent of helping the organization (Galperin 2012). Creative performance can be considered one of several different kinds of constructive deviance (Vadera et al. 2013). One example would be the violation of a managerial order to stop working on a new idea as it was the case with Pontiac's Fiero or 3 M's tape slitters (Mainemelis 2010). Despite the increasing importance of constructive deviance in organizations the majority of research still focuses on destructive deviant behaviors. Knowledge about the common causes and processes of constructive deviance is largely limited (Dahling and Gutworth 2017; Vadera et al. 2013). As Mainemelis (2010, p. 558) points out, "creativity and deviance researchers have rarely exchanged findings and insights to date". In a broad sense, every innovation begins as a deviation from existing norms. When these norms are not thought of as social norms in the sense of general values to maintain societal stability such as fairness,	Theoretical origins of deviance (Durkheim 1985 [1964]; Merton 1938) and positive deviance (Wilkins 1964) in sociology (Galperin 2003, 2012; Herington and van de Fliert 2018; Mertens et al. 2016; Spreitzer and Sonenshein 2004; Vadera et al. 2013; Warren 2003)

(continued)

Table 1.1   (continued)

Related construct	Brief description and differentiation from rule-breaking market behavior	Exemplary literature
	cooperation, or reciprocity; however, this is not what rule-breaking market behavior is about. It may be that rule-breaking market offerings also affect such values, but it is not to suggest that rule-breakers should deviate from fundamental societal merits. The idea is more to find different constructive ways to operate within the framework of generally accepted societal values by engaging in behaviors for the greater (corporate) good.	
Endogenous growth theory	As rule-breaking market behavior is under-stood as deviating from endogenous rules, a brief examination of possible similarities to endogenous growth theory seems appropriate. Discussions under the term endogenous growth encompass a vast body of theoretical and empirical work that emerged in the 1980s and stands in contrast to the neoclassical growth theory that focuses on technology as the engine of an economy's growth (Grossman and Helpman 1994). The endogenous growth theory posits that economic growth "is an endogenous out-come of an economic system, not the result of forces that impinge from outside", with the goal to "uncover the private and public sector choices that cause the rate of growth of the residual to vary across countries" (Romer 1994, p. 3). Economic theory models economic growth on a societal level, e.g. with their AK-model as the simplest endogenous model. The theory is distinct from endogenous rules in rule-breaking market behavior in some respects, such as level of analysis (economy vs. firm) and fundamental goals (modelling vs. procedural understanding).	Romer (1994)
Technology life cycle literature	Models of technical change use a life cycle metaphor to describe technological progress in an industry over time, starting with a technological discontinuity. The technology life cycle literature has, for the most part, neglected cognitive factors (Kaplan and Tripsas 2008) that would have been interesting for a better understanding of rule-breaking market behavior.	Kaplan and Tripsas (2008), Murmann and Frenken (2006), Suarez (2004), Tushman and Anderson (1986), Tushman and Rosenkopf (1992), and Utterback (1974)
Path dependency/ path breaking	The concept of organizational path dependence is used to explain change-inhibiting forces such as organizational rigidities, stickiness and structural inertia (Sydow et al. 2009). Path dependency stresses the imprinting effects of the past on future organizational behavior, with decisions being conceived of	Current perspectives (David 2001; Garud et al. 2010; Jean-Philippe and Rodolphe 2010; Schreyögg 2014;

(continued)

Table 1.1 (continued)

Related construct	Brief description and differentiation from rule-breaking market behavior	Exemplary literature
	as historically conditioned ("history matters") (Sydow et al. 2009). Another core concept lies in the dynamics of self-reinforcing social mechanisms, such as coordination, complementarity, learning, and adaptive expectation effects (Sydow et al. 2009). Path dependence is conceptualized to lead "into an organizational lock-in, understood as a corridor of limited scope of action that is strategically inefficient" (Sydow et al. 2009, p. 704). The possibility of escaping from or breaking a path depends on interrupting the logic and specific energy of the self-reinforcing patterns of organizational processes (Schreyögg 2014; Sydow et al. 2009). It is argued on a broad level that path dissolution may occur through unforeseen exogenous forces like shocks, catastrophes, or crises, which, by shaking the system, cause the organization to break away from the path (Arthur 1994). Furthermore, the literature refers to potential coincidental unlocking of organizational paths as a by-product of other decisions (Castaldi and Dosi 2006) and an insidious path dissolution by new organizational members because of their incomplete socialization (Tolbert and Zucker 1996). Apart from these more general statements, it is posited that "the conditions that are conducive to path dependence and possible ways of unlocking paths await further exploration" (Sydow et al. 2009, p. 705). A theory of path-breaking that could systematically show how to break paths does not yet exist (Schreyögg 2014). Starting off from a historical account, as discussed in the context of path dependence, could be one of many possible ways to get to rule-breaking market behavior. While both rule-breaking market behavior and path dependence are examined from a process perspective, the study of path dependence and path breaking primarily draws on studies of technological paths (fur further references, see Sydow et al. 2009). Path dependence started out as a study of technological standardization (Schreyögg 2014) and is anchored as a key concept in the genre of evolutionary economics.	Schreyögg and Sydow 2011; Sydow et al. 2009) exemplary early theoretical foundations (Arthur 1989, 1994; North 1990)
Disruption research	The theory of disruptive innovation has been introduced and popularized by Clayton Christensen in (1995, 1997) and is considered a powerful way of thinking about innovation-driven growth (Christensen et al. 2015). The theory has been called "one of the most influential modern business ideas" and is widely accepted far beyond the business world	Development of the fields intellectual core (Abernathy and Clark 1985; Bower and Christensen 1995; Christensen 1992, 1997, 2006;

(continued)

Table 1.1 (continued)

Related construct	Brief description and differentiation from rule-breaking market behavior	Exemplary literature
	(King and Baatartogtokh 2015). In a nutshell, disruption theory originally described a process in which a smaller company with fewer resources successfully challenges established incumbent businesses. More specifically, while incumbent companies are focusing on their most demanding customer segment and neglect or ignore the needs of others, these others are then targeted by new entrants who often deliver a cheaper, unproven or inferior alternative to mainstream products and services (low-end of the market) and then move upmarket. When the incumbent's mainstream customers adopt these offerings, disruption has occurred (e.g. Christensen et al. 2015). Today, disruption is seldom related to the original tenets of the theory but rather resembles a catch-all phrase used to describe any situation in which an industry is shaken up and previously successful companies stumble ("too many people who speak of 'disruption' have not read a serious book or article on the subject", (Christensen et al. 2015, p. 4). Moreover, the formal theory has aroused plenty of rich debate within academia, for instance about the definition and scope of disruptive phenomena (King and Baatartogtokh 2015; Yu and Hang 2010). Christensen's initial research was mainly based on the hard disk drive industry in the 1970s and 1980s (Christensen and Bower 1996). That is, besides the existing challenges with regard to disruptive innovation theory, that the fundamental locus of research (technology management) is different from the conceptualization of rule-breaking market behavior in this work.	Tushman and Anderson 1986) Exemplary reviews (Danneels 2004; Markides 2006; Yu and Hang 2010)
Entrepreneurship, opportunity recognition	According to the key references listed on the right, opportunity recognition is a key construct in entrepreneurship where opportunities are said to be triggered by environmental changes and recognized by individuals. Opportunity recognition involves the act of perceiving a possibility to create a new business or to significantly improve existing business to generate new profit potential associated with the cognitive processes of perception, discovery, creation, pattern recognition, and their interaction with new, novel, or ill-defined problems or situations requiring creativity. Opportunities involve identifying new combinations, new means, new ends, or new means-ends relationships that have the possibility of generating a profit for a new or existing business. Six influential factors are considered: Prior knowledge, social capital, cognition/personality traits, environmental	Baron (2006), Eckhardt and Shane (2003), Sardeshmukh and Smith-Nelson (2012), and Shane (2000) Recent review (Mary George et al. 2016)

(continued)

Table 1.1 (continued)

Related construct	Brief description and differentiation from rule-breaking market behavior	Exemplary literature
	conditions, alertness, and systematic search. In addition to the fact that key questions remain about what factors facilitate the recognition of opportunities, the perspective taken in opportunity recognition re-search is rather of the exogenous than endogenous kind: an individual is considered to potentially exploit technological, political and regulatory, social and demographic opportunities. Moreover, many discussions seem to revolve around the question of why some people and not others discover and exploit opportunities. Such a distinction across individual differences is not made in this work, however.	
Divergent thinking	The psychologist Guilford (1950, 1957, 1968) was the first to coin the terms divergent and convergent thinking. He defined divergent thinking as the ability to generate a large number (fluency) and wide assortment (flexibility) of original ideas or solutions (Titus 2018). Divergent thinking is considered to be one indicator of an individual's creative potential, meaning that someone can perform well on a test of divergent thinking but never actually perform in a creative fashion (Runco and Acar 2012). Divergent thinking tests are the major instrument for measuring an individual's creative potential (Zeng et al. 2011). As divergent thinking is a cognitive approach (a matter of cognitive style and ability; Anderson et al. 2014) leading to original ideas, it is more narrowly defined than the notion of rule-breaking market behavior. Most certainly, such thinking styles may be one mechanism of importance for the process of rule-breaking market behavior but the research design is more broadly oriented and not limited to this aspect only.	Baer (1993), Titus (2018), and Torrance (1962)
Lateral thinking	British psychologist Edward de Bono introduced lateral thinking in (1970), as a technique for creative and more effective problem solving by reformulating the problem or viewing if from a different angle (Colman 2015). Besides lateral thinking, de Bono developed several further techniques for deliberative creative thinking, such as the principle of Six Thinking Hats (Burgh 2014). Again, as in the previous example, it can be outlined that cognitive techniques comprise only one aspect of the process of rule-breaking market behavior, which is intended to be understood more holistically.	De Bono (1970, 2010)

(2006) further specifies that research, which is concerned with explaining a puzzling phenomenon without prior preconceptions, also described as Y-centered research, is much more open-ended. That is, a certain degree of openness regarding the study's outcome has been an inherent element throughout the underlying research endeavor.

Broadly defined, the overall objective of this work is to *systematically better understand the nature and process of the real-world phenomenon rule-breaking market behavior*. The realistic intention is to provide useful impulses for both scholars and practitioners alike and less to formally develop "The Theory of Rule-Breaking Market Behavior". Two overarching motives have been guiding the research process: To offer companies a new way to generate a revolutionary competitive advantage, and to address the mismatch between theory-building and theory-testing studies in management and marketing science.

Based on that, the following four specific research questions guide and will be discussed throughout the subsequent analysis.

1. What are the constitutive key characteristics of rule-breaking market behavior?

    First, it is essential to describe and conceptualize the underlying multifaceted phenomenon of rule-breaking market behavior in order to subsequently identify distinct cases for the empirical analysis. Common denominators are found within the extant literature that may serve as a foundation to understanding the nature of rule-breaking market behavior in a systematic and comprehensive way.

    While this initial step deals with the "what" component of theoretical contributions, the primary focus of the study is effectively further narrowed to the "how" of rule-breaking market behavior (see Whetten 1989, on the What, How, Why, Who, Where, and When as ingredients of theory).

2. What insight can be uncovered regarding the process of rule-breaking market behavior?

    From all four research questions, this question is the focal and most important one. The question aims at resolving of what the general creative and innovative process to rule-breaking market behavior is constitutive. Getting a better understanding of *how* to create rule-breaking market behavior is attempted. As outlined above, research endeavors often focus on descriptions of problems rather than solutions. By placing the emphasis on gaining a procedural understanding of a phenomenon, this is intended to be different here. Three analytical steps are involved that cover the following more specific enquiries.

    (a) Which individual mechanisms in the process of rule-breaking behavior can be derived from the empirical study?

        To begin with, it is of interest to get rich descriptions of particular empirical instances of rule-breaking behavior. This relates to the lessons that can be learned from individual examples of rule-breaking behavior, which are interesting and inspiring as such. Basically, this is a preparatory question for the much more central part (b).

    (b) Which generalizable patterns characterize the developmental process of rule-breaking behavior?

Most importantly, it is strived to reveal and capture a set of generalizable factors that are characteristic of the process leading to rule-breaking behavior. Such generative mechanisms are intended to be derived from possible patterns that can be observed in the empirical data.

(c) How do the empirical insights relate to existing theoretical frameworks?

Principally, step (c) is complementary to the empirical analysis. Transferring and comparing the identified databased patterns with existing research helps to classify and make statements about the generalizability of the empirical findings.

Corporate challenges are building the reference point for this study's contributions. That is why ultimately, after having gained a systematic empirical understanding of the phenomenon at hand, concrete suggestions regarding the development of rule-breaking market behavior shall be given to support companies in the process of creating a revolutionary competitive advantage.

3. Which normative recommendations can be provided for companies who would like to reach rule-breaking market behavior?

This is aimed at drawing managers' attention to key challenges in the process of rule-breaking market behavior, wishing to introduce a number of possibilities for managers to consider when examining routes for innovation development. Therefore, the goal is to provide a framework for thinking, debate and action, serving as a tool for improving innovation processes, breaking inertia and jolting conventional thinking.

4. What implications arise from the findings that could be related to other theoretical and practical problem spaces?

Indubitably, the fundamental need for breakthrough changes achieved through purposeful deviation from behavioral standards does not only apply to the context of marketing science and business practice. Thus, based on the findings, comparable challenges above and beyond the scope of this study have to be identified and reflected upon.

Overall, it can be summarized in modest analogy to Davis (1971) influential article on phenomenological research *That's Interesting!*: The purposeful deviation from existing behavioral standards to achieve a competitive advantage, as in rule-breaking market behavior, is interesting, relevant and understudied. What yet remains to be accounted for after all, is a rigorous analytical procedure to satisfactorily meet the top objective of this work by answering these four fundamental research questions.

1.3.2 Method and Analytical Process

The basic methodological approach in this work is to inductively uncover characteristic principles in the process of rule-breaking market behavior by analyzing multiple historical athletic cases, which then, by analogy, are transferred back to the managerial context.

To better outline these different methodological elements and set them in the particular context of this work, Fig. 1.2 gives an overview of the different steps. First of all, each methodological component will be briefly explained according to the numbers in ascending order. After that, the same picture will be filled with further information regarding key contents of each main chapter to provide a structured outline of this work's analytical process (see Fig. 1.3).

The analytical frame in Fig. 1.2 indicates a typical process of scientific research, displaying the level of abstraction on the vertical line and the analytical process on the horizontal line. Usually, the process begins in the lower left corner (A) with a single problem that can be observed, for instance in a company. Continuing with the upper left corner (B), scientists aim at raising the problem to an abstract level by systematically studying a (representative) sample of the phenomenon at hand. In theory-building approaches, the inquiry is exploratory at first (discovery) and moves on to the upper right corner (C) when hypotheses are tested (justification). These generalizable claims can then be transferred back to a more specific real-world context to find a solution for the original problem as well as similar ones (lower right corner, D). For the sake of this work, one further element has been added to the figure, which is the dotted line, indicative of the domain switch that has been made in the course of the analytical process (reasoning by analogy).

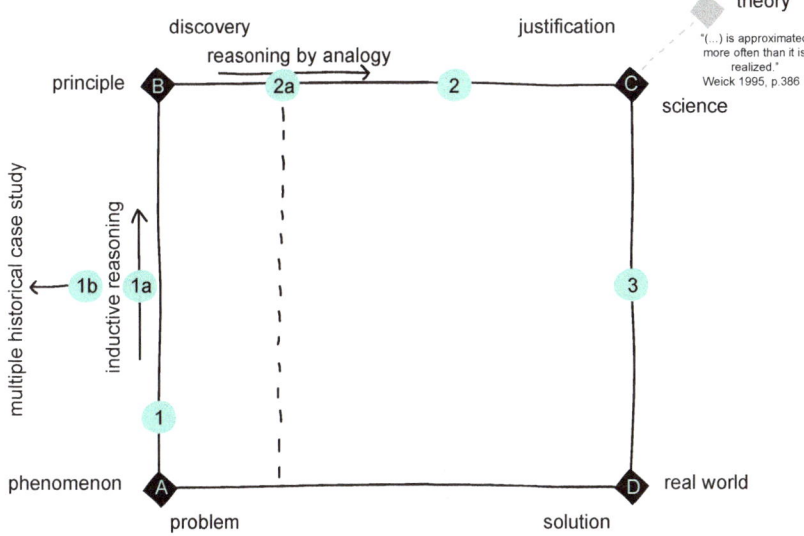

Note: The horizontal perspective displays the analytical process and the vertical perspective displays the level of abstraction. The four corners, A, B, C, and D, are building the frame for the analysis. The lines linking the four corners generally indicate that different processes take place to move from corner to corner. The particular processes employed in this work are added next to the general processes (i.e. inductive reasoning, multiple historical case study, reasoning by analogy). The numbers serve as a means to relate better the textual descriptions below

Fig. 1.2 Analytical framework (idea adapted from H. Schneider, source: author)

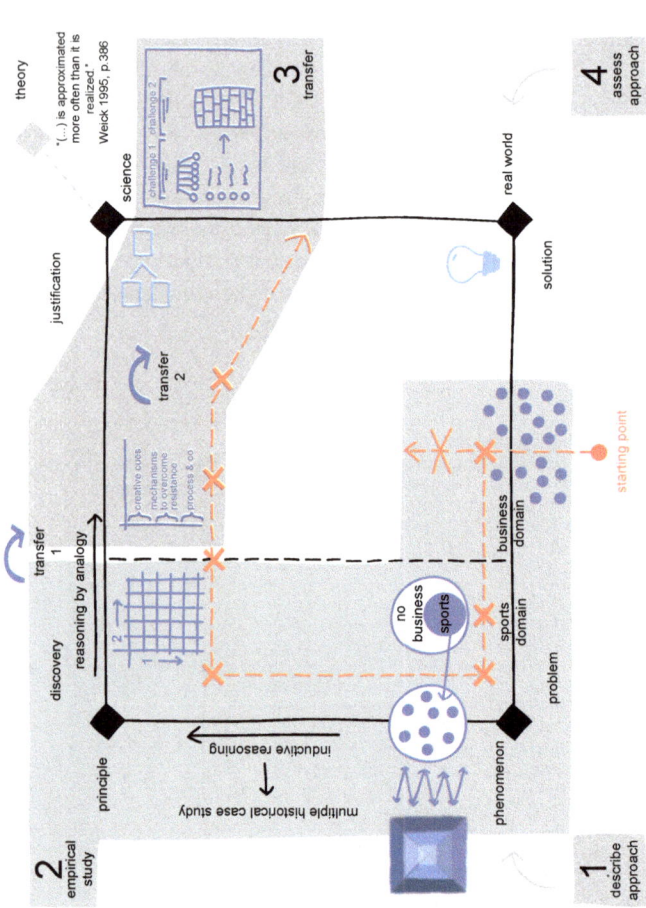

Fig. 1.3 Process and scope (source: author)

Note: Graphical elements in black visualize the general process of bottom-up scientific inquiries, starting in the lower left corner, ending in the lower right corner, with the level of abstraction displayed vertically and progress of the analytical process horizontally. Grey fields indicate where the four chapters of this work can be located on the graph. The orange path indicates the course of the research process. The blue drawings visualize important content-related elements of this work

Before turning to each point of Fig. 1.2, a brief note shall be given on the underlying philosophical paradigm that is guiding the research. Basically, any research endeavor is grounded in disciplinary research traditions that reflect the shared beliefs within a community of researchers about basic aspects of how research should be done (Kuhn 1996). The selected paradigm guides the researcher by providing him or her with higher-order philosophical assumptions, research objectives, selection of tools, instruments, and methods used in the study. A research paradigm sets the context for each study, affects an investigator's perspective and plays a substantial role in the research process. Being aware of a scientific endeavor's underlying philosophical foundations is likely to lead to better, more effective research (Hunt 1991). Thus, in order to better understand and assess the underlying thought processes it is essential to reveal the foundation accordingly.

The historical development of business studies has been accompanied by different philosophical schools of thought. Since around the middle of the twentieth century, Popper's critical rationalism, relativism, constructivism and, more recently, scientific realism have been considered relevant and discussed heavily in the literature (Eisend and Kuß 2017, p. 23). As a discussion of the different streams would exceed the scope of this work, the reader is referred to elaborate overviews of different approaches to philosophy of science, for example, given by Brown (2012), Chalmers (2013), Godfrey-Smith (2003), Hunt (2005), Schurz (2014). This research basically adopts a scientific realist orientation, assuming the existence of a single reality that is independent of any observer. "The fundamental tenet of scientific realism is that 'the long-term success of a scientific theory gives reason to believe that something like the entities and structure postulated by the theory actually exists'" (Hunt 2015, p. 22 with reference to McMullin 1984, p. 26). As Maxwell (2018) points out:

> . . . Most of us accept a realist ontology in our everyday lives. When our cars break down, we believe that there is a real problem that a mechanic can identify and repair. Most of us also believe that global warming is a real phenomenon that is occurring independently of our beliefs about this. Thomas Schwandt, in his *Dictionary of Qualitative Research*, argued that on a daily basis, most of us probably behave as garden-variety empirical realists—that is, we act as if the objects in the world (things, events, structures, people, meanings, etc.) exist as independent in some way from our experience with them. We also regard society, institutions, feelings, intelligence, poverty, disability, and so on as being just as real as the toes on our feet and the sun in the sky. (p. 20)

From the many varieties of realism across the philosophical landscape, scientific realism is, according to Hunt (2015), often used as an "umbrella term to include many of the specific versions of realism" (p. 22), such as methodological, critical or constructive realism. Much of what is described in key literature on case study research is also oriented towards a realist perspective (Yin 2014, p. 17).

In addition to the basic alignment with the idea of scientific realism, from a more practical orientation, this work is committed to the fundamental assumptions underlying the German "entscheidungsorientiertes Forschungsprogramm der Betriebswirtschaft" (for further information, see e.g. Heinen 1969). One of this research orientation's most important notions with relevance in the underlying scientific endeavor, is the need to reach beyond pure description by developing concrete recommendations for business or marketing practice. Similarly, Kotler (1972) distinguishes between marketing as a descriptive science, which studies "how transactions are created, stimulated, facilitated, and valued" (p. 52), and marketing management as a normative science, also "involving the efficient creation and offering of values to stimulate desired transactions" (p. 52). Thus, being also committed to such normative understanding of marketing science, this work attempts to provide guidelines for managers whenever possible.

[1] Coming back to the description of Fig. 1.2, the general process from (A) to (B) is discussed first. The left ordinate in the figure differentiates between phenomenon and principle,[4] with the level of abstraction being low with the former and high with the latter. As outlined by Titus (2018), abstraction generally "involves the act of removing or separating—that is, the process of extracting the inherent (abstract) qualities from an actual physical (concrete) object or concept to which they belong" (p. 242). The author further explains that, when transferred to a complex marketing problem, processes of creative abstractions entail the discovery of "novel or unfamiliar patterns and relationships between elements, facts, or attributes of the problem" (p. 242) which are then depicted in theoretical frameworks intended to give a simplified representation of the underlying phenomena. "As such, creative marketing abstractions often represent simplified versions of reality in much the same way as abstract paintings represent simplified visual representations of reality" (Titus 2018, p. 242). In line with Goldschmidt (2011), it can be concluded that "without abstraction it is hard to distance oneself from the source properties and transfer only the essential relationships" (p. 97) to a similar problem or phenomenon. To even better illustrate the idea of abstraction, one can think of the following analogy: Research in general and case study research in particular has oftentimes been compared to detective work (Mintzberg 1979; Truzzi 1976; Yin 1981). In order to solve a crime, the detective investigates the scene, collects reports from eye-witnesses and other related individuals, distinguishes relevant from irrelevant data, and further pursues important clues until eventually a plausible link of motive, opportunity and method can be established that better accounts for the facts than does any alternative explanation. In order to explain a real-world phenomenon, the case study researcher, analogously, accurately renders the facts of the case, considers alternative explanations and arrives at a conclusion that appears most congruent with the facts. In neither of the two processes there are fixed recipes for building explanations (Yin 1981). There is one important difference between the two domains, however, which is at the same time constitutive element of scientific endeavors: abstraction. Once detectives have identified the conjunction of events

---

[4]Other marketing scholars also refer to principles as "rules of thumb or high-level laws often distilled from experiences" (Challagalla et al. 2014, p. 5, with reference to Hunt 1991, Locke 2002). Here, the focus lies more on principles as general scientific theorems and as a fundamental truth or proposition that serves as the foundation for a system of belief or behavior (Principle n.d.).

that lead them to the perpetrator, they close the case and turn to the next crime. Scientists, on the other hand go "beyond the domain of experiences to the domain of structures and generative mechanisms that produced the cases" (Tsoukas 1989, p. 556). This is exactly what is intended in this work.

[1a] From Phenomenon to Principle: Different Modes of Reasoning. Basically, there are two ways of how to bridge gaps between concrete experience and abstract concepts, of how to relate data (phenomenon) and theory (principles). Researchers might either use existing theoretical knowledge to interpret and analyze their data, or they might attempt to ignore previous theoretical knowledge and discover patterns, themes, concepts, or theory from the data (Kennedy 2018). Such two approaches should be understood as opposite ends of a continuum in which researchers can be more or less close to one of the ends. The relation between data and theory is discussed in terms of deductive, inductive, and abductive reasoning (e.g. Mantere and Ketokivi 2013).

Deduction starts out with a specific theory and examines how the raw data support the existing theoretical framework. That is, the theory is employed as an analytical lens to make sense of the collected data. In quantitative research, this usually means that a hypothesis is deduced from theory and then empirically tested. In qualitative research, this often means that collected data are analyzed according to the existing theory.[5] In consumer research, the hypothetico-deductive approach is an esteemed and most dominant mode of scientific practice (Alba 2012; Eisenhardt et al. 2016). To illustrate the different ways of how to reason and make inferences, the American philosopher Charles S. Peirce, 1960 (as cited in Kennedy 2018) gave examples using beans. In his example of deduction, he explains: If according to the theory all beans from a particular bag are white, and all beans in our case have been taken from this particular bag, we can draw the conclusion that our beans are white.

In induction, the core emphasis lies on the emergence of theory from data by drawing general conclusions from specific observations (Sax 1968). The inductive logic sticks closely to the collected data and can reveal novel understandings of existing knowledge without specific a priori presumptions about the outcome (Kennedy 2018). Explained with the bean example, the inductive formation of a general statement based on the pattern found in the data could look like this: If we take out a couple of beans from the bag, we find that the beans are white, and we repeat this ten times with the same outcome, we would infer that it is plausible to assume that all the beans in the bag are white.[6] Inductive and deductive logic can be considered mirrors of one another, with the building of inductive theory producing new theory from data

---

[5]The distinction between qualitative and quantitative methods is commonplace in social sciences so that a separate explanation to understand better the different modes of reasoning has been used. To classify this work, the term *inductive* has been used to accentuate the core emphasis on the emergence of patterns from data, rather than to distinguish between *qualitative and quantitative work* which would merely refer to the type of data (for further elaboration see Eisenhardt et al. 2016).

[6]Of course, inductive conclusions are hypothetical and fallible. On the basis of a few empirical observations, we can never be sure that the sealed bag contains only white beans and not one or more red beans that we just have not yet observed (Kennedy 2018).

and deductive theory testing completing the cycle by using data to test theory. Therefore, inductive research naturally complements the mainstream deductive research imperative (Eisenhardt and Graebner 2007).

A third mode of inference, abduction, can be understood as the discovery of new concepts, ideas, and explanations by finding data that cannot be explained by pre-existing knowledge (Kennedy 2018). Here, Peirce's bean example illustrates the following: We see five bags and we know that each bag contains beans of a particular color; for instance, Bag A is filled with white beans. We then find three white beans lying in front of the bags, and we could instantly infer that the beans on the ground come from Bag A. However, we may discover further evidence (shoeprints on the floor, sealed bags) that would make us assume that there is another new and more plausible hypothesis that the beans do not come from any of the bags but from yet another source (somebody might have dropped them).[7] Basically, in abductive inference, researchers are trying to accomplish both striving to be open and sensitive to the data while also considering pre-existing theory as a source of inspiration to resolve surprising or puzzling data (Kelle 2014).

Under the assumption that theory can dominate research in a way that blinds the researcher to potentially informative observations (e.g. Greenwald et al. 1986; Rozin 2001), this work primarily pursues a bottom-up data driven, inductive reasoning approach to better understand the process of rule-breaking market behavior.[8]

[1b] Multiple Historical Case Study. One way to inductively explore a phenomenon is the case study approach (Eisenhardt 1989).[9] The research approach of inductive case studies derives from the tradition of grounded-theory research (Mantere and Ketokivi 2013), which can, in close resemblance with the above outlined inductive reasoning approach, be characterized as a systematic discovery of theory from data with less emphasis on a priori theoretical considerations (Glaser and Strauss 1967). A basic premise in inductive case research is the idea that theoretical insight can be gained from the underlying data by inductive reasoning mechanisms such as iterative tabulation, cross-case pattern search and replication (Eisenhardt 1989, p. 533). While within-case analyses primarily help gain familiarity with data and preliminary theory generation, cross-case pattern search "forces investigators to look beyond initial impressions and see evidence thru multiple lenses" (Eisenhardt 1989, p. 533). For reasons that will be further elaborated later, this work adapts a multiple case approach, enabling a look at the underlying phenomenon from both several single case perspectives and an overall cross-case perspective. The *historical* in multiple historical case studies refers to the fact that all

---

[7]For a detailed description of the example, see Thornberg and Charmaz (2014).

[8]At this point, it shall be acknowledged, that there is no "pure" induction in the strict sense (referred to as naïve inductivism by critics) because prior knowledge always shapes researcher's observations. As Chalmers (2013) points out, researchers are situated within a historical, ideological, and socio-cultural context, and thus bring their own lenses to interpret a specific set of data (for further information see also Maxwell 2018).

[9]Further inductive approaches for developing theory are imaginary experiments (i.e. disciplined imagination; Weick 1989) and thought experiments (Cornelissen and Durand 2014).

cases of rule-breaking behavior that will be chosen for the analysis have been developed in the past. Thus, the idea is to look back in order to look ahead. Past cases are intended to inform future processes of rule-breaking market behavior. In innovation research, for several reasons, this is a typical research approach. Often, changes that accompany innovations take place over years or even decades so that the analysis of historical cases helps to "provide the necessary distance to observe how an innovation both emerges from and reshapes its ... environment" (Hargadon and Douglas 2001, p. 476). Such a retrospective view is particularly valuable if one wishes to examine how radical the innovations have been by taking their long-term consequences into account (Rosenzweig 2017). In the underlying work, this perfectly serves the purpose of selecting only those cases for the analysis that are definite examples of rule-breaking behavior. Prior innovation studies, particularly in the realm of radical innovation, also used the historical methodology to shed light on innovations' developmental process (Chandy and Tellis 2000; Golder et al. 2009; Rosenzweig 2017; Sood and Tellis 2005).

[2] The Process of Developing Novel Theoretical Contributions. When regarded from a procedural perspective of how theories are generally built, this work can be considered the first part of a long and effortful journey to developing a Theory of Rule-Breaking Market Behavior. As indicated in Fig. 1.2, in general, "theory is approximated more often than it is realized" (Weick 1995, p. 386).Theory is commonly defined across different schools of thought and paradigms as an analytic structure or system of causal associations that attempts to account for, explain, and predict empirical phenomena (e.g. Sutton and Staw 1995). How theoretical contributions come into existence is one of the central questions researchers have been grappling with (e.g. Cornelissen and Durand 2014). Starting with Reichenbach (1938), both philosophers of science and marketing theorists have distinguished between the context of discovery and the context of justification (for more information on the historical background, see Hunt 2013). Discovery, or theory building, refers to how scientists go about creating or developing propositions, laws, and theories. Justification, or theory testing, denotes how scientists go about explaining and predicting phenomena, testing theories, and validating hypotheses, laws and theories (Eisend and Kuß 2017; Hunt 2013; Schickore and Steinle 2006). Together, both contexts play a role in advancing theory development (Yadav 2010). This work is focusing on the first context of the discovery-justification continuum. How this is actually done, remains an open question: As researchers concerned with the development of new discoveries, like Crittenden and Peterson (2012) or Hunt (2013) affirm, there is no fixed and no one best way to craft and establish a theoretical scientific discovery. Meheus (2009) states that, "a large majority of philosophers of science agrees that ... truly, novel discoveries are not the result of applying some standardized procedure ... [nor are they] produced by unstructured flashes of insight" (p. vii). Wilson (1998) advises novel scientists to "throw everything you can at the subject, so long as the procedures can be duplicated by others" (pp. 6–7). Hunt (2013) further specifies that the creative cognitive acts involved in theory generation resulting from insightful, constrained reasoning processes take place through time: "We went through iteration after iteration after iteration of the

model. There was no single, great, eureka! moment" (p. 70). As this is certainly also true for this work, more information regarding the analytical process of discovery will be given in the course of the following chapters in order to make the analytical process as transparent as possible.

[2a] Reasoning by Analogy. Analogical thinking is oftentimes associated as being helpful in the early, discovery-related stages of developing new theories (as cited in Cornelissen and Durand (2014): see, for example, Boxenbaum and Rouleau 2011; Cornelissen 2005; Okhuysen and Bonardi 2011; Shepherd and Sutcliffe 2011; Weick 1989). Analogical reasoning "is a process of mapping between a source and a target", (Haas and Ham 2015, p. 56). In that process, correspondences between structured representational elements of the two domains are set up and information is transferred accordingly (Jonassen 2010, p. 260). There is an abundant use of analogies throughout theory building endeavors for different purposes and in different parts of an argument (Ketokivi et al. 2017). For example, analogies are employed to comprehensively explain abstract and complex subjects, to convey new ideas, to derive explanations, to evoke a specific debate, to challenge a conventional way of thinking, or to elucidate some nonobvious point (Ketokivi et al. 2017). More broadly, Gentner (1982) distinguishes between expressive versus explanatory use of analogies. While the former applies analogies in a more metaphorical way, (i.e. to simply communicate or describe ideas), the latter is referred to as reasoning by analogy and often lies at the foundation of new theories. In that case, the original or source domain is understood to analyze and explain specific aspects in the target domain (Cornelissen and Durand 2014). Analogies are often referred to in the sense of, "think of x as if it were y" (Ketokivi et al. 2017). Ketokivi et al. (2017) offer three criteria to "examine whether a source domain can plausibly be bridged with a target domain to obtain insight on the latter" (p. 650): relevance, structural soundness and factual validity. With regard to heuristic analogies (i.e. analogies that are used to build theory) the three criteria are interpreted as follows (Ketokivi et al. 2017). First, the analogy must offer potential for insight and has to be familiar enough to be understood by the audience. Second, the analogy requires a sufficient number of similarities and no critical dissimilarities between the source domain and the target domain. Third, the analogy must be suited for empirical research in the target domain. Each criterion is considered in the selection of an adequate domain to empirically study rule-breaking behavior.

[3] Visual Artifact as an Attempt to Bridge the Academic-Practitioner Gap. The final step in the analytical process would then be to transfer the scientifically discovered findings back to the real world for them to be used as a means to hopefully better solve existing problems. Unfortunately, practitioners are said to rarely build on the artifacts developed in the academic literature (Lilien 2011). Such academic-practitioner divide has been discussed for decades in the area of marketing and management science, and the observation of Little (1970) still seems to be holding today: "The big problem with management science models is that managers practically never use them. There have been a few applications, of course, but the practice is a pallid picture of the promise" (p. B466). While this gap will not be overcome with this work, it is at least strived at proffering the findings in a way that

they may easily be adapted and used as a helpful guideline by managers who would like to get to rule-breaking market behavior.

In light of the foregoing discussion and the underlying research objectives, this study is structured as shown in Fig. 1.3. The analytical framework in black has been outlined in detail above. The grey fields indicate what parts of the process are intended to be accomplished in this work and which of the four chapters, 1, 2, 3, and 4, deal with the different stages. With the help of the blue drawings the story of this work can be outlined along the orange path.

Following the orange path in Fig. 1.3, the key contents of this work, displayed in blue, can be outlined as follows. As described above, the starting point for the research is the observation of a phenomenon in the context of business: companies deliberately depart from standard logic in the market in order to gain a competitive advantage. From an "innovation type" perspective, such deviations can be anything, a new product, a novel process, another business model, a different service, etc. What all these innovative and purposeful departures from the status quo have in common is that they are separate from the realm of technological progress. It is not to suggest that those companies, such as Amazon, IKEA, and Red Bull, do not engage in technology-related research and development (R&D) activities, but on top of that they also found novel solutions beyond mere technological progress in simply "doing things differently", as in "doing things like nobody else has done them before". Frequently, these innovations have breakthrough character leading to substantial changes in the marketplace. This work refers to such phenomena of insight innovations as rule-breaking market behavior. The goal is to gain a better understanding of the processes that underlie the development of rule-breaking market behavior. How is it created? Which major challenges have to be overcome? What can companies do to become rule-breaking players in their highly competitive environments? To find answers to such questions and learn more about general principles underlying rule-breaking market behavior, an empirical bottom-up approach has been chosen. The idea is to select a number of examples that are typical of rule-breaking market behavior and search for patterns across the data that are useful for companies in order to adapt a rule-breaking mindset.

For two main reasons, it has been decided to empirically investigate such phenomena outside the domain of business: data availability and making use of the virtues that reasoning by analogy from an interdisciplinary perspective can hold. Looking with fresh eyes at an existing issue or phenomenon might offer a new way of seeing. In consequence, these two basic assumptions underlie the empirical study: (1) that there are important commonalities in innovative processes and the way human actors deal with change across different domains and (2) that we can benefit by comparing research findings from disparate areas because different facets of kindred processes may come into focus as the perspective and level of analysis vary.

The objective of Chap. 2 is to conceptually understand and empirically explore rule-breaking (market) behavior. This entails both a derivation of the phenomenon's conceptual characteristics and an empirical analysis of eight rule-breaking cases. While, for clarity of explanation, these two elements are discussed linearly, they have been gradually developed in parallel with empirical insight from the cases further enriching the constitutive aspects of rule-breaking market behavior and vice versa. As graphically displayed in the lower left corner of Fig. 1.3, in a first step (Sect. 2.1), a taxonomy of four key characteristics will be depicted. These main characteristics not only help to distinguish rule-breaking market behavior from other concepts in the field of innovation but also, and more importantly, build the foundation to choose adequate cases for the empirical analysis. So that this can be conveniently done, the four key characteristics have been posed as questions and arranged in accordance with the logic of a decision tree. The resulting Four-Way-Rule-Breaking Test serves as a quick and easily applicable tool to categorize innovative phenomena and has proved to be a useful means to screen the vast pools of innovation examples for the case selection.

In a second step (Sect. 2.2), the empirical analysis will be prepared and conducted. Starting with multiple search spaces, the domain of sports is selected as the single most promising field for an analysis of rule-breaking behavior. Eight highly insightful historic athletic cases are carefully selected and systematically analyzed by collecting case data and conducting iterative comparisons of data and emerging patterns. The method fostered a vital mix of depth and breadth. Slowly moving from phenomenon to principle, the cases will first be analyzed in a single case fashion and then in a cross-case manner. The results are successively outlined in Sect. 2.3. Eight individual case narratives are provided first, a brief summary of all single cases is presented after that, and a cross-case description that gives a preliminary idea of more generalizable criteria playing a role in the process of rule-breaking behavior follows in the last step. As visualized in the upper left corner of Fig. 1.3, a comprehensive table including the most important case-based findings is the result of Chap. 2.

The objective of Chap. 3 is to transfer the empirical results that have been gained in the domain of sports back to the domain of business (see arrow "transfer 1" in Fig. 1.3). More specifically, the empirical cross-case findings are related to research in the context of creativity and innovation literature. In relating these results back to business, each cross-case criterion is assessed for whether it is of relevance in a corporate context and whether it can be assigned to a larger-order structure that generally applies to all cases of rule-breaking market behavior. In other words, under consideration of existing theories, concepts and discussions, the cross-case insight is not only contrasted with state-of-the-art research but also aggregated and structured further. The resulting three-part structure is used to organize Sect. 3.1 into some overall aspects (Sect. 3.1.2), and two challenges that are found to be characteristic of the process of rule-breaking market behavior (see Sect. 3.1.3 for challenge one: recognition of a new way and Sect. 3.1.4 for challenge two: overcoming resistance). The two challenges encompass this work's core findings. Formulated as research propositions, several ways to address both challenges, all grounded in the empirical cases, are discussed. That is, for challenge one, a perfunctory list of nine creative cues is suggested, and for challenge two, five exemplary mechanisms to overcome resistance are proposed. All of them are explained in detail and enriched with concrete measures that can be adapted by companies and individuals to more successfully engage in the process of rule-breaking market behavior.

In the second part of Chap. 3 (Sect. 3.2), the contributions are summarized and displayed in a Framework of Rule-Breaking Market Behavior. The latter serves as a managerial artefact to better discuss and implement the idea of rule-breaking market behavior into the set of existing business practices. As visually indicated by arrow transfer 2 in Fig. 1.3, this step can be seen as a second transfer approach from a scientific context back to managerial, real-world discussions that were the starting point of this work and is where the findings shall find application. As indicated by the two white spots at the upper and lower right of Fig. 1.3, for reasons of scope, two areas have been left out to fully account for a rigorous scientific journey. First, it has not yet been attempted to provide a rigorous test of the hypotheses but focused on the discovery-related elements toward building a theory only. Second, the results have not yet been applied and tested in a company to evaluate how much they assist in finding different and impactful solutions to existing problems and thus, actually help companies in creating a competitive advantage.

Finally, in Chap. 4, a retrospective look at the above-outlined research process is given in order to summarize and assess the approach. This includes both limitations and further research opportunities arising from this study.

References

Aarts H, Dijksterhuis A (2000) Habits as knowledge structures: automaticity in goal-directed behavior. J Pers Soc Psychol 78(1):53–63. https://doi.org/10.1037/0022-3514.78.1.53

Aarts H, Verplanken B, Knippenberg A (1998) Predicting behavior from actions in the past: repeated decision making or a matter of habit? J Appl Soc Psychol 28(15):1355–1374. https://doi.org/10.1111/j.1559-1816.1998.tb01681.x

Abernathy WJ (1978) The productivity dilemma: roadblock to innovation in the automobile industry. John Hopkins University Press, Baltimore, MD

Abernathy WJ, Clark KB (1985) Innovation: mapping the winds of creative destruction. Res Policy 14(1):3–22. https://doi.org/10.1016/0048-7333(85)90021-6

Ahlstrom D (2010) Innovation and growth: how business contributes to society. Acad Manag Perspect 24(3):11–24

Alba JW (2012) In defense of bumbling. J Consum Res 38(6):981–987. https://doi.org/10.1086/661230

Amabile TM, Pratt MG (2016) The dynamic componential model of creativity and innovation in organizations: making progress, making meaning. Res Organ Behav 36:157–183. https://doi.org/10.1016/j.riob.2016.10.001

Anderson N, Potočnik K, Zhou J (2014) Innovation and creativity in organizations: a state-of-the-science review, prospective commentary, and guiding framework. J Manag 40(5):1297–1333. https://doi.org/10.1177/0149206314527128

Arthur WB (1989) Competing technologies, increasing returns, and lock-in by historical events. Econ J 99(394):116–131. https://doi.org/10.2307/2234208

Arthur WB (1994) Increasing returns and path dependency in the economy. University of Michigan Press, Ann Arbor, MI. https://doi.org/10.3998/mpub.10029

Baas M, Koch S, Nijstad BA, De Dreu CKW (2015) Conceiving creativity: the nature and consequences of laypeople's beliefs about the realization of creativity. Psychol Aesthet Creat Arts 9(3):340–354. https://doi.org/10.1037/a0039420

Backhaus K, Schneider H (2009) Strategisches Marketing [strategic marketing], 2nd edn. Schäffer-
    Poeschel, Stuttgart
Backhaus K, Schneider H (forthcoming) Strategisches Marketing [strategic marketing], 3rd edn
Baer J (1993) Creativity and divergent thinking: a task specific approach. Lawrence Erlbaum,
    Hillsdale, NJ
Baron RA (2006) Opportunity recognition as pattern recognition: how entrepreneurs "connect the
    dots" to identify new business opportunities. Acad Manag Perspect 20(1):104–119. https://doi.
    org/10.5465/amp.2006.19873412
Becker MC (2004) Organizational routines: a review of the literature. Ind Corp Chang 13
    (4):643–678. https://doi.org/10.1093/icc/dth026
Benner MJ, Tushman ML (2003) Exploitation, exploration, and process management: the produc-
    tivity dilemma revisited. Acad Manag Rev 28(2):238–256. https://doi.org/10.2307/30040711
Bicchieri C (2006) The grammar of society: the nature and dynamics of social norms. Cambridge
    University Press, New York, NY
Bower JL, Christensen CM (1995) Disruptive technologies: catching the wave. Harv Bus Rev 73
    (1):43–53
Boxenbaum E, Rouleau L (2011) New knowledge products as bricolage: metaphors and scripts in
    organizational theory. Acad Manag Rev 36(2):272–296. https://doi.org/10.5465/amr.2009.0213
Brown JR (2012) Philosophy of science: the key thinkers. Continuum, London
Bucher S, Langley A (2016) The interplay of reflective and experimental spaces in interrupting and
    reorienting routine dynamics. Organ Sci 27(3):594–613. https://doi.org/10.1287/orsc.2015.
    1041
Burgh G (2014) Creative and lateral thinking: Edward de Bono. Encyclopedia of educational theory
    and philosophy, vol 1–2. Sage, Thousand Oaks, CA. https://doi.org/10.4135/9781483346229.
    n86
Carlile PR, Christensen CM (2004) The cycles of theory building in management research.
    Working Paper 05-057. Harvard Business School, Boston
Castaldi C, Dosi G (2006) The grip of history and the scope for novelty: some results and open
    questions on path dependence in economic processes. In: Wimmer A, Kössler R (eds) Under-
    standing change: models, methodologies and metaphors. Palgrave Macmillan, London, pp
    99–128. https://doi.org/10.1057/9780230524644_8
Černe M, Kaše R, Škerlavaj M (2016) Non-technological innovation research: evaluating the
    intellectual structure and prospects of an emerging field. Scand J Manag 32(2):69–85. https://
    doi.org/10.1016/j.scaman.2016.02.001
Challagalla G, Murtha BR, Jaworski B (2014) Marketing doctrine: a principles-based approach to
    guiding marketing decision making in firms. J Mark 78(4):4–20. https://doi.org/10.1509/jm.12.
    0314
Chalmers AF (2013) What is this thing called science? 4th edn. McGraw-Hill, Berkshire
Chandy RK, Tellis GJ (2000) The incumbent's curse? Incumbency, size, and radical product
    innovation. J Mark 64(3):1–17. https://doi.org/10.1509/jmkg.64.3.1.18033
Christensen CM (1992) Exploring the limits of the technology s-curve. Part I: component technol-
    ogies. Prod Oper Manag 1(4):334–357. https://doi.org/10.1111/j.1937-5956.1992.tb00001.x
Christensen CM (1997) The innovator's dilemma: when new technologies cause great firms to fail.
    Harvard Business School Press, Boston, MA
Christensen CM (2006) The ongoing process of building a theory of disruption. J Prod Innov
    Manag 23(1):39–55. https://doi.org/10.1111/j.1540-5885.2005.00180.x
Christensen CM, Bower JL (1996) Customer power, strategic investment, and the failure of leading
    firms. Strateg Manag J 17(3):197–218. https://doi.org/10.1002/(SICI)1097-0266(199603)
    17:3<197::AID-SMJ804>3.3.CO;2-L
Christensen CM, Raynor M, McDonald R (2015) What is disruptive innovation? Harv Bus Rev 93
    (12):44–53
Cirque du Soleil (n.d.) History. https://www.cirquedusoleil.com/about/history. Accessed 2 May
    2018

Colman AM (2015) Lateral thinking. A dictionary of psychology, 4th edn. https://www.oxfordreference.com

Cornelissen JP (2005) Beyond compare: metaphor in organization theory. Acad Manag Rev 30 (4):751–764. https://doi.org/10.5465/amr.2005.18378876

Cornelissen JP, Durand R (2014) Moving forward: developing theoretical contributions in management studies. J Manag Stud 51(6):995–1022. https://doi.org/10.1111/joms.12078

Crittenden VL, Peterson RA (2012) The AMS review: year 2. AMS Rev 2(2–4):45–47. https://doi.org/10.1007/s13162-012-0031-8

Crossan MM, Apaydin M (2010) A multi-dimensional framework of organizational innovation: a systematic review of the literature. J Manag Stud 47(6):1154–1191. https://doi.org/10.1111/j.1467-6486.2009.00880.x

Dahling JJ, Gutworth MB (2017) Loyal rebels? A test of the normative conflict model of constructive deviance. J Organ Behav 38(8):1167–1182. https://doi.org/10.1002/job.2194

Damanpour F (2014) Footnotes to research on management innovation. Organ Stud 35 (9):1265–1285. https://doi.org/10.1177/0170840614539312

Damanpour F, Aravind D (2012) Managerial innovation: conceptions, processes, and antecedents. Manag Organ Rev 8(2):423–454. https://doi.org/10.1111/j.1740-8784.2011.00233.x

Danneels E (2004) Disruptive technology reconsidered: a critique and research agenda. J Prod Innov Manag 21(4):246–258. https://doi.org/10.1111/j.0737-6782.2004.00076.x

David PA (2001) Path dependence, its critics and the quest for 'historical economics'. In: Garrouste P, Ioannides S (eds) Evolution and path dependence in economic ideas: past and present. Edward Elgar, Cheltenham, pp 15–40

Davis MS (1971) That's interesting! Towards a phenomenology of sociology and a sociology of phenomenology. Philos Soc Sci 1(2):309–344. https://doi.org/10.1177/004839317100100211

Day GS, Schoemaker PJH (2004) Driving through the fog: managing at the edge. Long Range Plan 37(2):127–142. https://doi.org/10.1016/j.lrp.2004.01.004

De Bono E (1970) Lateral thinking: creativity step by step. Ward Lock, London

De Bono E (2010) Lateral thinking: a textbook of creativity. Penguin, London

Dodge DL (1985) The over-negativized conceptualization of deviance: a programmatic exploration. Deviant Behav 6(1):17–37. https://doi.org/10.1080/01639625.1985.9967657

Duhigg C, Byrd A, Stark S (n.d.) The power of outsiders [video]. New York Times. https://www.nytimes.com. Accessed 21 Jun 2018

Durkheim É (1985 [1964]) The rules of sociological method (Solovay SA, Mueller JH, trans. Catlin GEG ed), 8th edn. Free Press, New York, NY

Eckhardt JT, Shane SA (2003) Opportunities and entrepreneurship. J Manag 29(3):333–349. https://doi.org/10.1016/S0149-2063(02)00225-8

Eisend M, Kuß A (2017) Grundlagen empirischer Forschung: Zur Methodologie in der Betriebswirtschaftslehre [Foundations of empirical research: methodology in business administration]. Springer, Wiesbaden. https://doi.org/10.1007/978-3-658-09705-9_4

Eisenhardt KM (1989) Building theories from case study research. Acad Manag Rev 14 (4):532–550. https://doi.org/10.2307/258557

Eisenhardt KM, Graebner ME (2007) Theory building from cases: opportunities and challenges. Acad Manag J 50(1):25–32. https://doi.org/10.5465/amj.2007.24160888

Eisenhardt KM, Graebner ME, Sonenshein S (2016) Grand challenges and inductive methods: rigor without rigor mortis. Acad Manag J 59(4):1113–1123. https://doi.org/10.5465/amj.2016.4004

Fagerberg J (2006) Innovation: a guide to the literature. In: Fagerberg J, Mowery DC (eds) The Oxford handbook of innovation. Oxford University Press, Oxford, pp 1–26. https://doi.org/10.1093/oxfordhb/9780199286805.003.0001

Fagerberg J, Verspagen B (2009) Innovation studies – the emerging structure of a new scientific field. Res Policy 38(2):218–233. https://doi.org/10.1016/j.respol.2008.12.006

Feldman MS, Pentland BT (2003) Reconceptualizing organizational routines as a source of flexibility and change. Adm Sci Q 48(1):94–118. https://doi.org/10.2307/3556620

Feldman MS, Pentland BT, D'Adderio L, Lazaric N (2016) Beyond routines as things: introduction to the special issue on routine dynamics. Organ Sci 27(3):505–513. https://doi.org/10.1287/orsc. 2016.1070

Galperin BL (2003) Can workplace deviance be constructive? In: Sagie A, Stashevsky S, Koslowsky M (eds) Misbehaviour and dysfunctional attitudes in organizations. Palgrave Macmillan, London, pp 154–170. https://doi.org/10.1057/9780230288829_9

Galperin BL (2012) Exploring the nomological network of workplace deviance: developing and validating a measure of constructive deviance. J Appl Soc Psychol 42(12):2988–3025. https:// doi.org/10.1111/j.1559-1816.2012.00971.x

Garud R, Kumaraswamy A, Karnøe P (2010) Path dependence or path creation? J Manag Stud 47 (4):760–774. https://doi.org/10.1111/j.1467-6486.2009.00914.x

Gentner D (1982) Are scientific analogies metaphors? In: Miall DS (ed) Metaphor, problems and perspectives. Harvester Press, Sussex, pp 106–132

Gerring J (2006) Case study research: principles and practices. Cambridge University Press, New York, NY. https://doi.org/10.1017/CBO9780511803123

Gladwell M (2013) David and Goliath: underdogs, misfits, and the art of battling giants. Little, Brown and Company, New York, NY

Glaser BG, Strauss AL (1967) The discovery of grounded theory: strategies for qualitative research. Aldine, Chicago, IL

Glăveanu VP (2012) Habitual creativity: revising habit, reconceptualizing creativity. Rev Gen Psychol 16(1):78–92. https://doi.org/10.1037/a0026611

Godfrey-Smith P (2003) Theory and reality: an introduction to the philosophy of science. University of Chicago Press, Chicago, IL

Golder PN, Shacham R, Mitra D (2009) Findings – innovations' origins: when, by whom, and how are radical innovations developed? Mark Sci 28(1):166–179. https://doi.org/10.1287/mksc. 1080.0384

Goldschmidt G (2011) Avoiding design fixation: transformation and abstraction in mapping from source to target. J Creat Behav 45(2):92–100. https://doi.org/10.1002/j.2162-6057.2011. tb01088.x

Greenwald AG, Pratkanis AR, Leippe MR, Baumgardner MH (1986) Under what conditions does theory obstruct research progress? Psychol Rev 93(2):216–229. https://doi.org/10.1037/0033-295X.93.2.216

Grossman GM, Helpman E (1994) Endogenous innovation in the theory of growth. J Econ Perspect 8(1):23–44. https://doi.org/10.1257/jep.8.1.23

Guilford JP (1950) Creativity. Am Psychol 5(9):444–454. https://doi.org/10.1037/h0063487

Guilford JP (1957) Creative abilities in the arts. Psychol Rev 64(2):110–118. https://doi.org/10. 1037/h0048280

Guilford JP (1968) Intelligence, creativity, and their educational implications. R.R. Knapp, San Diego, CA

Haas MR, Ham W (2015) Microfoundations of knowledge recombination: peripheral knowledge and breakthrough innovation in teams. In: Gavetti G, Ocasio W (eds) Cognition and strategy (advances in strategic management), vol 32. Emerald, Bingley, pp 47–87. https://doi.org/10. 1108/S0742-332220150000032002

Hargadon AB, Douglas Y (2001) When innovations meet institutions: Edison and the design of the electric light. Adm Sci Q 46(3):476–501. https://doi.org/10.2307/3094872

Hauser J, Tellis GJ, Griffin A (2006) Research on innovation: a review and agenda for marketing science. Mark Sci 25(6):687–717. https://doi.org/10.1287/mksc.1050.0144

Heinen   E   (1969)   Zum   Wissenschaftsprogramm   der   entscheidungsorientierten Betriebswirtschaftslehre [The scientific program of decision-oriented business administration]. Z Betriebswirt 39(4):207–220

Hennessey BA, Amabile TM (2010) Creativity. Annu Rev Psychol 61(1):569–598. https://doi.org/ 10.1146/annurev.psych.093008.100416

Herington MJ, van de Fliert E (2018) Positive deviance in theory and practice: a conceptual review. Deviant Behav 39(5):664–678. https://doi.org/10.1080/01639625.2017.1286194

Hodgson GM (2008) The concept of a routine. In: Becker MC (ed) Handbook of organizational routines. Edward Elgar, Cheltenham, pp 15–28

Hunt SD (1991) Modern marketing theory: critical issues in the philosophy of marketing science. South-Western, Cincinnati, OH

Hunt SD (2005) For truth and realism in management research. J Manag Inq 14(2):127–138. https://doi.org/10.1177/1056492605275242

Hunt SD (2013) The inductive realist model of theory generation: explaining the development of a theory of marketing ethics. AMS Rev 3(2):61–73. https://doi.org/10.1007/s13162-013-0040-2

Hunt SD (2015) Explicating the inductive realist model of theory generation. AMS Rev 5 (1–2):20–27. https://doi.org/10.1007/s13162-015-0064-x

Ireland RD, Hitt MA (1999) Achieving and maintaining strategic competitiveness in the 21st century: the role of strategic leadership. Acad Manag Exec 13(1):43–57. https://doi.org/10.5465/ame.1999.1567311

Jánszky SG, Jenzowsky SA (2010) Rulebreaker: Wie Menschen denken, deren Ideen die Welt verändern [Rulebreaker: how people think whose ideas change the world]. Goldegg, Berlin

Jean-Philippe V, Rodolphe D (2010) The missing link between the theory and empirics of path dependence: conceptual clarification, testability issue, and methodological implications. J Manag Stud 47(4):736–759. https://doi.org/10.1111/j.1467-6486.2009.00913.x

Jonassen DH (2010) Learning to solve problems: a handbook for designing problem-solving learning environments. Routledge, New York, NY

Jungbluth R (2006) Die 11 Geheimnisse des IKEA Erfolgs [11 secrets of ikea's success]. Campus, Frankfurt/New York

Kaplan S, Tripsas M (2008) Thinking about technology: applying a cognitive lens to technical change. Res Policy 37(5):790–805. https://doi.org/10.1016/j.respol.2008.02.002

Kelle U (2014) Theorization from data. The Sage handbook of qualitative data analysis. Sage, London. https://doi.org/10.4135/9781446282243

Kennedy BL (2018) Deduction, induction, and abduction. The Sage handbook of qualitative data collection. Sage, London. https://doi.org/10.4135/9781526416070

Ketokivi M, Mantere S, Cornelissen JP (2017) Reasoning by analogy and the progress of theory. Acad Manag Rev 42(4):637–658. https://doi.org/10.5465/amr.2015.0322Original

Keupp MM, Palmié M, Gassmann O (2012) The strategic management of innovation: a systematic review and paths for future research. Int J Manag Rev 14(4):367–390. https://doi.org/10.1111/j.1468-2370.2011.00321.x

King AA, Baatartogtokh B (2015) How useful is the theory of disruptive innovation? MIT Sloan Manag Rev 57(1):77–90

Klausen SH (2017) What is innovation? In: Shiu E (ed) Research handbook of innovation and creativity for marketing management. Edward Elgar, Cheltenham, pp 6–31. https://doi.org/10.4337/9780857937957.00008

Kotler P (1972) A generic concept of marketing. J Mark 36(2):46–54. https://doi.org/10.2307/1250977

Kotler P, Keller KL (2014) Marketing management, 14th edn. Pearson, Harlow

Krupka EL, Leider S, Jiang M (2017) A meeting of the minds: informal agreements and social norms. Manag Sci 63(6):1708–1729. https://doi.org/10.1287/mnsc.2016.2429

Kuhn TS (1996) The structure of scientific revolutions, 3rd edn. The University of Chicago Press, Chicago, IL

Labrecque JS, Wood W, Neal DT, Harrington N (2017) Habit slips: when consumers unintentionally resist new products. J Acad Mark Sci 45(1):119–133. https://doi.org/10.1007/s11747-016-0482-9

Larsen KR, How Bong C (2016) A tool for addressing construct identity in literature reviews and meta-analyses. MIS Q 40(3):529–A520

Lilien GL (2011) Bridging the academic-practitioner divide in marketing decision models. J Mark 75(4):196–210. https://doi.org/10.1509/jmkg.75.4.196

Little JDC (1970) Models and managers: the concept of a decision calculus. Manag Sci 16(8):B-466–B-485. https://doi.org/10.1287/mnsc.16.8.B466

MacInnis DJ (2011) A framework for conceptual contributions in marketing. J Mark 75 (4):136–154. https://doi.org/10.1509/jmkg.75.4.136

Mainemelis C (2010) Stealing fire: creative deviance in the evolution of new ideas. Acad Manag Rev 35(4):558–578. https://doi.org/10.5465/amr.35.4.zok558

Mantere S, Ketokivi M (2013) Reasoning in organization science. Acad Manag Rev 38(1):70–89. https://doi.org/10.5465/amr.2011.0188

Markides C (2006) Disruptive innovation: in need of better theory. J Prod Innov Manag 23 (1):19–25. https://doi.org/10.1111/j.1540-5885.2005.00177.x

Martin BR (2012) The evolution of science policy and innovation studies. Res Policy 41 (7):1219–1239. https://doi.org/10.1016/j.respol.2012.03.012

Mary George N, Parida V, Lahti T, Wincent J (2016) A systematic literature review of entrepreneurial opportunity recognition: insights on influencing factors. Int Entrep Manag J 12 (2):309–350. https://doi.org/10.1007/s11365-014-0347-y

Mascitelli R (2000) From experience: harnessing tacit knowledge to achieve breakthrough innovation. J Prod Innov Manag 17(3):179–193. https://doi.org/10.1016/S0737-6782(00)00038-2

Maxwell JA (2018) Collecting qualitative data: a realist approach. The SAGE handbook of qualitative data collection. Sage, London. https://doi.org/10.4135/9781526416070

Meffert H (2009) Erfolgreich mit den Großen des Marketings [successful with the greats of marketing]. Campus, Frankfurt a. M., Germany

Meheus J (2009) Foreword. In: Meheus J, Nickles T (eds) Models of discovery and creativity. Springer, Dordrecht, pp vii–viii. https://doi.org/10.1007/978-90-481-3421-2

Mertens W, Recker J, Kohlborn T, Kummer T-F (2016) A framework for the study of positive deviance in organizations. Deviant Behav 37(11):1288–1307. https://doi.org/10.1080/01639625.2016.1174519

Merton RK (1938) Social structure and anomie. Am Sociol Rev 3(5):672–682. https://doi.org/10.2307/2084686

Mintzberg H (1979) An emerging strategy of "direct" research. Adm Sci Q 24(4):582–589. https://doi.org/10.2307/2392364

Murmann JP, Frenken K (2006) Toward a systematic framework for research on dominant designs, technological innovations, and industrial change. Res Policy 35(7):925–952. https://doi.org/10.1016/j.respol.2006.04.011

Neal DT, Wood W, Labrecque JS, Lally P (2012) How do habits guide behavior? Perceived and actual triggers of habits in daily life. J Exp Soc Psychol 48(2):492–498. https://doi.org/10.1016/j.jesp.2011.10.011

Nelson RR, Winter SG (1982) An evolutionary theory of economic change. Harvard University Press, Cambridge, MA

North DC (1990) Institutions, institutional change, and economic performance. Cambridge University Press, Cambridge, NY

OECD (2015) The innovation imperative – contributing to productivity, growth and well-being. https://doi.org/10.1787/9789264239814-en

Okhuysen G, Bonardi J-P (2011) Editors' comments: the challenges of building theory by combining lenses. Acad Manag Rev 36(1):6–11. https://doi.org/10.5465/amr.36.1.zok006

Pentland Brian T, Feldman Martha S, Becker Markus C, Liu P (2012) Dynamics of organizational routines: a generative model. J Manag Stud 49(8):1484–1508. https://doi.org/10.1111/j.1467-6486.2012.01064.x

Porter ME (1990) The competitive advantage of nations. Harv Bus Rev 68(2):73–93

Prahalad CK, Ramaswamy V (2004) Co-creation experiences: the next practice in value creation. J Interact Mark 18(3):5–14. https://doi.org/10.1002/dir.20015

Principle (n.d.) In Oxford English Dictionary. https://en.oxforddictionaries.com/definition/princi ple. Accessed 1 Jun 2018

Reichenbach H (1938) Experience and prediction: an analysis of the foundations and the structure of knowledge. University of Chicago Press, Chicago, IL. https://doi.org/10.1037/11656-000

Ritter SM, Rietzschel EF (2017) Lay theories of creativity. In: Zedelius CM, Müller BCN, Schooler JW (eds) The science of lay theories: How beliefs shape our cognition, behavior, and health. Springer, New York, NY, pp 95–126. https://doi.org/10.1007/978-3-319-57306-9_5

Robinson SL, Bennett RJ (1995) A typology of deviant workplace behaviors: a multidimensional scaling study. Acad Manag J 38(2):555–572. https://doi.org/10.5465/256693

Romer PM (1994) The origins of endogenous growth. J Econ Perspect 8(1):3–22. https://doi.org/ 10.1257/jep.8.1.3

Rosenzweig S (2017) Non-customers as initiators of radical innovation. Ind Mark Manag 66:1–12. https://doi.org/10.1016/j.indmarman.2017.06.013

Rozin P (2001) Social psychology and science: some lessons from Solomon Asch. Personal Soc Psychol Rev 5(1):2–14. https://doi.org/10.1207/S15327957PSPR0501_1

Runco MA, Acar S (2012) Divergent thinking as an indicator of creative potential. Creat Res J 24 (1):66–75. https://doi.org/10.1080/10400419.2012.652929

Salter A, Alexy O (2014) The nature of innovation. In: Dodgson M, Gann DM, Phillips N (eds) The Oxford handbook of innovation management. Oxford University Press, Oxford, pp 26–49. https://doi.org/10.1093/oxfordhb/9780199694945.013.034

Sardeshmukh S, Smith-Nelson RM (2012) Opportunity recognition. Encyclopedia of new venture management. Sage, Thousand Oaks, CA. https://doi.org/10.4135/9781452218571.n142

Sax G (1968) Empirical foundations of educational research. Prentice-Hall, Englewood Cliffs, NJ

Schickore J, Steinle F (2006) Revisiting discovery and justification: historical and philosophical perspectives on the context distinction. Springer, Dordrecht

Schreyögg G (2014) Pfadabhängigkeit und Pfadbruch in Unternehmen [path-dependency and path-breaking in companies]. Schmalenbachs Zeitschrift für betriebswirtschaftliche Forschung 66 (S68):1–17. https://doi.org/10.1007/bf03373722

Schreyögg G, Sydow J (2011) Organizational path dependence: a process view. Organ Stud 32 (3):321–335. https://doi.org/10.1177/0170840610397481

Schumpeter JA (1911) Theorie der wirtschaftlichen Entwicklung [The theory of economic development]. Duncker & Humblot, Leipzig

Schumpeter JA (1934) The theory of economic development: an inquiry into profits, capital, credit, interest, and the business cycle. Harvard University Press, Cambridge, MA

Schumpeter JA (1942) Capitalism, socialism, and democracy. Harper & Bros, New York, NY

Schurz G (2014) Philosophy of science – a unified approach. Routledge, New York, NY

Shalley CE, Zhou J (2008) Organizational creativity research: a historical overview. In: Shalley CE, Zhou J (eds) Handbook of organizational creativity. Lawrence Erlbaum, Mahwah, NJ, pp 3–31

Shane S (2000) Prior knowledge and the discovery of entrepreneurial opportunities. Organ Sci 11 (4):448–469. https://doi.org/10.1287/orsc.11.4.448.14602

Shepherd DA, Sutcliffe KM (2011) Inductive top-down theorizing: a source of new theories of organization. Acad Manag Rev 36(2):361–380. https://doi.org/10.5465/amr.2009.0157

Simon HA (1976) Administrative behavior: a study of decision-making processes in administrative organization, 3rd edn. Free Press, New York, NY

Sluiter I (2017) Anchoring innovation: a classical research agenda. Eur Rev 25(1):20–38. https:// doi.org/10.1017/S1062798716000442

Solow RM (1985) Economic history and economics. Am Econ Rev 75(2):328–331

Sood A, Tellis GJ (2005) Technological evolution and radical innovation. J Mark 69(3):152–168. https://doi.org/10.1509/jmkg.69.3.152.66361

Spindler G-I (2016) Querdenker-Beispiele: Spielregeln erfolgreich geändert [lateral thinking examples: successfully changing the rules of the game]. In: Querdenken im Marketing: Wie Sie die Regeln im Markt zu Ihrem Vorteil verändern [Thinking outside the box in marketing: How to change the rules in the market to gain competitive advantage]. Springer, Wiesbaden, pp 121–207. https://doi.org/10.1007/978-3-658-08442-4_6

Spreitzer GM, Sonenshein S (2004) Toward the construct definition of positive deviance. Am Behav Sci 47(6):828–847. https://doi.org/10.1177/0002764203260212

Suarez FF (2004) Battles for technological dominance: an integrative framework. Res Policy 33 (2):271–286. https://doi.org/10.1016/j.respol.2003.07.001

Suddaby R (2010) Editor's comments: construct clarity in theories of management and organization. Acad Manag Rev 35(3):346–357

Sutton RI, Staw BM (1995) What theory is not. Adm Sci Q 40(3):371–384. https://doi.org/10.2307/2393788

Sydow J, Schreyögg G, Koch J (2009) Organizational path dependence: opening the black box. Acad Manag Rev 34(4):689–709. https://doi.org/10.5465/amr.34.4.zok689

The Economist (2016) Between Bentonville and Bezos: lessons from the two giants of American retailing. The Economist. https://www.economist.com

The World Bank and OECD (2009) Innovation and growth – chasing a moving frontier. OECD, Paris. https://doi.org/10.1787/9789264073975-en

Thornberg R, Charmaz K (2014) Grounded theory and theoretical coding. The Sage handbook of qualitative data analysis. Sage, London. https://doi.org/10.4135/9781446282243

Tidd J (2006) A review of innovation models. Discussion paper 1. Imperial College London, Tanaka Business School

Titus PA (2018) Exploring creative marketing thought: divergent ideation processes and outcomes. Psychol Mark 35(3):237–248. https://doi.org/10.1002/mar.21083

Tolbert PS, Zucker LG (1996) The institutionalization of institutional theory. In: Clegg SR, Hardy C, North CE (eds) Handbook of organization studies. Sage, London, pp 175–190

Torrance EP (1962) Guiding creative talent. Prentice-Hall, Englewood Cliffs, NJ

Truzzi M (1976) Sherlock Holmes: applied social psychologist. In: Sanders WB (ed) The sociologist as detective, 2nd edn. Praeger, New York, NY

Tsoukas H (1989) The validity of idiographic research explanations. Acad Manag Rev 14 (4):551–561. https://doi.org/10.5465/amr.1989.4308386

Tushman ML, Anderson P (1986) Technological discontinuities and organizational environments. Adm Sci Q 31(3):439–465. https://doi.org/10.2307/2392832

Tushman ML, Rosenkopf L (1992) On the organizational determinants of technological change: towards a sociology of technological evolution. In: Staw BM, Cummings LL (eds) Research in organizational behavior, vol 14. JAI Press, Greenwich, CT, pp 311–347

Utterback JM (1974) Innovation in industry and the diffusion of technology. Science 183 (4125):620–626. https://doi.org/10.1126/science.183.4125.620

Vadera AK, Pratt MG, Mishra P (2013) Constructive deviance in organizations: integrating and moving forward. J Manag 39(5):1221–1276. https://doi.org/10.1177/0149206313475816

Verplanken B (2006) Beyond frequency: habit as mental construct. Br J Soc Psychol 45 (3):639–656. https://doi.org/10.1348/014466605X49122

Verplanken B, Aarts H (1999) Habit, attitude, and planned behaviour: is habit an empty construct or an interesting case of goal-directed automaticity? Eur Rev Soc Psychol 10(1):101–134. https://doi.org/10.1080/14792779943000035

Verplanken B, Wood W (2006) Interventions to break and create consumer habits. J Public Policy Mark 25(1):90–103. https://doi.org/10.1509/jppm.25.1.90

Warren DE (2003) Constructive and destructive deviance in organizations. Acad Manag Rev 28 (4):622–632. https://doi.org/10.5465/amr.2003.10899440

Weick KE (1989) Theory construction as disciplined imagination. Acad Manag Rev 14 (4):516–531. https://doi.org/10.5465/amr.1989.4308376

Weick KE (1995) What theory is not, theorizing is. Adm Sci Q 40(3):385–390. https://doi.org/10.2307/2393789

Wendy W, Neal DT (2009) The habitual consumer. J Consum Psychol 19(4):579–592. https://doi.org/10.1016/j.jcps.2009.08.003

Whetten DA (1989) What constitutes a theoretical contribution. Acad Manag Rev 14(4):490–495. https://doi.org/10.5465/AMR.1989.4308371

Wilkins LT (1964) Social deviance: social policy, action, and research. Tavistock, London

Wilson EO (1998) Scientists, scholars, knaves and fools. Am Sci 86(1):6–7

Winter SG (1964) Economic "natural selection" and the theory of the firm. Yale Econ Essays 4 (1):225–272

Wood W, Rünger D (2016) Psychology of habit. Annu Rev Psychol 67(1):289–314. https://doi.org/10.1146/annurev-psych-122414-033417

Wood W, Quinn JM, Kashy DA (2002) Habits in everyday life: thought, emotion, and action. J Pers Soc Psychol 83(6):1281–1297. https://doi.org/10.1037/0022-3514.83.6.1281

Wood W, Tam L, Witt MG (2005) Changing circumstances, disrupting habits. J Pers Soc Psychol 88(6):918–933. https://doi.org/10.1037/0022-3514.88.6.918

Yadav MS (2010) The decline of conceptual articles and implications for knowledge development. J Mark 74(1):1–19. https://doi.org/10.1509/jmkg.74.1.1

Yadav MS (2014) Enhancing theory development in marketing. AMS Rev 4(1–2):1–4. https://doi.org/10.1007/s13162-014-0059-z

Yin RK (1981) The case study crisis: some answers. Adm Sci Q 26(1):58–65. https://doi.org/10.2307/2392599

Yin RK (2014) Case study research design and methods, 5th edn. Sage, Thousand Oaks, CA

Yu D, Hang CC (2010) A reflective review of disruptive innovation theory. Int J Manag Rev 12 (4):435–452. https://doi.org/10.1111/j.1468-2370.2009.00272.x

Zedelius CM, Müller BCN, Schooler JW (2017) The science of lay theories: how beliefs shape our cognition, behavior, and health. Springer, New York, NY. https://doi.org/10.1007/978-3-319-57306-9

Zeng L, Proctor RW, Salvendy G (2011) Can traditional divergent thinking tests be trusted in measuring and predicting real-world creativity? Creat Res J 23(1):24–37. https://doi.org/10.1080/10400419.2011.545713

Chapter 2
Conceptual and Empirical Exploration

Abstract An empirical analysis of the development of rule-breaking behavior leads to the choice of sports as the most promising domain. Selection criteria like the availability of cases and data, assumed degree of insight, and transfer potential privilege it over business and other domains. Within the sports domain, strict criteria of rule-breaking narrow the qualifying cases to eight: the Fosbury Flop in the High Jump, the Flip Turn in Backstroke Swimming, the O'Brien Shift in the Shot Put, the Skate Skiing Technique in Cross-Country Skiing, the Forward Seat in Equestrian Jumping, the Jump Shot in Basketball, the V-Style in Ski Jumping, and the Dolphin Kick in Butterfly Swimming. Based on secondary data, the eight cases are analyzed in depth individually and for cross-case commonalities. The resulting lessons learned are summarized in eight distinct narratives and 21 characteristics that contributed to successful rule-breaking behavior.

2.1 The Nature of Rule-Breaking Market Behavior

An attempt to explore the mechanisms underlying rule-breaking market behavior must start with a precise understanding of its constitutive elements. In Sect. 1.2, the definitional key characteristics of rule-breaking market behavior have already been briefly outlined to define the scope of the research and to better distinguish the underlying interest from other potentially related works. Now, the specific set of the four necessary and sufficient attributes of rule-breaking market behavior (Fig. 2.1) will be systematically outlined, closely aligning with current discussions in the creativity and innovation literature. In the research process, starting with a working definition, the four constitutive elements have been gradually refined with the help of empirical data on real-world rule-breaking and other innovations. By providing a clear conceptual definition (Podsakoff et al. 2016), the objective is to distinguish rule-breaking market behavior from other innovations. The intention is not to develop a measurement model with specific items and scales but rather to provide a guideline for the identification of rule-breaking behavior for empirical study. In the description, the features are phrased as questions to serve as a Four-Way-Rule-Breaking Test.

© Springer Nature Switzerland AG 2019   37
A.-K. Veenendaal, *Toward a Better Understanding of Rule-Breaking Market Behavior*, Contributions to Management Science,
https://doi.org/10.1007/978-3-030-16107-1_2

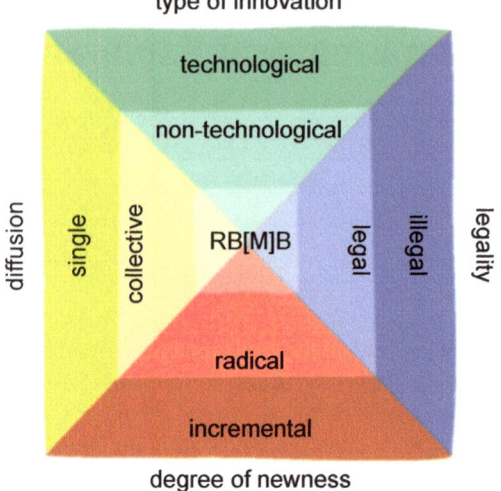

Fig. 2.1 Taxonomy of rule-breaking market behavior's key characteristics (source: author)

Note: RB[M]B (Rule-Breaking [Market] Behavior) can be identified with the help of the four inner square features. Feature 1 in green: Is it a non-technological innovation? Feature 2 in blue: Does the innovation comply with the formal set of rules? Feature 3 in red: Is the innovation radical? Feature 4 in yellow: Is the innovation collectively accepted?

2.1.1   Feature 1: Is It a Non-technological Innovation?

The first question to be answered in the course of investigating whether an innovation is rule-breaking or not is related to the type of innovation. Rule-breaking market behavior is concerned with insightful approaches to innovation; the focal interest is human insight rather than technological progress. Related to the field of innovation research, this contrast can be approximated by the existing distinction made between technologically and non-technologically induced innovation, which leads to the following question to be posed: Is it a non-technological innovation?

Research on innovation in organizations has predominantly followed a technological imperative (Damanpour and Aravind 2012). Many theories and models of innovation are thus based on technologically induced innovation, and other types of innovation have received less attention (Černe et al. 2016; Crossan and Apaydin 2010; Damanpour 2014; Keupp et al. 2012). There are several definitions and controversies regarding non-technological innovation. While some argue that innovation types may be artificial distinctions (Edquist et al. 2001), others do not consider the entire conceptual landscape of non-technological innovations. Many scholars, for example, follow the Oslo Manual definition (OECD 2005), depicting non-technology innovation as innovations in organizational structures, management techniques and marketing concepts or strategies. Following Černe et al. (2016), this work adopts a broader understanding (i.e. all innovation that includes a non-technical component). As an umbrella term, non-technological innovation has only recently become recognized by scholars and is currently considered an emerging field (Černe et al. 2016). More prevalent are some of the different sub-types of non-technological innovation such as administrative, organizational, management, marketing, process, social, ancillary, open, strategic, business model, and eco-innovations.[1] Research under the term "management innovation research" includes many of the abovementioned perspectives on non-technological innovation and can be considered a key concept (Damanpour and Aravind 2012; Volberda et al. 2014).

Contrary to the accusation that certain distinctions between different types of innovations are artificial, we see useful differences and goal-relevant specificities to non-technological (vs. technological) innovations. For instance, the development of non-technological innovations in firms is not limited to certain departments (e.g. R&D) but includes all employees as potential innovators. Non-technological innovation is related to implicit underlying assumptions in the sense of norms and behavioral standards instead of technological givens. That means, while technological innovation is (at least at some point) available to any firm, often going along with high investments, human insight or non-technological innovations are personal and unique to managers, other employees and firm-related agents. Furthermore, different patterns of antecedents and specific processual mechanisms can be assumed to be essential for successful non-technological innovations. Resources, knowledge and capabilities, for example, may be factors that play a role in both types of innovations but at different stages of the process and to different degrees.

Research regarding the relationship between non-technological and technological innovations is sparse. While some scholars argue that technological innovation is an antecedent of new non-technological solutions (Armbruster et al. 2008; Barañano 2003; Osterwalder 2004), others posit that technological innovations are enhanced by the non-technological counterpart (Camisón and Villar-López 2014; Damanpour et al. 2009; Mothe and Uyen Nguyen Thi 2010; Read 2000). As conceptualized in the introductory Sect. 1.1, this work considers both options as possibilities.

2.1.2   Feature 2: Does the Innovation Comply with the Formal Set of Rules?

From a semantic point of view, the term rule-breaking might be interpreted as behavior that violates the formal law and could, therefore, be legally sanctioned. However, this is explicitly not meant here. Deviations from behavioral standards that are illegal or harmful to society are explicitly excluded from the scope of the underlying analyses. Thus, when assessing an innovation in accordance with this

---

[1]Černe et al. (2016) provide a thorough review on the theoretical origins and intellectual structure of non-technological innovation which takes all the above-mentioned sub-types including conceptual overlaps into account.

criterion, the question to be posed is: Does the non-technological innovation lie within the formal set of rules?

Closely related to this, Backhaus and Schneider (2009) distinguish between exogenous and endogenous rules that determine or guide companies' behavior in a market. Exogenous rules have an external cause or origin; they regulate the actions of market members and are legally binding. Exogenous rules comprise all kinds of laws and codified rules, which may enforce by the imposition of penalties. Endogenous rules, on the other hand, have an internal cause or origin; they have been confined to a particular domain, such as a market or a company. Endogenous rules are interpreted as normative behavioral expectations, standard behavioral conventions in an industry, and typically, they are not codified. They reflect the way in which something is usually done; an oftentimes-implicit common agreement between market members that emerged over the course of the years. Rule-breaking behavior, in the sense of deviating from such endogenous rules, means pursuing novel behavioral paths without expecting legal sanctions.[2] Endogeneity here is not to be confused with endogeneity in the statistical sense.

Even though legal restrictions do not constitute a decisive part of this work, some brief remarks seem appropriate since they put constraints on the decisions that economic actors take and are, therefore, a central part of the institutional environment surrounding every transaction. While government-defined standards aim at protecting public interests, they may at the same time rule out certain rule-breaking ideas as unlawful beforehand. Backhaus and Plinke (1986) provide a basic systematization of legal impacts on marketing decisions by distinguishing between general regulations that relate to the organization of markets (property rights regulations and contract law) and regulations that intervene into market processes (protection of competition such as antitrust laws, protection of consumers or competitors) and, therefore, restrict the scope of marketing decisions.

A current business example to further illustrate this criterion is the case of Uber. Uber altered the transportation services industry dramatically by launching a private chauffeur solution. The company does not provide cabs to its drivers but employs private vehicles whose owners are registered with Uber as drivers. Uber is one of the leading transportation services and the highest valued start-up in the world (Blystone 2018). Due to legal restrictions, Uber services have been banned from several countries for unfair competition to licensed cab drivers. As London Business School Professor Birkinshaw (2017) points out: "When firms like Uber come up with new business models, they are—by definition—challenging the informal 'rules of the game' that incumbent firms are using. But Uber has taken a step further than most because it is also challenging the *formal* regulatory structure within which the game

---

[2]This does not imply that (endogenous) rule-breaking behavior does not get penalized at all. In fact, rule-breaking in the world of business can certainly lead to problems and punishment by relevant exchange partners (e.g. customers, suppliers, employees or other stakeholders) being reflected in the rule-breaking behaviors' market success (e.g. market rejects the rule-breaking behavior).

is being played" (cited in section "Strategy as breaking-the-rules"). Thus, Uber is not considered an example of rule-breaking market behavior as it is defined in this work.

In conclusion, rule-breaking market behavior exclusively refers to departures from endogenous rules that are not legally binding. While this second attribute further refines the origin of rule-breaking market behavior, it is a requirement for the rule-breaking attempt to become successful.

2.1.3   Feature 3: Is the Innovation Radical?

The third conceptual characteristic of rule-breaking market behavior refers to the magnitude of change. This is assessed by looking at both the process and the outcome of the new behavior (i.e. is the behavior fundamentally different and substantially better[3]). More specifically, rule-breaking market behavior is conceptualized to be distinct from current market practices and must lead to high impact for the innovative company. It is important to note that this stage only concerns the innovative individual or institution (not the subsequent process of innovation diffusion, which is a matter of the fourth feature). The question to be posed is whether the innovation is radical.

Discussions with regard to an innovation's magnitude of change occur under several different terms in the innovation literature, such as radicalness, degree of novelty, and newness. The degree of newness resulting from the innovation into the economic system is often thought to be the most crucial distinction in innovation research (Salter and Alexy 2014). The spectrum of novelty is typically modelled by the degree of discontinuity, ranging from radical innovations on one end of the continuum to incremental innovations on the other end (for a review on innovation typology and innovativeness terminology, see Garcia and Calantone 2002). Radical innovations are also described as groundbreaking, disruptive, breakthrough, divergent, really new, set-breaking, transformational, paradigm-shifting, discontinuous, substantially differing or changing the status quo. Incremental innovations, on the other hand, are referred to as adaptive, imitative, evolutionary, minor modifications, cumulative improvements or refinements of the current conditions (Anderson et al. 2014; Chandy and Tellis 1998; Damanpour and Aravind 2012; George 2007; Madjar et al. 2011; Mumford and Gustafson 1988; Rubera and Kirca 2012; Sternberg 1999; Unsworth 2001). While incremental changes are usually efficiency-driven, radical transformations are targeting a firm's effectiveness goals. According to Salter and Alexy (2014), the latter are often identified by a shift in the performance-price ratio

---

[3]The combination of those two elements results into four possible categories: fundamentally different and substantially better (!), fundamentally different but not substantially better, not fundamentally different but substantially better (?), not fundamentally different and not substantially better. When making an assessment as to whether a case is radical, when in doubt, the outcome (substantially better) is considered to be more important than the process (fundamentally different).

by a factor of five or even ten.[4] In most industries, radical innovations are an infrequent phenomenon occurring only every 30 years (Anderson and Tushman 1990). It is important to recognize that the purpose of distinguishing between different types of newness is not to suggest that one or the other may be superior, per se. It can be assumed, however, that the factors leading to one or another differ to a considerable extent. For example, radical creativity has been associated with willingness to take risks, career commitment and resources for creativity, while incremental creativity is generally predicted by organizational identification, presence of creative co-workers and conformity (Madjar et al. 2011).

The measurement of innovation newness is a problematic issue with a plethora of different methods employed (Garcia and Calantone 2002; Johannessen et al. 2001).[5] Both creativity and innovation are subjective, socially constructed phenomena, bound by historical time and place (e.g. Amabile 1983). Therefore, what is perceived as distinct, or fundamentally different from current market practices, depends on an individual or a group and varies as a function of what already exists in that particular domain. The individual perception of novelty can be influenced by several aspects (Zhou et al. 2017) and certainly defies an objective assessment. The question of whether a novel way is not just fundamentally different but also highly impactful is related to its contribution to the innovative company's performance outcomes and, thus, synonymous with (commercially) successful market behavior. Among other things, from a customer perspective, this requires that the rule-breaking market behavior fulfills their key needs better than existing products, viz. it provides substantially higher customer benefits (Chandy and Tellis 1998). The rule-breaking market behavior must be meaningful to a customer, denoting that it is personally valuable or relevant.

2.1.4 Feature 4: Is the Innovation Collectively Accepted?

Finally, in order to qualify as rule-breaking market behavior, a shift from the single level to a more collective level of acceptance is required. Basically, this means that the rule-breaking market behavior becomes a new rule; it has changed the competition. To investigate if that is the case, the fourth question to be asked is whether the innovation is collectively accepted.

---

[4]In quantitative statistics, the magnitude of a phenomenon is expressed by the effect size. Field (2013) defines an effect size as "an objective and (usually) standardized measure of the magnitude of an observed effect" (p. 874). While statistical significance determines that the observed effect is not due to random chance, the effect size quantifies the importance of an effect and can be compared to other effect sizes (even if particular variables or scales have been different across studies).

[5]Dahlin and Behrens (2005) list technology cycles (P. Anderson and Tushman 1990), s-curves (Foster 1986), technological trajectories (Christensen and Rosenbloom 1995; Dosi 1982), hedonic price models (Henderson 1993), expert panels (Dewar and Dutton 1986) and patent measures as the five most general methods to measure radicalness in the area of technology.

Whether rule-breaking market behavior has changed the competition refers to the "capacity of a new innovation to create a paradigm shift in the ... market structure in an industry" (p. 112) and is not just assessed from a micro firm related perspective (Garcia and Calantone 2002). In other words, it is conceptualized that the novel way to behave affects other market players as well, eventually leading to a change in the dominant logic of the market. By that, it is posited, that the impact of a new approach is reflected in its adoption by customers and other market actors. Thus, a shift from an individual, intra-subjective perspective to a more common, inter-subjective perspective is suggested. Of course, depending on the radicalness of the new behavior, other actors may not be quick to adopt the new behavior since it may require a substantial amount of time to implement and practice.

Ultimately, in the context of business, the success of innovations depends on consumers' accepting them (Hauser et al. 2006). In innovation research, two streams of literature exist. First, the literature on innovativeness focuses on adoption processes at the individual level, and second, the product diffusion literature focuses on adoption processes at the aggregate level.

Research on consumer innovativeness is concerned with the mental, behavioral, and demographic characteristics related to how fast or eagerly consumers are willing to adopt innovations (Hauser et al. 2006). Roehrich (2004) reviewed the concepts of consumer innovativeness and classified the findings on how to measure innovativeness into two groups: life innovativeness measures, which focus on the propensity to innovate at a general behavioral level (e.g. Kirton's 1976 innovators-adaptors inventory) and adoptive innovativeness scales, which focus specifically on the tendency to buy new products.

Rogers' (1962, 2003) seminal theory of innovation adoption is considered the most important work on product diffusion. The author provides explanations for when and how a novel idea, practice, or technique is accepted, rejected or reevaluated over time in a society. According to the framework, the decision to adopt an innovation is best predicted by the adopter's pre-adoption beliefs about or expectations from the innovation. Rogers (2003) describes the innovation diffusion process as "an uncertainty reduction process" (p. 232) with five attributes of innovations that may reduce the uncertainties: (1) relative advantage—"the degree to which an innovation is perceived as better than the idea it supersedes" (p. 15), (2) compatibility—"the degree to which an innovation is perceived as being consistent with the existing values, past experiences, and needs of potential adopters" (p. 15), (3) complexity—"the degree to which an innovation is perceived as difficult to understand and use" (p. 16), (4) trialability—"the degree to which an innovation may be experimented with on a limited basis" (p. 16), and (5) observability—"the degree to which the results of an innovation are visible to others" (p. 16).

In brief, question four sets in advance that the consequences of the novel behavior are required to affect the fundamental nature of current market givens in order to qualify as a pure version of rule-breaking market behavior. Once question four (in addition to the three prior questions) can be assessed as a given, the afore-described schematic conceptualization can be advanced by a new graphic element: see (a_1) new option in Fig. 2.2. The current options in a market to gain competitive advantage have been extended by a new option.

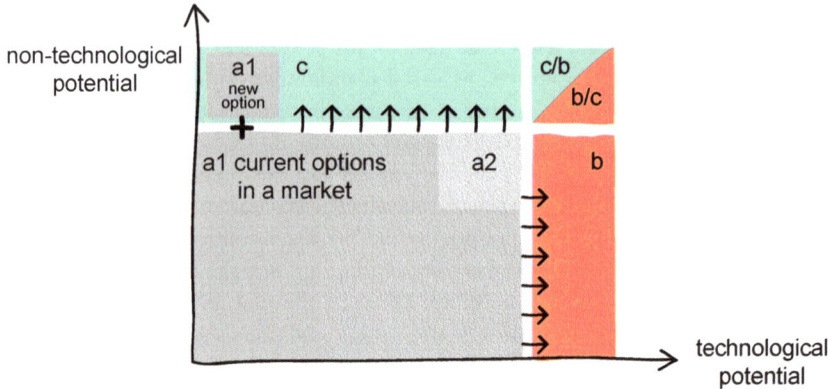

Note: a = current options in a market, b and c = expansion of the current options in a market. As in
Fig. 1.1, the color red indicates that technological innovation (b), and technological innovation that
leads to insight innovation (b/c) are not part of this work. Green indicates that insight innovation
(c) and insight innovation that leads to technological innovation (c/b) are part of this work. See Sect.
1.1 for a detailed explanation of the conceptualization. Here, (a1) new option has been added to the
figure

Fig. 2.2 Schematic conceptualization of the focal perspective, variant 2 (source: author)

2.1.5   *Further Elaborations Beyond the Conceptual Features*

These four attributes constitute the characteristics of rule-breaking market behavior
and are sufficient to form the concept's core. In the process of the analysis, many
prospective other differentiating features have been encountered and carefully
examined whether they would positively contribute to the conceptualization or
not. Although they do not qualify for distinguishing rule-breaking market behavior
from other innovative attempts, for the sake of an even better understanding of the
phenomenon, some of those criteria will be briefly outlined below.

Consider for example the number of actors involved in the development of the rule-
breaking behavior. Whether it is a rule-breaking attempt of a single creator or the result
of teamwork is regarded as irrelevant for the classification of the particular phenomenon
to be rule-breaking or not. Furthermore, the analyses have shown that it is not uncommon that different stages of the rule-breaking process trace back to the responsibility of
separate individuals or groups. For instance, rule-breaking behavior may be invented by
person A but popularized by person B, maybe even years or decades later. While such
characteristics will be acknowledged for a better understanding of the process, differences regarding agency, temporal and spatial dimensions do not lead to an inclusion or
exclusion of phenomena from the concept of rule-breaking market behavior.

Equally unimportant is a distinction among the number of behavioral changes
leading to rule-breaking behavior. Either one single or the sum of several incremental deviations from behavioral standards meets the requirements of the underlying
conceptualization. For example, whereas Red Bull (leaving their marketing efforts
aside), focusing on function instead of taste, has primarily changed one major feature

of the beverages market; Ryan Air, on the other hand, departed from several minor rules of the aviation industry.

A further criterion of no matter is whether the process of rule-breaking behavior has been started intentionally or coincidentally. While some scholars focus only on any one of the two features, this work is curious to learn more about both.

Lastly, the discovery of novel and impactful ways to solve a problem is often associated with a sudden appearance of a solution through insight, also famously known as the "aha" effect with its two characteristic features, suddenness and ease (Topolinski and Reber 2010). Both aspects can, but may not necessarily, apply for rule-breaking behavior: Neither have the rule-breaking ideas to pop into mind abruptly and surprisingly nor does the problem-related processing have to be fast and easy after a new way has been discovered.

2.1.6 Integration of the Decision Criteria in a Four-Way-Rule-Breaking Test

Based on the afore-outlined key characteristics and in preparation for a systematic selection of insightful cases of rule-breaking behavior, a decision tree is used. While decision trees are often applied to build classification algorithms in the context of machine learning (see Kotsiantis 2013, for an overview), in a simpler vein they can also serve as a graphical and analytical tool to systematize choices in a decision-making process. Here, the decision has to be made about which cases, from a large pool of innovations, are to be selected for the empirical analysis. Typically, a tree consists of nodes, branches, and endpoints. At each of the nodes, a decision has to be taken. The branches spreading out from the nodes represent the alternatives from which a choice can be made (Decision Tree 2017). Since the prospective empirical data to which the decision tree will be applied is primarily qualitative in nature, all stages (nodes) of the tree are based on logical considerations rather than mathematical algorithms. The tree can be thought of as a cognitive cluster analysis. The thought process leading to the final decision tree consisted of two basic stages. In a first step, individual questions have been generated and refined with the help of empirical data. In a second step, the rules have been evaluated as a collection[6] and refined, respectively. The decision tree is linear, applying a typical decision rule (Quinlan 1987):

> *if* non-technological:yes *and* legal:yes *and* radical:yes *and* collective:yes *then* rule-breaking [market] behavior.

The set of four exhaustive and mutually exclusive attributes is used to classify innovations. If there are unknown values for one or more of the attributes, either an

---

[6]"The performance of a simplification method can be assessed in terms of the clarity and accuracy of its final product" (Quinlan 1987, p. 229).

estimate is made or the specific example will be sorted out. The proposed hierarchical sequence of the questions has been chosen to solve the most differentiable classification task first. Moreover, the questions are sorted in a logical order based on the characteristics of the innovation processes. For instance, an illegal attempt to deviate from current market practices (which would be legal:no) means it is logically impossible to enter the next two stages in the decision tree because a departure from the set of formal rules will usually lead to a disqualification from competition. If the empirical analysis would have turned out to result in a final cluster of too many or few cases of rule-breaking behavior or a disproportionate imbalance between the categories, the questions were refined accordingly. Also, the questions have been deliberately phrased in a way that a positive answer (yes) advances the case to the next level of the selection funnel. This seemed reasonable because the development of rule-breaking market behavior is conceptualized to be a desirable means in a company's quest to achieve a sustainable competitive advantage.

A nominal scale to respond to the questions (yes/no) has been favored because it appeared to be the most accurate, simple, comprehensible, and opaque way to distinguish the focal phenomenon from other innovations and to select a range of suitable cases for the analysis. The explanations in Sects. 2.1.1–2.1.4 have already shown that the four bimodalities to innovation vary with regard to how easy they can be applied. Whether an innovation is technological versus non-technological or legal versus illegal is easier to assess than whether it is radical versus incremental or a single versus a collective phenomenon. Especially with regard to the magnitude of change, the higher difficulty in assessment can be partially attributed to the fact that the criterion lacks objectivity and tends to be thought of more in a continuous than binary fashion. In the real world there is a broad gray continuum that links the polarized concepts of radical and incremental innovations.

As the explanations have shown, the most important characteristic of rule-breaking market behavior is the deviation from established standards of behavior, which can also be functional for a company without being classified as radical and having to change entire sectors. However, in this work, the cases have been chosen to be of the most extreme kind because by making it really strict, there is no debate regarding the selection of the cases. All 16 possible combinations of the 4 decision criteria, for example, including the less radical second order rule-breaking market behavior, are displayed in Table 2.1.

Table 2.1 Combinations of rule-breaking key characteristics

Type	Legality	Novelty	Diffusion	Description
Non-technol.*	Legal*	Radical*	Collective*	Rule-breaking market behavior
Non-technol.*	Legal*	Radical*	Single	Rule-breaking exception
Non-technol.*	Legal*	Incremental	Collective*	Second order rule-breaking market behavior
Non-technol.*	Legal*	Incremental	Single	Idiosyncratic behavior
Non-technol.*	Illegal	Radical*	Collective*	Illegal breakthrough attempt
Non-technol.*	Illegal	Radical*	Single	Illegal breakthrough attempt
Non-technol.*	Illegal	Incremental	Collective*	Illegal innovative attempt
Non-technol.*	Illegal	Incremental	Single	Illegal idiosyncratic behavior
Technological	Legal*	Radical*	Collective*	Technological breakthrough
Technological	Legal*	Radical*	Single	Technological pioneer
Technological	Legal*	Incremental	Collective*	Incremental technological innovation
Technological	Legal*	Incremental	Single	Unique technological advance
Technological	Illegal	Radical*	Collective*	Illegal breakthrough technology
Technological	Illegal	Radical*	Single	Illegal technological pioneer
Technological	Illegal	Incremental	Collective*	Illegal, unique technological innovation
Technological	Illegal	Incremental	Single	Illegal, minor technological attempt

Note: The asterisks mark those criteria that have been answered with yes. Logically, there is one type with four asterisks (rule-breaking market behavior), four types with three asterisks (these four have been used as exemplary labels in Fig. 2.3), six types with two asterisks, four types with one asterisk, and one type with no asterisk at all. Not all combinations are meaningful (e.g. combinations of illegal + collective) but the overview helps picturing the spectrum of phenomena resulting from the four key characteristics

2.2   Research Setting, Data and Analysis

2.2.1   Rationale of a Multiple Case Study Beyond Business

Potentially being the first method of social science (Gerring 2006, p. x), the intensive study of very few cases lead to the construction of well-known theories in the course of the method's history. For instance, Freud's theory on human psychology relied on a close observation of a small number of clinical cases, Darwin's work on the process of human evolution built on his travels to a few chosen locations and Levi-Strauss's insights into human cultures based on several North and South American tribes (Gerring 2006, p. 40).

Deriving generalizable principles from case studies is a research strategy in which one or more cases are analyzed to create theoretical constructs, propositions and theory from case-based, empirical evidence (Eisenhardt 1989). According to Yin (2014), a case study is "an empirical inquiry that investigates a contemporary phenomenon (the "case") in depth and within its real-world context" (p. 16). Gerring (2017) specifies that, "a *case* connotes a spatially and temporally delimited phenomenon of theoretical significance" (p. 27). Not to be confused with teaching cases (Yin 2014, p. 18), scholars have long recognized the usefulness of case studies for generating research propositions and developing theory (e.g. George and Bennett

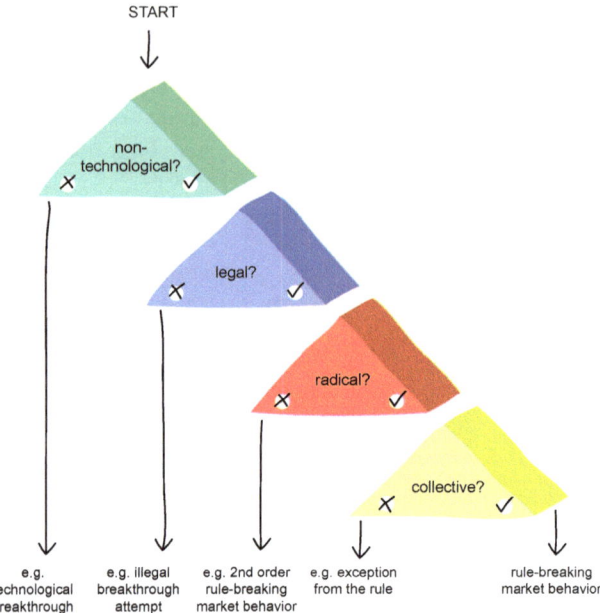

START

non-technological? ✗ ✓

legal? ✗ ✓

radical? ✗ ✓

collective? ✗ ✓

e.g. technological breakthrough

e.g. illegal breakthrough attempt

e.g. 2nd order rule-breaking market behavior

e.g. exception from the rule

rule-breaking market behavior

Note: The illustration displays the Four-Way-Rule-Breaking Test represented in form of a decision tree. The cross stands for no. The check mark stands for yes. The triangles symbolize the branches of a decision tree and at the same time, if they were put together, would result in the square shape that was initially introduced in Fig. 2.1. The colors match accordingly. The test starts at the upper left shape, continuing to the right from triangle to triangle if the example does not get sorted out earlier (by answering a question with no). The cluster names at the bottom of the arrows are exemplary, except for the right most cluster, rulebreaking market behavior. They are based on the assumption that any other question except the one where they have been sorted out would have been answered with yes (for further clarification see the full range of options in Table 2.1)

Fig. 2.3 Four-Way-Rule-Breaking Test (source: author)

2005). In a managerial context, case studies have been used to develop theoretical insight about topics as diverse as strategy, internal organization, and group processes (Eisenhardt and Graebner 2007; for a variety of popular examples from different contexts, see also Gerring 2017). Papers using the method are frequently highly regarded and among the most highly cited pieces in relevant outlets (Eisenhardt and Graebner (2007) exemplarily refer to Eisenhardt 1989; Gersick 1988) and sometimes even considered the "most interesting" research (Bartunek et al. 2006, p. 13). Often, case studies are the first line of evidence, aimed at recognizing the unexpected regarding a particular research question. "The product of a good case study is *insight*" (Gerring 2017, p. xvii). As Eisenhardt and Graebner (2007) point out, bottom-up research approaches "using cases typically answers research questions that address 'how' and 'why' in unexplored research areas particularly well (Edmondson and McManus 2007). By contrast, the research strategy is ill-equipped to address the questions of 'how often,' and 'how many' or questions about the relative empirical importance of constructs" (p. 27). A case study whose purpose is to explain how or why some condition came to be, as in the attempt to better understand the process of rule-breaking market behavior, is specified as an explanatory case study by Yin (2014). Although the case study method does not enable the observation of the underlying mental process that gives rise to people's innovative behavior, it is possible to witness many of its outward manifestations (Gerring 2006, p. 45).

Theoretical insights emerge from case studies by "recognizing patterns of relationships among constructs within and across cases *and* their underlying logical arguments" (Eisenhardt and Graebner 2007, p. 25). "The theory-building process occurs via recursive cycling among the case data, emerging theory, and later, extant literature" (Eisenhardt and Graebner 2007, p. 25). Eisenhardt and Graebner (2007) further state that, "although sometimes seen as 'subjective,' well-done theory building from cases is surprisingly 'objective,' because its close adherence to the data keeps researchers 'honest'" (p. 25).

Regarding the number of cases under study, two basic types of case study research can be distinguished: the *case study* in which either a single case or a small number of cases (i.e. multiple case study) is analyzed intensively and the *cross-case study* in which a larger number of cases is examined more superficially (Gerring 2006). Both variants can also be used as complements. From an abstract level, the decision regarding the number of cases to be studied is characterized by a breadth-depth tradeoff (Fig. 2.4): Under a fixed amount of resources, the study of an increasing (decreasing) number of cases leads to less (more) insight into each case but more (less) robust results (Fletcher and Plakoyiannaki 2010, hint at the breadth-depth tradeoff in a more general fashion).

Gerring (2006) provides a good overview on the differences regarding research goals and empirical and additional factors to distinguish between case studies and cross-case studies. A comparison of the factors with the underlying research goals shows that conducting a case study (either single case or multiple cases) is more suitable than a cross-case study. A case study aims at generating hypotheses or

Fig. 2.4 Breadth-depth dilemma (idea adapted from Schneider 2015, source: author)

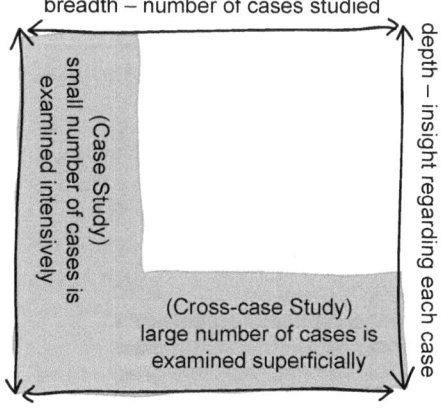

research propositions instead of testing them (Gerring 2006). This is in line with the underlying idea of better understanding the nature and process of rule-breaking market behavior. The scope of proportions in a case study is rather deep, pursuing a detailed, rich description of a phenomenon's causal mechanisms. That is, case studies focus on the detection of plausible pathways from X to Y, whereas effects, in the sense of a causal relationship's magnitude and the uncertainty of that estimation, cannot be detected by looking at a few cases only. Of course, single case insights are not appropriate to generalize to a population but can be used to set up theoretical propositions in a sense of analytically generalizing the case study's findings (Gerring 2006). With regard to the empirical givens at hand, too, conducting a case study can be considered more fruitful. Rule-breaking behavior is a comparatively rare phenomenon so it is desirable to know as much as possible about any given case. There is no database of rule-breaking behavior that could easily be used for a cross-case analysis, so data has to be extracted from a rather evidence-poor environment. With all these aspects in mind, a case study is considered the more promising approach in a pursuit of the underlying research goals. While some researchers consider multiple-case studies a different methodology from single-case studies, according to Gerring (2006) and Yin (2014) they are basically depicted as variants within the same methodological framework. Acknowledging the persuasive power of single case approaches (Siggelkow 2007), multiple-case designs provide a stronger base for theory building research (Yin 2014). For instance, multiple cases allow for a comparison of single case data to find out whether emergent findings are idiosyncratic or replicable (Eisenhardt and Graebner 2007). This gives insight into how the phenomenon under study might be affected by different environments and specific conditions under which the findings occur. Examining and comparing processes and outcomes across many cases leads to more compelling and powerful evidence relative to the results from a single case. Descriptions and explanations of underlying issues are typically more extensive (Chmiliar 2010). All in all, since multiple-case results are more deeply grounded in varied empirical evidence they are considered more robust, generalizable and testable (Eisenhardt and Graebner 2007; Yin 2014).

2.2.2 Research Context and Case Selection

The selection of cases is a crucial step in the process of theory building (Eisenhardt and Graebner 2007). The overarching goal of sampling in case study approaches is to search for a context in which the dynamics under study tend to be more visible than they might be in other contexts (Eisenhardt 1989). This work interprets the case selection procedure in a two-step hierarchical manner: First, a domain and then the particular cases in that domain need to be carefully selected.

2.2.2.1 Selecting the Most Promising Source Domain for the Analysis

The process of selecting the single most promising domain to study rule-breaking behavior has been guided by a number of criteria. Based on the study objectives, these criteria have been selected to account for both general logical requirements of bottom-up empirical research endeavors and specific needs related to the central tenets of analogical reasoning.

Three more generic aspects have been derived for choosing a domain: the novelty of the approach, the number of different domains sought for study, and data availability in the particular domain. First, it is obligatory that the same or similar study has not yet been conducted before to account for novelty and originality of the results. This has already been addressed in previous chapters but needs to be reevaluated once the domain is chosen. Second, to limit the scope of the research, to assure a rigorous analytic procedure and to provide a more elaborate and thorough line of reasoning, this study focuses on the development of a coherent set of recommendations in a single instead of multiple domains. Third, information-rich data on the focal phenomenon needs to be available in the specific context. The innovations should be well documented, with the documentation being publicly available, so that the analyses and findings can be replicated (Stuart et al. 2002). Thus, what is defined as rule-breaking behavior needs to exist in the particular domain, has to be visible, and a sufficient amount of data must be obtainable. If there is no such thing like rule-breaking behavior or information on the phenomenon is lacking, the context does not qualify.

The challenge is that there is no list of rule-breaking cases in any of the potential domains that could be compared across the domains to choose the most promising one. Consider another typical selection procedure we all face occasionally: choosing a restaurant for dinner in an unknown city. If we want to get a quick idea of the different cuisines we often walk from restaurant to restaurant, look at the menu, compare the dishes to our preferences and decide. In our case, there is no menu. No list of rule-breaking behavior exists in any of the potential domains; the menu has to be discovered first. Since we decided that we can only eat at one restaurant, it is necessary to derive further screening criteria to make an informed decision before entering the restaurant.

These guiding principles are based on two diametric criteria: originality of the research or degree of insight to be gained in the chosen source domain and the ability to transfer information from the source domain back to the context of management. According to Corley and Gioia (2011), originality is a critical concern for the assessment of theoretical work with insight being either incremental or revelatory. In order to get closer to the revelatory end of the spectrum, it is deemed important to change perceptions (Mintzberg 2005), to reveal what otherwise may not have been conceivable (Corley and Gioia 2011), to surprise, and to be interesting (Davis 1971). As Cornelissen and Durand (2014) point out, "more distant domains may provoke surprisingly new and revelatory insights and inferences" (p. 1001). On the other hand, different contexts follow different logic so that it needs to be assured that

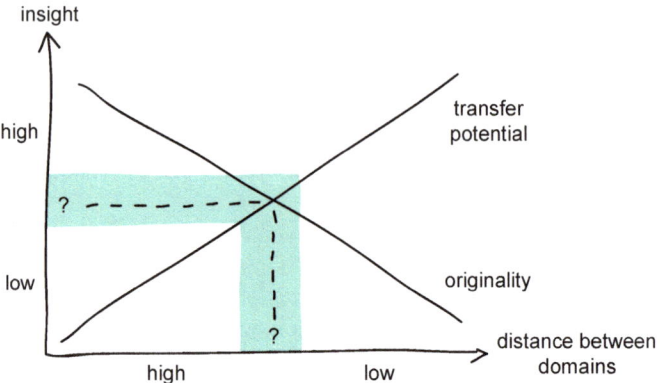

Fig. 2.5 Tradeoff between originality and transfer potential (source: author)

correspondences between structured representational elements of domains can be set up to transfer information guided by common relational structure (Jonassen 2010, p. 260). This would imply that a domain needs to be chosen that corresponds, at least regarding basic representational elements, to the context of innovation in business. The tradeoff is schematically displayed in Fig. 2.5.

In order to find a domain at the intersection of the two criteria [visualized with the "?" in Fig. 2.5] that provides both a certain degree of insight and, at the same time, can be linked back into the reference system of innovation in the context of management, four further criteria have been derived: application orientation, non-technological focus, objective performance measurement, and scope. The criteria will be explained further below. With all these aspects in mind, the corridor of disciplines has systematically been narrowed. The process followed for the selection of the source domain is presented in Fig. 2.6 and described in detail further below.

On the left, the figure displays the five selection criteria, which have been applied to systematically narrow the pool of prospective domains. Moving from top to bottom, the filter process started out with all disciplines. In the first stage, business studies have been filtered from the set of domains because, as explained above, the idea is to select a context that is remote from the corporate landscape, assuming that by doing this, insight can be revealed that would not be visible in cases of rule-breaking behavior in business. All domains without business remained for further investigation. Next, the still broad range of disciplines has been limited to applied sciences because it has been assumed that data availability on real-world break-through innovations may be larger in contexts that are more application oriented than in more abstract theoretical sciences, which are primarily concerned with the development of new theories and models on an abstract level. At the next stage of the filter, a distinction between domains focusing on technological versus non-technological aspects has been made. Reflected in the first characteristic of rule-breaking market behavior (see Sect. 2.1.1), the domain should provide data

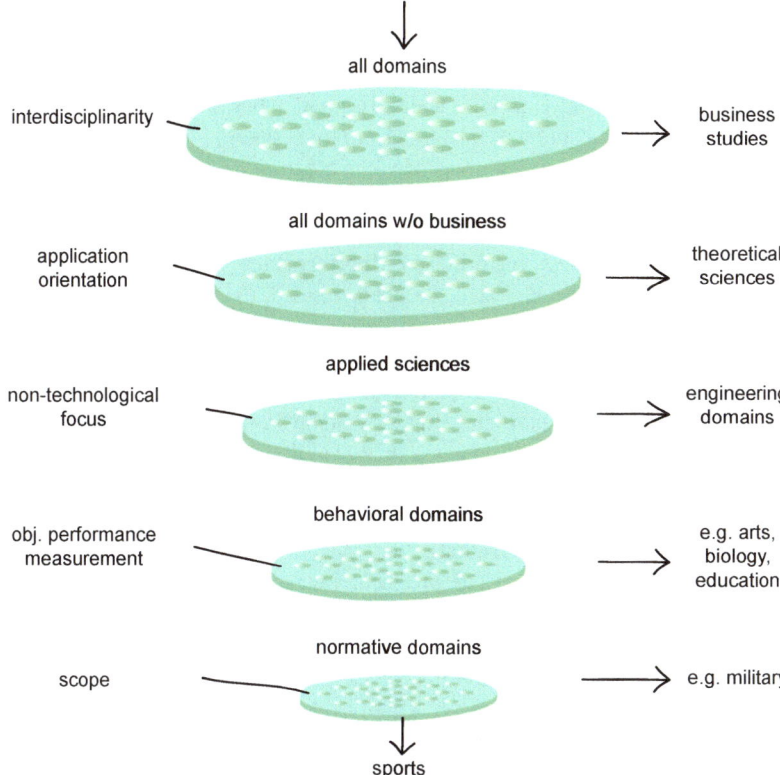

Fig. 2.6 Flowchart of the systematic search to select the source domain (source: author)

on changes in behavioral standards rather than changes induced by technological progress. Thus, it seemed meaningful to exclude all engineering domains. After that, the remaining domains have been evaluated more closely according to key characteristics of the target domain. As objective performance measurement is very important to evaluate whether a case is rule-breaking or not, all disciplines that defy such precise criteria have been eliminated from the list. Last but not least, scope also played a role when the final domain was selected, as it was considered desirable that the mechanisms that would be uncovered are not limited to a unique context only.

To further clarify and elaborate on the last two stages in the filter process, it can be added that the process of discipline selection has not been as straightforward as depicted in Fig. 2.6 but, like the rest of the study, was characterized by a more circular back and forth procedure. The filter emerged from a combination of bottom-up and top-down investigation of several domains. For instance, initially a more multifaceted approach has been pursued, planning to take several disciplines into account. Arts and military sciences were two of the domains that have been investigated more deeply. At first sight, creative arts seemed highly suitable to gain better understanding into the underlying phenomenon because the idea of deviating from existing norms, traditions or standards is deeply entrenched in any creative activity. Great artists stand out by pursuing their individual way of behaving and not necessarily complying with state-of-the-art work and market givens. A lot may be derived for the context of business from that domain—it is not by chance that the scientific interest in arts as sources of value creation for business is growing (for further information see, for instance, the recent special edition of *Journal of Business Research*, Volume 85, April 2018). However, for the fundamental mismatch between arts and business regarding the performance measurement (subjective vs. objective), this work excluded all areas related to arts as insight has been considered to be less easily transferrable back to marketing. Moreover, military sciences appeared to be a fruitful domain but, after having interviewed an expert on the development of military operational thinking at the Center for Military History and Social Sciences of the Bundeswehr in Potsdam and having studied a book dealing with operational changes in the military, it turned out to be a less effective domain to study (e.g. because of the rather game-theoretic characteristics and a limited scope of applications due to the national character of a rather regulated and hierarchical military organization).

To sum up, other domains had promise, but sports seemed the single most promising source domain to investigate rule-breaking behavior and transfer the insights back to the target context of business. The domain of sports wins for being highly application-oriented, for providing clear cases of innovation that do not require technological progress but simply rely on changes to behavioral standards, for entailing a large number of sports disciplines that can be measured objectively ("Citius, Altius, Fortius", "Faster, Higher, Stronger" as the Olympic motto), for being less complex than innovation in a corporate context, and for being a potential source of inspiration from an analogy perspective since sports is a domain everybody usually can somehow positively relate to. Hence, the idea of rule-breaking behavior in the domain of sports can be thought of as if it were the attempt to win gold in the Olympics or set a new world record by developing a completely new and different technique (as in an innovative way to move the body) that challenges or replaces the dominant style in the sports domain respectively.

2.2.2.2 Selecting Cases of Rule-Breaking Behavior in Sports

Sampling in case study research is guided by the goals of a particular study and entails decisions regarding the sampling strategy, the number of cases and the definition of the unit of within-case analysis (Fletcher and Plakoyiannaki 2010).

First, the sampling procedure for theory building bottom-up approaches often relies on a logic of purposeful, non-random selection of information-rich cases (e.g. Fletcher and Plakoyiannaki 2010). This means that cases are chosen because they are considered particularly likely to offer theoretical insight on a phenomenon (Eisenhardt and Graebner 2007). While there is a plethora of different techniques under the umbrella of purposeful case selection in the literature (e.g. typical, extreme, deviant, and most-similar cases; see Gerring and Cojocaru 2016; Yin 2014), this work follows the logic of the decision tree to select adequate cases (see Sect. 2.1.6). That is, examples of non-technological sports innovations that fulfill the set of rule-breaking criteria have been systematically searched: complying with the formal rules, being substantially different compared to the prior state-of-the-art, and leading to better results and having become (one of) the dominant style(s). Apart from these content-related selection criteria, adequate cases are also required to be information-rich. Hence, unlike theoretical sampling in grounded theory terms, the cases have not been selected according to categories emerging from the data, but the sampling mechanism has been specified up front. While these content-related boundaries lead to certain homogeneity among the selected cases, there is still a substantial amount of heterogeneity remaining. For instance, cases may differ regarding criteria such as the sport's complementary requirements (e.g. ball, ski, bike, or horse), the venue (inside versus outside), the athlete's gender (men versus women), the sport's organizational form (single athlete versus team), or the originator of the invention (coach versus athlete, professional versus amateur). Without suggesting that the cases chosen are typical, it can be stated that they are symptomatic—that is, influential and potentially inventive in their respective sport's domains.

Second, the adequacy of sample size in case study research depends on the underlying goal of the research (Fletcher and Plakoyiannaki 2010). Since it is costly to conduct a case study, it is reasonable to reflect on the minimum number of cases that is required to obtain the desired quality of the research (Royer 2010). Due to the individual features and goals of each case study research endeavor, there are, of course, no precise rules regarding the number of cases that should be selected in a multiple case study. Recommendations in the literature range from 4 to 15 cases. A more general heuristic suggests that cases should be added up to the point where theoretical saturation and information redundancy are attained (Fletcher and Plakoyiannaki 2010). Royer (2010) concludes that case selection is mainly guided by two criteria, internal validity (rejecting alternative explanations across cases) and generalization of findings (replicating findings across cases). This is particularly true for studies that are focusing on explanation rather than exploration of certain phenomena. Here, a number of 8 cases including 18 different innovators build the sample. They resulted from the comprehensive selection procedure that will be outlined below. Against the background of the study's exploratory character, the sample has been assessed to be sufficient regarding both its quantitative (total amount of information) and qualitative character (information-richness). A final evaluation will take place in Chap. 4.

A third aspect of case study sampling is related to the case's specific entities, which will be analyzed in the study, and is also referred to as within-case sampling. While holistic case studies focus on a rather global nature of a phenomenon (i.e. gaining insight on rule-breaking behavior in general), embedded case studies involve an analysis of particular subunits (i.e. addressing single perspectives of individuals and institutions involved in the process of rule-breaking behavior). This case study focuses on studying rule-breaking behavior from the athlete's perspective. Subject to available data, it is preferably aimed at drawing an extensive picture of the whole process emerging from the case study findings, including information on other entities such as coaches, official institutions or social groups involved (Fletcher and Plakoyiannaki 2010).

Against this background, the details of the case selection procedure in the domain of sports will be systematically described in the remainder of this chapter. Starting with a rather broad population of innovations in sports, the four key features of rule-breaking behavior (see Sect. 2.1) build the content-related framework to identify potentially interesting cases. Three different approaches have been used to find suitable cases: (a) consulting with sports enthusiasts, coaches and athletes in both the researcher's extended private and professional environment, (b) contacting German sports professors[7] from different sports related faculties such as history, sociology, pedagogy, and management of sports, and (c) conducting a thorough search by screening relevant sports media and applying pertinent key words in online resources. Each of the three ways proved as fruitful, eventually resulting in a comprehensive though not all-encompassing database of sports innovations (see Sect. 2.2.3.1). While approaches (a) and (b) are mostly self-explanatory, the course of the systematic search is outlined in more detail subsequently. In a first step, the scope of sports disciplines relevant for a more extensive search will be derived by choosing an appropriate starting point and defining disciplines on which to focus. After that, search criteria such as key words and resources will be briefly outlined.

All Olympic sports are considered as starting points for the identification of cases.[8] The Olympic Charter requires that a sport must be widely practiced in order to become a competing event at the Olympic games (for men: on four continents in no fewer than 75 countries, and for women: on three continents in at least 40 countries). Many other rules, such as bans on particular kinds of sports (mind sports, e.g. chess, or sports reliant on mechanical propulsion, e.g. automobile racing) apply and various criteria are taken into consideration by the Olympic Program Commission (How Are Sports Chosen for the Olympics? 2018; IOC 2017b). Without intending to demote other non-Olympic sports, this approach is considered to meet the underlying goals and assumptions best. Not only is it necessary to focus on a smaller range of sports from an efficiency-perspective but more importantly, Olympic sports provide an interpersonally accepted, broad variety of disciplines that reflect a certain maturity level (which is better suited to find historical cases), follow a transparent logic of competition and underlie explicit

---

[7]A list of current sports professors provided by the sports faculty of the University of Hamburg has been used as a starting point to contact the experts. Six out of 11 professors replied to the inquiry. Every comment and remark has been followed up on. The faculty of sports historians at the University of Münster invited to present and discuss this work at their research colloquium with more than 15 faculty members and graduate students. They provided further examples, insight into sports historians' way of thinking and helpful feedback on the research endeavor.

[8]The Olympic Games are considered the most preeminent international multisport event worldwide. In the first Games in Athens in 1894, 241 athletes from 12 countries competed in 43 events (Fay 2011). In 2016, the Olympic Games in Rio welcomed 11,238 athletes from 207 countries and territories contesting in 306 different events (IOC, "Rio" 2016).

regulations regarding performance measurement. An overview of the current Olympic Summer and Winter sports disciplines is provided in Fig. 2.7.

Each of the 57 sports disciplines listed in Fig. 2.7 is further divided into separate events. These range substantially across the different sports in terms of number. While handball, for instance, is only divided into men's and women's events and can, therefore, be analyzed as a whole, there are more than 20 different track-and-field events. All in all, this leads to a large number of events to be analyzed, so the scope needed to be narrowed again. It seemed meaningful to prioritize the disciplines by looking at obvious differences between the logics of sports and business.

To facilitate the transfer of the insights back to the target domain, all sports that do not comply with the "Faster, higher, further"-idea and thus differ from general logic of performance management in business, have been given less attention in the screening process. First, this concerns one-on-one combat sports where a contestant wins by scoring more points (subjective evaluation) or disabling the opponent. And second, all sports that are primarily characterized by subjective metrics, in which the performance measurement relies more on individual opinions and feelings rather than being independent of the observer using timing or distance measures. For instance, sports such as high jump or beach volleyball use completely objective measures like meters or goals scored. Diving or gymnastics, on the other hand, are solely evaluated according to subjective measures. Others combine both, for instance ski jumping and karate. Sports that have been screened less intensively are indicated by a transparent overlay in Fig. 2.7.

Following a three-step procedure, all remaining sports, sport disciplines and sport events have been scanned for leads to rule-breaking behavior. In an initial step, it has been attempted to identify cases by screening three more general sources related to sports. First, the official website of the Olympics (http://www.olympic.org) provides short editorials for all sports, which highlight important characteristics and milestones. Second, in many cases, the Wikipedia entries of each sport contain a section on the history of important techniques. Third, the Encyclopedia Britannica proved to be an eligible outlet for condensed but extensive information on major developments in the sports. These sources only served as a starting point for further research in which all findings have been validated by at least two other credible sources. In a second step then, a key word search in both Google and Google scholar has been conducted by applying the name of the sport plus the following terms (separate and in different combinations): tactic*, revolution*, record, style, innovation, history, technique, breakthrough. Finally, credible and more detailed sources for validation and further investigation of any potential case have been consulted. Often, only after this stage of further validation and, therefore, after a substantial amount of time has been invested, could one be sure whether the case could be considered a bona fide example of rule-breaking behavior or not. Whether the potential case qualified as such an example has been assessed with the help of the decision tree.

The above-explained analytical screening procedure has been conducted sport by sport, little by little filling the database of rule-breaking behavior. Since the identification of each case already required a substantial amount of data analysis, the lines between case selection, data collection and data analysis (see Sect. 2.2.4.2 for more

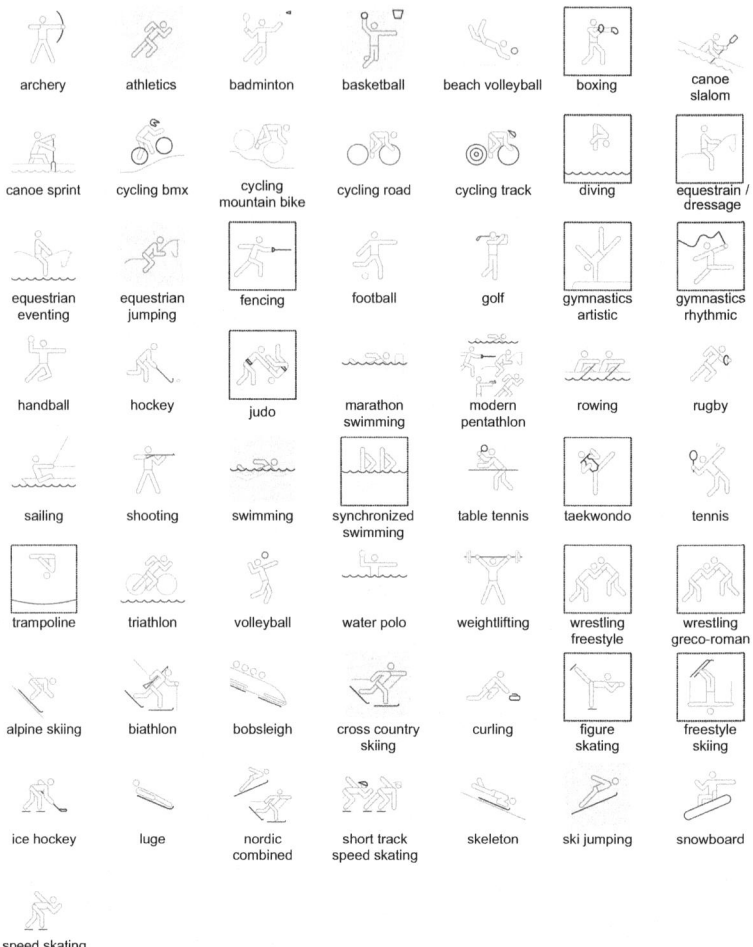

archery   athletics   badminton   basketball   beach volleyball   boxing   canoe slalom

canoe sprint   cycling bmx   cycling mountain bike   cycling road   cycling track   diving   equestrain / dressage

equestrian eventing   equestrian jumping   fencing   football   golf   gymnastics artistic   gymnastics rhythmic

handball   hockey   judo   marathon swimming   modern pentathlon   rowing   rugby

sailing   shooting   swimming   synchronized swimming   table tennis   taekwondo   tennis

trampoline   triathlon   volleyball   water polo   weightlifting   wrestling freestyle   wrestling greco-roman

alpine skiing   biathlon   bobsleigh   cross country skiing   curling   figure skating   freestyle skiing

ice hockey   luge   nordic combined   short track speed skating   skeleton   ski jumping   snowboard

speed skating

Note: By the time the analysis has been conducted, 57 sports are contested at the Olympic summer and winter games. Images in the figure are taken from https://www.olympic.org. Grey highlights indicate that cases of rule-breaking behavior have been identified in these sports disciplines. The numbers in the upper left corner stand for the number of examples taken from that category. The dotted lines signal that these disciplines have been given less attention in the analysis since they are considered to be more structurally different to the logic of business than the others

Fig. 2.7 Olympic sports disciplines (figures from https://www.olympic.org)

details) were sometimes blurry in the course of the research. For the purpose of a clear and logical structure, however, both steps have been clearly separated in the report. Without anticipating too much, credible data could not be obtained easily in any of the cases. In some cases, even, available data had to be deemed insufficient to qualify for the case study even though the example may have had rule-breaking characteristics.

Finally, Fig. 2.8 displays the process of case selection by applying the Four-Way-Rule-Breaking Test. All preliminary examples that resulted from the three-step screening procedure (experts, key word search, sports enthusiasts) entered the filter process at the top of the graph. According to the four key features, the examples have been divided into five different clusters, as visually indicated at the bottom of the figure. The eight multicolored cases in the right bottom represent the final sample. In the next section, both a description of the whole database including all clusters and of the eight focal cases is presented.

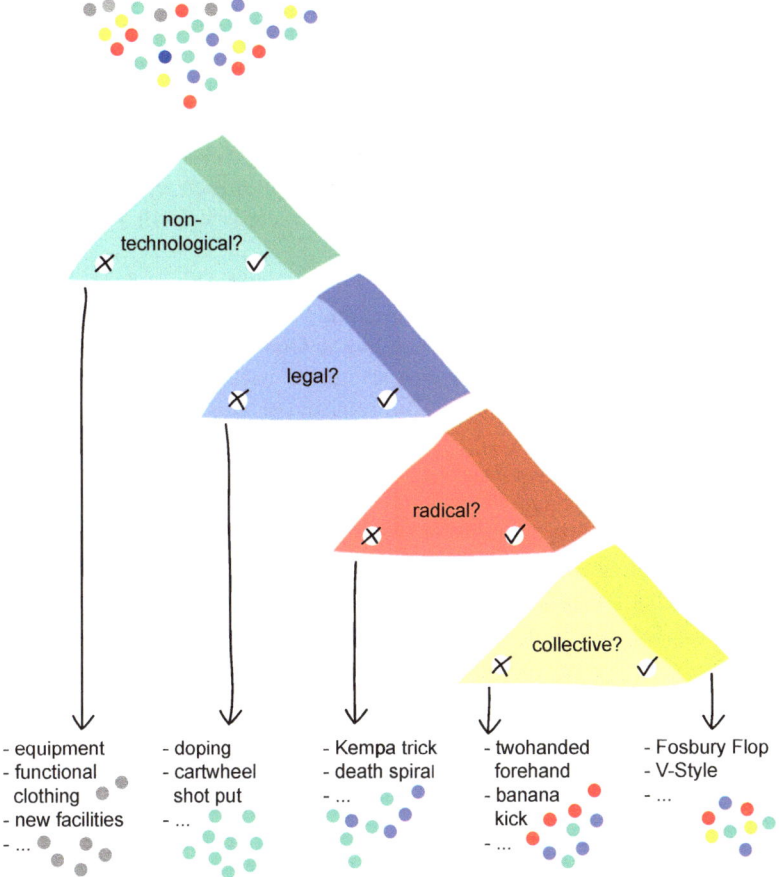

Fig. 2.8 Application of the Four-Way-Rule-Breaking Test (source: author)

2.2.3 Data Description

2.2.3.1 A Database of Historical Sports Innovations

The final database comprises 74 examples of different sports innovations.[9] Using the Four-Way-Rule-Breaking Test, all examples have been clustered into five categories (in line with Sect. 2.1). The database includes the name, year, discipline, a brief description, further insight on the origins, and a four-way-rule-breaking (quick)-check for each of the examples (see Table A.4 in the Appendix). The list also encompasses innovative training methods, although they have not been taken into account for further analysis. The content of the database is summarized in Table 2.2.

2.2.3.2 Description of the Selected Sample

Most sports evolve over a long period of time: Rules are changed, patterns of play alter, techniques are adjusted. Only rarely does a sport take a great leap forward at one point (IOC, "High Jump" n.d.). The triangular case selection procedure resulted in eight focal cases reflecting a broad variety of different sports disciplines. Only the most extreme and clear examples of rule-breaking behavior in their purest form (no training methods or dietary changes) have been considered for the sample. Table 2.3 lists all cases, including a short description of each technique's key rule-breaking features. A detailed outline of the characteristics will follow in Sects. 2.3.1.1–2.3.1.9.

The eight examples of rule-breaking behavior in sports derive from six Olympic disciplines: ski jumping and cross-country skiing in Olympic winter sports; athletics, basketball, equestrian jumping and swimming in Olympic summer sports. Athletics and swimming are represented by two examples each, contested in a different sub-discipline or event respectively. The sample contains seven individual sports and one team sport.

It is important to note that the eight cases, in fact, comprise 18 individuals to be analyzed because in some cases several individuals have been associated with the development of the novel technique.[10] Two agents have been identified in the Forward Seat, Dolphin Kick, and V-Style, and eight individuals have been analyzed for the Jump Shot. With the Fosbury Flop, Flip Turn, Skate Skiing Technique and O'Brien Shift, the innovation has primarily been traced back to a single athlete.

---

[9]Please note that the database is not all-encompassing and further research is likely to yield more examples, especially regarding clusters one to four because the underlying selection procedure has been focusing on the identification of rule-breaking cases.

[10]This is neither an uncommon nor occurrence specific for sports innovations. In science, too, there are plenty of examples in which individuals were not the first or only agents to make their respective discovery but are associated with it (e.g. as outlined by Weisenfeld (2009), "Fleming . . . as well as Pfizer's employees . . . were not the first or only agents to make their respective discovery [penicillin and Viagra] but both are associated with it", p. 141).

Table 2.2 Essence of sports innovations database

#	Cluster	n	Brief description	Exemplary case
1	Technological innovations	8	Technological advances in sports equipment (e.g. functional clothing, shoes, rackets, skis, and new facilities) serving as performance-enhancing means or to prevent injury and protect against harm	Gloves/mufflers in boxing
2	Illegal innovative attempts	10	Violations against the official rules such as performance-enhancing drugs and other forms of illegal behaviors leading to a disqualification of the athlete; this cluster also includes novel techniques that caused a change in the formal rules and were declared illegal afterwards, e.g. because of sporting dominance or safety concerns	Doping; cartwheel shot put (rendered illegal because of safety concerns)
3	Second order rule-breaking behavior	31	New styles or techniques with incremental rather than radical impact on the discipline	Kempa trick in handball
4	Exceptions from the rule	12	Styles or techniques with radical character that occurred only once, seem idiosyncratic or are used by a small number of athletes only	Biwott in 3000 m steeplechase, two-handed forehand in tennis
5	Rule-breaking behavior	13	Pool of examples that meet all four criteria of rule-breaking behavior; to qualify for the final sample these cases further have to comply with other above-outlined criteria like data richness and objective performance measurement	Fosbury Flop in high jump

All inventors of the rule-breaking techniques were male. Most athletes came from the U.S., the other four were Europeans (Federico Caprilli from Italy, Pauli Siitonen from Finland, Jan Boklöv from Sweden, and Miroslaw Graf from Poland).

The cases took place in the course of the twentieth century, covering a rough time span of 80 years. Occurring around the century's turn, the Forward Seat is the oldest example, followed by the Jump Shot, Flip Turn, and Dolphin Kick in the later first half of the twentieth century. O'Brien and Dick Fosbury started inventing their new styles at the beginning of the second half of the twentieth century, the former winning Olympic gold in 1952, the latter in 1968. The two Winter sports date back to the 1980s and are thus the most recent examples of the study.

Taken together, the sample of rule-breaking cases comprises a broad range of different sports contexts, providing a solid base for an analysis to better understand the underlying focal phenomenon of the study. Table 2.3 gives an overview of the eight cases indicating the time period when the innovation took place, the sports discipline, the inventor(s) including their country of origin, and a brief description of the technique.

Table 2.3 Case study overview sports

Case, time period	Sports discipline	Inventor(s), country of origin	Short description
Fosbury Flop, 1960s	High jump	Dick Fosbury, U.S.	Running in a curve and jumping backwards over the bar
Jump Shot, 1930s	Basketball	Several	Shooting the basketball while jumping
Forward Seat, 1900s	Equestrian jumping	Tod Sloan, U.S. Federico Caprilli, IT	The rider's weight is centered forward in the saddle over the horse's withers
Flip Turn, 1930s	Backstroke swimming	Albert Vande Weghe, U.S.	Going under water with the head when turning
Dolphin Kick, mid 1930s	Butterfly swimming	Dave Armbruster/ Jack Sieg, U.S. Volney Wilson, U.S.	Beating the legs in unison, similar to a fish tail
Skate Skiing, 1980s	Cross-country skiing	Pauli Siitonen, FIN (Bill Koch, U.S.)	Pushing off the edges of the ski as in ice skating
V-Style, 1980s	Ski jumping	Jan Boklöv, SWE Miroslaw Graf, POL	Spreading the tips of the skis into a "V" shape throughout the jump
O'Brien Shift, 1950s	Shot put	Parry O'Brien, U.S.	Facing away from the direction of the throw, turning by 180°

2.2.4 Data Collection and Data Analysis

2.2.4.1 Process of Data Collection and Sources

In case study research, multiple sources of evidence and numerous forms of data collection are utilized to systematically gather information on a given case from different perspectives. Potential resources range from any kind of historical or contemporary secondary data source such as archival records, books, news articles, guidelines, reports, memos, web pages, posters, or diaries to newly collected primary data from interviews, observations, questionnaires, or focus groups to name but a few. Often, the data comprises a mix of textual, visual and audible material (McGinn 2010; Yin 2014).

To better understand rule-breaking behavior in the context of sports, this work is primarily making use of secondary data. Apart from the fact that data collection would be very costly, many protagonists have already passed away. Prevailing data on the cases may not always be easily retrieved because it is scattered across a plethora of different databases and bears the risk of being subjectively biased. However, all data can ultimately be considered to provide a rich context for better understanding this research's underlying focal phenomenon.

The entire process of data accumulation lasted more than one and a half years, starting in summer 2016 with the selection of the first cases and ending in early 2018 after the cross-case analysis had been finished. That is, not only have the eight focal cases been part of the iterative process of data collection and interpretation but also a substantial amount of insight has been accumulated above and beyond that.

The initial stage of the data collection process was characterized by extensive desk research to circularly define the phenomenon and identify suitable cases accordingly (see Sect. 2.2.4.2 for further description). Popular science, articles in local as well as international newspapers, sports magazines and blogs turned out to be helpful early on. At a more advanced stage of investigation, data sources expanded to biographies, books on the history of sports disciplines, scientific research in managerial and sports related journals, and podcasts and interviews with protagonists in written or audible format. Librarians, registrars and historians from several German and U.S.-American institutions have been consulted, accounting for both an effective and efficient search strategy. For example, several days have been spent at the central library for sports sciences at the German Sport University Cologne, which is the largest specialized library of sport and exercise sciences worldwide (German Sport University Cologne n.d.). Other libraries of sports sciences throughout Germany granted support with contemporary documents from the early and mid nineteenth century as well. Last but not least, experts and organizations (e.g. International Swimming Hall of Fame, International Ski Federation) have been contacted to retrieve personal reports and gain access to archives that are not publicly accessible.

All data sources have been assessed in terms of their reliability. If possible, each key insight has been referenced by at least two different sources, which is invariably true for data from sources such as newspapers or magazines but less so for information such as archival records from the ISHOF. Insight into the data collection procedure and exemplary sources of each focal case is summarized in Table 2.4.

All in all, a substantial number and broad variety of secondary sources has been taken into consideration. It is difficult to give an estimation regarding the total scope of material that has been used for the analysis in terms of how many pages have been read and converted (sometimes manually transcribed), how many videos have been watched (and transcribed), how many podcasts have been listened to, how many sources have been screened and dismissed as inadequate or unhelpful, and how many lines have been coded until just the very essence of information remained that eventually could be considered to sufficiently capture the unique stories for the purpose of this work. Roughly and pessimistically approximated, around 100 case-related sources have been cited in this work and the Excel tables that have been used for data collection and analysis contain around 50,000 words,[11] many of them transcribed by hand.

2.2.4.2   Data Analysis

When analyzing case study evidence, there is no fixed procedure to guide the researcher. Much depends on the individual style of rigorous empirical thinking

---

[11]To compare: This work comprises around 80,000 words excluding the Appendix; 100,000 words in total.

Table 2.4 Data collection

Case	Insight into data collection procedure	Exemplary sources
Dick Fosbury, Fosbury Flop	Most prominent example; relatively much data available including interviews with Dick Fosbury	Scientific paper (Goldenberg et al. 2010), audiovisual media such as podcast (BBC World Service 2011) and video interviews (IOC 2014b)
Albert Vande Weghe, Flip Turn	Difficult to retrieve reliable information from publicly available sources; personal contact to U.S. Aquatic Historian and ISHOF	Material from the ISHOF archives such as letters and pictures (accessed in 2017), aquatic online magazines like usms.org (2000) and swimmingworldmagazine.org (2002)
Parry O'Brien, O'Brien Shift	A variety of sources created during the period of the invention as well as more contemporary narratives on the development of the technique from both scientific and track and field related outlets have been used	Historical newspaper articles such as the Time Magazine cover story (Dec. 1956) and Sports Illustrated article by Merell Noden (1955), IAAF paper on Shot Put Techniques (1990), IAAF and USATF Hall of Fame, thesis submitted at Sport University Cologne (1953), obituaries in major newspapers like The New York Times, LA Times, and the guardian (all 2007)
Pauli Siitonen, Skate Skiing	As the attempt to gain access to material on the development of the Skate Skiing technique from the FIS archives remained unsuccessful, the analysis is based on publicly available information only	Worldlopped Ski Federation's anniversary book on 30 years of skiing around the world (2007), International Skiing Association sources, several books on cross-country skiing techniques, dictionary entries like Britannica academic and the historical dictionary of skiing
Federico Caprilli, Tod Sloan Forward Seat	In spite of being the most historic case, data availability was adequate	(Scientific) books, expert blogs and encyclopedias on horsemanship, John Dizikes' (2000) biography on Tod Sloan, Caprilli papers
Jan Boklöv, Miroslaw Graf, V-Style	Even though this is the most recent example of rule-breaking behavior data availability is sparse; a compilation of newspaper articles, historical articles by Skiing experts and blog entries built a sufficiently detailed foundation for this work's purpose	Tim Ashburner's History of Ski Jumping (2003), articles in Skiing Heritage Journal (2011) and Juncture (2007), reports in major German and Nordic news magazines such as Welt (2015), FAZ (2008), Deutschlandfunk (2013), Tagesspiegel (2008), Sportevent Gellivare Lapland (2017)
Eight jump shooters, Jump shot	Finding the origins of the jump shot in basketball turned out to be a challenging undertaking which several sports historians tried to attempt; their comprehensive investigations have been used as the basis for the case study	Two major books on the origins of the jump shot, both based on yearlong research and a vast array of primary sources: Christgau's (1999) The Origins of the Jump Shot—Eight Men Who Shook the World of Basketball, and Shawn Fury's (2016) Rise and Fire: The Origins, Science, and Evolution of the Jump Shot—And How It Transformed Basketball Forever

(continued)

Table 2.4 (continued)

Case	Insight into data collection procedure	Exemplary sources
Armbruster/ Sieg, Volney Wilson Dolphin Kick	Insight on Armbruster and Sieg's development of the Dolphin Kick could be found in several reliable resources, a little less has been found with regard to Volney Wilson's case	Two scientific papers ("Odyssey of the Butterfly" (2008) and Armbruster and Sieg's (1935) elaborations on the Dolphin Breast Stroke in the Journal of Health and Physical Education), a number of historical and contemporary newspaper articles and books, swimmingworldmagazine.org, ISHOF sources

together with a sufficient outline of case insight and careful consideration of alternative explanations (Yin 2014, p. 133). In an attempt to distill explanations from the data that are as objective as possible, the analysis followed established guidelines for inductive, theory-building research. These can be found in the context of grounded theory (Corbin and Strauss 2008; Glaser 1965, 1978; Glaser and Strauss 1967; Locke 2015), in articles provided by management scholars (e.g. Carlile and Christensen 2004; Colquitt and Zapata-Phelan 2007; Corley and Gioia 2011; Cornelissen and Durand 2014; Crittenden and Peterson 2011a, b, 2012, 2013; Gioia et al. 2013; Gioia and Pitre 1990; Peterson and Crittenden 2012; Weick 1995), and in the context of philosophy of science or theory building in marketing (e.g. Anderson 1983; Chalmers 2013; Curd and Psillos 2013; Eisend and Kuß 2017; Hunt 1990, 1991, 2011, 2012, 2013, 2015; Kuß 2013; Locke 2007; Van de Ven 1989, 2007). Moreover, Jonsen et al. (2018) recently reviewed and assessed selected inductive studies published in leading academic journals on what constitutes convincing qualitative research. Their list containing around 30 articles has been reviewed to find further guidance for the whole process of data analysis and writing that goes beyond the more general directions on bottom-up data driven theory-building as in the literature referred to above.

Following such guidelines, the cases have been analyzed by recursively moving between the data and an emerging structure. Various data has been woven together into a coherent picture by iteratively (back and forth) and accumulatively (growing by gradual increase) aggregating and interpreting the data in order to explore the process of rule-breaking behavior from the cases of non-technological sports revolutions. In the course of the data analysis, the large amount of unstructured data from the eight different cases has been compressed dramatically. Basically, the 50,000 words referred to above (which already are the selection from a much broader pool of data) have been systematically reduced into just a few general principles that easily fit onto one single page, giving an overview of the key findings (Sect. 3.2.3). Such processes of data reduction naturally contain a substantial loss of information. One important way to ensure reliability and validity in such procedures is to incorporate several researchers and experts into the process. Here, besides consulting with historians and experts from the area of sports and other doctoral candidates, I most importantly regularly met my advisor and committee members to discuss the specific case characteristics, emerging key insights and potential patterns that evolved gradually. Memos have been kept to record the gist of the discussions (Charmaz 2006) and the typical three-stage process of coding the data, which will be outlined in detail below, has been followed.

Figure 2.9 gives insight into the three main steps of the research process. From left to right it shows how the analysis has been conducted, illustrating several iterative processes between data collection, data analysis, and theory throughout the study (a similar depiction of the bottom-up analytic process can be found in Harrison and Rouse 2014). Accordingly, Fig. 2.10 shows each stage's key outputs in tabular display, which basically is a zoom-in into the highlighted boxes in Fig. 2.9's data analysis mode. Here is a brief description of what both figures display (a more detailed description of the three stages is given further below). As visualized in the lower left corner of stage one, the analytic process began with an interest in studying rule-breaking market behavior based on observations in the real world [I]. First, data has been collected on eight cases, one after the other, each taking several sources into account [II]. This resulted into eight unique case narratives [III]. When looking at the outlined table in Fig. 2.10, one can think of it as a column-wise analysis (from top to bottom) in which the most important case insight is told in a coherent story, independently from what happened in other cases [IV]. The stickmen indicate that, in some cases, more than one individual has been analyzed. Second, back to Fig. 2.9, these individual cases have been combined in order to find differences and similarities across the cases [V]. To do so, the individual themes have been merged, which at some points also required returning to data collection mode [iterations between V and VI] and accumulate new data to fill possible gaps [VI]. When zooming into the highlighted data analysis mode field and looking at the outlined table in Fig. 2.10 again, one can think of it as a row-wise analysis (from left to right) in which each row has been given a label and briefly described accordingly [VII]. Third, the still rather extensive cross-case insight needed to be aggregated further in order to derive generalizable themes [VIII]. This required leaving the data collection and analysis mode and returning to theoretical concepts in the domain of business [IX]. There, the cross-case insight has been aggregated further, resulting in three areas (see different colors) that provide general insight into the process of rule-breaking market behavior. The preliminary labels from stage two have been replaced by research propositions [X].

Again, the interplay among these stages was not as linear and straightforward as suggested by the figure and the following in-depth description of the three analytic stages. Often, events were recursive and overlapped in time.

In stage 1, the data analysis began by building individual case studies. With no specific a priori hypothesis to test, it has allowed a structure to emerge that describes the process of rule-breaking behavior experienced by each of the 18 innovators. There are two different approaches in multiple-case design: a parallel design where all cases are selected in advance and conducted at the same time and a sequential design where the case studies follow each other (Chmiliar 2010). Each case has been treated separately in this work, trying to make sure that in this stage of the analysis the following cases were not informed too much by the outcome of the previously

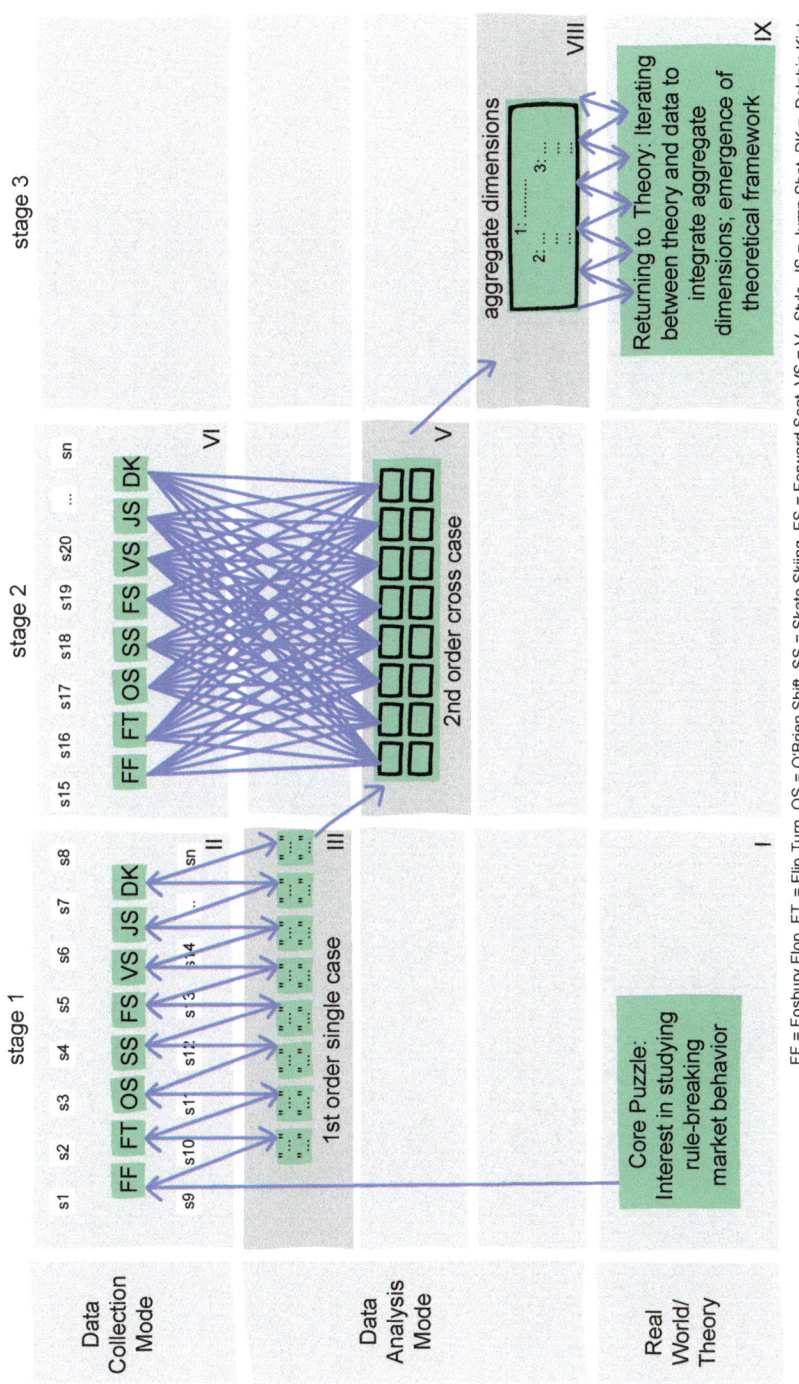

Fig. 2.9 Three stages of data collection and analysis—process perspective (source: author)

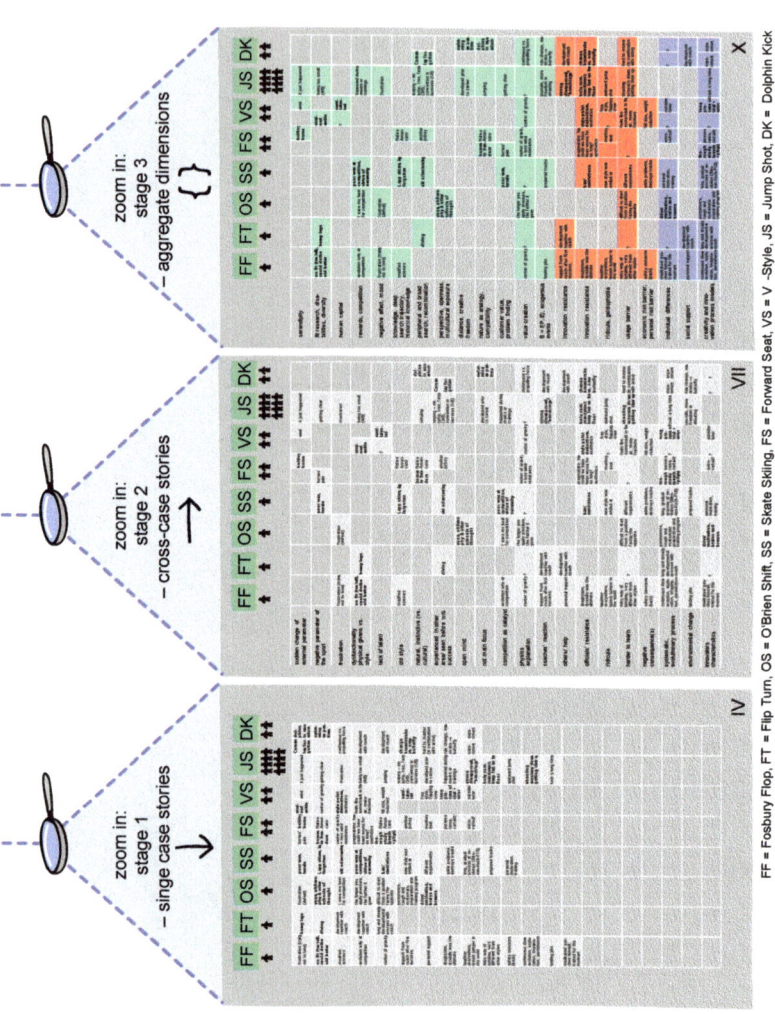

FF = Fosbury Flop, FT = Flip Turn, OS = O'Brien Shift, SS = Skate Skiing, FS = Forward Seat, VS = V -Style, JS = Jump Shot, DK = Dolphin Kick

Note: The two figures can be read in combination, with Fig. 2.10 zooming into the three boxes of Fig. 2.9 that are visualized in darker grey (i.e. fields III, V, and VIII). The Roman numerals are indicative of the order in which the boxes have been described in the text. Readable versions of the tables in Fig. 2.10 can be found in Appendix A.1

Fig. 2.10 Three stages of data collection and analysis—outcome perspective (source: author)

completed cases. One way to do so is by allowing for temporal breaks between the analyses of each case. The order of the cases has been chosen randomly (i.e. in an unsystematic way): those cases which have been identified first (and provided sufficient data), have been examined first.

Technically, this initial step of analysis comprises open coding of the underlying data using in vivo codes or verbatim statements, a process that "is designed to break open the data to consider all possible meanings" (Corbin and Strauss 2008, p. 59). To best access a variety of meanings, the basic notion of intercoder-agreement has been considered. For each case, all quotes that were directly and indirectly related to the underlying phenomenon have been extracted from the data. It has been decided to interpret the data independently beforehand (by developing so called first-order concepts) and to present the plain and roughly structured text passages (without codes). To avoid biasing the second researcher during his act of interpretation, i.e. by verbal emphasis or utilized terms, the quotes have not been read out loud but displayed on the computer screen. The subjectively derived alternative interpretations have been compared in each case, followed by a final agreement (Nemeth et al. 2001). This careful process of data examination and interpretation in each single bounded case included a prioritization of crucial elements. The approach has been repeated for each single case that has been incorporated in the final sample. The setup was informed by prior experience with grounded theory from a former research project as well as consultation with experienced qualitative researchers during a methodological seminar on grounded theory. Moreover, throughout the process, two cases have been randomly picked to have a research-experienced student conduct an individual search which was followed by 60-min discussion sessions on contents and research methodology afterwards. Once an acceptable point of saturation was reached, the data was organized into a comprehensive description as a unique, holistic entity. The results of this stage are outlined in Sects. 2.3.1.1–2.3.1.9. All eight narratives entail (1) a descriptive report of structural details that closely adhere to the underlying facts and (2) a more normative portrayal of the key dynamics leading to rule-breaking behavior, which have been constructed on the basis of the above explained intuiting and interpretation processes. These two elements are woven together in eight coherent stories that are kept as precise, illustrative and brief as possible.

The next level of the study, the cross-case analysis, only began once all case write-ups were completed. This stepwise procedure maintains the independence of the replication logic across cases (Brown and Eisenhardt 1997), which applies if patterns of variables or themes transcend the cases (Eisenhardt and Graebner 2007). This second stage comprises two steps: the integration of the single case's first-order codes and the discovery of second-order themes.[12] Therefore, in a stepwise manner, the case data first has been merged into an integrated picture. Starting with case one, all codes were put in a table. The high-priority codes are highlighted by using bold

---

[12]Nag and Gioia (2012) describe second-order themes as "theoretically distinctive, researcher induced concepts, formulated at a more abstract level, albeit with an attempt to apply informant labels if those labels represented theoretical concepts" (p. 427).

font (see process of prioritizing in step 1) and the case-specific content is summarized in each cell. Continuing with case two in a similar vein, homogenous codes were located next to each other and empty cells (resulting from different initial codes in each case) were filled if possible. With this procedure, it can be assured that the unique aspects of each particular case remain and inter-case similarities and differences become visible at the same time (Eisenhardt 1989). During that process, codes were solidified and irrelevant ones were removed. Eliminated from further analysis were all codes that were considered too general to play a role with regard to the underlying research goal of parsimony and at the same time occurred in less than three cases. At the end of the process, each single case data was reevaluated to ensure that all of the important issues had been captured. After all cases were accumulated accordingly, the search for links between and among the single cases was begun by logically rearranging and grouping first-order concepts together and further aggregating the codes into second-order themes. The resulting table, including information on all eight cases, was then rearranged and further consolidated in several iterative steps. Again, this process of comparing and contrasting was guided by various meetings for consultation and interpersonal confrontation regarding the evolving results. As with all steps in the analysis process, this was not a linear but "recursive, process-oriented, analytic procedure" (Locke 1996, p. 240) that continued until the data overview accounted for only the most important single case characteristics and a rough first order of emerging themes. Data collection ended with the completion of this step. The results of stage two are described in Sect. 2.3.2.

Stage 3 proceeded with the results perspective to the development of more general principles. More specifically, focal theoretical dimensions have been derived by clustering the cross-case data into a meaningful set of more simplified, complementary groupings. The goal is to look for even more common characteristics in the data expressed by similarities across cases. This process was characterized by cycling between data and relevant literature more frequently to enrich and refine the patterns that became visible in the data (Gioia et al. 2013). To do so, in a first step, the codes and themes have been colored according to several potentially distinctive features. By looking at the data from such different perspectives, alternative conceptual frames have been tested, which helped to evaluate data characteristics and support the logical process of condensation. For instance, the data has been structured using the idea of a "temporal bracketing" strategy that organizes the data into successive phases (Langley 1999). In another attempt, the cross-case themes have been divided into person-related aspects and context-related aspects. All in all, the sample has been reorganized several times, striving to find a suitable aggregation logic to the process of rule-breaking behavior by de-/re-/co-constructing the cross-case data until all second-order constructs had been assembled into an overarching logic fitting the underlying evidence. Emergent frameworks have again been discussed with other researchers as further validity checks for the different interpretations. The results of stage three are outlined in Chap. 3, as this step requires returning to existing theoretical concepts in the context of business. More detailed insight into how the transfer between the two contexts has been analytically approached will also be given.

2.3   Empirical Results

2.3.1   Single Case Analysis: Insight into Eight Historical Sports Innovations

2.3.1.1   Fosbury Flop in High Jump

In the early nineteenth century, high jump competitions started to become common in Scotland (IAAF, "High Jump" n.d.). The athletic event was contested for the first time in the inaugural modern Olympic Games in 1896 (IAAF, "High Jump" n.d.). Compared to other track and field events, the high jump is said to have experienced the most radical changes of techniques, obvious even to the outside observer (IAAF, "High Jump" n.d.; Keil and Killing 2014). Figure 2.11 displays an overview of different high-jumping styles. It can be seen that the bar can be cleared in several different ways: in an upright, sideways, backwards, face down, tucked, or stretched way, with either head, feet or arms first. Moreover, the approach, takeoff and landing can be different depending on each technique (Keil and Killing 2014).

The high jump went down in history after the 1968 Olympics in Mexico (Goldenberg et al. 2010). This was when Dick Fosbury won gold (2.24 m, his personal best) with a back-first jump, which was seen here for the first time in a major contest (a video of his jump can be retrieved under IOC, "Mexico 1968" n.d.). Though he did not set a world record with the jump, the new technique is deemed a revolutionary innovation, soon to replace the other approaches to jumping (Goldenberg et al. 2010; IAAF, "High Jump" n.d.). In the 1972 Olympic games, almost all other high-jumpers had adopted the Fosbury Flop.[13] In 1978, Vladimir Yashchenko was the last jumper to set a world record with the Straddle, and that record lasted 2 years (IOC, "Revolutionary Fosbury" n.d.). According to Fuqua (2014), Fosbury said: "The last straddler at the elite level was at the Olympic Games in 1988, when a decathlete jumped the same height I did in 1968" (para. 23). Today, the Fosbury Flop is still pre-eminent (IAAF, "High Jump" n.d.). After the introduction of the flop, no other promising high jump technique followed (Keil and Killing 2014). Goldenberg et al. (2010) further elaborate that other elite-level jumpers needed time to adapt and change to the new style. They had invested many hours in practicing their own technique so that the majority of the early adopters of the Fosbury Flop came from secondary-level jumpers. In an interview, Fosbury recalls, "After four decades, the technique is what all of the high jumpers are using. They all have their own individual way of jumping but they're using more or less the generic form, and it's exciting for me to watch" (Turnbull 2008, para. 5). Goldenberg et al.

---

[13]In a BBC interview Dick Fosbury gives insight into how the style became known as Fosbury Flop: "And they asked, Dick what is this technique called and there had been a photograph in our local newspaper and the caption said 'Fosbury Flops Over the Bar'. And personally, I kind of liked the conflict. Flop is typically a failure and here I was winning." (BBC World Service 2011, from 5:20).

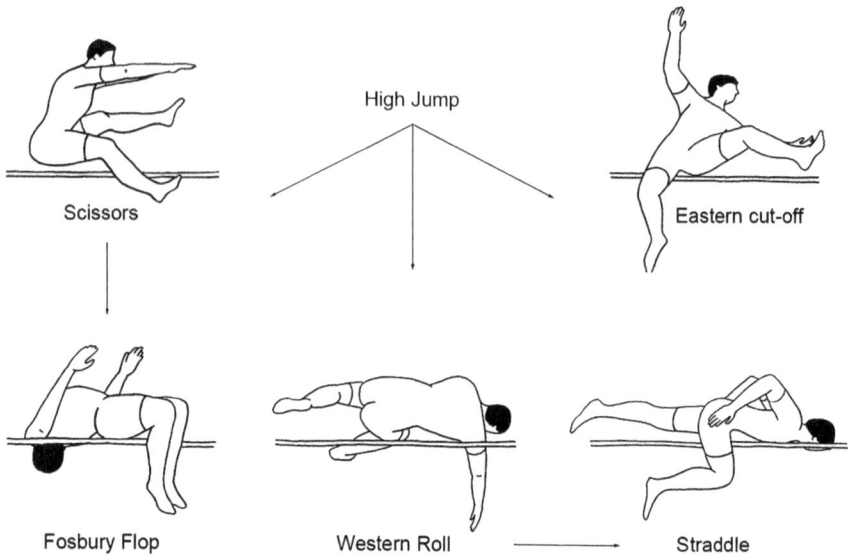

Note: The arrows indicate that some techniques have been developed on the basis of others (e.g. the Fosbury Flop is a modified version of the Scissors). The authors (Keil & Killing 2014) give an insightful overview on the development and key characteristics of each style, incorporating even more variants than just the five above displayed major high jumping techniques

Fig. 2.11 Development of different high-jumping styles (based on Keil and Killing 2014, p. 15)

(2010) found a significantly faster pace of world record setting after the introduction of the Fosbury Flop compared to the world records achieved with previous styles.

By 1968, the Straddle technique ("diving" over the bar face first) was the dominant jumping style. Other jumping approaches previously used by the world's elite were the Eastern Cut-off (variant of the Scissors style in which jumpers leap high and almost sit on the bar before scissor kicking their legs over) and the Straddle's predecessor, the Western Roll (see Fig. 2.12). In contrast to the prevalent sideways and forward style, Dick Fosbury approached the bar in a curve and jumped backwards (Goldenberg et al. 2010; IAAF, "High Jump" n.d.; Reid 1986; Turnbull 2008). Other jumpers are said to have developed the same technique independently of Fosbury (BBC World Service 2011; IOC, "Dick Fosbury" n.d.; Richard Douglas Fosbury 2018).

At high school competitions, Richard Douglas "Dick" Fosbury (U.S., *1947) failed to master the state-of-the art straddle-roll jumping style. He found it compli- cated and frustrating and felt that the straddle technique did not go along with his abilities or personal style. At an earlier age, Fosbury employed the scissors style and eventually his coach allowed him to go back to the older approach he had started out with to improve both his performance and confidence (Goldenberg et al. 2010; Zarkos 2004). "Instead of adopting the widespread style, he looked for a familiar style that felt safer to him. As Fosbury himself recalls: 'What did I have to lose?'" (Goldenberg et al. 2010, p. 39). "I felt I was falling behind, so out of desperation and

Note: The Straddle was the dominant way to jump by the time Dick Fosbury developed the backwards technique

Fig. 2.12   Straddle technique (left) vs. Fosbury Flop (right) (source: author)

frustration, toward the end of the season, that's when I went to Dean and asked him for permission to go back to the scissors," Fosbury said. "He said 'don't give up, it's your choice'." (Fuqua 2014, para. 8). However, since the Scissors style was less efficient, he knew he had to change his body position when facing the actual heights being cleared in competitions (Fuqua 2014; Goldenberg et al. 2010).

This was the starting point of gradually transforming the antiquated technique into something new. Fosbury was 16 years old by that time. With the scissors style, he typically knocked off the bar with his behind or the movement of the legs, so he started lifting the hips higher, consequently making his shoulders drop (Goldenberg et al. 2010; Zarkos 2004). "This first day I wasn't jumping backwards. All I was doing was going from sitting up to laying down or laying out over the bar. So, I was really trying to search for this better form." (BBC World Service 2011, 2:17–2:33). A step-by-step, continuous slow evolution in the technique took place. When he was trying a curved approach to the bar, this eventually made him turn his shoulder away, then he cleared with his body in a 45° angle to the bar and no longer parallel to it. Having no role model to follow, each attempt looked different, the technique developed continuously over the course of several years. The actual clue is a physical one: By stretching out on his back his center of gravity is lowered, allowing for higher jumps (BBC World Service 2011; Durso 1986; Koppenwallner 1968). "It was not by design at all," Fosbury confided. "It was just simply intuition. It was not based on science or analysis or thought or design. It was all by instinct. It happened one day at a competition." (Turnbull 2008, para. 8).

His coach first discouraged his use of the unorthodox approach, but as Fosbury cleared higher and higher, he and his practicing team began to support him (Fuqua 2014; Goldenberg et al. 2010; IAAF, "High Jump" n.d.; Zarkos 2004). Fosbury reports that the whole process of evolutionary improvement solely took place at competitions, never during practice. In a competitive environment he was more concentrated and more intense (Goldenberg et al. 2010; Zarkos 2004). The introduction of foam landing beds in the early 1960s allowed jumpers to be more focused on the bar and less concerned about the landing (Goldenberg et al. 2010; Keil and Killing 2014; Zarkos 2004).

He was highly ridiculed for his jumping style (BBC World Service 2011; Burnton 2012; Fuqua 2014; Schneider 2017; Turnbull 2008), regarded skeptically by judges and coaches (BBC World Service 2011; IOC, "Mexico 1968" n.d.) and his technique was considered dangerous because of safety concerns regarding the landing on the back (Burnton 2012; USATF Hall of Fame, "Dick Fosbury" n.d.; Zarkos 2004). On the other hand, he received great support from his home town and later on his team (BBC World Service 2011). In 1993 he was elected to the U.S. Olympic Hall of Fame (Richard Douglas Fosbury 2018).

Fosbury was not considered an exceptional athlete, one reason being his physical measurements (i.e. his tall height of 1.93 m) (IOC 2014a; Zarkos 2004). His focus is said to have been rather presence-directed, never clearly envisioning becoming an Olympic athlete or star but concentrating on immediate goals (BBC World Service 2011; Goldenberg et al. 2010; Zarkos 2004). Before and during the jumps, mental motivation and positive thinking played an important role for him (Durso 1986; Schneider 2017; Zarkos 2004). From a very early age, Fosbury showed an aptitude for science and mathematics (IOC 2014a). He studied physics and engineering and became a civil engineer after his athletic career (Sports Reference, "Dick Fosbury" n. d.). "What I like is solving problems. In engineering you have a primary responsibility to the public to design infrastructure and make it safe," he said (Zarkos 2004, in section "Back home"). After his professional career he continued to contribute to track and field by serving on committees and setting up youth clinics (Fuqua 2014).

2.3.1.2 Flip Turn in Backstroke Swimming

Swimming goes back to the stone age and began to be more widely practiced by the beginning of the early nineteenth century (Swimming 2018). Today, four different strokes are used in competition: freestyle, breaststroke, backstroke and butterfly. Freestyle (crawl) and breaststroke were part of the inaugural Modern Olympic Games in 1896, backstroke first appeared officially in the 1904 Games, and butterfly was the last of the four that appeared in the Olympics at the 1956 Games in Melbourne (IOC, "Swimming" n.d.; for further information, see Lohn 2010).

The flip turn[14] is one of the turns in swimming that is used to reverse the swimming direction at the end of the swimming pool. It was first invented in backstroke and has subsequently been adopted by freestyle swimmers (Wigo 2017a, b). Prior to the development of the flip turn, backstroke swimmers turned with their head out of the water. Only when their body was guided around and their feet touched the wall, was the head dropped back under water to go ahead with a powerful push. With the flip turn, the swimmer's head stays underwater for the whole turning procedure, knees drawn up towards the chin in a tuck position while the feet whip out of the water when propelling the body around (Wigo 2017a). Figure 2.13 schematically visualizes the differences between the two turns.

---

[14]The flip turn is also known under various other names such as somersault turn, rollover turn, tumble turn and turntable turn (e.g. Wigo 2017a).

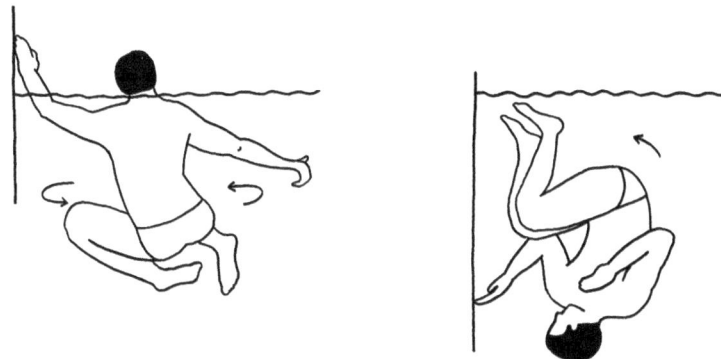

Fig. 2.13 Old Backstroke Turn (left) vs. Flip Turn (right) (source: author)

The development of the flip turn has rule-breaking character. The graphical display of the two turns shows that they are substantially different. Swimming turns have been identified to be a crucial factor in overall race performance, especially when longer distances are evented (Chow et al. 1984). In freestyle events, for example, swimmers spend between 38% and 50% of the competition time executing turns (Araujo et al. 2010). Maglischo (2003) indicates that an optimization of the turn technique can reduce times by at least 0.20 s per lap. What is most characteristic of the Flip Turn's superiority over prior turns is the fact that it has become the standard for competitive backstroke and freestyle swimming and has not been altered substantially since. Only recently, Ryan Lochte, 12-time Olympic medalist (six gold, three silvers, three bronze, see IOC, "Ryan Lochte" n.d.) ranking second behind Michael Phelps (IOC, "Michael Phelps" n.d.), slightly changed the turn and saved almost another second from his lap time. In competitive swimming, this is considered a vast difference (for more information, see an interactive report in *The New York Times* 2016). The International Swimming Federation (FINA), however, adjusted its rules and made the "Lochte Turn" illegal in individual medley races (e.g. *Swimming World Magazine* 2015).

The International Swimming Hall of Fame (ISHOF) is crediting the development of the under-water turn to Albert Vande Weghe (U.S., *1916–†2002) and his coach Maxwell "Mickey" Vogt. Before becoming the aquatics director and swimming coach at the famed Newark Athletic Club (New Jersey), Vogt had been a Metropolitan AAU diving champion.

In a letter (taken from the ISHOF archive), Albert Vande Weghe remembers:

> I am not certain I was the originator, but I know I had never seen it done before Mickey Vogt and I developed it while practicing at the Newark AC late in 1933. I always had trouble swinging my heavy legs around with the old turn, and while training with Mickey I started bringing them out of the water. This was so much easier and faster for me that I used it thereafter. I know I was the only one using it in the 1934 NAAU meet in Columbus, Ohio, at the Ohio State University. At that national meet I gave a number of demonstrations of the turn. After that it became common to all backstrokers. (Wigo 2017a, para. 3)

The tuck position of the turn is said to have been influenced by the back flip in diving. As well as Vogt himself, many swimmers in those days practiced both swimming and diving. Albert Vande Weghe also started out as a diver and only came to backstroke after swimming freestyle first (Wigo 2017a).

While still in high school, he was the first man ever to finish the 100-yard backstroke in under a minute. He set six world records between 1934 and 1939 (ISHOF, "Albert Vandeweghe" n.d.). At the 1936 Olympics in Berlin, Vande Weghe won a silver medal in the 100-m backstroke behind Adolph Kiefer. The following two Olympic Games in 1940 and 1944 have been omitted because of World War II and Albert was a member of the USA National and honorary USA Olympic team (Kopsky 2002). He chose to attend Princeton University as an All-American right after the Berlin Games, graduating with academic honors in chemical engineering. After that he pursued a business career with the DuPont Company and continued with competitive swimming in the Masters (Kopsky 2002; USMS 2000; Wigo 2017a). Albert married and had three children (USMS 2000). Several other members of the Vande Weghe family, such as Tauna Vande Weghe (swimmer), Kiki Vande Weghe (basketball), Coco Vande Weghe (tennis) and Ernie Vande Weghe (basketball), were also athletically successful. Albert Vande Weghe was inducted into the International Swimming Hall of Fame as an Honor Swimmer (USA) in 1990 (ISHOF, "Albert Vandeweghe" n.d.).

Due to his success at the Berlin Games in 1936, many historians credit Adolph Kiefer for inventing the flip turn. However, according to ISHOF's records, he was the one perfecting the turn. At the AAU 1934 indoor Nationals, when Albert Vande Weghe set a new world record employing the flip turn, Kiefer was too young to attend, but his future coach Stan Brauninger watched Albert Vande Weghe's flip turn.

2.3.1.3 O'Brien Shift in Shot Put

Shot put has been an athletics Olympic event since the first modern Olympics 1896 and has its origins in the ancient sport of putting the stone (Shot Put 2018). In the 1950s, at the age of around 20, Parry O'Brien (U.S., *1932–†2007) invented a new throwing technique in shot put by facing away from the direction of the throw and turning by 180° (Athletics: The Shot Put 2018; Gemer 1990). The glide has been named the O'Brien Shift (or O'Brien Glide), ensuring its originator's fame (Athletics: The Shot Put 2018). Prior to that, it had long been conventional that athletes began their throw by facing forward at a right angle to the direction of the shot, turning 90° before releasing the ball (Shot Put 2018). Figure 2.14 compares the O'Brien Shift and its predecessor in the first part of the shot put, the starting point for the preliminary movement that is generally called the "glide". To "establish the most favourable position from which to begin the putting action" is the most important task for the thrower during the glide (Gemer 1990, p. 32).

By all means, the O'Brien Shift can be considered a prime example of rule-breaking behavior. The effect it had on the athletics discipline is manifested in the

Fig. 2.14 Prior Shot Put Technique (left) vs. O'Brien Shift (right) (source: author)

fact that today, the modern shot-putting era is divided into two periods: The period *before* 1953, when the shot putters stood sideways at the back of the circle with the hips, shoulders and the left arm facing and pointing towards the direction of the throw (as displayed on the left in Fig. 2.14), and the period *after* Parry O'Brien had introduced his technique in which the athlete turned completely away from the direction of the throw by facing the back of the circle when beginning with the glide and thus setting the starting point for many important modifications to follow (for more information on the evolution of different shot put techniques, see, e.g. Gemer 1990).

With Parry O'Brien's success, his style was almost universally adopted by other shot putters and became the new standard (Parry O'Brien 2018; Shot Put 2018; *TIME Magazine* 1956). It is said, however, that few other shot putters enjoyed similar success (Elliott 2007). Parry O'Brien is considered the most important shot putter in history (Sports Reference, "Parry O'Brien" n.d.). He increased the record from 17.95 m to 19.30 m and won three Olympic medals, gold in 1952 and in 1956, silver in 1960 (Athletics: The Shot Put 2018). He was the first athlete for more than 40 years who managed to repeat as Olympic champion (IAAF, "Shot Put" n.d.). For all of his accomplishments, he was inducted into the U.S. Olympic Hall of Fame, USA Track and Field Hall of Fame, and his alma mater's USC Athletic Hall of Fame. Between 1953 and 1959 he broke the world record 17 times, and won 17 American titles in shot put and one in discus (USATF Hall of Fame, "O'Brien" n.d.).

In 1956, a *Time Magazine* cover story gives insight into O'Brien's life and the development of his technique (*TIME Magazine* 1956). According to the article, athletics have not always been O'Brien's main focus. His father played baseball and would have liked his son to follow his footsteps. Parry, however, started out with football and won a scholarship to USC instead. It is said that O'Brien gradually lost interest in football (e.g. because of difficulties with his coaches) and eventually a kick in his stomach during a game led him away from the team sport back to the shot put, which he had already practiced in high school. When USC's 1948 Olympic shot put winner Wilbur Thompson saw O'Brien working out with the track team, he encouraged him to focus solely on shot put. "I wanted to be able to take the credit or the blame for what I did myself. I always wanted to be a soloist.", Parry admits later (*TIME Magazine* 1956, p. 37). Being considered a person who organizes his life with a compulsive neatness, at USC Parry O'Brien systematically scheduled his life around the sport (*TIME Magazine* 1956). *Sports Illustrated* recites that much of his success can be traced back to hard work with daily practices including "insane" 150 puts. "I don't quit until my hands bleed, and that's the god's truth," Parry once said (Noden 1997, para. 1). His practice at USC is reported to have been at any time and any place: Outside his home, in an alley in front of his fraternity house, alone at the Coliseum (after sneaking over the fence), at 3 a.m. by street lights on a vacant parking lot, on his way to dinner or dance, even during dates. In those days, he still put the shot just like everyone else (*TIME Magazine* 1956).

One day in 1951, it is reported that he returned to his parent's home in Santa Monica, California, ruminating over his failure after having been defeated by Otis Chandler at a collegiate meet (Litsky 2007). He figured there must be some better way to put the shot. That night, after having been woken up by repeated earth shaking, his father found his only son practicing outside. "I think I've discovered something!" Parry shouted. "I couldn't wait till morning" (*TIME Magazine* 1956, p. 38). The theoretical clue of the glide Parry is said to have discovered that night was an application of physics: "The longer you apply pressure or force to an inanimate object, the farther it will go" (*TIME Magazine* 1956, p. 38).

Deemed extraordinary at that time, Parry was said to have combined mental attitude and physical aptitude, by gathering input from various schools of thought and philosophy such as studies of physics and aerodynamics, yoga and Ayurveda, different religions, self-hypnosis, nocturnal rites, psychological warfare and Afro-Cuban drumming (Noden 1997; *TIME Magazine* 1956). He has constantly been looking for tricks that enable him to "dig deep into what you might call an inner reserve of strength" (*TIME Magazine* 1956, p. 38). Furthermore, Parry's fierce concentration and determination (*TIME Magazine* 1956), consistency (Elliott 2007) and competitiveness (Carlson 2007) have been pointed out. He always made sure to save his "best for competition" and to "not put well in practice", he said according to Maule (1960, para. 9). Others suggest that his "unique and systematic preparation and well-designed strength training programme, rather than … his technical innovations" led to his success (Gemer 1990, p. 33). *TIME Magazine* (1956) summarizes: "He is the epitome of the spirit of single-minded pursuit of perfection idealized in the Olympic reed, a loner who has consecrated his life to shot-putting farther than anyone" (p. 37).

O'Brien graduated from University of California, majoring in business administration (*TIME Magazine* 1956). He stopped competing in shot put in 1966 and pursued a business career in banking, real estate and civil engineering (Elliott 2007; Sports Reference, "Parry O'Brien" n.d.). He got married, had two stepsons and two daughters (Noden 1997).

2.3.1.4 Skate Skiing Technique in Cross-Country Skiing

Cross-Country Skiing is the oldest type of skiing and originated in Norway. During the wintertime, skis were used as a way to move in snow-covered areas, to chase game, gather firewood, or keep social contact. The advent of skiing as a sport dates back to the end of the nineteenth century. The first recorded race is reported to have taken place in 1842. The Holmenkollen ski festival commenced in 1892 with Nordic combined events only and was expanded with cross-country competitions in 1901. The Olympic debut of cross country skiing was at the first Winter Games in Chamonix in 1924 (IOC, "Cross Country Skiing" n.d.).

For more than a 100 years, cross-country skiers had universally used the classic diagonal stride in which skiers alternately kick and glide, following parallel tracks (Bengtsson n.d.; Hottenrott and Urban 2004; Nordic Skiing 2018). Then, in the 1970s, the skating technique found its way to cross-country skiing. It first appeared in a preliminary version, the Siitonen step, also called Finnstep or Halfskating Step, where the skier takes one-sided lateral pushes on the skis for propulsion (Theiner and Karl 2002). One ski slides in the track of the cross-country ski run and the other ski crosses the side. This movement is performed on both sides, which leads to a kind of skating movement, called Skate Skiing Technique (Allen 2012, pp. 9, 10). Over the years, several variations of Skating techniques have evolved (Kuhn 1997; Schlickenrieder and Elbern 2003). The Classic technique and the Skating technique are shown in Fig. 2.15.

The Skating Technique spread rapidly in cross-country skiing. Within 5 years, the World Championships and Olympic competitions in cross-country skiing were entirely transformed (Bengtsson n.d.; Hottenrott and Urban 2004; Paal and Corradini

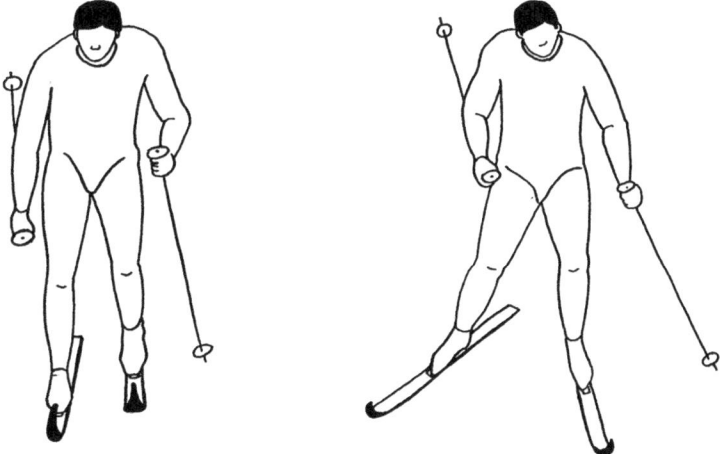

Fig. 2.15 Classic Technique (left) vs. Skating Technique (right) (source: author)

2007; Theiner and Karl 2002). One of the reasons is reported to be the dynamics of the new style. The skating stride is more efficient, so skiers can race much faster (Bengtsson n.d.; Nordic Skiing 2018), gaining up to 40 km/h on trails and up to 70 km/h downhill (Hottenrott and Urban 2004; Theiner and Karl 2002). Concerns regarding inevitable strain injuries (especially ankle joints, knee joints, hip joints) resulting from the skating style have not been confirmed (Hottenrott and Urban 2004). While the classic technique can be applied on both undisturbed and tracked snow, for skate skiing, smooth and firm surfaces are needed (Schlickenrieder and Elbern 2003). Therefore, the advent of prepared trails in 1968 facilitated considerably the diffusion of the skating style (Hottenrott and Urban 2004).

Officials ensured that the classical step was not replaced entirely though. Fearing that the skate skiing technique would eliminate classic cross-country skiing, officials were trying to restrict skating as much as possible (Hottenrott and Urban 2004; Paal and Corradini 2007; Schlickenrieder and Elbern 2003; Theiner and Karl 2002). This process eventually lead to an official divide of cross-country skiing into two sub-disciplines: classic and freestyle (Bengtsson n.d.; Paal and Corradini 2007).

The development of the Skate Skiing Technique has been a long and gradual process of evolution. The Scandinavian Pauli Siitonen and the American Bill Koch are said to have been the most important contributors to the new technique. The basic idea of skating, however, has existed for hundreds, maybe even thousands, of years (Hottenrott and Urban 2004; Kuhn 1997; Paal and Corradini 2007; Theiner and Karl 2002). A picture of a Lapp skier from 1675 shows uneven skis, the long one used for standing, the short one for pushing. In that vein, the skier moved via single-sided skating step (Paal and Corradini 2007). In the earlier twentieth century, skating was still used regularly. After that, however, the traditional technique was either forgotten or ignored by racers, until it was reintroduced in the 1970s (Bengtsson n.d.; Paal and Corradini 2007).

Pauli Siitonen (FIN, *1938) is credited with popularizing the so-called Siitonen-step, which is the precursor to the present skating technique (Paal and Corradini 2007). Siitonen grew up in southern Finland and was considered a promising skier in his junior years. Being portrayed as tough and relentless, he trained hard. Before coming to cross-country skiing, his alpine career started with ski-orienteering, where he had learned to ski with a single-sided free technique, in which the athletes parallelly study the map to plan the route. When he started taking part in marathon cross-country races, he eventually used the same skiing style (Paal and Corradini 2007). It is reported that after problems with his waxing[15] at a ski race in 1972, Pauli Siitonen started using the ancient propulsion technique (Abele 2005; Haffner 2004). As Allen (2012) remarks, "[He] had used the wrong wax, so he kept one ski in the track and skated with the other ... and won!" (p. 170). Among other successes, he won the Koenig-Ludwig-Lauf (the largest German long distance cross-country ski race) six times between 1974 and 1981 (Paal and Corradini 2007).

---

[15] At the higher levels of competitive skiing, waxing is an integral aspect and considered the biggest problem with the classic style (Hottenrott and Urban 2004).

William Conrad "Bill" Koch (U.S., *1955) is said to have popularized the skating technique (Nordic Skiing 2018). He started out competing in Nordic Combined, which is a combination of cross-country skiing and ski jumping but decided to focus on cross-country skiing at the age of 16, competing at an international level (Paal and Corradini 2007). At the 1976 Innsbruck Olympic Games, he became the first and so far only American to win an Olympic medal (silver) in cross-country skiing (IOC, "Bill Koch" n.d.). It is reported that at a Swedish marathon, he observed the Siitonen step and perfected it (Bengtsson n.d.; Paal and Corradini 2007; Theiner and Karl 2002). With the new technique he was around 10% faster (Paal and Corradini 2007). Apart from his Olympic success, he won several major competitions, (e.g. the 1981 Engadin Skimarathon and the 1982 World Cup of Cross-Country skiing; Bengtsson n.d.; Paal and Corradini 2007).

2.3.1.5 Forward Seat in Equestrian Jumping

Equestrian Jumping is rooted in fox hunting. After the Enclosures Act had been introduced in England in the eighteenth century, fences were built by landowners. This lead to a situation where hunters could not just pursue foxes galloping across the fields but required jumping horses to overcome the new obstacles (IOC, "Equestrian Jumping" n.d.). Horses were already part of the Ancient Olympic Games in 680 B.C., eventing in chariot racing. Equestrian was incorporated into the 1912 Modern Olympic Games for the first time. In the initial years, jumping was dominated by the military (IOC, "Equestrian Jumping" n.d.).

With the prior Classical seat, riders would lean back and pull the reins when jumping a fence. This technique, however, was unnatural and uncomfortable for the horse (Caprilli 1901). In the Forward seat position instead, the rider's weight is centered forward in the saddle, over the horse's withers. This allows the horse to move freely without its forward impulse being impeded by the interference of the rider. Therefore, the horse can extend, move more freely and, in consequence, perform better (Self 1946, p. 133, "Forward Seat"; 1952, p. 169). Figure 2.16 schematically displays how the Forward seat differs from the prior Classic seat (e.g. regarding the rider's position and the length of stirrups and reigns).

The beginnings of the Forward seat are often ascribed to two people: infamous American jockey Tod Sloan who dominated racing by using the Forward seat and Italian cavalry officer Federico Caprilli who conducted an extensive scientific study of horses in the natural environment during his work at the military. Information on both is outlined in the following paragraphs.

The American jockey Tod Sloan (U.S., *1874–[†]1933)[16] is considered to be the first person having used the Forward seat in racing (Self 1952, p. 169). John Dizikes, an emeritus professor of American studies at the University of California, Santa

---

[16]For more information about Tod Sloan, see his reprinted and edited autobiography Sloan (1988) and Dizikes (2000).

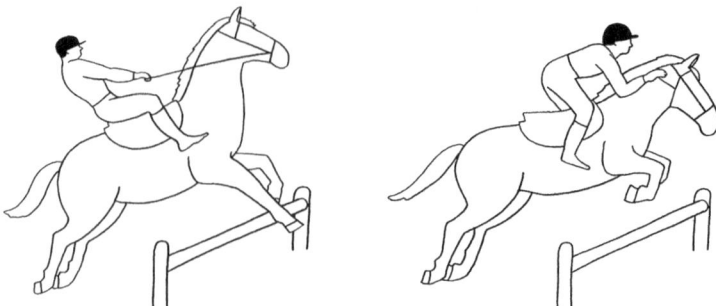

Fig. 2.16 Classic Seat (left) vs. Forward Seat (right) (source: author)

Cruz, portrays Sloan in his book *Yankee Doodle Dandy: The Life and Times of Tod Sloan* (2000, first edition 1932). It is primarily based on Tod Sloan's autobiography (1988) and further enriched with contemporary information. According to his writings, Sloan's discovery can be pinned down to one dramatic moment. While galloping his horse together with another jockey, Sloan's horse started to bolt. In an attempt to regain control, he left the saddle and crouched onto the horse's neck. Both jockeys laughed at the strange sight but Sloan also got the feeling that in such a position, riding seemed to be easier for both the horse and the rider (Dizikes 2000). Tod Sloan recalls (Dizikes 2000, with reference to the original source Sloan (1915) "Tod Sloan by Himself"):

> I put two and two together and thought there must be something in it, and I began to think it out, trying all sorts of experiments on horses at home. The "crouch seat," or the "monkey mount," or the thousand and one other ways it has been described, was the result. Then the time came when I determined to put it into practice. But I couldn't screw up enough courage the first time I had a chance. I kept putting it off. At last, though, I did really spring it on them. Everybody laughed. They thought I had turned comedian. But I was too cocksure to be discouraged. I was certain that I was on the right track. I persevered, and at last I began to win races! (p. 58).

There remain, however, open questions and other versions of the story. For instance, Dizikes (2000) points out the puzzling fact that contemporary media accounts seem to have not mentioned anything like the invention of a Forward seat. Also, Sloan himself insisted that he did not ride in an actual Forward seat but only in a "*somewhat* forward position" (Dizikes 2000, p. 62). Regarding the origins of the Forward seat, Tod Sloan also gave some credit to jockey Harry Griffin whom he had seen riding in a similar, more forward leaning manner. It is also asserted by writers and observers at the time, that Tod got inspired by white and African-American stable boys who were riding untrained and without equipment—similar to Native Americans who rode bareback up on their horse's necks. For instance, J. Huggins, a popular American trainer in those days, referred to roots in indigenous American racing styles (Dizikes 2000, p. 63). Some years after the Forward seat had gained more acceptance and had already become associated with Tod Sloan as the inventor, a writer argued that Frank Van Ness, horse owner and trainer, supposedly taught the style to Tod Sloan and, therefore, should be credited instead (Dizikes 2000, p. 67). All in all, Dizikes (2000) summarizes that the new Forward riding style "revealed itself gradually, as a continuous evolution, not a single moment" (p. 62).

While Sloan, assumingly in part also because of his overall jockey skills and racing success, is credited with popularizing the forward seat as a jockey, he made no study of the scientific reasons for the horse's behavior (Self 1952, p. 169). It was Italian cavalry officer Federico Caprilli in the 1900s (IT, *1868–†1907) who is said to have systematically developed and formalized the Forward seat after long years of observing horses in freedom and studying the natural movements of the horse, regarding the horse's balance and axis of gravity (Fox and Mickley 1987, p. 97; Self 1946, pp. 133, 239, 1952, pp. 8–9). Lieutenant Federico Caprilli is, therefore, often regarded as the "father of modern riding" (Caprilli 1901; IOC, "Equestrian Jumping" n.d.), and the change from Classic Seat to Forward Seat is also called the Caprilli Revolution. Caprilli wrote very little and little is known about him. His fundamental principles have been publicized by his pupil Piero Santini in Italian (Caprilli Papers). Entering the military at an early age, he was schooled in the militaries equestrian principles and eventually became chief instructor at the Italian Cavalry School of Tor di Quinto. This is where the major part of his studies took place.

Despite the tentativeness regarding the emergence of the style, the groundbreaking character of the Forward seat leading to major changes in horsemanship cannot be dismissed. The Forward seat completely revolutionized the entrenched belief system in which the horse was asked to conform to the rider's center of gravity and not the other more natural way around (Horsemanship 2018, p. 169; Self 1952). It took a while before the new method was accepted universally, however (Dizikes 2000, Chap. 6; Fox and Mickley 1987, p. 97). Standing in opposition to the established system, the new technique was controversial at first and suffered from resistance (Fox 2017). For 200 years, jockeys had ridden the "languidly elegant classical style" (p. 59), sitting far back in the saddle with long stirrups and long reins (Dizikes 2000). It was the only style existing and "tradition's power was so great that intelligent observers refused to accept its overthrow" (Dizikes 2000, p. 59). Dizikes (2000), with reference to "Notes", *Badminton Magazine*, January 1899, p. 26–27, provides an exemplary quote for the functionary's resistance: "It may be insular, narrow-minded, prejudiced, and the rest of it but I cannot believe that, generation after generation, jockeys have been sitting on the wrong part of a horse's back, that the best place for the saddle is not where it has always been, and that at the end of the nineteenth century the theory and practice of horsemanship as applied to racing is to be revolutionized" (pp. 59–60).

Eventually, however, the Italian method (known as il systema in Italy) has been adopted by practically all schools of riding and is now recognized as a revolutionary contribution to horsemanship (Self 1946, pp. 133, 239, 1952, pp. 8–9, 169). To this date, the technique is the one most frequently used, especially for Equestrian Jumping (Horsemanship 2018).

2.3.1.6   V-Style in Ski Jumping

Ski jumping was incorporated into the first Olympic Winter Games in Chamonix Mont-Blanc in 1924. Since then, ski jumping has developed tremendously with different jumping styles leading to ever greater distances (IOC, "Ski Jumping" n.d.; for historical background information regarding the development of jumping techniques, see Macarthur 2011). In 1964, the Olympic event was split into large-hill jumping and normal or small-hill jumping (Ski Jumping 2018). Until the early 1990s, the standard ski jumping technique used by most jumpers was the "parallel skis" or Daescher method. In the parallel position, jumpers lean far forward from the ankles with knees straight, holding the skis parallel and arms backward. While the parallel technique already minimizes wind resistance and, therefore, leads to an aerodynamic lifting effect, the V-style provides even more lift. When going down the hill with a V-Style, the jumpers spread the ski tips outward in the opposite direction, literally creating a V-shape (Ski Jumping n.d.; for more information regarding performance factors in ski jumping, see Müller 2008). Both styles are visually juxtaposed in Fig. 2.17.

In most references, Swedish jumper Jan Boklöv (SWE, *1966) is credited for having popularized the V-style (e.g. Ashburner 2003; Nedo 2016; Ski Jumping 2018; Svensson n.d.).[17] The stuttering, epileptic (Eiberle 2010; Svensson n.d.) and reportedly semi-talented (Eiberle 2010; Wittmann n.d.) Swede started ski jumping at the age of 11 (Wittmann n.d.). He never craved the spotlight (Geiler 2015) and was considered to be rather reserved (Nedo 2016). That may be the reason why some initially ignored his style, dismissing it as some kind of peculiarity (Nedo 2016).

By his own account, he came to discover the new style by chance (Haack 2015; Nedo 2016; Svensson n.d.; Voigt 2008). In a training session in his early twenties, a sudden wind squall caused a seemingly faulty jump. To prevent a crash, Jan Boklöv instinctively leaned his body forward so that his skis opened at the front (Boecker 2010; Haack 2015; Nedo 2016; Voigt 2008; Wittmann n.d.). He flew 90 m, which was a substantial improvement over the average 70 m that jumpers usually achieved on that hill in Falun (Svensson n.d.). Together with his coach, he tried to figure out what happened. The investigative process took several years (Geiler 2015; Nedo 2016; Voigt 2008), including a number of fractures and other injuries (Haack 2015; Wittmann n.d.). Some reports mention different analogies he used during that thought process, such as thinking about it like surfing, as in being in front of the wave (i.e. wind), allowing it to push the body forward (Svensson n.d.), or like being a kite (Eiberle 2010). Eventually Boklöv managed to refine the style and started

---

[17]There is also some account that Polish ski jumper Miroslaw Graf discovered the V-technique as early as 1969, without it becoming adopted or popular, however (Johnson 2008). One reason why he never got successful is said to be ascribed to the fact that the increased distance of his jump could not overcompensate the loss of style points the judges penalized the new technique with (Macarthur 2011). It is recorded that he began to use his skis in a V because he had fractured his ribs and ankles (Maryniak et al. 2009; *Skijumping* 2006).

Fig. 2.17 Parallel Style (left) vs. V-Style (right) (source: author)

using it in competitions. As Macarthur (2011) points out, "Soon, Boklöv was jumping farther than anyone else in regular ski jumping competitions" (p. 23).

In the beginning, however, his distance advantage he achieved with the V-Style was decreased by low style points in competitive events. According to Macarthur (2011), decreasing style points for new styles is "a ski jumping tradition" (p. 24). The FIS reportedly also deducted points for the initial presentations of the Kongsberg and Daescher techniques because they were judged unaesthetic. In the case of the V-Style, the FIS objected to this break with tradition as well (Eiberle 2010; FAZ 2008; Wittmann n.d.), and judges deducted style points because the new style to them looked neither safe nor attractive (Ashburner 2003; Haack 2015; Voigt 2008). Boklöv was not just punished during competitions but also highly ridiculed for his nontraditional style (Haack 2015; Nedo 2016; Ski Jumping 2018). For example, he was called a "flapping crow", or "clown" or "frog king", and the new technique was labelled "frog style" (FAZ 2008; Svensson n.d.; Wittmann n.d.). Boklöv, however, believed in himself and continued to jump with his technique, enduring all resistance, frustration and humiliation (Haack 2015). At last, Boklöv's success in the World Cup sparked a wide-ranging mental change (Nedo 2016): An increasing number of ski jumpers adapted the V-Style and eventually the new technique was officially considered acceptable by the officials (Macarthur 2011). Other jumpers are said to have acknowledged his accomplishments even earlier (Haack 2015).

Winning the 1988/1989 World Cup in Lahti remained Boklöv's biggest success, he never became a star athlete (Ashburner 2003; Geiler 2015; Wittmann n.d.). His prototype version of the new jump was soon considerably improved by other jumpers (Ashburner 2003; Nedo 2016). Boklöv had to stop ski jumping because of physical problems (Haack 2015). After his sports career, he became a nursery teacher and took care of his two sons (Geiler 2015).

Once the new V-Style jumping method had been accepted, it rapidly changed the sport. Starting with its first official introduction in the 1988/1989 annual World Cup competition, only a couple of years later in the 1992 Olympics, all medalists were using the style (Ashburner 2003; IOC, "Ski Jumping" n.d.). Even though it was harder to learn (Michalek 2017), ski jumpers, especially the young, started to imitate Boklöv's style—some groups liking the technique more (Japanese, who soon noticed the fit of the style and their slim physiques) than others ("traditionalists voicing concern that a sport of elegance and beauty could degenerate into a crude form of gymnastics", Ashburner 2003, p. 84).

Despite these more subjective objections, the V-Style without doubt lead to longer jumps. Many hills had to be revised to extend the landing slopes at considerable cost in consequence of the much longer jumps (Ashburner 2003; Haack 2015; Macarthur 2011). Different figures have been reported regarding the increased lift resulting from the V-configuration. Macarthur (2011) summarizes that jumping in a V is leading to "anywhere from 26 to 33% more lift" (p. 23). Moreover, according to Walter Hofer, director at the German Ski Association, ski jumping has become much safer with substantially fewer accidents after the V-Style had been introduced (Voigt 2008). All in all, the invention of the V-style is said to be the most decisive innovation in ski jumping (Pfister 2007). Jens Weißpflog, triple winner of Olympic gold and four-time winner of the World Cup, even compares its importance to the Fosbury Flop in high jump (Nedo 2016).

2.3.1.7   Jump Shot in Basketball

In 1891, James Naismith, a PE teacher at Springfield College, invented basketball using peach baskets in Springfield, Massachusetts (USA). Basketball has been an Olympic event since the 1936 Games in Berlin. The inaugural tournament was hosted outdoors on the clay courts of the tennis stadium. In those days, the ball was still a lot bigger, heavier and not perfectly round (IOC 2017a). The invention of the jump shot is considered one of basketball's most important changes (Christgau 1999, p. xi). As a result of the change, basketball games have become a lot faster, ending with substantially higher scores. In the time before, defenders controlled the sport and the number of baskets was comparable to the amount of goals in a football game (Fury 2016; Pennington 2011). Today, as basketball players usually score points during the game using the jump shot, the shot is still considered to be the most important element of technique in basketball, requiring a high level of performance (Struzik et al. 2014).

For around 40 years, basketballers would only take set shots with both feet firmly on the ground (Fury 2016, p. 11). Players orthodoxically shot multiple quick passes from a standing position with two hands held chest high (Pennington 2011). With a jump shot, the player intends to score a basket by leaving the ground, jumping high in the air and throwing the ball, typically with one hand (e.g. Christgau 1999; Fury 2016). Figure 2.18 schematically displays both the set shot and the jump shot.

The early jump shooters did not induce an instant revolution, rather it was a shot that had been emerging for years (Fury 2016). Basketball historians ascertain that the incubation period was the early 1930s. A decade later, it was not just a college game phenomenon anymore but slowly arrived into the mainstream (Pennington 2011). With the beginning of the 1950s, the jump shot is said to have "found a home in basketball" (Fury 2016, p. 37). It emerged in small towns and migrated to the big cities (Fury 2016, p. 12). By the end of the incubation period, basketball fans divided

Fig. 2.18 Set Shot (left)
vs. Jump Shot (right)
(source: author)

into two groups. Some thought the new shot made the game more exciting and others concluded that it would destroy the game by turning it into a mere contest of basket shooting, which is usually won by the team with the most accurate shooters. Opponents also regarded the shot as unfair, mitigating the importance of teamwork (Fury 2016, pp. 37–38).

The jump shot disobeyed two "basketball commandments", which were deeply entrenched in the whole basketball system during that time: staying on the floor and shooting with two hands (e.g. pp. 194; 201). Physical educators played a major role in the development of basketball. They taught the game and, therefore, had a considerable impact on the sport's growth in the United States. The typical way of playing basketball was said to have been quite scientific, originating from the textbooks that were used (Fury 2016, p. 12). In 1922, Walter E. Meanwell's (professor of physical education from England) book *The Science of Basketball for Men* was published and "became the bible for basketball in the United States" (Christgau 1999, p. 12). In the book, standard shots were described to be two-handed without leaving the floor. The One-Hand Push Shot (in which the player should jump toward the basket) was discussed briefly. In the following years, other publications emerged in which the wish for more freedom in shooting slowly started to be expressed (Fury 2016, pp. 13–17).

A second aspect is related to the mechanical characteristics of the jump shot. The following quotation gives insight into the major concerns (Fury 2016):

> "Any time you can do something on the ground, it's better," he said, "Once you leave the ground, you've committed yourself." Jump shot critics discouraged players from flying into the air because they feared the indecision that came when someone left their feet. They feared the bad passes from players who jumped with no clear plan of what they'd do in the air. Staying grounded meant fewer mistakes. It was simply a safer way to play the game, if not as exciting. (p. 42)

Early jump-shooters faced strong resistance in terms of doubts and fear, angry coaches and benchings. They were "ridiculed or scolded into conformity" (Pennington 2011, para 12). More detailed information on the contemporary developments is provided below with the help of individual cases.

The search for the originator of the jump shot has been troubling sports historians for a long time. The innovation cannot be traced back to a single person. For years, the American author John Christgau interviewed over a hundred players, coaches and fans, finally identifying eight players who, according to his research, were among the earliest pioneers (Christgau 1999, see also Fury 2016, p. 11). Based on Christgau's research (if not quoted otherwise), six stories are outlined subsequently. The other two are excluded from the analysis because it is explicitly stated that they did not come up with the idea themselves but watched and imitated other players (Joe Fulks "watched Robert Goheen score repeatedly with an exciting, two-handed leaping shot", p. 111; Johnny Adams saw Gaylon Smith coming to the gym and "remembered him as the very same player with an unusual leaping shot" whom he had seen in a game 1 year earlier, p. 144). The early shooters are said to have developed their shots independent of each other, from the little media that existed, not being aware of what happened elsewhere in the country (Fury 2016, p. 10).

Myer "Whitey" Skoog's (U.S., *1926) father had emigrated from Norway. The family lived in the USA but still preserved their native country's culture in terms of friends, deep religious faith, the language spoken at home, and leisure activities such as cross-country skiing and ski jumping. At school, Myer's beginning was difficult, culminating in a note from his teacher to his parents: "If you want your son to be an American, you're going to have to start speaking English at home" (p. 9). So, they did. According to the records, his Norwegian character was rather quiet and selfless but also competitive in nature. Myer won his first contest in the fourth grade: the city marble championships—soon to be followed by success in high jumping at high school (being heralded as one of his school's all-time greats). It is reported that he had developed an "explosive leaping ability" (p. 12) on ski jumps. He started playing basketball on the eight-grade basketball team in junior high school but had a hard time in the beginning. His ski-jumping instincts for jumping and soaring were considered highly inappropriate and lead to strong disapproval from his coach, admonishing him that in basketball "except for rebounding, ... you kept your feet on the floor", benching and calling him "hot dog" (p. 11). The embarrassment deeply entrenched in his mind and for not again violating both the code of basketball and his traditionally rooted Nordic demeanor (never call attention to yourself), he intended to be fully compliant in the future. At a high school game in 1944, however, the violation of the basketball traditions happened again. Almost without thinking, he crouched and jumped, releasing an awkward shot that was much too short. "'I'm gonna put that shot away,' he told himself, 'I'll never do it again!'" (p. 25). It took four further years until he threw another leaping shot, coming as spontaneously as the first one but with two alterations: the shot was good and did not leave him with regret. Sportswriters who saw it mistakenly reported it as his first jump shot. Skoog started refining it in daily practices from then on (Christgau 1999, pp. 1–29).

   John Burton (U.S., *1926–†2014), often called Mouse Gonzales because of his height, was ascribed with "mosquito like quickness" (p. 32) and good coordination. His ancestors were Spanish and his parents got divorced when he was 7 years old. Spending most summers of his childhood at his grandparents' lively house reportedly made him "irrepressible and wild" (p. 31). On his first high school day, the basketball coach chose him as the tiniest from a long row of freshman and said, "I'm gonna make you a basketball player" (p. 34). He began practicing a lot, was taught moves and fundamentals by the coach, got into a circle of taller, more experienced basketballers, but still being the smallest, he remained a bench substitute and played little. While practicing games in his free time, he found that he easily managed to get to the basket but found his shot being blocked by the taller men most of the times. "Getting clear was the main thing on his mind as he walked" (p. 38). At one of the next games, in the middle of an action, he suddenly stopped, disconnected from the flow of the game, leaped quickly and rose high up, and with the ball over his head he released the shot. He thought it was stupid. His coaches shouted directions "'Bounce passes, bounce passes!'" (p. 42) making it clear that staying on the floor was critical. Afterwards he could not grasp what had happened during that jump but he was aware of one thing: "I'm a little man in a big man's game. But now I have a shot nobody can touch." (p. 43). He started experimenting, trying to reconstruct the mechanics of the shot that seemingly came by accident rather than by design. When he watched another player catching a rebound, jumping back and hanging for a second before throwing the ball he finally knew how to do it and further developed his leaping shot. Burton was called one of the finest players of that golden age but came to decide that his own family was more important to him than basketball (Christgau 1999, pp. 30–53).

   Bud Palmer (U.S., *1921–†2013) is depicted as having loved athletic challenges from an early age. At the age of six, he and his friends set up a boxing ring in a backyard. Basketball came after that, and their games were characterized by fierce fighting that they had used as boxers before. He was too small and weak to throw a ball into the basket, so he supported his movement with a leap. His parents got divorced by the time their son was born, so he grew up with his Mother Blanche who was portrayed as settled but unforgiving and rigid. Neither money nor academics had ever been an issue. At the age of eight, they moved to Switzerland where he attended an exclusive private school on Lac Léman. His father, Lefty Flynn, was considered a semi-successful actor who drank heavily, married four times and is said to have been theatrical, restless but also warmhearted. He taught his son the importance of invention and spontaneity and most importantly living fully, never doing anything with only half a heart. When Bud got back to the U.S., he went to Phillips Exeter and then attended Princeton where he started playing college basketball, among the smallest in his team (Christgau 1999, pp. 54–78). Christgau (1999) reports that Bud Palmer could not identify the exact moment he had discovered the jump shot but that he memorized the following:

> He could remember playing lacrosse and disobeying one of its commandments, which was that you shot only with your strongest arm, and he could remember with perfect clarity telling himself "Well, hell, why can't I shoot from *both* sides?" and then immediately doing it. He could remember that basketball suffered from strict commandments, too, command-ments which weren't for him a cause of frustration. Instead, they were a departure point for the spirit of originality . . . . He could remember the exact thought that preceded his discovery of the jump shot, which was, *If I dribble, and stop, and jump, I will have an advantage.* (pp. 68–69)

He played three seasons and after that enlisted in the United States Navy during World War II. He was the first captain of the New York Knicks and went on as a successful sportscaster after his NBA career (Martin 2013).

Dave Minor (U.S., *1922–†1998) grew up in the custody of his three aunts because his father left when he was born and his mother died. They were highly devoted in teaching him good manners and kindliness, the importance of indepen-dence and enterprise, and insisted on regular attendance at the church. He is described as a bookish boy, a math genius but also talented in athletics such as pole vault, high jump, broad jump, hurdles and sprint. At one point, he set an Indiana state high jump record of six-feet four-inches that stood for 16 years (p. 88). To entertain his friends, he jumped over high spear-tipped fences—an exercise that seemed easy and not the least threatening to him. His first jump shot attempt happened during a practice game. It is said to have occurred instinctively, not deliberately planned: "He was driving straight up the middle when he leaped for the shot with the same explosive spring that had carried him over the . . . fence" (pp. 82–83). His coach interrupted the game by calling for a time out, asking him whether he knew what he did. Dave did not really remember except that he attempted to make the basket. He did not stop leaping, however, although he was not explicitly aware of the underlying mechanics. His teammates secretly tried to also learn the shot but had a hard time. Their coach eventually announced during one game: "'I don't want you shootin' that shot'" . . . 'No one shoot that damn shot!' . . . 'Except Minor'" (p. 86). After all, his running short-handers were considered electrifying and unconventional. Dave Minor was among the first blacks in the NBA. He married, had four kids, and took over the real-estate business from his aunt (Christgau 1999, pp. 79–105).

Belus Smawley (U.S., *1918–†2003) grew up on a farm with his parents and six siblings. In his freshman years, he was tall and able to jump higher than any other boy, trying to improve his leaping ability by touching higher and higher limbs of the oak tree on their farm. Their father expected unquestioning obedience and did not accept recreational activities as part of their son's lives. They still managed to sneak off to play with other kids in the abandoned passenger waiting room nearby. This is where his first jump shot attempt is said to have taken place (Christgau 1999):

> Then he stopped and went into the same deep crouch he had used to explode off both feet when he jumped to touch higher and higher oak limbs. . . . He exploded upward with a leap that shook the old floor. As he rose, the habit of reaching to touch an oak limb was too powerful to ignore, and he extended the ball in his two stiff arms, as if he were reaching again for a limb. For a split second at the top of his leap he experienced the sharp feeling of hovering over everybody else. (p. 171)

His friend told him he could not do that shot again because they were not able to guard him that way. Soon they were trying to imitate Belus, without mastering it, however. So, they urged his friend to untangle his secret, but he was not able to give more than an unsatisfying advice: "'Well, I can hesitate . . . I can *hold in the air*,' he said. 'You have to practice it'" (p. 172).

When Belus Smawley started using his shot regularly, he became the leading scorer. At the age of 18, he got accepted for a position on an AAU[18] basketball team. He finished high school afterwards and got an All-American athletic scholarship for Appalachian State University (majoring in history and physical education). He became player-coach until he went to the Navy. He started playing in their basketball team and refined his jump shot. He got married and either worked as a high school teacher and basketball coach or further pursued his NBA basketball career playing fulltime for several teams (e.g. St. Louis, Syracuse, Baltimore). Eventually he focused on family and his teaching career, becoming the principal of a junior high school (Christgau 1999, pp. 156–186).

Kenny Sailors (U.S., *1921–†2016) grew up on a farm together with his mother and his one-foot taller, older brother Bud. Both siblings were dedicated to playing basketball and practiced outside on the farmyard gravel next to their farm's windmill whenever they found the time in between helping their mother to keep the farm going. Their parents got divorced when they were young. She taught them that "'it doesn't make any difference if you get knocked down seven times. *You get back up again*'" (p. 190). She set a perfect example of the importance of hard work and perseverance. Kenny, small and quick, was considered a masterful dribbler, darting and spontaneous. Bud, in contrast, was tall and deliberate regarding his movements. They could both jump; as a junior the older brother was the best high school jumper in Wyoming. Never leaving the floor was "a basketball commandment as rigid as what he heard in church" (p. 194), insistently imposed on them by their coach. Bud never challenged his coach, mostly because he could easily score without jumping. It was different for his smaller brother, however. Christgau (1999) reports the following key scene in which Kenny jumps for the first time:

> Meanwhile, he had already suffered too many losses, already been knocked down too many times not to get up again, *way up*—exactly the way his brother could high jump. The pause for the drink had given Kenny time to set it in his mind: *I can shoot over him if I can get up in*

---

[18]"The Amateur Athletic Union (AAU) is a multisport organization that focuses on the promotion and delivery of amateur sport for participants of all ages in the United States" (Daprano 2011, p. 49).

the air. Minutes later, Kenny tried the first shot. It came at the end of a long and apparently aimless course of dribbling and circling. Bud stepped back and watched with awe, because his little brother's talent was spectacular. The ball seemed fixed to the rapid flutter of his hand by an invisible rubber band. But Bud also couldn't help but watch with amusement, because it was all useless dazzle. When Kenny finally decided to shoot, Bud was confident he could slap the ball away easily, just as he had always done. Then Kenny stopped suddenly and jumped. For a moment, Bud stood watching as if he were transfixed by the surprising sight of his brother rising high in the air. Then Bud realized it was not a pointless, acrobatic leap. It was the prelude to a shot! But before he could close and bat the shot away, the ball was sailing over his long arms. Much later, Bud would laugh deeply and insist that his little brother's first awkward jump shot hadn't reached the backboard, or even hit the windmill. (p. 195)

Despite his coaches reservations, Kenny went on practicing his new shot until he finally had developed an "uncanny accuracy" (Christgau 1999, p. 201). More than a decade after his first "crude and desperate" jump shot, a picture of Kenny hanging high in the air above the floor of Madison Square Garden was published in *Life Magazine* and became historic (Christgau 1999, pp. 205–206). Millions of young players saw the picture of how Kenny jumped and shot, "causing a chain reaction in basketball" (Christgau 1999, p. 206). Even though it took some more years until professional athletic journals recognized the shot, young basketballers began to practice the shot everywhere. Kenny played professional basketball for a long time, being among the league's leading scorers each year (Christgau 1999, p. 209). In his mid-40s, he and his wife settled in the Alaskan wilderness (Christgau 1999, p. 211).

Apart from Christgau's investigations, several other names of players who are supposedly related to the development of the jump shot occur. The NCAA collegiate archives, for instance, honor John Miller Cooper as the first jump shooter and credit Hank Luisetti for popularizing the shot (e.g. Pennington 2011). Therefore, a short profile of those two players is also added below and incorporated into further analysis.

John Miller Cooper (U.S., *1912–†2010) grew up on a cattle farm in Kentucky. It is reported that he discovered the jump shot by accident: "He went up to catch a pass, didn't see anyone to dish off to, and fired the ball at the basket" (Fury 2016, p. 16). According to his son, Cooper used his twisting jumper with two hands above his head to shoot over taller opponents. "'My feet left the hardcourt surface, and it felt good. It was free and natural, and I knew I had discovered something'" (Fury 2016, p. 17). His coach at the University of Missouri benched Cooper after he saw his first attempt in a college game and admonished him to never shoot like that again. "'It was a rule, and it was a time in America when rules didn't get broken.'" (Pennington 2011, para 10). That is why Cooper reportedly complied first, but eventually he jumped again and his coach conceded. The shot's impact was indisputable, leading to his schools highest score for almost 20 years. Other coaches complained about the unfairness of the shot, pointing out that "'legal defense against the shot is virtually impossible'" (Fury 2016, p. 17). After college, Cooper focused on an academic career working as a researcher, instructor and author of basketball textbooks— sometimes being called the "father of biomechanics" (Fury 2016, p. 17).

Hank Luisetti (U.S., *1916–†2002) did not create the jump shot and insists that he actually never had a jump shot but just a "running one-hander" (Fury 2016, p. 15). It is reported that he adapted the style on the playground while playing against older and taller opponents. In the 1930s, he started for Stanford and scored high in a normally low-scoring era (Fury 2016). On average, he obtained 16.1 points per game and was the first college player to ever score 50 points in a single game (Naismith Memorial Basketball Hall of Fame n.d.). When coach Nat Holman saw Luisetti's style, his judgment was clear, "I'd quit coaching before I'd teach a one-hand shot to win a game. Nobody can convince me a shot that is more a prayer than a shot is the proper way to play the game. There's only one way to shoot—the way we do it in the East. With two hands" (Fury 2016, p. 14).

2.3.1.8 Dolphin Kick in Butterfly Swimming

The Butterfly stroke is one of the four swimming techniques used in major competitions (IOC, "Swimming" n.d.). Originally emerging from the breaststroke, the technique was recognized as a distinct competitive swimming stroke in 1953 (Swimming 2018). The first official appearance at the Olympic Games took place in Melbourne in 1956 (IOC, "Swimming" n.d.). In the butterfly, the swimmer's arms are brought forward above the water, from back to front in a windmill fashion. Initially, the legs were moved in an accustomed frog kick style in butterfly swimming. Later, this was replaced by a fishtail or dolphin kick (Swimming 2018). The two different leg kicks are schematically visualized in Fig. 2.19. Butterfly's two components (arms and legs) evolved separately. Taking the origins of the arm's propulsion mostly aside, the following descriptions focus on the genesis of the leg's movement.

In a dolphin kick, the swimmers keep their legs together and propel them down "like a flipper" (Swimming 2018). D.A. Armbruster and Sieg (1935) compare the movement to the crawl stroke: "Instead of 'fluttering' the legs up and down alternately they are 'fluttered' up and down simultaneously" (p. 23). As "the most effective attempt so far by humans to adopt a swimming technique from nature" (Colwin 2002, p. 95), the dolphin kick is considered a milestone in the history of swimming. Jack Sieg's early speed time trials already showed the performance differences between the fish-tail kick and the regular breaststroke kick (Barney and Barney 2008, p. 18): in 40 yards distance, the dolphin kick was 2.3 s faster (0:21.3 vs. 0:23.5); in 100 yards distance, the dolphin kick was 4.9 s faster (1:04.1

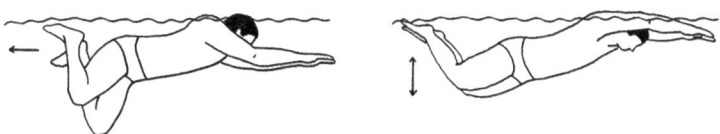

Fig. 2.19 Frog Kick (left) vs. Dolphin Kick (right) (source: author)

vs. 1:09.0); and in 200 yards distance, the dolphin kick was 8.0 s faster (2:29.0 vs. 2:37.0). Today, in world-record terms, the butterfly technique is the second fastest swimming style after the front crawl (FINA, n.d.). Just considering the legs, the dolphin kick is recognized as the fastest kick in swimming (Buchanan 2017). The underlying physical explanation appears simple: "In the historical breast-stroke kick, one unit of force is exerted intermittently, while in the Dolphin (fish-tail) kick, force is being exerted continuously, with no lost efficiency of effort or movement in relation to propelling force" (Armbruster and Sieg 1935, p. 25).

While the development of the kick itself evolved relatively quickly (description follows below), it was a long process until official acceptance was gained. Being first declared a violation of competitive rules, it took almost three decades from the style's first appearance in the mid-1920s to be declared autonomous in the mid 1950s (Barney and Barney 2008). The dolphin kick was declared illegal because the legs moved vertically (Colwin 2002). Barney and Barney (2008) use the analogy of an Odyssey to describe the process of gaining acceptance for the dolphin kick: "from origin to emergence as an autonomous stroke, butterfly's evolution was marked by measures of xenophobia, controversy, frustration, angst, argument, and gnashing of teeth, not to mention other disorders, most of them having to do with conflicting semantic interpretations of various rules books" (p. 11). Barney and Barney (2008) further hypothesize why the process to official recognition took so long:

> If Armbruster had couched the dolphin kick in language introducing the idea of an entirely new competitive stroke, instead of attaching it to the idea of altering, yet once again, the historically-oriented breaststroke, we might have seen the introduction of what we know today as the butterfly stroke by the mid-1930s instead of almost 20 years later. Regardless, Armbruster embraced high hopes for the inclusion of the new kick in breaststroke swimming, which, he thought, "had the potential to surpass the backstroke in speed, thus becoming the second fastest of the competitive strokes" (p. 20)

Thus, for 21 years a stroke with high potential existed in swimming but could not be legally exercised because no such event existed in any official competition (Colwin 2002).

The International Society of Olympic Historians recognizes swimming coach David Armbruster and his swimmer Jack Sieg as the creator of the dolphin kick (Barney and Barney 2008). Reportedly it all started in 1911 when Dave Armbruster met George Corsan at a swim clinic in Toronto where the latter demonstrated the movement of a fish-tail kick. By that time, Corsan was thinking of it as an alternative for the prevailing freestyle kicking patterns (Barney and Barney 2008, p. 6). George H. Corsan Sr. is "a Canadian who did more than any single person to popularize swimming in North America during the first 25 years of this century" (ISHOF, "George Corsan" n.d.). He popularized swimming on a mass scale and was the first swimming teacher recognized as a professor (Corsan 1924). Five years after that demonstration took place, Dave Armbruster started his 42 year career as head swimming coach at the University of Iowa, also incorporating a 20-year study on "The Science of Swimming" (Barney and Barney 2008, p. 25). In the 1930s, more than two decades after his first encounter with Corsan's leg kick, Armbruster and his swimmer Jack Sieg started experimenting with what later would be known as the dolphin kick (Barney and Barney 2008, p. 13). Sieg started by first swimming on the side beating his legs like a fish's tail. Later, they trained the leg movements face down in the water pairing it with the breaststroke arm motion first. Eventually, swimmers combined butterfly arms and dolphin legs (e.g. Barney and Barney 2008; Doezema 2016; *The Washington Post* n.d.).

In other references, (e.g. by historian Richard Rhodes 2012), physicist Volney Wilson is recognized as the originator of the dolphin kick (see also e.g. Joseph 2016; Schrader 2006). It is reported that Wilson was keen in swimming and studied dolphins' behavior at the Shedd Aquarium in Chicago. Based on his observations, he started experimenting with new leg movements. He combined the side-wave legs with the customary arm movement of the breaststroke and eventually demonstrated the kick at swim meets, even winning the Olympic trial in 1938. However, the technique was considered illegal and he was disqualified (Joseph 2016; Rhodes 2012). Regarding his actual occupation as a physicist, Wilson is most famous for his work on The Manhattan Project (Atomic Heritage Foundation n.d.).

2.3.1.9   Synopsis of All Single Cases

In the preceding sections, narratives on this work's focal cases of rule-breaking behavior in the domain of sports have been provided: Fosbury Flop, Flip Turn, O'Brien Shift, Skate Skiing, Forward Seat, V-Style, and the Dolphin Kick. By that, the context, characteristics and creation of the eight cases have been taken into account. While this has already been a considerable condensation of the underlying information, the following paragraph will provide no more than the gist.

The Fosbury Flop can be considered a prime example of rule-breaking behavior. Literally turning his back on track and field conventions, Dick Fosbury, by running in a curve and jumping backwards over the bar, created a jumping technique that was both different and far-reaching. While he could only win gold at the Mexican Olympics in 1968, many world records (including the current one, by the time this work has been published) have been set with the Fosbury Flop. It has prevailed as the dominant style in high jump. Technically being a modified scissor style combined with a curved running approach, the transformation that Fosbury initiated began with a step backward, reverting to an obsolete and less efficient form. That decision lay rooted in an incompatibility of his physical givens and the state-of-the-art straddle technique (clearly evident by poor jumping performance employing the latter). Caused by frustration, the subsequent developmental process undertaken by a competitive athlete with affinity towards engineer-typical tinkering was intuitive in nature, took several years, and held many small, consecutive alterations before the ultimate flop evolved. Without the advent of foam mats, the success of the Fosbury Flop would possibly not have been realizable.

Based on the available information from the International Swimming Hall of Fame, the Flip Turn is not only a relevant case sui generis but also unambiguous regarding the origins of its invention. Turning upside down (i.e. head under water, feet whipped up out of the water) was substantially different compared to the prior style and lead to a considerable improvement in times once being mastered. Other swimmers in both backstroke and freestyle adapted the approach and keep using it even today. Talented swimmer Albert Vande Weghe is credited for having created and popularized the technique. During backstroke races he noticed that his turns were impaired by a feeling of heavy legs. Together with his coach, he systematically looked for other ways, eventually coming up with a technique that is closely related to the tuck movement he applied in his former diving practices.

The O'Brien Shift has ushered in a new era in shot put by replacing prior sideways approaches with a technique that is primarily characterized by facing away from the direction of the throw in the starting position. The style has been quickly adopted and became standard. The development of the new technique literally took place overnight: O'Brien is said to have discovered it at 3 a.m. outside his parents' house after he came home frustrated because he had been defeated in a meet. What has been conveyed is that O'Brien was an exceptional shot putter with a very unique character. Hard training, a combination of "brains and brawn", dabbling into various schools of thought that are seemingly unrelated to athletics, and an exceptionally high degree of motivation are some of his characteristics that stood out in the underlying data.

The process of gaining official acceptance for the new and distinct Skate Skiing Technique has not been a straightforward endeavor. Officials, who feared that the faster and more exciting skating style would make the traditional diagonal technique obsolete, tried to formally ban its use or restrict it otherwise. When the majority of racers started to use the technique, however, its breakthrough could not be prevented. Eventually, cross-country skiing was split into two separate categories, classic and freestyle, so that both the diagonal and skating technique could be practiced and contested in parallel. Interestingly enough, skating was not a completely new invention but had lain forgotten in marathon races for several decades. Pauli Siitonen is said to have reactivated the technique. He employed some form of the skating step in ski orienteering before, but when he turned to cross country skiing, he applied the discipline-specific Classic diagonal technique accordingly. In the course of one race, however, after problems with waxing, he is said to have recalled and spontaneously switched to a precursor of the skating technique. By making a virtue of necessity, he managed to win the race. The renowned American skier Bill Koch copied and refined Siitonen's Halfskating-step, being known for popularizing it thereupon.

Although being a rather simple innovation, the Forward Seat distinctly classifies as what this work terms rule-breaking behavior. The non-technological innovation has been in accordance with formal rules, completely changed horsemanship and lead to a sustainable improvement in lap times. Nowadays, the Forward Seat is universally the most frequently used, especially in Equestrian Jumping. Interestingly, the two key actors seem to have discovered the Forward Seat in an almost opposing manner. Tod Sloan's discovery is portrayed to have risen like a phoenix from the ashes in one single moment (as a reaction to his bolting horse). Based on the underlying data, it can be assumed, however, that he saw a similar way of riding before—be it by the stable boys with Native-American background or some other famous jockey. In contrast to this more intuitive approach, Federico Caprilli comprehensively studied horses' natural behavior and systematically developed a functional way of rider and horse interplay. By abandoning the common convention that the horse had to comply with the rider's seating position and not the other way around, from a conceptual perspective, the new style re-interpreted the mental model of the interplay between two production factors (here: horse and rider) replacing a norm-oriented behavior with a more natural approach (less inference into natural movements).

The V-Style differs substantially from the prior diagonal ski jumping technique and lead to considerably longer jumps, which eventually initiated a major change process in ski jumping. Records regarding the V-Style's creation are controversial. Often, Jan Boklöv is reported to be the inventor and the advent of the style depicted as a somewhat natural epiphany. It is said that in a training session, a sudden environmental change (i.e. strong gust of wind) caused his skis to spread in a V shape so that by actually preventing himself from tumbling he jumped much longer than he typically did. Making use of several techniques (e.g. wind tunnel tests) and analogies (such as surfing, kiting) he and his coach intentionally repeated the "error" and systematically refined the style in the following months and years to come. Jan Boklöv was attributed modest talent and depicted an outsider rather than a wide-known hero. Besides, some references point out that Miroslaw Graf had jumped in a V-Style already. In his case the technique has reportedly been a result of a strained ankle. Either way, the most critical aspect is that the diffusion of the new jumping technique was impeded by traditional shibboleths of ski jumping. Officials and judges tried to prevent the ongoing challenge of the norm using style point deductions to diminish the impact of the much longer jumps. The regulatory measure delayed a wide-ranging adoption of the style but could not prevent its spread.

The addition of the Jump Shot to basketball players' repertoire of shots dramatically changed the game. It became faster with much higher scores. Assessed from a distant perspective, *jumping* is actually more likely to be considered a natural and obvious movement instead of being regarded as particularly groundbreaking. Yet, even after the Jump Shot had been discovered, a relatively long adaption period followed. Two overarching causes are prevalent. First, staying on the ground and shooting with both hands was not just a mere habit but a very strong, deeply rooted, almost pious convention in basketball. The textbooks suggested a very scientific way to play basketball and all coaches followed it rigorously. Second, even though the Jump Shot increased the probability of getting clear and not being blocked, it at the same time decreased the likelihood of a steady shot with an accurate trajectory. The latter skill typically required a substantial amount of training to be mastered, even for the more talented players. Hence, the probability of scoring is not higher per se. While the underlying case literature suggests that the invention, in some instances, happened accidentally, any of the eight players who is reported to have invented the Jump Shot or some precursory variant of it shows at least one aspect that is related to the above-mentioned case characteristics (jumping as obvious natural behavior, rigid conventions, getting clear as a problem, and shooting accuracy while jumping). John Burton, Kenny Sailors, Miller Cooper and Hank Luisetti faced an apparent physical inferiority (being smaller than their opponents) so that getting clear became the major issue they have been pondering and trying to solve. Bud Palmer had experienced in lacrosse that individual behavior can be limited by potentially counterproductive (under the assumption that winning the game is the primary goal of basketball players) conventions. Dave Minor, Myer Skoog and Belus Smawley inhibited a strong natural jumping instinct since they had practiced their leaping ability in other contexts. The individual efforts to change the basketball landscape have been accompanied by calls for more freedom in shooting and a broader variety of shots in pertinent contemporary basketball literature.

Despite the fact that the dolphin kick first did not initially go along with the official rules, its advent has substantially altered the sport. It is being recognized as the fastest kick in swimming and athletes keep refining the movements (Michael Phelps' recent efforts and successes). As the name suggests, the style imitates dolphins' motions. Different documentations regard either Volney Wilson or David Armbruster and his swimmer Jack Sieg as creators of the style, both being keen in scientific work. For Volney Wilson who was a physicist as his main occupation, swimming was the favorite pastime. After having observed dolphins in an aquarium, he is said to have started experimenting with a similar leg movement, even winning the Olympic trials although later disqualified. Armbruster, on the other hand, was a yearlong fulltime swimming coach working at the University of Iowa. Two decades before he and his talented swimmer Jack Sieg started experimenting with dolphin-like leg kicks, Armbruster had seen a similar fishtail movement demonstrated by the famous swimming professor George Corsan. Yet, not the development of the new style itself but the official acceptance of the dolphin kick turned out to be the biggest challenge. It is hypothesized that an immediate introduction of the dolphin kick as a new swimming style rather than yet another attempt to change the traditional breaststroke-kick could have substantially stream-lined the process.

The vade mecum of the eight single cases merely focuses on insights that have been assessed to be directly relevant for a further analysis of rule-breaking behavior *before* the cases have been analyzed from a cross-case perspective. As explained in Sect. 2.2.4.2, more information has been added for each case during the cross-case analysis. Thus, what has been described above, was the starting point for the following cross-case analysis and, if the reader wishes to make a connection between the textual description and the following table including all relevant empirical data, can be found in the dark grey boxes of Table 2.5 (slightly different wording used for the sake of a brief tabular display). The light grey boxes in Table 2.5 convey all such information that has been added for each case in the course of the cross-case analysis then. Exemplary quotes for all eight cases can be found in Appendix A.3.

Table 2.5 Summary of cross-case data

	Fosbury Flop (Dick Fosbury)	Flip Turn (Albert Vande Weghe)	O'Brien Shift (Parry O'Brien)	Skate Skiing (Pauli Siitonen)	Forward Seat — Caprilli	Forward Seat — Sloan	Forward Seat — Graf	V-Style (Boklöv several players)	Jump Shot (several players)	Dolphin Kick — Sieg/Armbr.	Dolphin Kick — Wilson
Sudden change of external parameter					bolting horse			wind	it just happened		
Negative parameter of the sport				poor wax, terrain		horses' pain			getting clear		
Frustration	frustration (trying not to lose)		frustration (defeat)						frustration		
Dysfunctionality physical givens vs. style	no fit (too tall), could do the old better	heavy legs						strained ankle	being too small (4/8)		
Lack of talent							?	semi-talented			
Old style	modified scissors			Lapp skiers, lay forgotten	Native Americans						
Natural, instinctive (vs. cultural)					horses in freedom	Native Americans			jumping		dolphins in aquarium
Experienced in other area/ seen before w/o success		diving		ski orienteering		another jockey			leaping – ski jump, tree, fence (3/8), convention in lacrosse (1/8)	Corsan	lay forgotten
Open mind			yoga, philosophy & other schools of thought								
Not main focus									developed prior to career		swimming as pastime
Competition as catalyst	evolution only at competition		I save my best for competition	poor wax at competition, virtue of necessity					happened during meets or trainings		
Physics explanation	center of gravity	?	the longer you apply pressure, the farther it goes	?	center of gravity + less wind resistance			center of gravity	?	continuous vs. propelling force	
Coaches' reaction	support from coach after first success	development together with coach							strong disapproval, "benchings"	development with coach	
Others/ help	personal support	development together with coach								development with coach	
Officials' resistance	skepticism, straddle was the ultimate			ban/ restrictions	pragmatists: how could we have been wrong for so long? aesthetics			style point deductions, aesthetics	holy commandment: keep feet on the floor	change breaststroke vs. new butterfly	
Ridicule	laughter everywhere, laziest jumper in the world			new style was smiled at		monkey seat	?	frog style, flapping crow	awkward jump shot		
Harder to learn	risky way of jumping, very different from other styles	?	difficult to start from a position facing the opposite	different requirements		?		feels like somersault in the air, many fractures	shooting accuracy down, getting clear up	hard to master, (in combination with arms)	
Negative consequence(s)	safety concerns (back)			ankle problems, destroys tracks				hill size, weight reduction			
Systematic, evolutionary process	continuous slow evolution, exploration, imagination, persistence	long and steady developmental process with coach	persistence, tough and systematic preparation and training program	long, gradual process of evolution (Siitonen-Koch-FIS)	thorough study (psych +phys)	perseverance, certainty	?	long process of trial + error	took a long time (e.g. long adaption period)	experiment	experiment
Environmental change	landing pits			prepared tracks					journals, more freedom in shooting	rule change, new stroke → butterfly	
Innovators characteristics	meditates/ psyches himself, trained for the moment	?	drive/ motivation, brains and brawns	personal motivation, training		extroverted?	?	outsider loner		?	?

2.3.2   Cross-Case Analysis: In Search of Patterns and General Explanations

Starting from the eight single case narratives that have been outlined in both an in-depth and more aggregated way, the data will now be analyzed from a cross-case perspective. The goal is to search for patterns and general explanations that fit each or a group of individual cases even though the details among the cases vary (Yin 2014). To do so, as described in Sect. 2.2.4.2, in the course of a comprehensive analytic process trying to make meaning of the data, the single case insight has been consolidated, prioritized and (re)ordered in multiple iterative steps. The results of the data consolidation procedure are summarized in Table 2.5.

From a horizontal perspective, the first two rows in Table 2.5 present the eight cases and innovators that have been analyzed, except for the Jump Shot where for purposes of presentation, the information on all eight jump shooters is displayed together.

From a vertical perspective, the first column on the left side lists 21 different criteria. In the broadest sense, these criteria were chosen because they inform us about the process of rule-breaking behavior in the domain of sports. That is, the information in all 21 rows is considered helpful in getting a better understanding of the processes underlying rule-breaking behavior. The criteria relate to different aspects like challenges the athletes had to face, factors that enabled or facilitated the developmental process, and characteristics that were evaluated as important drivers or preconditions. The codes are not displayed in random order but logically sorted to facilitate the subsequent line of argumentation.

In brief, the selection of exactly these 21 criteria out of many others results from two prior analytical steps: (a) independent coding of the eight single cases and (b) aggregation of all codes that have either been considered essential for any of the cases or occur in at least three different cases. That is, first, whenever a piece of information in a single case was deemed particularly important, it was incorporated in the table, no matter if other cases conveyed similar characteristics. As noted earlier, this priority information is visually emphasized by bold typeface. Second, all other criteria required relevance in more than two cases to be incorporated into the table. Consequently, there is no row that contains less than three grey fields unless one of the fields contains key information in bold typeface.

Over the next pages, Table 2.5 will be described in detail. By looking into the case data from such an integrated perspective, several observations can be made. These primarily relate to structural characteristics and more general preliminary interpretations that can already be drawn at this stage of analysis. It is important to mention that a more nuanced, further structured and theoretically grounded interpretation will follow when all these criteria are transferred to the context of business.

This stage can be thought of providing a descriptive summary from a cross-case perspective in the domain of sports. The discussion has exploratory character with labels, such as terms of the 21 criteria in the left column, all subject to be changed later on. The idea is (1) to make the stepwise process of data aggregation more transparent and (2) to serve as a mental preparation (viz. developing data-based cognitive working propositions that are as unbiased from existing concepts and theories as possible) for the following transfer to the context of business.

Column-wise, all relevant information regarding the eight single cases is displayed in abbreviated textual version, as both a detailed and a condensed description of the case stories have already been given.[19] However, some column-wise aspects that become visible in this cross-case perspective shall be drawn attention to. To begin with, it is apparent that there are no cases that fill the exact same cells. Along with the seemingly rather unique descriptions in Sect. 2.3.1, this does not come as a surprise. Each case tells a somewhat unique story. Second, there is a noticeable difference in the number of cells on which each case gives information. For instance, while the flip turn provides information regarding five aspects, skate skiing and the Fosbury Flop fill 15 cells each.[20] Fewer filled cells do not automatically indicate poor or incomplete case data. Whenever information is missing, this is indicated by a question mark. The difference in number of filled cells neither indicates that we can learn more from some of the cases than from others because, for example, the 21 codes are not operating on the same level (i.e. they are not necessarily equally important). The difference in number of filled cells per case may, however, be partly related to the presumption that we can see various procedural paths to rule-breaking behavior—some consisting of less and some of more stages. Third, there are no evident blank spots when looking at a within-case distribution of the filled cells. Knowing that the 21 variables are deliberately arranged in some sort of process perspective means that none of the cases have absolutely incomplete information.

The following row-by-row examination will describe the specifics of each of the 21 criteria. As all themes have already been discussed in the course of the single case analysis, this is not entirely new in content but places the case information in another context.

When looking for generalizable patterns in data, the aim is to find features that all cases have in common. A brief glance at Table 2.5 reveals, at first sight, that at this level of analysis, there seem to be only a few potential data patterns that apply to all cases. Thus, the data would need to be aggregated further in order to arrive at such general characteristics. When taking the number of filled cells per criteria into account, it can be analytically distinguished between four types of criteria: (1) zero cells are filled, which can be precluded because it is opposed to the underlying logic of code selection, (2) one of the cells is filled, which could indicate a specific or idiosyncratic case-lesson, (3) all cells are filled, which could indicate a potential generalizable variable, and (4) any number of cells larger than one but less than all

---

[19] As explained before, the dark grey boxes include information that directly derived from the single case analysis (see descriptions in Sect. 3.1), the light grey boxes have been added during the cross-case study.

[20] The large amount of information in the Jump Shot case is related to the fact, that for purposes of presentation, all eight cases are displayed together.

cells is filled, which could indicate a potential case cluster (i.e. a pattern that applies to some of the cases).

Starting with type two, just one of the 21 criteria at this level of data aggregation applies to one single case only: open mind. The small number is due to the fact that after an initial aggregation of the first-order codes, the remaining single-cell-codes that were not considered particularly relevant have been excluded from the list for reasons of parsimony. Being open to other schools of thought that are seemingly unrelated to sports, or at least do not show an immediate impact on the athlete's better performance, such as yoga, philosophy or religious studies, has been considered a possible important factor in Parry O'Brien's case and is, therefore, supposed to be included in further investigations.

Regarding type three, two potential cross-case patterns are evident at this level of data aggregation. First of all, it is true for all cases that basic rules of physics (e.g. change in center of gravity with Fosbury Flop, V-Style and Forward Seat) play a role in explaining the performance increase resulting from the new technique. Without further elaborating on the biomechanical details, it can be noted that in none of the three cases the inventor was explicitly aware of this. Although some rule-breakers were described to have affinity with engineering, they realized the physical explanations retrospectively only. Secondly, all cases have in common that the innovations were developed in some kind of systematic, incremental manner— even if these evolutionary elements occurred at different stages of the innovative processes. It appears that the slow and gradual process took place in three different instances: to understand a seemingly coincidental event (e.g. V-Style), to deliberately search for and master a new technique (e.g. Dolphin Kick, Forward Seat, O'Brien Shift, Fosbury Flop, Jump Shot), or to gain acceptance for the new style (e.g. Jump Shot, Skate Skiing, Flip Turn). While a simultaneous occurrence of the first two instances can be logically ruled out, it is possible and true for some of the cases that the gradual character appeared twice during the process of rule-breaking behavior (e.g. V-Style, Dolphin Kick).

All other variables on the list fall in category four, meaning that data on those criteria has been found in more than one but less than all cases. Light will now be shed on these cases, particularly on explaining what is meant with every variable using particular case data as exemplary evidence.

Sudden changes in external parameters, such as strong wind, a bolting horse or a specific situation in the middle of a basketball meet are said to have triggered the invention of the V-Style (Boklöv), the Forward Seat (Sloan), and the Jump Shot (e.g. Cooper). To prevent themselves from negative consequences, such as tumbling or falling, the affected actors are reported to have automatically reacted in an instant: by spreading the skis, leaning forward over the horse's withers, or jumping in the air before releasing the ball. In those cases, it is typically concluded that the idea came up by chance, referring to the notion of Eureka.

The single case analyses revealed that the precursory variants of Skate Skiing (i.e. classic style), of the Forward Seat (i.e. classical seat), and of the Jump Shot (i.e. set shots) all held a fundamentally negative parameter that could cause substantial problems. Classical cross-country skiers had trouble with waxing and poor terrain. The Classical seat dramatically impaired the horse, and with set shots, basketballers had a hard time getting clear.

Apart from such overall problems regarding certain techniques, more individual issues were stated as well. Frustration, resulting from comparatively poor performance in general or in a specific match, reportedly played a role in three cases. Parry O'Brien had been defeated the night before he discovered the new technique, Dick Fosbury was eagerly trying not to lose when he employed the Straddle, and some of the early jump shooters, despite their talent, struggled keeping up with their competitors. According to the underlying data, the latter two examples are presumably closely linked to the next criterion, which gives case-specific information on dysfunctionalities between physical givens (e.g. long legs, little height) and the dominant style. Dick Fosbury felt a misfit of his tall height and the Straddle, the frustrated jump shooters have reportedly been relatively small, Albert Vande Weghe noticed "heavy legs" when turning with the old backstroke turn, and Miroslaw Graf is said to have started ski jumping in a V-Style because of a strained ankle. Closely related but distinctly assessed are reports on the athletes' talents (Boklöv, who invented the V-Style is described as semi-talented at most).

All these first variables have been fairly focused on rule-breakers problems, so the next section encompasses the codes that give insight into potential solutions instead. The Fosbury Flop, Skate Skiing technique, and Forward Seat all have in common that the new technique was not actually as new as it first seemed. Dick Fosbury reverted to the old Scissors technique and used it as a starting point to develop a more productive technique thereafter. The Skating style has been used by Nordic natives at least hundreds if not thousands of years ago and the Forward Seat was already applied by indigenes (e.g. native Americans). In those two cases, the old styles simply lay forgotten and could be successfully revitalized. Both techniques were not just old but also shared yet another characteristic, which is covered by the next variable: They departed from culturally-construed behavior and went back to a more natural, instinctive approach.

Besides cross-country skiing and equestrian, three more cases contain corresponding insight: Skiing the way Lapps skied, observing horses in freedom or riding the way native Americans rode, watching dolphins' way of swimming in an aquarium, or making use of a basic human motion (jumping) when playing basketball. In five cases, the new technique was not completely new for the innovator. They had either experienced a similar movement in another area already: Vande Weghe's flip turn resulted from the tuck position he and his coach had used in diving before, Siitonen had previously applied the skating technique in ski orienteering, three jump shooters had practiced their leaping ability independent from basketball. Or they had seen a demonstration of a closely related movement before and only applied it (much) later: Sloan saw a fellow jockey riding in a similar fashion and Armbruster had seen a demonstration of a fishtail kick many decades before. Furthermore, in two cases, the idea of the new style arose before the innovator chose to actually pursue an athletic career. Volney Wilson was employed as a physicist and only practiced swimming in his pastime when he started experimenting with the Dolphin Kick, and the early jump shooters started jumping at a young age prior to their prospective future basketball career. An additional insightful fact is that competition has explicitly been stated as a catalyst in four different cases. This is true for Dick Fosbury who only evolved his style at competition, for O'Brien who deliberately saved his best for competition, for the Jump Shot, which in each case happened during meets or trainings, and for Skate Skiing, which was applied in the middle of a race, making it a virtue of necessity.

Coaches, as a matter of course, can play a decisive role in the process as well. The data reveals that they can be both supporting and opposed to the rule-breaking athlete's endeavor. Fosbury's coach encouraged him to revert to a style he felt better with but was hesitant regarding the first steps in the direction of a backwards jump. When Dick Fosbury proved little successes of the technique-in-evolution by jumping higher, his coach and team supported Fosbury's attempt. In the Flip Turn, Vande Weghe and his coach developed the technique together. That is also true for Armbruster and Sieg and their development of the Dolphin Kick. More so, in that case, the coach even played the leading role, especially when it came to the stage that official acceptance for the new technique had to be gained. With the Jump Shot, however, coaches acted as strong advocates of the traditional way to play basketball. In many cases, they highly disapproved of and sanctioned individual leaping attempts. Closely related, not only coaches but also officials, in particular, were potential actors who displayed resistance to the new techniques. Their opposition ranged from mere skepticism to explicit restrictions and bans. The Fosbury Flop was taken with a grain of salt since the Straddle was regarded as the ultimate technique to jumping. Traditionalists in horsemanship just could not believe they had been wrong for such a long time and were complaining about the lack of aesthetics when riding in a Forward Seat. An absence of aesthetics (among other things) has also been contemplated when the V-Style emerged, resulting in style point deductions and a substantial delay in the style's diffusion. In Skate Skiing, functionaries' reactance led to temporarily bans and restrictions. The Dolphin Kick was considered rule-abiding at first, and in basketball, the convention of keeping the feet on the floor had almost obtained religious dimensions. Moreover, ridicule and humiliation had been typical fare when a substantially different style got introduced. Dick Fosbury's presentation of his jump was accompanied by laughter in the audience and he was depicted the laziest jumper in the world. Tod Sloan's Forward Seat attempt was referred to as monkey seat, Jan Boklöv was called a flapping crow, and the V-Style was renamed frog style. The Skate Skiing Technique has been smiled at and early jump shooters faced bursts of laughter by their fellow teammates when they saw the first awkward jump shot experiments. Especially this latter case is seemingly related to the fact that new styles may be hard(er) to learn, different training elements are required, and certain risks or uncertainties can prevail. While it was easier for early jump shooters to get clear, their shooting accuracy initially declined. The reports show that learning to jump and at the same time shoot precisely could not be mastered immediately or by everybody. Similar difficulties apply for the other techniques as well but to various degrees. The Fosbury Flop has been considered a risky way of jumping, starting from a position facing the opposite direction is considered challenging, especially for young shot putters or combined event athletes (O'Brien Shift), the

Dolphin Kick is said to be comparatively difficult to master in combination with butterfly arms, Skate Skiing demands different physical requirements (e.g. muscles which are used), and Boklöv endured many fractures to understand and learn the V-Style.

Further negative consequences such as safety concerns and substantial environmental adjustments came on top of that in some cases. To name a few, serious back injuries were feared when jumping backwards like Dick Fosbury did, Skate Skiing was assumed to cause major ankle problems and a destruction of the prepared tracks, all major ski jumping hills had to be restructured to enable long and safe jumps, and the ski jumpers' alarming weight reductions came along as challenges for the discipline as well. Also, the advent of the new techniques was in some cases facilitated by environmental changes in the landscape of the different sports: landing pits in the high jump, prepared tracks in cross-country skiing, rule changes in swimming (acceptance of butterfly as fourth stroke), and contemporary basketball journals' discussions on more freedom in shooting. Last but not least, individual characteristics of different athletes might have influenced the development and are thus subsumed in the last row.

In summary, Table 2.5 displays both the most important single case insights in brief version, when analyzed from a vertical perspective, and preliminary cross-case evidence regarding 21 systematically selected criteria, when analyzed from a horizontal perspective. At this point, the analysis in the domain of sports is finalized. While the single case analysis can be considered to be complete, the cross-case analysis, which aims to derive generalizable propositions for a better understanding of rule-breaking behavior needs to continue further. To do so, the case-based insight will now be critically (re)examined, (re)structured and further aggregated in light of managerial literature in the context of creativity and innovation. How this has been accomplished and which lessons can be learned for the developmental process of rule-breaking market behavior will be outlined in Chap. 3.

References

Abele R (2005) Ski-Langlauf: In frischer Spur voran [Cross-country skiing: Fresh track ahead]. Frankfurter Allgemeine Zeitung, March 10, https://www.faz.net

Allen EJB (2012) Historical dictionary of skiing. Scarecrow Press, Lanham, Toronto, Plymouth

Amabile TM (1983) The social psychology of creativity: a componential conceptualization. J Pers Soc Psychol 45(2):357–376. https://doi.org/10.1037/0022-3514.45.2.357

Anderson PF (1983) Marketing, scientific progress, and scientific method. J Mark 47(4):18–31

Anderson P, Tushman ML (1990) Technological discontinuities and dominant designs: a cyclical model of technological change. Adm Sci Q 35(4):604–633. https://doi.org/10.2307/2393511

Anderson N, Potočnik K, Zhou J (2014) Innovation and creativity in organizations: a state-of-the-science review, prospective commentary, and guiding framework. J Manag 40(5):1297–1333. https://doi.org/10.1177/0149206314527128

Araujo L, Pereira S, Gatti R, Freitas E, Jacomel G, Roesler H, Villas-boas J (2010) Analysis of the lateral push-off in the freestyle flip turn. J Sports Sci 28(11):1175–1181. https://doi.org/10.1080/02640414.2010.485207

Armbruster DA, Sieg JG (1935) The dolphin breast stroke. J Health Phys Educ 6(4):23–58

Armbruster H, Bikfalvi A, Kinkel S, Lay G (2008) Organizational innovation: the challenge of measuring non-technical innovation in large-scale surveys. Technovation 28(10):644–657. https://doi.org/10.1016/j.technovation.2008.03.003

Ashburner T (2003) The history of ski jumping. Quiller Press, Shrewsbury

Athletics: The Shot Put (2018) In Encyclopaedia Britannica. https://academic.eb.com. Accessed 25 Sep 2017

Atomic Heritage Foundation (n.d.) Volney D. Wilson. https://www.atomicheritage.org. Accessed 16 Jan 2018

Backhaus K, Plinke W (1986) Rechtseinflüsse auf betriebswirtschaftliche Entscheidungen: Ein Lehrbuch zur allgemeinen Betriebswirtschaftslehre [Legal influence on business decisions: a textbook on general business administration]. Kohlhammer, Stuttgart

Backhaus K, Schneider H (2009) Strategisches Marketing [Strategic marketing], 2nd edn. Schäffer-Poeschel, Stuttgart

Barañano AM (2003) The non-technological side of technological innovation: state-of-the-art and guidelines for further empirical research. Int J Entrep Innov Manag 3(1–2):107–125. https://doi.org/10.1504/IJEIM.2003.002223

Barney DE, Barney RK (2008) A long night's journey into day: the odyssey of butterfly. J Olympic Hist 16(3):11–25

Bartunek JM, Rynes SL, Ireland RD (2006) What makes management research interesting, and why does it matter? Acad Manag J 49(1):9–15. https://doi.org/10.5465/amj.2006.20785494

BBC World Service (2011) The Fosbury Flop [audio podcast]. https://www.bbc.co.uk. Accessed 12 Oct 2017

Bengtsson BE (n.d.) Cross-country skating: how it started. https://www.skiinghistory.org. Accessed 2 Mar 2018

Birkinshaw J (2017) Uber – a story of destructive creation. Forbes, October 16, https://www.forbes.com

Blystone D (2018) The story of Uber. Investopedia, May 24, https://www.investopedia.com/articles/personal-finance/111015/story-uber.asp

Boecker A (2010) Physik des Skispringens – der Ritt auf dem Luftpolster [Physics of ski jumping – a ride on the air cushion]. Süddeutsche Zeitung, May 17, https://www.sueddeutsche.de

Brown SL, Eisenhardt KM (1997) The art of continuous change: linking complexity theory and time-paced evolution in relentlessly shifting organizations. Adm Sci Q 42(1):1–34. https://doi.org/10.2307/2393807

Buchanan J (2017) The butterfly: a complex history for a complex stroke. Swimming World Magazine, May 25, https://www.swimmingworldmagazine.com

Burnton S (2012) 50 stunning olympic moments no28: Dick Fosbury introduces the flop. The Guardian, May 8, https://www.theguardian.com

Camisón C, Villar-López A (2014) Organizational innovation as an enabler of technological innovation capabilities and firm performance. J Bus Res 67(1):2891–2902. https://doi.org/10.1016/j.jbusres.2012.06.004

Caprilli F (1901) Per l' equitazione di campagna [For riding in the field]. Translation from the Italian by Dan Gilmore, Originally Published in Revista di Cavalleria, January–February, https://www.gilmorehorsemanship.com/caprillinaturalsystem.html

Carlile PR, Christensen CM (2004) The cycles of theory building in management research. Working Paper 05-057. Harvard Business School, Boston, https://www.hbs.edu

Carlson M (2007) Obituary: Parry O'Brien. The Guardian, June 14, https://www.theguardian.com

Černe M, Kaše R, Škerlavaj M (2016) Non-technological innovation research: evaluating the intellectual structure and prospects of an emerging field. Scand J Manag 32(2):69–85. https://doi.org/10.1016/j.scaman.2016.02.001

Chalmers AF (2013) What is this thing called science? 4th edn. McGraw-Hill, Berkshire

Chandy RK, Tellis GJ (1998) Organizing for radical product innovation: the overlooked role of willingness to cannibalize. J Mark Res 35(4):474–487. https://doi.org/10.2307/3152166

Charmaz K (2006) Constructing grounded theory: a practical guide to qualitative analysis. Sage, Thousand Oaks, CA

Chmiliar L (2010) Multiple-case designs. Encyclopedia of Case Study Research. Sage, Thousand Oaks, CA. https://doi.org/10.4135/9781412957397.n216

Chow JWC, Hay JG, Wilson BD, Imel C (1984) Turning techniques of elite swimmers. J Sports Sci 2(3):241–255. https://doi.org/10.1080/02640418408729720

Christensen CM, Rosenbloom RS (1995) Explaining the attacker's advantage: technological paradigms, organizational dynamics, and the value network. Res Policy 24(2):233–257. https://doi.org/10.1016/0048-7333(93)00764-K

Christgau J (1999) The origins of the jump shot: eight men who shook the world of basketball. University of Nebraska Press, Lincoln, NE

Colquitt JA, Zapata-Phelan CP (2007) Trends in theory building and theory testing: a five-decade study of the academy of management journal. Acad Manag J 50(6):1281–1303. https://doi.org/10.5465/AMJ.2007.28165855

Colwin CM (2002) Breakthrough swimming. Human Kinetics, Champaign, IL

Corbin J, Strauss A (2008) Basics of qualitative research: techniques and procedures for developing grounded theory, 3rd edn. Sage, Thousand Oaks, CA

Corley KG, Gioia DA (2011) Building theory about theory building: what constitutes a theoretical contribution? Acad Manag Rev 36(1):12–32. https://doi.org/10.5465/amr.2009.0486

Cornelissen JP, Durand R (2014) Moving forward: developing theoretical contributions in management studies. J Manag Stud 51(6):995–1022. https://doi.org/10.1111/joms.12078

Corsan GH (1924) The diving and swimming book. A. S. Barnes, New York, NY

Crittenden VL, Peterson RA (2011a) The AMS review. AMS Rev 1(1):1–3. https://doi.org/10.1007/s13162-011-0001-6

Crittenden VL, Peterson RA (2011b) Ruminations about making a theoretical contribution. AMS Rev 1(2):67–71. https://doi.org/10.1007/s13162-011-0014-1

Crittenden VL, Peterson RA (2012) The AMS review: year 2. AMS Rev 2(2–4):45–47. https://doi.org/10.1007/s13162-012-0031-8

Crittenden VL, Peterson RA (2013) Scientific progress in marketing. AMS Rev 3(1):1–2. https://doi.org/10.1007/s13162-013-0037-x

Crossan MM, Apaydin M (2010) A multi-dimensional framework of organizational innovation: a systematic review of the literature. J Manag Stud 47(6):1154–1191. https://doi.org/10.1111/j.1467-6486.2009.00880.x

Curd M, Psillos S (2013) The Routledge companion to philosophy of science, 2nd edn. Routledge, New York, NY

Dahlin KB, Behrens DM (2005) When is an invention really radical? Defining and measuring technological radicalness. Res Policy 34(5):717–737. https://doi.org/10.1016/j.respol.2005.03.009

Damanpour F (2014) Footnotes to research on management innovation. Organ Stud 35(9):1265–1285. https://doi.org/10.1177/0170840614539312

Damanpour F, Aravind D (2012) Managerial innovation: conceptions, processes, and antecedents. Manag Organ Rev 8(2):423–454. https://doi.org/10.1111/j.1740-8784.2011.00233.x

Damanpour F, Walker RM, Avellaneda CN (2009) Combinative effects of innovation types and organizational performance: a longitudinal study of service organizations. J Manag Stud 46(4):650–675. https://doi.org/10.1111/j.1467-6486.2008.00814.x

Daprano CM (2011) Amateur athletic union. In: Swayne LE, Dodds M (eds) Encyclopedia of sports management and marketing, vol 1. Sage, Thousand Oaks, CA, pp 50–51. https://doi.org/10.4135/9781412994156.n19

Davis MS (1971) That's interesting! Towards a phenomenology of sociology and a sociology of phenomenology. Philos Soc Sci 1(2):309–344. https://doi.org/10.1177/004839317100100211

Decision Tree (2017) A dictionary of economics, 5th edn. Oxford University Press, New York, NY

Dewar RD, Dutton JE (1986) The adoption of radical and incremental innovations: an empirical analysis. Manag Sci 32(11):1422–1433. https://doi.org/10.1287/mnsc.32.11.1422

Dizikes J (2000) Yankee doodle dandy: the life and times of Tod Sloan. Yale University Press, New Haven, CT

Doezema M (2016) The murky history of the butterfly stroke. The New Yorker, August 11, https://www.newyorker.com

Dosi G (1982) Technological paradigms and technological trajectories: a suggested interpretation of the determinants and directions of technical change. Res Policy 11(3):147–162. https://doi.org/10.1016/0048-7333(82)90016-6

Durso J (1986) Fearless Fosbury flops to glory. The New York Times, October 20, https://www.nytimes.com

Edquist C, Hommen L, McKelvey MD (2001) Innovation and employment: process versus product innovation. Edward Elgar, Cheltenham

Eiberle H (2010) Typen und Tüftler, Teil I – Wie ein Papierdrachen [Types and tinkerers, part I – Like a paper kite]. Süddeutsche Zeitung, May 10, https://www.sueddeutsche.de

Eisend M, Kuß A (2017) Grundlagen empirischer Forschung: Zur Methodologie in der Betriebswirtschaftslehre [Foundations of empirical research: methodology in business administration]. Springer Gabler, Wiesbaden. https://doi.org/10.1007/978-3-658-09705-9_4

Eisenhardt KM (1989) Building theories from case study research. Acad Manag Rev 14(4):532–550. https://doi.org/10.2307/258557

Eisenhardt KM, Graebner ME (2007) Theory building from cases: opportunities and challenges. Acad Manag J 50(1):25–32. https://doi.org/10.5465/amj.2007.24160888

Elliott H (2007) Parry O'Brien, 75; Champion revolutionized shotput throw. Los Angeles Times, April 23, https://www.latimes.com

Fay T (2011) Olympic organization. In: Swayne LE, Dodds M (eds) Encyclopedia of sports management and marketing, vol 3. Sage, Thousand Oaks, CA, pp 1038–1040. https://doi.org/10.4135/9781412994156.n520

FAZ (2008) Jan Boklöv: Clown, Revolutionär und Erfinder des Victory-Stils [Jan Boklöv: Clown, revolutionizer, and inventor of the victory-style]. Frankfurter Allgemeine Zeitung, December 12, https://www.faz.net

Field AP (2013) Discovering statistics using IBM SPSS statistics: and sex and drugs and rock'n'roll, 4th edn. Sage, Los Angeles, CA

FINA (n.d.) Swimming records. https://www.fina.org/content/swimming-records. Accessed 5 Jun 2018

Fletcher M, Plakoyiannaki E (2010) Sampling. Encyclopedia of case study research. Sage, Thousand Oaks, CA. https://doi.org/10.4135/9781412957397.n307

Foster RN (1986) Timing technological transitions. In: Horwitch M (ed) Technology in the modern corporation: a strategic perspective. Pergamon Press, Elmsford, NY, pp 35–49. https://doi.org/10.1016/B978-0-08-034239-9.50008-6

Fox BE (2017) Caprilli – during his time. https://www.theridinginstructor.net. Accessed 8 Jan 2018

Fox MW, Mickley LD (1987) Advances in animal welfare science 1986/87, vol 3. Martinus Nijhoff, Dordrecht, Netherlands. doi:https://doi.org/10.1007/978-94-009-3331-6

Fuqua B (2014) Fosbury takes track and field to new heights. The Corvallis Gazette-Times, March 29, https://www.gazettetimes.com

Fury S (2016) Rise and fire: the origins, science, and evolution of the jump shot – and how it transformed basketball forever. Macmillan, New York, NY

Garcia R, Calantone R (2002) A critical look at technological innovation typology and innovativeness terminology: a literature review. J Prod Innov Manag 19(2):110–132. https://doi.org/10.1016/S0737-6782(01)00132-1

Geiler C (2015) Jan Boklöv, der Erfinder des V-Stil [Jan Boklöv, inventor of the v-style]. Der Kurier, February 18, https://www.kurier.at

Gemer GV (1990) Overview of the shot put technique. IAAF New Stud Athl 5(1):31–34

George JM (2007) Creativity in organizations. Acad Manag Ann 1(1):439–477. https://doi.org/10.1080/078559814

George AL, Bennett A (2005) Case studies and theory development in the social sciences. MIT Press, Cambridge, MA

German Sport University Cologne (n.d.) Library. https://www.dshs-koeln.de/english/university-facilities/library/. Accessed 21 Jun 2018

Gerring J (2006) Case study research: principles and practices. Cambridge University Press, New York, NY. https://doi.org/10.1017/CBO9780511803123

Gerring J (2017) Case study research: principles and practices, 2nd edn. Cambridge University Press, Cambridge

Gerring J, Cojocaru L (2016) Selecting cases for intensive analysis: a diversity of goals and methods. Sociol Methods Res 45(3):392–423. https://doi.org/10.1177/0049124116631692

Gersick CJG (1988) Time and transition in work teams: toward a new model of group development. Acad Manag J 31(1):9–41. https://doi.org/10.5465/256496

Gioia DA, Pitre E (1990) Multiparadigm perspectives on theory building. Acad Manag Rev 15 (4):584–602. https://doi.org/10.5465/amr.1990.4310758

Gioia DA, Corley KG, Hamilton AL (2013) Seeking qualitative rigor in inductive research: notes on the Gioia methodology. Organ Res Methods 16(1):15–31. https://doi.org/10.1177/1094428112452151

Glaser BG (1965) The constant comparative method of qualitative analysis. Soc Probl 12 (4):436–445. https://doi.org/10.2307/798843

Glaser BG (1978) Theoretical sensitivity: advances in the methodology of grounded theory. Sociology Press, Mill Valley, CA

Glaser BG, Strauss AL (1967) The discovery of grounded theory: strategies for qualitative research. Aldine, Chicago, IL

Goldenberg J, Lowengart O, Oreg S, Bar-Eli M (2010) How do revolutions emerge? Int Stud Manag Organ 40(2):30–51. https://doi.org/10.2753/IMO0020-8825400202

Haack M (2015) Jan Boklöv, Erfinder des V-Stils, im Interview: "Geächteter, V-Mann, Revoluzzer" [Interview with Jan Boklöv, inventor of the v-style: "Outlaw, v-man, revolutionary"]. Die Welt, February 18, https://www.welt.de

Haffner S (2004) Tricks von gestern: Revolutionen und Marotten [Tricks of yesteryear: Revolutions and quirks]. Frankfurter Allgemeine Zeitung, January 10, https://www.faz.net

Harrison SH, Rouse ED (2014) Let's dance! Elastic coordination in creative group work: a qualitative study of modern dancers. Acad Manag J 57(5):1256–1283. https://doi.org/10.5465/amj.2012.0343

Hauser J, Tellis GJ, Griffin A (2006) Research on innovation: a review and agenda for marketing science. Mark Sci 25(6):687–717. https://doi.org/10.1287/mksc.1050.0144

Henderson R (1993) Underinvestment and incompetence as responses to radical innovation: evidence from the photolithographic alignment equipment industry. Rand J Econ 24 (2):248–270. https://doi.org/10.2307/2555761

Horsemanship (2018) In Encyclopaedia Britannica. https://academic.eb.com. Accessed 8 Jan 2018

Hottenrott K, Urban V (2004) Das grosse Buch vom Skilanglauf [The big book of cross-country skiing]. Meyer & Meyer Verlag, Aachen

How Are Sports Chosen for the Olympics? (2018) In Encyclopaedia Britannica. https://www.britannica.com/story/how-are-sports-chosen-for-the-olympics. Accessed 20 Jun 2018

Hunt SD (1990) Truth in marketing theory and research. J Mark 54(3):1–15. https://doi.org/10.2307/1251812

Hunt SD (1991) Modern marketing theory: critical issues in the philosophy of marketing science. South-Western, Cincinnati, OH

Hunt SD (2011) Developing successful theories in marketing: insights from resource-advantage theory. AMS Rev 1(2):72–84. https://doi.org/10.1007/s13162-011-0007-0

Hunt SD (2012) Explaining empirically successful marketing theories: the inductive realist model, approximate truth, and market orientation. AMS Rev 2(1):5–18. https://doi.org/10.1007/s13162-012-0023-8

Hunt SD (2013) The inductive realist model of theory generation: explaining the development of a theory of marketing ethics. AMS Rev 3(2):61–73. https://doi.org/10.1007/s13162-013-0040-2

Hunt SD (2015) Explicating the inductive realist model of theory generation. AMS Rev 5 (1–2):20–27. https://doi.org/10.1007/s13162-015-0064-x

IAAF "High Jump" (n.d.) High jump. https://www.iaaf.org. Accessed 12 Oct 2017

IAAF "Shot Put" (n.d.) Shot put. https://www.iaaf.org. Accessed 5 Jun 2018

IOC (2014a) Leap of faith: Dick Fosbury on how a new jump style changed his sport forever. April 11, https://www.olympic.org

IOC (2014b) Leap of faith: Dick Fosbury on how a new jump style changed his sport forever [video interview]. April 11, https://www.olympic.org

IOC (2017a) Olympic basketball's muddy beginnings. https://www.olympic.org. Accessed 10 Feb 2018

IOC (2017b) Olympic charter. https://www.olympic.org/documents/olympic-charter

IOC "Bill Koch" (n.d.) Bill Koch – cross country skiing. https://www.olympic.org. Accessed 21 Jun 2018

IOC "Cross Country Skiing" (n.d.) Cross country skiing. https://www.olympic.org. Accessed 14 Jan 2018

IOC "Dick Fosbury" (n.d.) Richard Douglas "Dick" Fosbury: Dick Fosbury revolutionised the high jump. https://www.olympic.org. Accessed 7 Jun 2018

IOC "Equestrian Jumping" (n.d.) Equestrian jumping. https://www.olympic.org. Accessed 1 Feb 2018

IOC "High Jump" (n.d.) Dick Fosbury – high jump men – athletics [video and text]. https://www.olympic.org/videos/dick-fosbury-high-jump-men-athletics. Accessed 20 Nov 2017

IOC "Mexico 1968" (n.d.) Mexico 1968 athletics high jump men [video]. https://www.olympic.org. Accessed 17 Oct 2017

IOC "Michael Phelps" (n.d.) Michael Phelps. https://www.olympic.org. Accessed 1 Jan 2018

IOC "Revolutionary Fosbury" (n.d.) Revolutionary Fosbury raises the bar. https://www.olympic.org. Accessed 7 Jun 2018

IOC "Rio" (2016) Rio 2016. https://www.olympic.org. Accessed 19 Jun 2018

IOC "Ryan Lochte" (n.d.) Ryan Lochte. https://olympic.org. Accessed 20 Jan 2018

IOC "Ski Jumping" (n.d.) Ski jumping. https://www.olympic.org. Accessed 5 Jun 2018

IOC "Swimming" (n.d.) Swimming. https://www.olympic.org. Accessed 5 Jun 2018

ISHOF "Albert Vandeweghe" (n.d.) Albert Vandeweghe. https://ishof.org. Accessed 4 Jan 2018

ISHOF "George Corsan" (n.d.) George Corsan, Sr. https://www.ishof.org. Accessed 15 Jan 2018

Johannessen J-A, Olsen B, Lumpkin GT (2001) Innovation as newness: what is new, how new, and new to whom? Eur J Innov Manag 4(1):20–31. https://doi.org/10.1108/14601060110365547

Johnson W (2008) White heat: the extreme skiing life. Simon and Schuster, New York, NY

Jonassen DH (2010) Learning to solve problems: a handbook for designing problem-solving learning environments. Routledge, New York, NY

Jonsen K, Fendt J, Point S (2018) Convincing qualitative research: what constitutes persuasive writing? Organ Res Methods 21(1):30–67. https://doi.org/10.1177/1094428117706533

Joseph F (2016) Our dolphin ancestors: keepers of lost knowledge and healing wisdom. Bear & Company, Rochester, Vermont

Keil J-G, Killing W (2014) Vom Hocksprung zum Speedflop: Hochsprung im historischen Wandel. Teil 1 [From squat to speed-flop: Historical development of the high jump. Part 1]. Leichtathletiktraining: die Lehre der Leichtathletik 25(6):10–17

Keupp MM, Palmié M, Gassmann O (2012) The strategic management of innovation: a systematic review and paths for future research. Int J Manag Rev 14(4):367–390. https://doi.org/10.1111/j.1468-2370.2011.00321.x

Kirton M (1976) Adaptors and innovators: a description and measure. J Appl Psychol 61 (5):622–629. https://doi.org/10.1037/0021-9010.61.5.622

Koppenwallner L (1968) Erfinder eines neuen Stils [Inventor of a new style]. Olympisches Feuer 10 (Oct):52–53

Kopsky J (2002) Olympian, masters great al Vandeweghe passes away. Swimming World Magazine, August 17, https://www.swimmingworldmagazine.org

Kotsiantis SB (2013) Decision trees: a recent overview. Artif Intell Rev 39(4):261–283. https://doi.org/10.1007/s10462-011-9272-4

Kuhn W (1997) Structuring cross-country skiing techniques on the basis of motor-program theory. In: Kornexl E, Muller E, Raschner C, Schwameder H (eds) Science and skiing. Chapman & Hall, London, pp 70–79

Kuß A (2013) Marketing-Theorie: Eine Einführung [Marketing theory: an introduction], 3rd edn. Springer Gabler, Wiesbaden

Langley A (1999) Strategies for theorizing from process data. Acad Manag Rev 24(4):691–710. https://doi.org/10.5465/AMR.1999.2553248

Litsky F (2007) Parry O'Brien, pioneer in shot-putting technique, dies at 75. The New York Times, April 23, https://www.nytimes.com

Locke K (1996) Rewriting the discovery of grounded theory after 25 years? J Manag Inq 5 (3):239–245. https://doi.org/10.1177/105649269653008

Locke EA (2007) The case for inductive theory building. J Manag 33(6):867–890. https://doi.org/10.1177/0149206307307636

Locke K (2015) Pragmatic reflections on a conversation about grounded theory in management and organization studies. Organ Res Methods 18(4):612–619. https://doi.org/10.1177/1094428115574858

Lohn J (2010) Historical dictionary of competitive swimming. Historical dictionaries of sports, No. 1. Scarecrow Press, Lanham, Toronto, Plymouth

Macarthur PJ (2011) Taking flight – the evolution of sky flying, from the first recorded jump to the latest world record. Skiing Herit J (March–April):20–25

Madjar N, Greenberg E, Chen Z (2011) Factors for radical creativity, incremental creativity, and routine, noncreative performance. J Appl Psychol 96(4):730–743. https://doi.org/10.1037/a0022416

Maglischo EW (2003) Swimming fastest. Human Kinetics, Champaign, IL

Martin D (2013) Bud Palmer, jump shot pioneer, dies at 91. The New York Times, March 22, https://www.nytimes.com

Maryniak J, Ładyżyńska-Kozdraś E, Tomczak S (2009) Configurations of the Graf-Boklev (v-style) ski jumper model and aerodynamic parameters in a wind tunnel. Hum Mov 10(2):130–136. https://doi.org/10.2478/v10038-009-0012-4

Maule T (1960) The shotput explosion. Sports Illustrated, April 25, https://www.si.com

McGinn MK (2010) Data resources. Encyclopedia of case study research. Sage, Thousand Oaks, CA. https://doi.org/10.4135/9781412957397.n102

Michalek G (2017) Die Geburtsstunde des V-Stils [The birth of the v-style]. https://www.deutschlandfunk.de. Accessed 29 Sep 2017

Mintzberg H (2005) Developing theory about the development of theory. In: Smith KG, Hitt MA (eds) Great minds in management: the process of theory development. Oxford University Press, Oxford, pp 355–372

Mothe C, Uyen Nguyen Thi T (2010) The link between non-technological innovations and technological innovation. Eur J Innov Manag 13(3):313–332. https://doi.org/10.1108/14601061011060148

Müller W (2008) Performance factors in ski jumping. In: Nørstrud H (ed) Sport aerodynamics. Springer, Wien, pp 139–160

Mumford MD, Gustafson SB (1988) Creativity syndrome: integration, application, and innovation. Psychol Bull 103(1):27–43. https://doi.org/10.1037/0033-2909.103.1.27

Nag R, Gioia DA (2012) From common to uncommon knowledge: foundations of firm-specific use of knowledge as a resource. Acad Manag J 55(2):421–457. https://doi.org/10.5465/amj.2008.0352

Naismith Memorial Basketball Hall of Fame (n.d.) Angelo "Hank" Luisetti. https://www.hoophall.com. Accessed 20 Jan 2018

Nedo J (2016) Der V-Stil im Skispringen: Jan Boklöv: Per Zufall zum Visionär [The v-style in ski jumping: Jan Boklöv: Visionary by chance]. Tagesspiegel, December 28, https://www.tagesspiegel.de

Nemeth C, Brown K, Rogers J (2001) Devil's advocate versus authentic dissent: stimulating quantity and quality. Eur J Soc Psychol 31(6):707–720. https://doi.org/10.1002/ejsp.58

Noden M (1997) Shot put champion Parry O'Brien March 21, 1955. Sports Illustrated, August 18, https://www.si.com

Nordic Skiing (2018) In Encyclopaedia Britannica. https://www.academic.eb.com. Accessed 14 Jan 2018

OECD (2005) Oslo manual: the measurement of scientific and technological activities – guidelines for collecting and interpreting technological innovation data, https://www.oecd.org

Osterwalder A (2004) The business model ontology: a proposition in a design science approach. Doctoral dissertation, University of Lausanne, https://doc.rero.ch/record/4210/files/1_these_Osterwalder.pdf

Paal E, Corradini A (2007) Worldloppet – 30 years of skiing around the world. Worldloppet International Ski Federation, Estonia, http://www.worldloppet.com/magazines/pdf/WL-anniversary-book-full.pdf

Parry O'Brien (2018) In Encyclopaedia Britannica. https://academic.eb.com. Accessed 20 Jun 2018

Pennington B (2011) In search of the first jump shot. The New York Times, April 2, https://www.nytimes.com

Peterson RA, Crittenden VL (2012) On the impactfulness of theory and review articles. AMS Rev 2 (1):1–4. https://doi.org/10.1007/s13162-012-0025-6

Pfister G (2007) Sportification, power and control: ski-jumping as a case study. Junctures J Thematic Dialogue 8:51–67

Podsakoff PM, MacKenzie SB, Podsakoff NP (2016) Recommendations for creating better concept definitions in the organizational, behavioral, and social sciences. Organ Res Methods 19 (2):159–203. https://doi.org/10.1177/1094428115624965

Quinlan JR (1987) Simplifying decision trees. Int J Man-Mach Stud 27(3):221–234. https://doi.org/10.1016/S0020-7373(87)80053-6

Read A (2000) Determinants of successful organisational innovation: a review of current research. J Manag Pract 3(1):95–119

Reid P (1986) The high jump. New Stud Athl 1(1):47–53

Rhodes R (2012) Making of the atomic bomb. Simon and Schuster, New York, NY

Richard Douglas Fosbury (2018) In Encyclopaedia Britannica. https://www.academic.eb.com. Accessed 10 Jan 2018

Roehrich G (2004) Consumer innovativeness: concepts and measurements. J Bus Res 57 (6):671–677. https://doi.org/10.1016/S0148-2963(02)00311-9

Rogers EM (1962) Diffusion of innovations. Free Press, New York, NY

Rogers EM (2003) Diffusion of innovations, 5th edn. Free Press, New York, NY

Royer I (2010) Number of cases. Encyclopedia of case study research. Sage, Thousand Oaks, CA. https://doi.org/10.4135/9781412957397.n231

Rubera G, Kirca AH (2012) Firm innovativeness and its performance outcomes: a meta-analytic review and theoretical integration. J Mark 76(3):130–147. https://doi.org/10.1509/jm.10.0494

Salter A, Alexy O (2014) The nature of innovation. In: Dodgson M, Gann DM, Phillips N (eds) The Oxford handbook of innovation management. Oxford University Press, Oxford, pp 26–49. https://doi.org/10.1093/oxfordhb/9780199694945.013.034

Schlickenrieder P, Elbern C (2003) Skilanglauf: Das Trainingsprogramm (Nordic walking) [Cross-country skiing: The training program (Nordic walking)]. Ehrenwirth, Bergisch Gladbach

Schneider H (2015) HWAIW: Eine kommentierende Einführung ins Marketing [Introduction to marketing – a comment]. BoD – Books on Demand, Norderstedt

Schneider J (2017) Rückwärts in die Zukunft: Der Erfinder des Fosbury Flops Dick Fosbury wird 70 [Backwards into the future: Dick Fosbury, the inventor of the Fosbury Flop turns 70]. SPOX, March 6, https://www.spox.com

Schrader DM (2006) Obituary of Volney Colving Wilson. Physics Today, May 5, https://physicstoday.scitation.org

Self MC (1946) The horseman's encyclopedia. A.S. Barnes, New York, NY

Self MC (1952) Horsemastership: methods of training the horse and the rider. A. S. Barnes, New York, NY

Shot Put (2018) In Encyclopaedia Britannica. https://www.acedemic.eb.com. Accessed 6 Jan 2018

Siggelkow N (2007) Persuasion with case studies. Acad Manag J 50(1):20–24. https://doi.org/10.2307/20159838

Ski Jumping (2006) Ewolucja stylów w skokach narciarskich [The evolution of styles in ski jumping]. https://www.skijumping.pl/wiadomosci/5349/Ewolucja-stylow-w-skokach-narciarskich%2D%2D-cz3/. Accessed 12 Jan 2018

Ski Jumping (2018) In Encyclopaedia Britannica. https://www.academic.eb.com. Accessed 21 Jun 2018

Sloan T (1988) Tod Sloan by himself. San Diego State University Press, San Diego, CA

Sports Reference "Dick Fosbury" (n.d.) Dick Fosbury. https://www.sports-reference.com. Accessed 11 Oct 2018 2017

Sports Reference "Parry O'Brien" (n.d.) Parry O'Brien. https://www.sports-reference.com. Accessed 25 Sep 2017

Sternberg RJ (1999) A propulsion model of types of creative contributions. Rev Gen Psychol 3 (2):83–100. https://doi.org/10.1037/1089-2680.3.2.83

Struzik A, Pietraszewski B, Zawadzki J (2014) Biomechanical analysis of the jump shot in basketball. J Hum Kinet 42(1):73–79. https://doi.org/10.2478/hukin-2014-0062

Stuart I, McCutcheon D, Handfield R, McLachlin R, Samson D (2002) Effective case research in operations management: a process perspective. J Oper Manag 20(5):419–433. https://doi.org/10.1016/S0272-6963(02)00022-0

Svensson H (n.d.) Evolution of skiing – ski jump. http://www.sporteventgellivare.com/en/evolution-of-skiing/evolution-of-skiing-ski-jump/. Accessed 25 Sep 2017

Swimming (2018) In Encyclopaedia Britannica. https://academic.eb.com. Accessed 15 Jan 2018

Swimming World Magazine (2015) Fina officially makes "Ryan Lochte turn" illegal in IM races. Swimming World Magazine, September 8, https://www.swimmingworldmagazine.com

The New York Times (2016) The fine line: Ryan Lochte swimming [interactive material and YouTube-video]. The New York Times. https://www.nytimes.com. Accessed 5 Jun 2018

The Washington Post (n.d.) The development of the modern stroke. The Washington Post, https://www.washingtonpost.com

Theiner E, Karl C (2002) Skilanglauf: Geschichte, Kultur, Praxis [Cross-country skiing: History, culture, practice]. Die Werkstatt, Göttingen, Germany

TIME Magazine (1956) Faster, higher, farther. TIME Magazine, December 3, pp 36–41

Topolinski S, Reber R (2010) Gaining insight into the "aha" experience. Curr Dir Psychol Sci 19 (6):402–405. https://doi.org/10.1177/0963721410388803

Turnbull S (2008) Olympics: four decades later, we're all still doing the Fosbury Flop. The Independent, July 26, https://www.independent.co.uk

Unsworth K (2001) Unpacking creativity. Acad Manag Rev 26(2):289–297. https://doi.org/10.5465/amr.2001.4378025

USATF Hall of Fame "Dick Fosbury" (n.d.) Dick Fosbury. https://www.usatf.org. Accessed 12 Oct 2017

USATF Hall of Fame "O'Brien" (n.d.) William (Parry) O'Brien. https://www.usatf.org. Accessed 26 Sep 2017

USMS (2000) Remembering Albert Vandeweghe. http://www.usms.org. Accessed 4 Jan 2018

Van de Ven AH (1989) Nothing is quite so practical as a good theory. Acad Manag Rev 14 (4):486–489. https://doi.org/10.5465/amr.1989.4308370

Van de Ven AH (2007) Engaged scholarship: a guide for organizational and social research. Oxford University Press, Oxford

Voigt B (2008) Und plötzlich öffneten sich die Ski: Vor 20 Jahren hat der Schwede Jan Boklöv mit dem V-Stil seine Sportart revolutioniert [And suddenly the skis opened: Twenty years ago the swede Jan Boklöv revolutionized his sport with the v-style]. Tagesspiegel, December 30, https://www.tagesspiegel.de

Volberda HW, Van Den Bosch FA, Mihalache OR (2014) Advancing management innovation: synthesizing processes, levels of analysis, and change agents. Organ Stud 35(9):1245–1264. https://doi.org/10.1177/0170840614546155

Weick KE (1995) What theory is not, theorizing is. Adm Sci Q 40(3):385–390. https://doi.org/10.2307/2393789

Weisenfeld U (2009) Serendipity as a mechanism of change and its potential for explaining change processes. Manag Rev 20(2):138–148. https://doi.org/10.1688/1861-9908_mrev_2009_02_Weisenfeld

Wigo B (2017a) History of the backstroke flip or somersault turn. [Information compiled by the ISHOF past president for the purpose of this work]. Taken from letters in the ISHOF archive. Copy in possession of author

Wigo B (2017b) History of the freestyle somersault turn. [Information compiled by the ISHOF past president for the purpose of this work]. Taken from letters in the ISHOF archive. Copy in possession of author

Wittmann U (n.d.) Jan Boklöv: Der V-Mann [Jan Boklöv: The v-man]. https://www.nordicsports.de. Accessed 25 Sep 2017

Yin RK (2014) Case study research design and methods, 5th edn. Sage, Thousand Oaks, CA

Zarkos J (2004) Raising the bar: a man, the 'flop' and an olympic gold medal. Sun Valley Guide, https://www.svguide.com

Zhou J, Wang XM, Song LJ, Wu J (2017) Is it new? Personal and contextual influences on perceptions of novelty and creativity. J Appl Psychol 102(2):180–202. https://doi.org/10.1037/apl0000166

Chapter 3
Toward a Rule-Breaking Managerial Framework

Abstract The findings from the eight sports cases are extrapolated from the domain of sports to the managerial context, specifically to the overlapping domains of creativity and innovation. Each of the 21 cross-case insights from Chap. 2 is linked to corresponding scholarly discussions by comparing the present empirical findings to existing research. Additionally, normative recommendations for strategic actions, derived from the case-based insights, describe how firms can help individual employees in the process of rule-breaking behavior. The key insights are visualized in the Framework of Rule-Breaking Market Behavior that contains a precis of the findings.

3.1 Transferring the Insights: From Sports to Business

3.1.1 Logic and Structure of the Transfer

Twenty-one criteria have emerged as a result of the single case and cross-case analysis of eight examples of rule-breaking behavior in the source domain sports. They build the basis for the transfer to the target domain of business and innovation. The objective of the transfer is to converge further, derive propositions, and find managerial suggestions on behaviors that are based on the underlying database but generalize over and above the individual cases and the domain of sports. Figure 3.1 schematically displays the two basic cognitive steps to go from case data to managerial implications: (1) relating each of the 21 criteria to discussions in the creativity and innovation literature and (2) deriving managerial implications that help managers to create competitive advantage by adapting the idea of rule-breaking market behavior.

As displayed on the left in Fig. 3.1, the two-step process of transferring the case data starts out with Table 2.5, which has been thoroughly explained in the previous chapter. First, each of the 21 criteria has been transferred to equivalent concepts and discussions in the context of creativity and innovation. In other words, it has been individually analyzed for each criterion whether the case-based insight from the domain of sports can, by analogy, also be considered meaningful in the context of

© Springer Nature Switzerland AG 2019
A.-K. Veenendaal, *Toward a Better Understanding of Rule-Breaking Market Behavior*, Contributions to Management Science,
https://doi.org/10.1007/978-3-030-16107-1_3

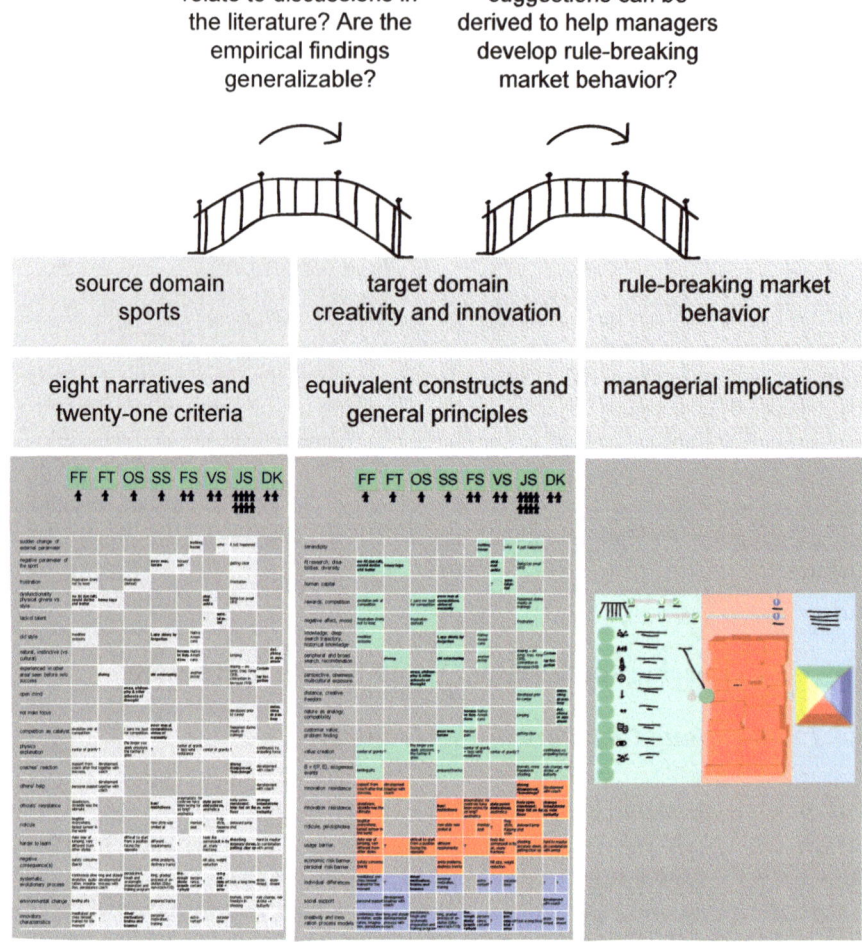

How does the criterion relate to discussions in the literature? Are the empirical findings generalizable?

Which managerial suggestions can be derived to help managers develop rule-breaking market behavior?

source domain sports

target domain creativity and innovation

rule-breaking market behavior

eight narratives and twenty-one criteria

equivalent constructs and general principles

managerial implications

FF = Fosbury Flop, FT = Flip Turn, OS = O'Brien Shift, SS = Skate Skiing, FS = Forward Seat, VS = V -Style, JS = Jump Shot, DK = Dolphin Kick

Note: In principle, this figure adds a further step to Fig. 2.10, where the first two of the above displayed stages have already been explained. Here, the visualization focuses more on transfer-related aspects and gives a brief preview of the managerial framework. Again, the readable versions of the two tables can be found in Appendix A.1.

Fig. 3.1 Building bridges from sports cases to managerial implications (source: author)

business. The guiding questions were the following: How does the criterion relate to discussions in creativity and innovation? Is there evidence that the criterion is generalizable? An overview of the concepts that have eventually been logically connected to the sports-findings is given hereafter in Table 3.1. This is indicated visually by the bridge that goes from the first to the second of the three steps. What can also be seen, is that in the second step, the long list of criteria has been divided

Table 3.1 Overview of transfer-related contents and structure

Second order themes (21 criteria)	Equivalent in the (creativity and innovation) literature	Aggregation and structure	Discussed in sections
Challenge one in the process of rule-breaking behavior: recognizing the new way			
Sudden change of external parameter	Serendipity	Serendipitous cues	Serendipitous Cues
Dysfunctionality physical givens vs. style	Fit research, disabilities, diversity	Incompatibility cues	Incompatibility Cues
Lack of talent	Human capital	Motivational cues	Motivational Cues
Competition as catalyst	Rewards, competition		
Frustration	Negative affect, mood	Affective cues	Affective Cues
Old style	Knowledge, deep search trajectory, historical knowledge	Cognitive cues	Cognitive Cues
Experienced/seen before w/o success	Peripheral search, recombination, broad perspective	Experiential cues	Experiential Cues
Open mind	Perspective, openness, multicultural exposure		
Not main focus	Distance, creative freedom		
Natural, instinctive (vs. cultural)	Nature as analogy, compatibility	Cultural cues	Cultural Cues
Negative parameter of the sport	Customer value, problem finding	Functional cues	Functional Cues
Physics explanation	Value creation		
Environmental change	B = f(P, E), exogenous events	External cues	External Cues
Challenge two in the process of rule-breaking behavior: overcoming resistance			
Coaches' reaction	Innovation resistance	Active and passive innovation resistance	Active and Passive Innovation Resistance
Officials' resistance	Innovation resistance		
Ridicule	Ridicule, gelotophobia		
Harder to learn	Usage barrier		
Negative consequence(s)	Economic risk barrier, personal risk barrier		
Overall aspects			
Innovators characteristics	Individual differences	Overall aspects	A Brief Overview of Creativity and Innovation Literatures
Others/help	Social support	Overall aspects	A Brief Overview of Creativity and Innovation Literatures
Systematic, evolutionary process	Creativity and innovation process models	Overall aspects	Systematic Evolutionary Process

into three parts (indicated by the three colors, green, red and blue). This structure, which further subsumes the themes, stood out clearly after all criteria had been transferred to the domain of business. As will be outlined later, the discussions in the remainder of Chap. 3 will follow exactly that three-part structure. Finally, in the third and last step, the following question has been posed: Which managerial suggestions can be derived to help managers create competitive advantage by developing rule-breaking market behavior? Thus, in addition to the propositions that have been derived, each theme is enriched with concrete measures that can be taken by managers and other corporate individuals. All contributions will be summarized in a template, referred to as the Framework of Rule-Breaking Market Behavior, and graphically foreshadowed on the right in Fig. 3.1.

Next, Table 3.1 gives an overview of the transfer-related contents and structure. It displays the 21 criteria in the left column, divided into three sections: two major challenges: (1) recognition of the new way and (2) overcoming innovation resistance and (3) overall aspects. A brief description of the three sections will be given thereafter, followed by an in-depth discussion of each criterion in the remainder of Sect. 3.1.

The three-part structure (green, red, blue in Table 3.1) is resulting from the empirical analysis. The underlying cases have revealed that rule-breaking behavior first requires athletes to recognize a new way (green in Table 3.1). This recognition entails two further elements: the rule-breaking approach needs to be discovered (i.e. to be seen) and to be pursued subsequently. Nine creative cues have been identified to aid in this quest. Generally, cues can be thought of as a trigger to the solution of a problem. More specifically, they either give a signal for action or indicate how to behave. The nine different categories of creative cues mostly consist of more than one single cue. For instance, four cues have been identified as related to motivation: failure, competition, limited talent, and situational constraints. All cues that have been identified in the case study have been classified in order to not provide a long list but a useful categorization accounting for homogeneity among and heterogeneity across the different cue categories. Consequently, the nine different categories of cues consist of slightly varying cues that will all be explained and discussed separately. The different cues are not mutually exclusive. That is, one single cue could fall into more than one cue category, but each cue has been classified according to the highest weight of the cue's characteristics. It is more to be thought of as a distinction among different characteristics of cues than that any of the single cues is completely unique (i.e. selective in their capability to differentiate).

Second, the case study has shown that novel ways to behave, no matter how effective they are, often face resistance (red in Table 3.1). Five of the twenty-one criteria have been related to this challenge. Compared to challenge one, the sports cases provided less insight into how to actually overcome the challenge. That is why an equivalent to creative cues is missing in Table 3.1. However, when transferred to existing literature, some case-based hints lead to a number of potentially helpful mechanisms, which will be outlined respectively.

The three overall aspects at the top of the table could neither be classified under challenge one nor under challenge two (blue in Table 3.1). Individual differences and social support will, therefore, be generally addressed in the introductory remarks on how the results generally classify within the current research. The notion of a systematic, evolutionary process, which is, besides the two challenges, the third overall generalizable finding, will also be explored against the background of creativity and innovation process models.

3.1.2 Overall Aspects

3.1.2.1 A Brief Overview of Creativity and Innovation Literatures

Since Schumpeter's seminal work on the importance of innovation for economic development in 1911, scholars from several different domains including sociology, psychology, business administration, and public management have shown continuously growing interest in research on innovation (Damanpour and Aravind 2012). Especially over the recent decades, research on change- and novelty-related constructs has increased exponentially (Amabile and Pratt 2016; Anderson et al. 2014; Blomberg et al. 2017; Potočnik and Anderson 2016). Despite the vast and expansive research efforts, the state of the science is "far from congruent" (Ramos et al. 2016, p. 477). This refers, for instance, to a lack of definitional clarity, a diverse number of (not always functionally operationalized) concepts (Potočnik and Anderson 2016), and fragmentation (Hennessey and Amabile 2010).

In line with the conceptualization of rule-breaking market behavior, creativity and innovation are viewed as different parts of essentially the same process. Creativity is defined as the production of novel and useful ideas, and innovation as the successful implementation of creative ideas within an organization (Amabile and Mueller 2008; Amabile and Pratt 2016; Drazin et al. 1999; Van de Ven 1986; West 1990). While there remains a general lack of consent between researchers, this notion is shared by most scholars of organizational creativity and innovation.[1]

Creativity and innovation are complex, multilevel, and emergent phenomena (Anderson et al. 2014), and the predictors of the two stages are likely to differ (Zhou and Hoever 2014). Several attempts have been made to comprehensively integrate existing findings. Recent reviews on the state-of-the-science reveal large numbers of (enhancing, inhibiting, and either-or[2]) factors that are found to have

---

[1]Anderson et al. (2014) give a brief overview on prevalent discussions concerning definitional aspects. Their proposal of an integrative definition goes along with and expands the definition used above: "Creativity and innovation at work are the process, outcomes, and products of attempts to develop and introduce new and improved ways of doing things. The creativity stage of this process refers to idea generation, and innovation refers to the subsequent stage of implementing ideas toward better procedures, practices, or products. Creativity and innovation can occur at the level of the individual, work team, organization, or at more than one of these levels combined but will invariably result in identifiable benefits at one or more of these levels of analysis" (p. 1298).

[2]For more information on the paradoxical nature of organizational creativity's antecedents, see Blomberg et al. (2017).

influence on innovation and creativity in organizations. Anderson et al. (2014) summarize extant research between 2002 and 2011, resulting in a tabular overview encompassing more than 70 dimensions affecting individual, team, organizational, or multilevel creativity and innovation in the workplace. Zhou and Hoever (2014) refer to an equally large number of direct and multiple interacting effects in their review on empirical work related to workplace creativity in the realm of organizational psychology and innovation, published since 2000. Amabile and Pratt (2016) list a number of particularly important elements of the work environment for creativity used in their theoretical model (creativity stimulant "catalysts" and creativity obstacle "inhibitors"). Blomberg et al. (2017) cover an equally large number of major drivers of and barriers to organizational creativity across the individual level, group level, organizational level, and macro level.[3] In their meta-analytic review focusing on organizational culture and innovation alone, Büschgens et al. (2013) identified an array of more than 40 cultural values supposedly related to innovation.

All in all, in creativity and innovation, a plethora of forces are in play, each of which is rewarded a particular stream of research. Integrating all of them into a comprehensive theory of business success is considered a high ambition unlikely to be attained anytime soon (King and Baatartogtokh 2015).

Thus, theoretical perspectives and models, in contrast to the plethora of single predictor studies, are comparatively sparse (Anderson et al. 2014). Anderson et al. (2014) discern six prominent theoretical frameworks across the creativity and innovation literature, which all emphasize the role of different determinants at different stages of the innovative process (viz. idea generation versus idea implementation). In order to create a solid foundation for the subsequent classification of the empirical results, the key tenets of five different theoretical concepts will be outlined briefly below.

The *Componential Theory of Organizational Creativity and Innovation* (see Fig. 3.2) has been first articulated by Amabile (1983, 1988). According to Amabile and Pratt (2016), it is the oldest and only widely-cited theory of creativity and innovation in organizations. In essence, the 1988 model specifies that creativity should be highest when four aspects apply: (1) an intrinsically motivated person with (2) high domain relevant skills (e.g. knowledge, expertise, technical skills, intelligence, and talent) and (3) a high skill in creative thinking (e.g. cognitive style and personality characteristics favorable of independence, risk-taking, and a disciplined work style) works (4) in a highly creativity-supportive social environment (e.g. characterized by a sense of positive challenge, collaborative work teams, diverse skills and idea focus, freedom in how to carry out work, innovation-encouraging supervisors, etc.) (Amabile 1983, 1988, 2012; Amabile and Mueller 2008). Most empirical attention has been given to the motivational component of the model (Anderson et al. 2014; Shalley et al. 2004; Zhou and Shalley 2003). In 2016, the theory was revised, including four new or radically modified elements:

---

[3]Other comprehensive narrative reviews or quantitative meta-analyses on the topic (either less recent or more specific) include but are not limited to: Anderson et al. (2004), Andriopoulos (2001), Hauser et al. (2006), Hennessey and Amabile (2010), Mumford and Gustafson (1988), Shalley et al. (2004), Zhou and Shalley (2003).

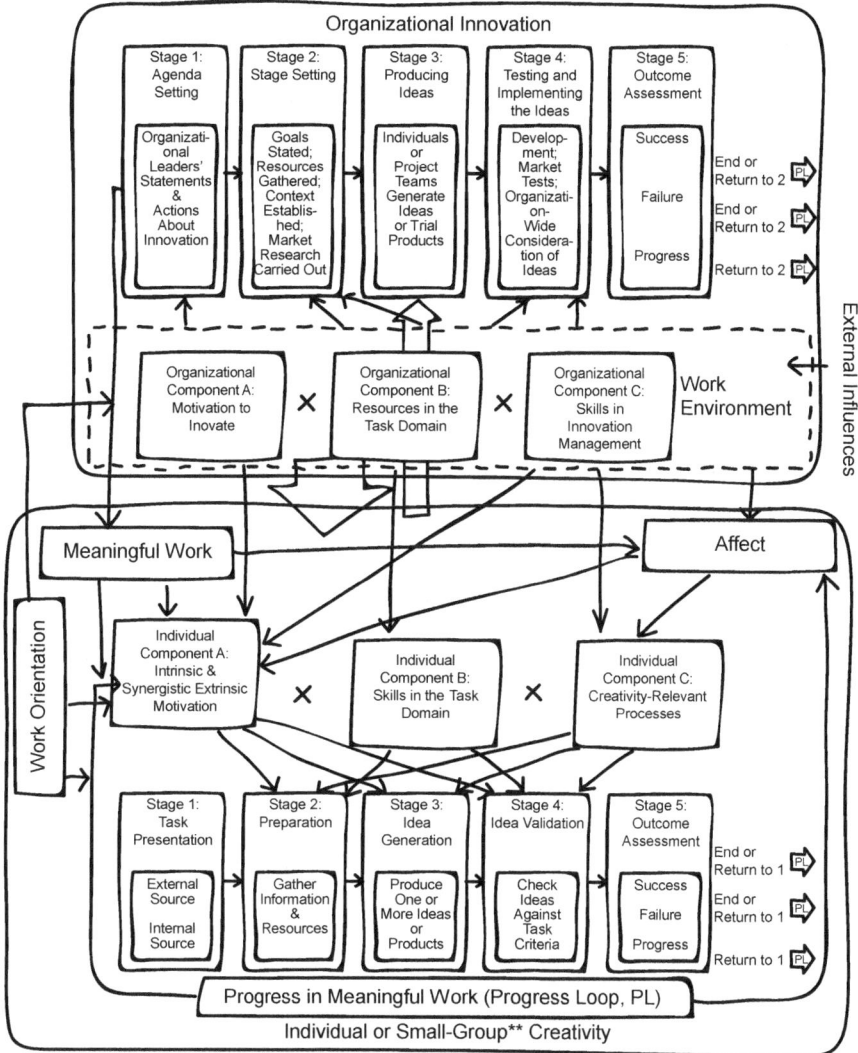

Fig. 3.2 Componential theory of organizational creativity and innovation (adapted from Amabile and Pratt 2016)

introduction of a greater degree of dynamism (i.e. progress loop), work meaningfulness and affect are added to the model, and the former near-exclusive focus on intrinsic motivation is expanded by an extrinsic component (Amabile and Pratt 2016). Much of what the model proposes has not yet been examined empirically (Amabile and Pratt 2016).

The *Interactionist Perspective of Organizational Creativity* (see Fig. 3.3) by Woodman et al. (1993) is one of the most frequently used frameworks when it comes to the

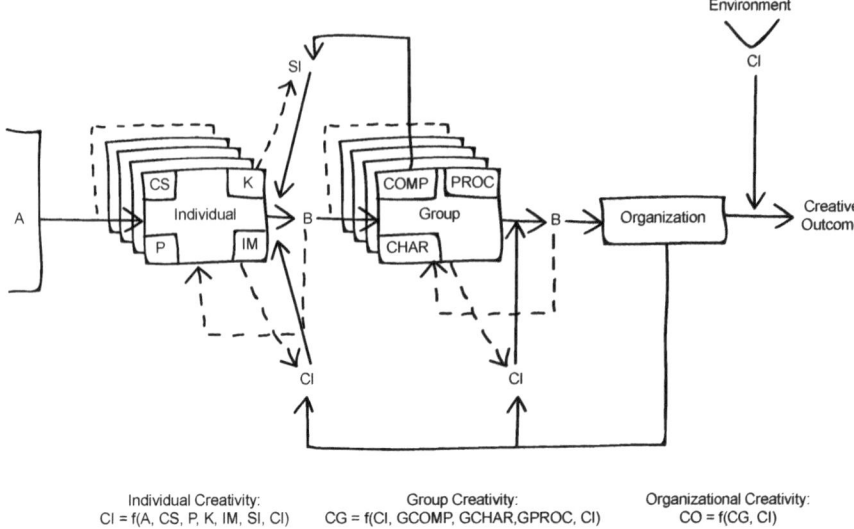

$$CI = f(A, CS, P, K, IM, SI, CI) \qquad CG = f(CI, GCOMP, GCHAR, GPROC, CI) \qquad CO = f(CG, CI)$$

Individual Creativity: Group Creativity: Organizational Creativity:

Note: A = Antecedent Conditions, B = Creative Behavior, CS = Cognitive Style/ Abilities, P =Personality, K = Knowledge, IM = Intrinsic Motivation, SI = Social Influence, CI = ContextualInfluences, G_{COMP} = Group Composition, G_{CHAR} = Group Characteristics, G_{PROC} = Group Processes.

Fig. 3.3 Interactionist model of organizational creativity (adapted from Woodman et al. 1993)

question of how interactions between individual and contextual factors (instead of treating the two variables separately) might influence creative work at different levels of the organization (Anderson et al. 2014; Yuan and Woodman 2010; Zhou and Shalley 2011). At the individual level, creativity is modeled as a function of antecedent conditions (e.g. past reinforcement history, biographical variables), cognitive style and ability (e.g. divergent thinking, ideational fluency), personality (e.g. locus of control, self-esteem), relevant knowledge, motivation, social influences (e.g. social rewards, social facilitation), and contextual influences (e.g. physical influences, task and time constraints). At the group level, creativity is viewed as a function of all individual level parameters plus group composition (i.e. interaction between the group members), group processes (e.g. approaches to problem solving), group characteristics (e.g. norms, size, degree of cohesiveness) and contextual influences (e.g. characteristics of group task). Finally, the organizational level comprises both the aforementioned individual and group creativity parameters plus, again, contextual influences (e.g. organizational culture, reward systems, resource constraints).

In his *Model of Individual Creative Action* (see Fig. 3.4), Ford (1996) makes a fundamental distinction between either being creative or undertaking routine, habitual actions. Whether an individual pursues creative or habitual action is, according to his framework, determined by the joint influence of three mandatory factors: sense making, motivation, and knowledge and ability. Sense making refers to an individual's interpretive processes. Motivation is further determined by goals, receptivity beliefs (i.e. expectation that creative actions are rewarded), capability beliefs (i.e. confidence that one is capable of being creative) and emotions (e.g. interest

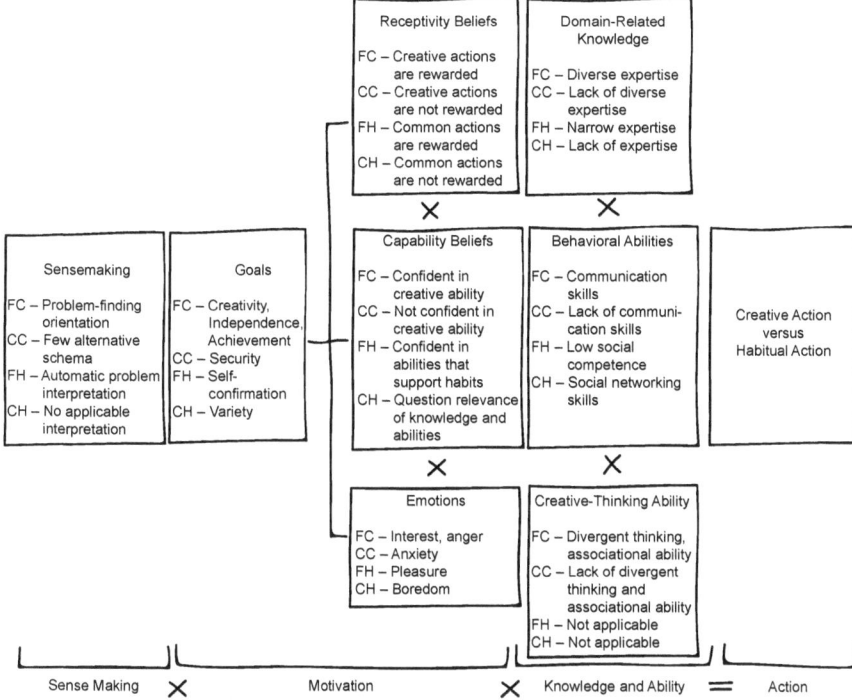

FC – Facilitates creativity, CC – Constrains creativity, FH – Facilitates habits, CH – Constrains habits

Fig. 3.4 A theory of creative individual action (adapted from Ford 1996)

and anger facilitating creativity, anxiety inhibiting creativity). Knowledge and ability is a function of an individual's domain-related knowledge (e.g. expertise), behavioral abilities (e.g. communication skills, social competence), and creative-thinking ability (e.g. divergent thinking).

Ford's theoretical perspective has attracted less empirical research attention than the interactionist and componential framework, which could, according to Anderson et al. (2014), partly be related to the model's complexity.

West (1990) proposed the *Four-Factor Theory of Team Climate for Innovation*, positing that the four factors, vision, participative safety, task orientation, and support for innovation, facilitate innovation (see also West and Anderson 1996). In brief, the theoretical concept proposes that innovation is facilitated if (a) the work group vision is clear, readily attainable, shared and has a valued outcome, (b) team members feel save to propose new ideas and problem solutions without being judged and criticized, (c) the group commits to excellence in task performance involving aspects like stimulating debate and discussion of several possible solutions that lead to improvements of established policies, procedures and methods, and (d) the expectation, approval and practical support of innovative attempts is both articulated and enacted (Anderson et al. 2014; Anderson and West 1998). West's theory has been widely applied in team-level innovation research (Hülsheger et al. 2009).

More recently, Bledow et al. (2009a, b) further advocated *ambidexterity theory* to successfully manage conflicting demands pervasive throughout organizational innovation.[4] On the most general level, being ambidextrous means that an organization is able to reconcile the dichotomy of explorative variability creation (e.g. search, variation, experimentation, and discovery) and exploitative variability reduction (e.g. refinement, efficiency, selection, and implementation) both needed for a company's sustainable success (Anderson et al. 2014; Bledow et al. 2009a, b; O'Reilly and Tushman 2008, 2013; Raisch and Birkinshaw 2008; Raisch et al. 2009). Thus, ambidexterity theory aids coping with paradoxes related to managing creativity of which plenty can be found in that context. One such dilemma managers are facing is how to exploit existing competencies while avoiding their dysfunctional rigidity effects by renewing and replacing them with entirely new competencies needed for the inauguration of breakthrough ideas (Atuahene-Gima 2005).[5] Another paradox is related to the different stages of the creativity and innovation process. The requirements for activities in the beginning of the innovation process compared to those in the later stages have been shown to be contradictory (Miron-Spektor et al. 2011). For instance, the stages in the beginning of the innovation process (e.g. idea generation) associated with breaking away from existing paradigms and an exploration of novel solution spaces require different personal attributes and managing instruments than later stages in which innovations are implemented into the company or brought to the market. In fact, the personal characteristics associated with creativity have been shown to have no effect or even a negative effect on performance outcomes related to innovation (i.e. idea implementation) (Miron et al. 2004)[6]. In consequence, different factors can inhibit a dual role in the process of rule-breaking behavior.

What seems to be universally accepted throughout the change-related literature is the distinction between individual, team, organizational, and multi-level analysis. These different levels of analysis are reflected throughout the above outlined theoretical accounts. As highlighted by Crossan et al. (1999), insights usually first occur to individuals before they are shared at the team level and subsequently institutionalized at the organizational level. Thus, individual-level processes at the root of the multilevel phenomenon typically lay the foundation for the dissemination of new behavior through several societal levels (Lewandowsky et al. 2012). The analysis of the underlying rule-breaking sports innovations has predominantly been conducted from the perspective of individual athletes. Hence, the social nature of innovation processes (i.e. how dynamic and interactive team processes contribute to the development of innovations) is not thoroughly investigated in this work (for reviews on the team levels of analysis, see Anderson et al. 2014; Hülsheger et al. 2009; Rosing et al. 2011; Widmann et al. 2016). One aspect from a group level perspective has been identified and included into the list

---

[4]For a brief outline of the evolution of organizational ambidexterity research, see Raisch and Birkinshaw (2008).

[5]For further insight on the management of innovation paradoxes, see for instance Andriopoulos and Lewis (2010), Knight and Harvey (2015).

[6]Caniëls et al. (2014), too, show that antecedents of creativity indeed have different roles in different stages of the creative process and that antecedents that are helpful in one stage of the creative process can be detrimental for another stage.

of 21 second-order constructs: social support. Support for creativity, the extent to which individuals aid and encourage employees' creative performance, is considered an important social condition influencing creativity (Amabile et al. 1996). Much of the research has been focusing on support from individuals inside the organization, such as coworkers and supervisors (for a brief overview including relevant studies, see Anderson et al. 2014). Additionally, explicit support from non-work individuals (e.g. family members and friends) has also been shown to make an independent contribution, viz. over and above the support from people in the workplace, to an employee's creative performance (Madjar et al. 2002). In the latter case, the positive relationship between support and creativity has been explained through a mood state perspective: social support shapes employees moods, which then enhances their creativity (Madjar et al. 2002). Especially with regard to completely new ways of solving a problem, where no particular task-oriented help is available, such support seems to be crucial.

Even though the individual level perspective will be the focus in the subsequent elaborations, individual differences (how much of the innovative behavior is due to the "person") will not be further investigated. It is commonly accepted that individuals differ in their individual characteristics, for instance regarding their cognitive style (Armstrong et al. 2012), the way they solve problems (Isaksen et al. 2016) and make decisions (Appelt et al. 2011), their capacity of memory systems and the flexibility of stored cognitive structures (Zhou and Shalley 2011), selective attention (McIntyre and Graziano 2016), whether ridicule is perceived as a threat or not, and whether they are more likely to persist or quit after having experienced failure (Markman and Baron 2003). However, even though creativity in persons has trait-like stable aspects, it is also considered a state subject that can be influenced by the social environment (Hennessey and Amabile 2010). In their review, Zhou and Hoever (2014) suggest that even when organizations select employees with a particular inclination to be creative, an unsupportive context will prevent them from realizing their potential. On the other hand, workers regarded as lacking the natural inclination to be creative may become so in a supportive environment. Thus, even if some employees do have more creative potential than others, creativity is something that can be developed, for example, through training (Ritter and Rietzschel 2017). Therefore, based on Zhou and Shalley's (2011, p. 286) premise, that "all individuals have the capacity to be creative", the sphere of individual differences will not be further investigated. Instead it will be focused on effective strategies, practical tools and managerial techniques that can be applied by anybody.

3.1.2.2   Systematic Evolutionary Process

Multiple pathways can lead to innovation (Bledow et al. 2009a), and the underlying case study, too, has shown that there is more than one path to rule-breaking behavior in the domain of sports. How the case results can be transferred to and interpreted with regard to existing process models, and which specific findings can be highlighted for the process of rule-breaking market behavior, will be shown below. Basically, a distinction between creativity and innovation process models is to be made. This view is also reflected in the athletic cases and will, for instance, be expressed in the distinction between the two key challenges later.

Many different frameworks regarding the different stages of the creative thought process, the sequence of thoughts and actions that leads to a novel creation, have been suggested (see Lubart 2001 for an overview). The classical model originally formulated by Graham Wallas (1926), who was inspired by the writings of mathematician Henri Poincaré (Verhaeghen et al. 2017), continues to serve as the most important fundamental model to understand the creative process. It contains four linear stages of creative thinking: preparation (e.g. examination of the problem, setting up goals, gathering knowledge; process), incubation (e.g. setting problems consciously aside but unconsciously working on it; unconscious process), illumination (e.g. seeing the solution, often referred to as "aha effect"; event), and verification (e.g. using logic and knowledge to assess and refine the idea into an appropriate solution; process) (Zhou and Shalley 2011). Zhou and Shalley (2011, p. 287) summarize that despite slight variations across the different creativity models, they all "include some identification of a problem or opportunity, gathering information, generating ideas, and evaluating ideas".

The innovation process, too, has been conceptualized in many different ways. The most prominent model of innovation diffusion has been introduced by Rogers (2003). His conceptualization includes five stages: knowledge, persuasion, decision, implementation, and confirmation. In the knowledge stage (1), consumers are exposed to an innovation and gain awareness and knowledge about it. In the persuasion stage (2), consumers form their favorable or unfavorable attitude toward the innovation based on an evaluation of their individual expectations compared to the impression they formed during information processing. In the decision stage (3), consumers refine their perception of the innovation and make a decision about whether they intend to adopt or reject it. In the implementation stage (4), these intentions form into concrete behavior (i.e. purchase or not purchase). In the confirmation stage (5), consumers continue, stop, or reverse their initial behavior. The adoption process ends if the consumer uses the innovation or will not purchase it at any later time.

While early models portrayed innovation as a linear sequence of functional activities, it is now widely acknowledged that the processes are iterative and evolving, including complex, interactive activities such as reflection and action, improvising, experimenting, feedback loops, false starts, recycling between stages, and dead ends (Amabile and Pratt 2016; Lubart 2001; Tidd 2006; Zhou and Shalley 2011). The same is true of innovation (Amabile and Pratt 2016). Creativity is a process that even others close to the person, such as supervisors and coworkers, often only notice and observe at later stages when creative outcomes have already been produced (Zhou and Shalley 2011, p. 279). Consequently, the stories about a creative idea or innovation emerging in a single flash and becoming a success overnight can be considered pure myths (Amabile and Pratt 2016; Ashton 2015). This view is reflected in the underlying cases. Each of the 18 individual paths that have been analyzed shows at least one longer sequence of either conscious sensemaking or unconscious incubation. All eight breakthrough cases are characterized by elements of gradual, incremental development. Thus, here, the processes of radical innovation are characterized by "day-to-day"[7] continuous and rigorous processes of

---

[7]In an analogy, one may compare this to the process of plant growth. Before the seed breaks forth from the soil and the plant becomes visible, it is first in a dormant and then sprouting stage under the earth.

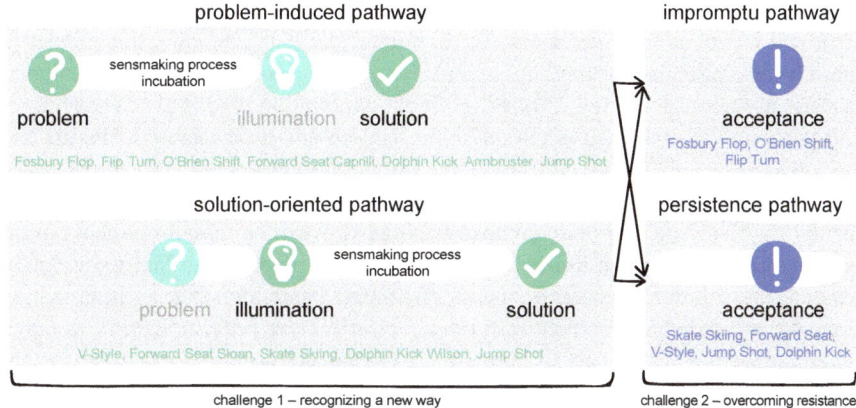

Note: The white graphic elements symbolize enduring systematic process elements (i.e. these stages are characterized by effort rather than occurring in an ad-hoc fashion).

Fig. 3.5 Challenges of rule-breaking behavior in a process view (source: author)

development rather than sudden strokes of ingenuity following extraordinary styles of thought (for a similar discussion, see Goldenberg et al. 2004). As will be shown based on the case data, what is often referred to as flashes of insight can be part of the creativity and innovation process, but they are still embedded in a systematic process (for more information on the unconscious foundations of the incubation period, see, e.g. Ritter and Dijksterhuis 2014; Ritter and Rietzschel 2017).

Figure 3.5 summarizes the process view that has been derived from the case data, independently from the above outlined theoretical process models already existing in the context of creativity and innovation literature. It shows how the different stages observed in the underlying cases of athletic rule-breaking behavior can be systematized. Horizontally, the two distinctive challenges that have been identified during the coding process are schematically displayed. The different length of the two boxes containing the two process steps does not imply that challenge one generally takes longer than challenge two but is simply due to illustration purposes. Statements concerning the typical length of such processes are highly idiosyncratic to different cases and cannot be made on the basis of the empirical data at hand. The different steps of the process (i.e. problem, sensemaking, illumination, etc.), too, are displayed in a stylized way to focus on the quintessential message. Vertically, two different variants have been distinguished regarding both major challenges. This is to highlight the abstract differences, which have been distilled from the cases of rule-breaking behavior in sports.

In challenge one, a problem-induced pathway and a solution-oriented pathway have been identified. First, the problem-induced pathway to rule-breaking behavior starts out with some kind of prevalent difficulty or issue: Fosbury did not feel comfortable with the state-of-the art jumping technique, O'Brien was not satisfied with the results he achieved with this technique and additionally frustrated because of having been defeated in a meet, Caprilli was worried about the horses' pain,

Armbruster's legs felt too heavy, and some of the jump shooters just could not get clear and lost over and over again. To disentangle the Gordian knot, the athletes in these cases consciously started out to make sense of the situation and find a solution to their problem, involving effortful in-depth exploration of different possibilities and perspectives with their attention being focused and their search deliberate and systematic. Eventually, the athletes found a solution to their problem, either with or without having had a particularly illuminating event during the systematic developmental process. In a corporate context, this pathway can be thought of as a typical institutionalized approach to innovations ("here's the problem, go find a solution"). Second, the solution-oriented pathway, in contrast, starts out with an illuminating event for a task or process that must not necessarily have been thought of as being erroneous before. This is not to imply that there has not been a problem before, but the problem was either not perceived consciously or not deliberately intended to be solved: Jan Boklöv has been surprised by a sudden wind in a training session and intuitively adapted to the changed environment, Tod Sloan reportedly reacted to his bolting horse by riding in a Forward seat fashion, Wilson watched dolphins in an aquarium, and some of the jump shooters proclaim that they just left the floor without having thought about it before. Other than in the problem-induced pathway, which followed a systematic search procedure, the solution-oriented pathway is characterized by a period of sensemaking after the illumination event. Due to the fact that the insight occurred comparatively sudden in these cases, the athletes had yet to figure out how to successfully reproduce and master the novel style. As there is no apparent problem that could be structured and addressed, this approach can be considered a more anarchic one, with less controlling rules or principles to give for initiating the pathway. Here, the bottom line is that, in most cases, there seems to be the opportunity to find a different and more impactful way to solve a problem.

In challenge two, an impromptu pathway and a persistence pathway have been identified. The impromptu pathway is characterized by ad-hoc acceptance, namely there is comparatively little resistance to be overcome by the rule-breaking attempt to become adapted by others. In the athletic cases this has been observed with the Fosbury Flop, the O'Brien Shift and the Flip Turn. By no means does ad-hoc or impromptu imply that from one day to the other, every athlete changed his or her style. However, it suggests that there have been comparatively fewer official objections, and the amount of reluctance toward the new technique was relatively smaller. In a corporate world, the impromptu pathway can probably be considered a rare occasion. The majority of innovative attempts, termed persistence-pathway here, require perseverance and effort until (e.g. group, company, market, or societal) acceptance will be gained. In the sports cases, a great deal of barriers had to be overcome until the Skating Technique, the Forward Seat, the V-Style, the Jump Shot and the Dolphin Kick had been officially allowed, broadly accepted and adapted by others.

Much more detailed information regarding the two challenges, above and beyond this more general classification into the context of creativity and innovation process models and how to address them, will be provided in the remainder of this chapter.

3.1.3   Rule-Breaking Market Behavior Challenge 1: Recognizing the New Way

Proposition 1   The first challenge in the process of rule-breaking market behavior is to recognize a new way with the potential of leading to fundamental change.

The first major challenge that generalizes across all cases of rule-breaking sports behavior empirically examined here is to recognize a new way. Recognizing a new way can be linked to the creativity process, which is typically the first part in the process of innovation. The term recognizing explicitly entails both situations, if a person creates or discovers a novel attempt for the very first time or if a person acknowledges the value of an existing approach and intends to further pursue it as a strategic or operative option to gain a competitive advantage. By that, this first challenge also incorporates those situations in which somebody, maybe years after an approach had been first invented, re-discovers the rule-breaking attempt and pursues it further. Sports cases in which more than one innovator played a role are examples of this. For instance, even if there are some accounts that Dick Fosbury was not the first one to jump in a backwards manner, yet he seems to have been the one to recognize and further pursue it successfully.

Visualized with the help of the schematic conceptualization that was introduced at the beginning of this work, the recognition of a new way is represented by the arrows in the slightly altered graph (Fig. 3.6 vs. Fig. 1.1). For reasons of simplicity, the technological options to expand current options in a market on the right have been left out. The focus now is on how the new way to behave (i.e. how companies go from the grey to the green field) comes to fruition. Recognizing the new way is conceptualized to be the first step in this endeavor, here referred to as the rule-breaking impulse.

3.1.3.1   Conceptualizing Creative Provocations

Firms, and because of the legacy of their experiences and the path-dependencies involved, particularly established firms, have been theorized to become entrapped in persisting behaviors and mindsets that consign them to incremental refinements

Fig. 3.6 Schematic conceptualization of the focal perspective, variant 3 (source: author)

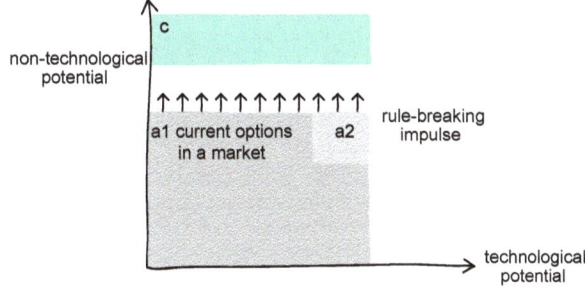

rather than breakthrough innovations (Perra et al. 2017). One of the reasons for that is that individuals generally are subject to strong inertial forces, spending most of their lives in a state of low attention or low consciousness (Davis 1971; Garfinkel 1967). Accordingly, Van de Ven (1986) pointed out that one of the central challenges in the management of innovation is the management of attention. Standardized daily behavioral processes incur the risk of mindless application (Alba 2012). Individuals gradually adapt to their environments and by that their awareness of need deteriorates and their action thresholds reach a level, which is said to only be surmountable by crisis (Van de Ven 1986). Dawkins (1998), too, cautioned against the "anaesthetic of familiarity, a sedative of ordinariness, which dulls the senses" (p. 6), and suggests to "recapture that sense of having just tumbled out to life on a new world by looking at our own world in unfamiliar ways" (p. 7).

How to break such inertial states and spark creative processes, above and beyond crises, strong environmental jolts, market disequilibrium, other environmental forces and external agents (e.g. consultants), is of central interest in the organizational creativity and innovation research. The eight sports cases have been carefully analyzed regarding the ideas or events that triggered an observable sequence of events eventually leading to rule-breaking behavior. These creative stimuli are termed creativity cues in this work. Literally, cues can be interpreted as a signal for action or a hint about how to behave (Cue n.d.).[8] That is, they either interrupt an individual's routines or indicate a different and useful way to do something by initiating a cognitive or behavioral alteration, stimulating action, and activating a particular perspective or lens that helps one to step out of habitual thinking. Cues can be provided by particular encounters and events, either tangible (e.g. people, places, artifacts) or intangible (e.g. memories, facts, emotions) in form (Titus 2018). Nine examples, which can be thought of as search and thinking trajectories will be outlined subsequently (Sect. 3.1.3.2).

3.1.3.2 Nine Creative Cues for Rule-Breaking Market Behavior

Subsequently, the creative cues will be discussed in the following order: serendipitous, incompatibility, motivational, affective, cognitive, experiential, cultural, functional, and external cues. The sequence has been chosen for purposes of explanation (e.g. cognitive and experiential cues are outlined successively to highlight conceptual links) but is not supposed to give an indication of the cue's importance or originality.

---

[8]Cues are also used as a term in the context of habits (habit cuing). In both cases, cues are understood as some kind of trigger event. What they are triggering, however, is highly different, almost contrary. In the context of habit, cues cause individuals to automatically behave in a certain, habitual way. In the context of this work, cues cause individuals to be creative, to initiate the process of rule-breaking behavior and to explicitly overcome habitual or routine states.

Serendipitous Cues

Proposition 1.1   (Making sense of) a surprising encounter may trigger the process of rule-breaking market behavior.

The factor of accident repeatedly occurs throughout the case data that builds the foundation of this work: "Cooper discovered the jump shot by accident" (Fury 2016, p. 16), Minor's "shot came from instinct, not deliberation" (Christgau 1999, p. 86), Jan Boklöv became "visionary by chance" (Nedo 2016), and Tod Sloan's discovery "merged into one dramatic moment" (Dizikes 2000, p. 58). The Forward Seat has been prompted by a sudden bolting of the horse and the V-Style has been triggered by an unexpected strong wind.

In the social sciences, an accidental or unexpected discovery of something valuable is referred to as serendipity (Merton and Barber 2004; Stebbins 2013; Van Andel 1992; Yaqub 2018). Frequently cited scientific examples are Fleming/Dubos' discovery of the enzyme lysozyme in 1932 and penicillin from the mold Penicillium notatum in 1928, the Bell Lab scientists Arno Penzias' and Robert Wilsons' identification of cosmic background radiation and Christian Ørsted's finding that electric currents create magnet fields (Crease 1989; Murayama et al. 2015).

As a term, serendipity was coined by novelist Horace Walpole in 1754 and is based on the Persian fairy tale *The Travel and Adventures of Three Princes of Serendip*[9]. Serendipity is regarded as a particular type of discovery (along with other methods such as exploration, trial and error, or metaphoric reasoning (Stebbins 2013), in which observation, sagacity and chance come into play within a certain context (Weisenfeld 2009). Most of what we know about serendipity is based on U.S. American sociologist Robert K. Merton's work. According to his posthumous book on serendipity with Elinor Barber in 2004, sagacity can either refer to finding something of value while searching for something else or finding a solution in an unexpected place or manner (Merton and Barber 2004). Drawing on the Merton archives, which comprises hundreds of examples of serendipity, papers and countless notes, Yaqub (2018) provides a typology to accentuate different degrees of serendipity, distinguishing between the nature of the inquiry and the solution (Table 3.2).

Regardless of the type of serendipity, what is important for the process of rule-breaking market behavior is a subsequent follow-up of the serendipitous event so that it does not sink without trace, but the latent potential can be turned into an

---

[9]Serendip is the ancient name of Ceylon (now Sri Lanka) and serendipitous discovery (in the sense of making discoveries of things that they were not in quest of) is happening frequently throughout the tale. As quoted in Merton and Barber (2004), Horace Walpole wrote: "This discovery, indeed, is almost of that kind which I call Serendipity, a very expressive word, which, as I have nothing better to tell you, I shall endeavor to explain to you: you will understand it better by the derivation than by the definition. I once read a silly fairy tale, called the three Princes of Serendip: as their Highnesses traveled, they were always making discoveries, by accidents and sagacity, of things which they were not in quest of: for instance, one of them discovered that a mule blind to the right eye had traveled the same road lately, because the grass was eaten only on the left side, where it was worse than on the right—now do you understand Serendipity?" (pp. 1–2).

Table 3.2 Typology of serendipity (based on Yaqub 2018)

Solution of the given problem (the discovery leads to the solution of a given problem via an unexpected route) *"By 1837, Goodyear had been searching for a decade for a way to make rubber thermostable, when he accidentally allowed a mixture of sulphur and rubber to touch a hot stove and discovered vulcanization"* (Yaqub 2018, p. 171).	Solution of a different problem (discovery of things that the discoverers were not in search of, unanticipated and unexpected) *"In 1897, whilst searching for a way of extracting proteins from bacteria for immunization, Buchner discovered that cell-free yeast extract could still convert sugar to alcohol and carbon dioxide. This discovery proved that whole cells were not necessarily required for fermentation and thereby inaugurated the field of enzymology"* (Yaqub 2018, p. 170).
Solution of a pre-existing problem (discovery leads to a not sought-for solution because the research was un-targeted or not intended to be research) *"In 1895, Roentgen was preparing to recreate phenomena documented by Crookes, and tinker with them. In his emulation, he noticed a mysterious glow, a new form of radiation he called X-rays"* (Yaqub 2018, p. 171).	Solution of waiting for a problem (neither the problem nor the solution existed prior to the serendipitous episode) *"In 1903, Benedictus dropped a flask. The flask shattered but … the fragments of glass did not fly apart, the flask remained almost in its original shape. He found that it had a film on the inside to which the broken pieces of glass had adhered. … [that] had come from the evaporation of a solution of collodion … [inside the flask]. After the incident, Benedictus learned of automobile accidents, with serious consequences from flying glass. This was the problem for which his solution was waiting, and his non-shattering flask became safety glass"* (Yaqub 2018, p. 171).

opportunity. Often, serendipity is misunderstood as referring only to the accidental nature and the delight and surprise of an unexpected event.[10] Equally important, however, is the subsequent synthesis of the accident into insight (Fine and Deegan 1996). To account for the fact that serendipity involves both chance and sagacity, Calhoun (2004, Summer) paraphrased it into "accidental wisdom" in his book review.

Weisenfeld (2009) transfers the idea of serendipity into the context of strategic management and summarizes five crucial processual elements of an accidental discovery to become effective: accident or clue, observation (seeing), sagacity (knowing, sense making), motivation (pursuing the chance element, doing something about it), and an environment conducive to the adaption of the discovery.

---

[10]In his theory of reflective practice, Schön (1983) also elaborates on the role of surprising encounters: "Something falls outside the range of normal expectations … the practitioner allows himself to experience surprise, puzzlement or confusion in a situation, which he finds uncertain or unique. He reflects on the phenomena before him, and on the prior understandings, which have been implicit in his behaviour. He carries out an experiment that serves to generate both a new understanding of the phenomena and a change in the situation" (p. 68).

Although serendipity apparently happens randomly, it does not imply that it is not manageable. Understanding the importance of and recognizing chance elements in change processes is vital. While accidents are commonplace, they are often either overlooked (Stompff et al. 2016) or seen as detrimental to developments so that positive side effects of unplanned events are not fully harnessed. A retrospective streamlining of such serendipitous accounts of discovery in order to trace their cause, look for principles and possible use cases behind observations is considered an important mechanism, potentially leading to rule-breaking market behavior. Since serendipity is conceivably available for everyone (Stebbins 2013), the lever of those unanticipated encounters and observations can prove to be central and have far-reaching consequences for the development of breakthroughs. I am not suggesting that any serendipitous finding shall lead to a change in any initial research plan per se, but that, by weighing the options at hand regarding their expected impact on the objectives of the company, an informed managerial choice shall be made whether to pursue the accidental encounter or not.

Incompatibility Cues

Proposition 1.2 A mismatch, for example between a person and his or her environment, may trigger the process of rule-breaking market behavior.

Four of the underlying cases show a lack of fit between the athletes' physical givens and the requirements of the current technique, which, in turn, lead to the development of the rule-breaking behavior successively: Dick Fosbury felt that he was too tall to properly execute the Straddle, Albert Vande Weghe had difficulties with his heavy legs when turning, four of the analyzed early jump shooters were too small to get clear, and Miroslaw Graf reportedly opened his skis into a V-shape because he had a strained ankle.

Transferred to the organizational literature, such phenomena of compatibility or match between individuals and some aspect of their environment is being broadly discussed in "fit research"[11], which is grounded in the interactionist theory of behavior (Chatman 1989; Muchinsky and Monahan 1987). A wide range of specific fits has been investigated at different levels: personal interests versus vocational characteristics, individual values versus organizational cultures, individual preferences versus organizational systems, individual knowledge, skills, and abilities versus demands of a job, individual needs versus work-provided supplies, personality of individuals versus personality of peers or supervisors (for a review on person-environment fit, see Kristof-Brown and Guay 2011). While the domain of strategic management typically deals with fit between organizational and environmental variables, most fit research in the domain of organizational behavior incorporates individual level variables (De Castro and Brigham 2003; Kristof 1996). The

---

[11]Fit is also termed congruence (O'Reilly et al. 1991), compatibility (Cable and Parsons 2001), confluence, or similarity (Kristof 1996).

broadest level, person-environment fit, is defined as the compatibility that occurs when individual[12] and work environment characteristics are well matched (Kristof-Brown et al. 2005). Misfit, on the other hand, refers to the degree of mismatch between any such two parameters (Chan 1996). Generally, higher levels of person-environment fit are considered positive for both the organization and the individual (Kristof-Brown and Guay 2011). Consequently, the concept of fit continues to be a primary concern for a company's hiring decisions (Tomoki 2007). Cognitive style is stable, or at least only very slowly to be altered (Chan 1996). When individuals experience cognitive misfit, they tend to employ adaptive behaviors as part of their coping mechanisms. But these coping mechanisms are not sustainable; they are a source of great stress, typically making individuals return to their preferred style (Kirton 1976).

In research on creative behavior, the concept of person-organization fit has received comparatively little attention, especially when it comes to an empirical examination of the relationship (De Castro and Brigham 2003). While some scholars argue that congruence between persons and the environment in relevant dimensions positively influences creative behavior (Tierney et al. 1999), others suggest that high levels of fit might lead to a lack of innovation and strategic myopia (Kristof 1996; Schneider et al. 1995).

When focusing more on physical than behavioral misfits, as in the case of the V-Style, yet another area of interest can be mentioned: the role of people with disabilities in the context of innovation. Contrary to old myths that people with disabilities are a burden on society, inventive history provides us with various examples of people with disabilities who substantially advanced science, technology or other fields (the following three examples are taken from Girma 2017). In nineteenth century Italy, the inventor Pellegrino Turri developed one of the first working mechanical typewriters so that his blind lover Countess Carolina Fantoni da Fivizzano could send him secret love letters. In the 1980s, hearing-impaired Vinton "Vint" Cerf searched for a good alternative to communication over the phone and lead the way for creating the first commercial email service. He is widely known as one of the fathers of the Internet, and since 2005, served as a vice president and chief Internet evangelist for Google (Internet Hall of Fame n.d.). Further, blind astronomer Wanda Diaz Merced developed a non-visual system for studying stellar radiation by converting complex space data into sound (sonification). The tool to "hear the stars" also benefits non-disabled colleagues in finding patterns in the data using visual techniques in tandem with sonification (Merced 2017).[13] Such examples show that treating disabilities as a design challenge, no matter whether with regard to within-

---

[12]Personal attributes may encompass personality traits, values, cognition, beliefs, interests, and individual preferences. According to Chan (1996), organizational attributes may include the climate, culture, norms, values, structure, strategic needs, and other expectations or demands in the work environment (see also Bowen et al. 1991; Bretz et al. 1989; O'Reilly et al. 1991; Rynes and Gerhart 1990).

[13]Further examples of innovative solutions that have been designed for impaired people but were also useful in other contexts are provided by Newell and Gregor (1999).

company processes or current products on the market, might not only support the idea of diversity but also lead to spillover effects to regular markets or activities.

Another discussion on how to "deal with misfit" is taking place under the umbrella of diversity. Consistent with the "value-in-diversity" thesis in the diversity literature (Anderson et al. 2014), a line of work in innovation supports the idea that cultural diversity promotes divergence, and divergence is facilitative of creativity (Stahl et al. 2010). In an organizational innovation context, diversity is usually discussed on a group level and covers aspects such as the skills, functional or hierarchical positions, knowledge, and background of the group members (Blomberg et al. 2017). While diversity can negatively influence the creative process (e.g. by causing misinterpretation of other group members' ideas) heterogeneous groups are typically found to be more likely to develop creative ideas than homogenous groups with overlapping skills (Blomberg et al. 2017).

In summary, it is proposed that a mismatch between two parameters, such as an individual and his or her respective environment, can trigger the process of rule-breaking market behavior. Especially in times of constant (organizational) change, it appears that the idea of fit loses relevance since the environmental variable of the two parameters is constantly varying (for further information, see Caldwell et al. 2004, who study person-environment fit as an outcome of organizational change). As shown above, disabilities, as a particular kind of misfit, create a constraint, and embracing constraints can spur inventive solutions. Thus, it is suggested to reframe misfit as an opportunity and catalyst for innovation. However, this is not to imply that well-known approaches and practices to fit have become obsolete or ineffective but rather that breakthroughs may not be created with traditional organizational practices only.

Motivational Cues

Proposition 1.3 Failure, limited talent, rewards, and situational constraints may trigger the process of rule-breaking market behavior.

Looking at all sports historical cases that have been analyzed in the study, the motivation to win (or at least not to lose) appears to be a central underlying tenet of rule-breaking behavior. In current conceptualizations of creativity and innovation, motivation and so-called self-management factors (believing in one's own creative capability, e.g. self-efficacy, self-esteem, self-regulation, creative identity, self-concordant goals) are commonly accepted individual level factors that are found to have significant effects on creative and innovative performance (Anderson et al. 2014; Blomberg et al. 2017; Zhou and Shalley 2011). In his theory of creative individual action, Ford (1996) posits that an individual's overall motivation to undertake a particular course of action is determined by the interaction among goals, emotions and expectations related to those intentions. In Woodman et al.'s (1993) model, intrinsic motivation is one of the seven parameters influencing individual creativity. In both Amabile's original and updated componential theory of creativity (Amabile 1988, 1996; Amabile and Pratt 2016), motivation is considered a core construct. Traditionally, her work was based on the intrinsic motivation principle[14] only. This basic assumption has now been refined by positing that in particular situations, intrinsic and extrinsic rewards are not necessarily antagonistic, a claim that is supported by the meta-analysis of Cerasoli et al. (2014). Amabile and Pratt (2016) radically modified their componential model of innovation, acknowledging that extrinsic motivation, too, can play a positive role in the creative process. Specifically, they introduce two likely mechanisms by which extrinsic motivation potentially has additive positive effects on creativity: *"extrinsics in service of intrinsics"* (p. 176, focus on informational vs. controlling extrinsic motivators, such as recognizing value of the work with a wall of honor or funding a new pet project) and the *"motivation-work cycle match"* (p. 176, extrinsic motivation is likely to be facilitative only at certain stages of the creative process, for instance when activities might be particularly tedious). To sum up, there is general agreement that motivation is a relevant factor with influence on creativity, but there are differing views on the roles and right balance of intrinsic and extrinsic motivation (Blomberg et al. 2017).

Motivation can arise from several different sources. Four of them have been identified in the underlying sports cases and will be outlined below: competition as a catalyst, failure as a motivation to explore novel approaches, "lack of talent" as an outlet for the pursuit of unconventional ways, and the experience of resource constraints as the trigger for rule-breaking improvisation, including how to make a virtue of necessity.

Competitive events such as meets or contests reportedly played an important role for the development of the Fosbury Flop, the O'Brien ("I save my best for competition", Maule 1960, para. 9), the Jump Shot, and the Skate Skiing Technique. It may be common sense that competition can bring out the best in athletes, but whether extrinsic incentives (e.g. winning a competition) lead to higher creativity in an organizational context has been a contentious, decades-old debate (Gross 2016). On the one hand, scholars argue that the common effects of reward on performance do not apply to creativity by positing that strong extrinsic incentives impair creativity because they diminish intrinsic motivation (see Hennessey and Amabile 2010 for a review) or cause agents to choke under pressure (Ariely et al. 2009). Conti et al. (2001) summarize that negative effects of extrinsic incentives appear "when they are perceived as constraining, controlling, or when they are accompanied by negative competence information" (p. 1274). On the other hand, incentives are said to enhance creativity because they, for instance, recognize the creative individual's personal competencies or make the task more interesting or challenging (Conti et al. 2001; Eisenberger and Cameron 1996). Empirical evidence has shown support for both accounts (Bradler et al. 2016; Byron and Khazanchi 2012; Erat and Gneezy 2016; Shalley et al. 2004,

---

[14]The intrinsic motivation principle states that people are most creative when they are motivated primarily by the interest, enjoyment, satisfaction, and challenge of the work itself, and not by extrinsic pressures or motivators in the social environment (see Amabile 1996, adapted from Amabile and Pratt 2016). Extrinsic, on the other hand, refers to any motivation that arises from a source outside the work itself, including expected evaluation, contracted-for reward, external directives, or any of several other, similar sources (as stated in Amabile and Pratt 2016).

pp. 939–940). More generally, Paulus (2000) acknowledged competition to be a social stimulator that leads to high creativity in groups. Market competition, too, has been found to foster organizational innovation (Anderson et al. 2014; Damanpour 2010).

Against this background, it can be concluded that innovation prize competitions (such as "take a rule-breaking look at '___(insert e.g. product or process)___'") or other competitive mechanisms for innovation need to be handled with care. Gross (2016) states that they have to be managed properly in order to be effective (e.g. balanced competition, "too little, and high-performers lack incentive to develop new ideas; too much, and agents stop investing effort altogether", p. 19).

A second motivational cue could be failure. In organizations, failure (in contrast to success) is defined as performance that falls below (in contrast to exceeds) some aspirational level (Cyert and March 1963; March and Simon 1958). According to organizational theory, failure experience challenges the existing organizational knowledge (e.g. models of the world) and motivates the search for new ways that better represent reality (Cyert and March 1963; March and Simon 1958). Such problemistic search to close a specific gap in organizational knowledge usually comes with a sense of urgency and is, therefore, more likely to lead to the adoption of new and divergent ideas (Cameron 1984; March 1981). In short, failure can motivate organization members to correct problems, challenge assumptions, and innovate (Sitkin 1992).[15] Complete failure can, on the other hand, also end a creative process. Amabile and Pratt (2016) argue that re-engagement in the creative process usually only takes place if the setback leads to increased intrinsic motivation and learning of domain-relevant skills. For that to happen, a high degree of psychological safety is typically needed (Edmondson 1999). Psychological safety is understood as a shared sense in the group that failing and making mistakes is acceptable because those failures and mistakes are commonly treated as opportunities without derision of the individuals involved (Edmondson 1999). Creative failures are learning experiences that may lead to success in the long-run (Amabile and Pratt 2016).

As a consequence of failure being an important trigger of innovative behavior, tolerance for failure should be an essential pillar of any innovative company's culture. Levinthal and March (1993) point out that it is important for firms to provide safety nets because the fear of carrying the burden of failure in a punitive climate is likely to dampen innovative behavior. By regarding failure as an inevitable and beneficial by-product of breakthrough innovation, employees may be emboldened to engage in exploring new directions instead of sticking with the "tried and true" (Rita Gunther McGrath 1999).[16]

---

[15]From an individual differences perspective, the continuation of effortful action despite failures, impediments, or threats, either real or imagined, is referred to as persistence. Persistence entails two aspects: first, the decision to continue to pursue a particular endeavor, and second, doing so in face of opposing motivational factors (see Samuel et al. 2016 for an overview in the context of entrepreneurship).

[16]"Action is more salient than the absence of action. As a result, attributions of causality and blame are drawn to those individuals (or groups) who have acted and failed, more than to those who have failed to act. ... Problems that result from taking risks often lead to individual punishment, whereas problems that result from the avoidance of risky action are rarely traced to individuals and less often lead to punishment." (Sitkin 1992, pp. 234–235).

With regard to the age of the references, one might argue that this should by now be part of any company's cultural DNA. However, empirical evidence shows that learning from failure is the exception rather than the norm (Bennett and Snyder 2017; Edmondson 2011; McGrath 2011). Amabile and Pratt (2016), for instance, report that a high degree of psychological safety was rare in their comprehensive diary study conducted across 26 teams in a chemicals firm. Also, more than 10 years after her seminal article on psychological safety, Edmondson (2011) quotes: "When I ask executives to … estimate how many of the failures in their organizations are truly blameworthy, their answers are usually in single digits—perhaps 2–5%. But when I ask how many are *treated* as blameworthy, they say (after a pause or a laugh) 70–90%. The unfortunate consequence is that many failures go unreported and their lessons are lost" (p. 50). An extreme case of mitigating minor mistakes leading to (late) learning from extreme failure is provided by the National Aeronautics and Space Administration (NASA). When they launched their 113th space shuttle *Columbia* on January 16, 2003, a piece of foam broke off and struck the orbiter's left wing. Upon reentering the earth's atmosphere after the 16-day mission, the damaged left wing failed and caused the disintegration of the space shuttle. None of *Columbia*'s crew of seven survived. The failure disrupted NASA's long history of successful launches, which had lead the company's decision makers to "flawed decision making, self-deception, introversion, and a diminished curiosity about the world" (CAIB 2003, p. 102). Before, smaller anomalous events had failed to change the status quo, but the disaster triggered massive rethinking (example and reference adapted from Madsen and Desai 2010).

In the article, *Failing by Design*, McGrath (2011) provides normative recommendations on helpful mechanisms to implement the idea of intelligent failure:

> You should decide what success and failure would look like before you start a project. Document your initial assumptions, test and revise them as you go, and convert them into knowledge. Fail fast—the longer something takes, the less you'll learn-and fail cheaply, to contain your downside risk. Limit the number of uncertainties in new projects, and build a culture that tolerates, and sometimes even celebrates, failure. Finally, codify and share what you learn. These principles won't give you a means of avoiding all failures down the road-that's simply not realistic. They will help you use small losses to attain bigger wins over time. (p. 137)

In their research on the recombination of routines for creative efficiency, Cohendet and Simon (2016) also refer to the "fail faster" principle, which is in common practice in firms such as IDEO and IBM. To do so, they specifically promote a culture of risk taking and quick learning through sharing, probing and testing ideas locally without waiting for formal validation by top management.

In brief, even though there are differences between the responsibilities and consequences athletes and employees have to face when failing (e.g. athletes are mostly responsible for their own fate whereas employees act on behalf of the company), the literature shows that a transfer of this case-based insight is legitimate and necessitated. If companies intend to get to rule-breaking market behavior, it appears to be important that the negative affect associated with failure is mitigated. Reinterpreting failure as learning and as an important type of progress helps in creating an environment with a high degree of psychological safety conducive to rule-breaking market behavior. Stories[17] such as Thomas Edison's quote "I have not failed, I've just found 10,000 ways that won't work" (p. 178) are potentially crucial tools in facilitating the reinterpretation of failure as learning and preventing irrational perseveration (as cited in Amabile and Pratt 2016). It is likely to assume that at one point or another in the pursuit of rule-breaking behavior, failure will play a role, which is why fostering intelligent failure throughout the organization (failing cheap and fast, and not making the same mistake twice) appears to be a much more realistic and supportive framework. Disguising mistakes and failed attempts of any kind prevent the organization from analyzing the causes and origins and, therefore, mitigates possible paths to rule-breaking market behavior (and may lead to serious consequences, as shown in the NASA case).

Third, what has been summarized under lack of talent might be another cue to open up novel ways of behaving. Jan Boklöv developed a rule-breaking behavior in ski jumping despite (or maybe because) he was not considered very talented. In the literature, talent refers to "a native aptitude for some special kind of work and implies a relatively quick and easy acquisition of a particular skill within a domain" (Genius 2018, para. 5). Talent in an organizational context are, for instance, related to discussions regarding human capital, defined as the knowledge, skills, and abilities residing with and utilized by individuals (Schultz 1961). In the domain of innovation research, talent belongs to the category of individual level variables, usually referred to as abilities (e.g. networking ability, creative-thinking capabilities; for exemplary studies see Baer 2012; Choi et al. 2009). Amabile and Pratt (2016) specify that creativity and innovation each require three components: basic resources or raw materials, a set of processes or skills for combining these in novel ways, and a driver. Each component includes both relatively stable and relatively amenable elements. Domain-relevant talents are, together with an individual's expertise or factual knowledge and technical skills for doing work, subsumed under basic raw material. Thus, it is suggested, that a putative lack of talent does not necessarily prevent individuals from rule-breaking market behavior but may even be facilitative (e.g. when it leads to increased intrinsic motivation for being creative). This could, for instance, lead to a re-thinking when hiring employees, building teams, allocating tasks and assigning responsibilities.

The experience of resource constraints is the fourth specificity in the case study that has been subsumed under the umbrella of potential motivational forces leading to the recognition of a new way to behave. The competitive cross-country skiing situation in which Siitonen applied a precursor of the Skate Skiing technique is particularly characteristic of that. After he had problems with his waxing in the classical technique, he improvised and went on with a skating-like style. In common parlance, the expression "necessity is the mother of innovation" would be used to describe the situation, and pertinent research, too, suggests that constraints can stimulate creative behavior (Keupp and Gassmann 2013; Weiss et al. 2011). While it has typically been argued that

---

[17]See Shalley and Perry-Smith (2001) for insight on how creativity can be stimulated by exposure to creative examples and models.

resource constraints, such as financial, knowledge, and time constraints (Baer and Oldham 2006; Byron et al. 2010), have an inhibiting effect on creativity and innovation (e.g. Amabile 1996; Damanpour 1991), another perspective suggests that organizations less well endowed with resources are more likely to explore new trajectories, especially when they operate in competitive environments (Keupp and Gassmann 2013). Keupp and Gassmann (2013) list several studies that have shown that radical innovation "can be developed efficiently despite—or even *because of*—resource constraints" (p. 1457). Much has been written about improvisation in both everyday situations of discovery and crisis situations, "where time is an obvious scarce resource and spontaneity is at a premium" (Dusya and Crossan 2005, p. 205). The difference with behaving à l'improviste or all'improvviso, is that the attention is focused on the very moment when things take shape (Dusya and Crossan 2005). Thus, improvisation is characterized by spontaneity and a realtime nature (Weick 1998). Improvisation has been identified as a key area of new development in the field of innovation (Poolton and Ismail 2000). More on improvisation as "Making Do" and "Letting Go" can be learned from Dusya and Crossan (2005).

Affective Cues

Proposition 1.4 Frustration or other negatively connoted emotion may trigger the process of rule-breaking market behavior.

Dick Fosbury was frustrated and at times the worst athlete in his team; he was just trying not to lose. O'Brien developed the new shot put technique right after he came home from a defeat, and with some of the early jump shooters, their first attempt has reportedly also been directly triggered by (a series of) frustrating individual losses. In the literature, the most commonly used expressions for such examples of emotional phenomena are affect, mood, and emotion (Baas et al. 2008). Affect is the most general term and refers to a subjective feeling state that includes both long-lasting mood states (e.g. cheerfulness or depression) and specific mood states (e.g. happiness or anger) (Frijda 1993). Mood and emotion are regarded as subtypes of affect, with emotions, in comparison to mood, being more strongly directed toward a specific stimulus. For example, Parry O'Brien was probably angry and frustrated because he got defeated (emotion) and not just generally grumpy for no specific reason (mood). The link between affect and creativity has been widely studied and highly debated (Amabile and Pratt 2016; Blomberg et al. 2017). The traditional research approach predominantly investigated positive dimensions of affect as antecedents to creativity (Amabile and Pratt 2016; Zhou and Shalley 2011), with Alice Isen as a particularly active scholar in this arena (see, for instance, Isen 1999a, b; Isen et al. 1987, 1985). While many studies revealed a positive relationship between positive affect and creativity, not all studies confirmed this relationship. Some organizational theorists, for instance, have introduced mechanisms by which negative affect is facilitative of creativity (for more details on research regarding the relationship between affect and creativity, see Amabile and

Pratt 2016). Broadly speaking, in that context negative affect is said to alert employees to problems, to focus on the current situation instead of their preexisting assumptions, and to exert high levels of effort to make improvements (for further references, see Amabile and Pratt 2016; George and Zhou 2007; Zhou and Shalley 2011). Positive moods, on the other hand, are posited to allow employees to be playful with ideas, facilitate divergent thinking and unusual associations, enhance willingness to take risks and explore novel ways of doing things (ibid.).

Not just focused on affect alone but with a more general regard to negative emotional dimensions, Anderson et al. (2004) suggest in their review on the innovation literature's state-of-the-science, that distress-related variables such as negative mood states, job dissatisfaction, role conflict and ambiguity (individual level), intergroup competition, minority dissent and task-related conflict (group level), turbulent environment, reduced slack and budget deficiencies (organizational level), trigger innovation by stimulating novel ways of doing something. But again, empirical evidence on the relations between negatively connoted events and creativity is sparse (Zhou and Shalley 2011). In his meta-analysis, Davis (2009) predominantly focuses on the effects of positive mood an creativity. All in all, there seems to be common agreement that much research is needed in order to better understand the conditions under which different types of affect might positively or negatively influence the creativity and innovation process (Amabile and Pratt 2016).

Relatedly, Clancy et al. (2012) refer to the paradoxical tension surrounding disappointment and how creativity can be sustained when facing fears and anxieties about failure and disintegration. They argue that while the "existing literature usually frames disappointment as a potential threat to organizational effectiveness and morale and as something that needs to be managed and controlled. ... it can also, however, be a potential source of creativity, learning and renewal" (Clancy et al. 2012, pp. 518, 519). Amabile and Pratt (2016) further point out that "finding creative work meaningful (positive and significant) may be paramount in helping individuals who are experiencing negative outcomes—whether from setbacks or negative feedback—to persist in their creative endeavors" (p. 174).

More generally, frustration has been addressed in discussions regarding the process perspective of innovation. Some authors have suggested that frustration occurs when the analytic mind reaches its limit, stops actively dealing with the problem and, consequently, induces the incubation phase (Lubart 2001). A "point of creative frustration" (p. 24) between incubation and the moment of illumination has also been referred to by Sapp (1992).

Despite existing controversies in the literature, the underlying cases give evidence for the positive role that negative affect can play in the process of rule-breaking market behavior. It is, therefore, concluded that both positive and negative affect can be functional for creativity in the workplace. While a deliberate provocation of constructive controversy (e.g. by trying to induce stress) does not appear to be the first-choice implication to be made, this insight may certainly help to positively reframe (e.g. frustration as a catalyst, for more information on reframing, see section "Reframing" and overcome stages of frustration and anger in the pursuit of innovation.

Cognitive Cues

Proposition 1.5 Both deep and broad knowledge search trajectories may indicate a
way to rule-breaking market behavior.

Knowledge is considered a crucial precondition for creativity (e.g. Amabile 1996;
Mumford et al. 2012; Woodman et al. 1993).[18] Organizational knowledge can be
interpreted as an organization's internal representation of the world (Daft and Weick
1984), as the set of expectations and assumptions held about the cause-and-effect
linkages in the underlying domain of activity (Huber 1991; Walsh and Ungson 1991).

   Both negative and positive effects of existing knowledge on creativity have been
identified. On the one hand, previous knowledge or experience might cause functional fixedness (Woodman et al. 1993) or result in more habitual thinking (Ford
1996), which consequently prevents individuals from creative solutions. On the
other hand, creative behavior cannot occur without knowledge, as "Invention is
little more than a new combination of those images which have been previously
gathered and deposited in the memory. Nothing can be made of nothing. He who has
laid up no material can produce no combination" (Sir Joshua Reynolds, 1732–1792;
quoted in Woodman et al. (1993, p. 301). Accordingly, many theories of creative
process suggest that creation rarely ever "occurs *de novo*" (p. 1) but rather is a
combination of previously available ideas (Verhaeghen et al. 2017). With specific
regard to breakthrough innovation, too, it has oftentimes been suggested that it
results from recombining different streams or pieces of knowledge in novel ways
(for a range of references, see Perra et al. 2017). The pursuit of deep search
trajectories can be conducive to innovation as well (Davis and Eisenhardt 2011;
Dosi 1982; Fleming 2001; Katila and Ahuja 2002).

   Two categories of knowledge that promote creativity can be distinguished:
knowledge of the domain in which one is operating and intends to create and
knowledge of other domains, which can be useful (e.g. for creating analogies)
(Smith et al. 2000). When looking at the rule-breaking sports cases, the development
of the new styles has been facilitated separately by the depth and breadth of the
athletes' knowledge. Here, breadth refers to the spectrum of knowledge domains,
whereas depth characterizes the knowledge regarding each domain. The notion of
depth will be further addressed below, and breadth will be reviewed in the course of
the experiential cue afterwards.

   The most prevalent example of how deep domain-related knowledge and experience can provide the starting point for rule-breaking behavior has been provided by
the Fosbury Flop. Dick Fosbury did not establish his new style from scratch but
reverted to the former, less effective Scissors high jumping technique that was
modified into the Fosbury Flop. He built his idea on the basis of his own deep
existing knowledge and experience. His individual expertise was critical for the

---

[18]In the strategy literature, the knowledge-based view of the firm is a central paradigm positing that
an organization's knowledge resources are important determinants of sustained competitive advantage (Eisenhardt and Santos 2006; Grant 1996; Spender 1996).

change or recombination of the existing approach into a novel application. Similar with the Skating technique and the Forward Seat: the new styles were not completely new. Lapp skiers had used a precursory variant of the Skating style in ancient times and other alpine sports had employed a similar technique; Native Americans already rode in a manner comparable to the Forward Seat. That is, the seemingly novel styles simply lay forgotten, were unrecognized or neglected. Comparable examples of seemingly novel ways to behave, which at a closer look had not actually been new at all can also be traced down in the inventive history of business and science. Leonardo Da Vinci's scientific discoveries were sealed off from society for two centuries and had, therefore, been forgotten and unused for a long time (White 2000, p. XII). Electric cars were first designed at the end of the nineteenth century and were only revived years later under different socio-cultural circumstances (Sluiter 2017). For whichever reasons once existing knowledge becomes dormant, the afore-stated examples reveal that it can be functional for the development of breakthroughs to look back, to have a sense of history. Especially in times of fast-rotating leadership, valuable knowledge and experience may not always be passed on. Moreover, antiquated and abandoned routes ("old styles") are potential outlets to be considered for the creation of new ideas. The discovery of the past (e.g. regarding former behavioral standards or unsuccessful attempts to change existing behavioral standards) can be a fruitful starting point for future rule-breaking market behavior.

Differences among individuals comprising deep versus broad knowledge have for instance been prominently discussed in works contrasting generalists versus specialists and experts versus novices. The classic conceptualization of the proverbial multifaceted renaissance man, also referred to as one-man multidisciplinarian (Pettitt 2015), a person with deep expertise in many different domain areas, seems to be an ideal difficult to achieve (Boh et al. 2014). According to Melero and Palomeras (2015), the majority of innovators are narrow specialists. It has been argued, that generalist inventors with a broad knowledge set make a particularly valuable contribution to the development of innovations in uncertain contexts (i.e. where the procedures for solving problems are not clearly established Melero and Palomeras 2015, p. 155). This is due to the idea that generalists expectedly have a comparative advantage over specialists in combining different knowledge elements. Thus, teams including generalist inventors have been found to produce more economically relevant innovations in high-uncertainty contexts, whereas comparable teams produce less economically relevant innovations in low-uncertainty contexts (Melero and Palomeras 2015). Experts and novices, too, differ with regard to creativity and innovation relevant parameters: for example, they differ in their decision making (Shanteau 1992a, b) and problem solving (Larkin et al. 1980). Expertise alters the perceptual experience (Kukla 2013, p. 441). A trained musician, for instance, is said to perceive, "in any composition whether great or mundane, a structure, development, and rationale that is lost on the untrained ear" (Churchland 1988, p. 179). There are different perspectives on whether and to which extent mastery of a specific domain helps creative performance. It is often concluded that expertise may very well be a necessary but not sufficient condition for creativity (e.g. Simonton 2003). However, "too much expertise" (p. 229) has also been argued to possibly turn out to be detrimental for creative activity (Simonton 2003) because expertise may lead to increased inflexibility and narrowness in thinking and action (referred to as "cognitive entrenchment" by Dane 2010). In their work on expert performance in chess, Chase and Simon (1973) discovered that players need approximately a decade of practice before great achievement, which, as later on confirmed, is related to creative activity in several domains and lays the foundation to reach a level of "creative greatness" (for an overview, see Glăveanu 2017; quote as in Kaufman and Kaufman 2007, p. 114). "In order to function well within the creative system, one must internalize the rules of the domain and the opinions of the field" (Csikszentmihalyi 1999, p. 332). Amabile et al. (1996) postulate the interactive character between both domain-general and domain-specific skills in the course of creative action.

One particular aspect in which experts and novices tend to differ is abstract thinking (Chi et al. 1981, who have also underscored the creative problem-solving benefit of abstract thinking). They found that novice students tended to classify problems on the basis of the domain's elementary properties, whereas experts, on the contrary, tended to classify the same problems on the basis of theoretical or shared principles of the domain. Thus, the experts' abstractions represent higher order theoretical summaries or simplifications of problems.

To conclude, it does not seem to be a binary issue of preferring generalists over specialists or novices over experts. Cases can be made for either one of them. The literature seems to converge towards balancing depth and breadth accordingly. One way to do so and solve the tension is provided by ambidexterity theory. While this cannot be conclusively outlined in the scope of this work, it can be summarized that both deep and broad knowledge are important to support the process of rule-breaking market behavior. With the help of the sports cases, the consideration of seemingly antiquated and abandoned or simply forgotten ways from the past has been outlined to be a potential avenue for the creation of novel behaviors.

Experiential Cues

Proposition 1.6 Experience in another domain and/or distance to the problem space may help identifying a way to rule-breaking market behavior.

> Remember to look up at the stars and not down at your feet, try to make sense of what you see . . . be curious.—quoted from Stephen Hawking's last message

While cognitive cues are conceptualized to be more focused on domain-related deep search trajectories, experiential cues are conceptualized to be stronger related to the breadth end of the search spectrum. The sports cases have given insight into three particular ways to rule-breaking behavior, which have been summarized under this theme: prior experience in another area, being actively open for different perspectives and approaches, and having developed the technique outside the realm of professional athleticism.

Across the sports cases, several accounts have been found where the athletes had either seen or experienced a similar technique in a different domain or unrelated context before. Albert Vande Weghe applied a tuck position he had previously learned in diving, Siitonen had employed a move similar to the Skating-technique in ski orienteering, some jump shooters brought serious leaping abilities with them and one of them had experienced a convention change before in Lacrosse. At some point, Tod Sloan saw another jockey ride in a Forward Seat and Armbruster had watched another swimmer demonstrate a fish kick many years earlier. Similar connections of knowledge or experiences from apparently unrelated domains have led to innovative solutions in the business context as well (examples adapted from Haas and Ham 2015). By connecting ideas from traditional banking with ideas from the supermarket business, Merill Lynch revolutionized retail brokerage. The Reebok Pump basketball shoe was created by combining conventional shoe design with medical device technologies, such as inflatable splints and intravenous bags. Scientists at MIT connected e-commerce data mining algorithms used in book recommendations to predict crystal structures of materials. More revolutionary, the Phage Group integrated physics and biology leading to the molecular biology revolution and the formation of a whole new discipline (Griffith and Mullins 1972).

It is widely acknowledged that the development of breakthrough innovation can often be characterized by the recombination of ideas from distant, previously disconnected domains (Abernathy and Clark 1985; Nelson and Winter 1982; Weick 1979). This could possibly be achieved in many ways (e.g. cooperation, consultancies, interdisciplinary research) but there is another, more simple approach that often is not fully exhausted: making use of intra-company potentials by accessing employees' peripheral knowledge. While the importance of employees' knowledge that is directly related to the job or the task has been widely recognized in innovation research (Bunderson and Sutcliffe 2002; Hambrick et al. 1996), less attention has been given to an individual's or team's other areas of expertise and experience outside the organization's core domain (Haas and Ham 2015).

As it has been the case with the above-mentioned rule-breakers in the domain of sports, individuals in firms, too, typically bring with them knowledge in seemingly irrelevant domains that could be used for the development of rule-breaking solutions. Such knowledge is referred to as peripheral knowledge by Haas and Ham (2015) and can come from several sources: other professional and educational expertise (e.g. work as a yoga teacher or ski instructor, university degree in a different domain), distinct personal experience (e.g. medical knowledge through particular illnesses, cultural and geographical insights through travel or foreign exchanges), hobbies and personal interests (e.g. athletic, artistic, or mechanical skills), and other habits or activities leading to exposure to a particular domain (e.g. activities with kids or social connection to family, friends or acquaintances of certain professions with unique sets of knowledge and experience). In order to not only access the resulting wide variety of knowledge but explicitly recognize relevant aspects, Haas and Ham (2015) suggest using the mechanism of analogical reasoning and "translate such analogical exemplars into an assemblage that can function in their local environment" (Glaser 2017, p. 2145).

Two other specific instances in the sports cases are closely related to the general idea of peripheral experience but highlight yet another aspect that can be potentially important for the process of rule-breaking market behavior: the innovator's distance to the task domain or problem space. Many different scholarly discussions under a diverse array of terms like perspective, proximity versus distance, freedom, and familiarity are related to this.

The particular case of Parry O'Brien can be associated with openness to different perspectives and learning orientation. Whenever Parry O'Brien studied different philosophical schools of thought, did yoga and pursued several religions, he distanced himself from the domain of shot put and gained a novel perspective. Perspective shifting can inspire the rearrangement of prevalent concepts and lead to radically new ways of solving a problem (Amabile 1988). Innovation thrives by looking at one problem from several different angles. In the context of strategic change, Hamel (1996) used the aphorism "perspective is worth 50 IQ points" (p. 79), pointing out that helping individuals to look at the world through different lenses can be crucial for the creation of revolutions. "What one sees from the mountaintop is quite different from what one sees from the plain" (Hamel 1996, p. 80). Openness to experience has been found to be a personality trait positively related to creativity across several domains (Anderson et al. 2014; Feist 1998). The predictor is usually associated with the Five Factor Model that captures to which extent individuals are broad-minded, curious, imaginative, and original (Costa and McCrae 2008; McCrae 1987). They seek out new and varied experiences, are in quest of unfamiliar situations and, therefore, have access to a variety of ideas and perspectives (McCrae and Costa 1997). One typical way of perspective changing is multicultural experience. In a series of studies, Leung et al. (2008) show that exposure to multiple cultures can foster creativity in several ways: broadening the range of accessible ideas and concepts used in problem solving, helping to realize that the same form can have different functions and implications, weakening and questioning established associations, increasing the willingness to look for ideas from diverse outlets, and building cognitive complexity.

It is widely acknowledged that creative acts seem to require a certain independence from rules, restrictions, and maybe even close social relationships (Harrison and Rouse 2014). The link between creativity and freedom has deep intellectual roots, discussed by Aristotle, Hobbes and Locke, Epicurius and Kant, to name but a few (Harrison and Rouse 2014; Rose 1997). When one of the early jump shooters started leaping in the air as a child, he acted completely independent from basketball rules and conventions. And when Volney Wilson developed the Dolphin Kick, even though he was not a professional swimmer, he presumably also had a certain distance to the habits and typical practices in the aquatic domain.

With regard to current innovation research, the idea of creative freedom is typically discussed in the context of work autonomy (e.g. Hammond et al. 2011) or independence as personality variable associated with creative work (see Ford 1996 for a range of further references). In their review, Blomberg et al. (2017) sum up that providing employees with sufficient freedom and autonomy has been mostly discussed as a driving force of creative behavior. When individuals work in a supportive, nonthreatening, and challenging environment they will invest more, are more willing to take risks, more open to new ideas and opinions, and adopt a more explorative thinking style by which they are actively looking for possible alternatives and improvements (Amabile 1996; Shalley and Zhou 2008). However, too much freedom and autonomy may become a barrier (e.g. when task complexity leads to a reliance on mental shortcuts) so that finding a suitable balance between freedom and control for the specific task is important (Blomberg et al. 2017).

In summary, a number of lessons for the process of rule-breaking market behavior can be taken away from the above discussion related to experiences in the broadest sense. The following outline of possible means is far away from being exhaustive but is intended to serve as a source for developing and incorporating mechanisms related to experiential cues into a particular corporate context. First of all, the broad pool of employees' experience in peripheral domains can be the starting point of break-through ideas and should, therefore, be more strongly supported and used. Analogical reasoning can be used as a tool to transfer relevant elements from one domain to the other. Both deep (as discussed in the context of cognitive cues) and broad search trajectories (as addressed in the above discussion) can be the starting point for creative ideas. Thus, balancing instead of just focusing on individual profiles according to breadth and depth may be helpful.

Another way to cue rule-breaking market behavior is to go on physical and mental journeys, above and beyond daily business. Distance from the taken-for-granted assumptions, processes, rules and standards can, for instance, be gained by a guided monthly trip to the metaphorical moon. This might help people see with new eyes and should necessarily include relating the lessons learned back to the original domain and problems at hand. Another way to encourage creative solutions to a problem is to provide employees with a certain amount of freedom and independence to determine which procedures should be used to carry out a task. As long as the goal will be achieved with equal or, in a long-term view, preferably with a better input-output ratio, any fresh approach should be appreciated ("this is what we are aiming for" instead of "this is how we do it"). A particular use case is the onboarding process of new employees. It is generally acknowledged that when an outsider comes in with an open mind and different prior interests, it can lead to very illuminating results. When the usual approach to a problem is unknown, it is easier to come up with a different and maybe rule-breaking solution ("principle autodidact"). While it is commonsense to provide new employees with the best possible introduction to the values, goals, and relevant processes at the company, it should be considered equally important to reverse the process, making use of the fresh and unbiased perspectives (reverse onboarding).

Cultural Cues

Proposition 1.7 Questioning dysfunctional culturally imposed behavioral standards may indicate a way to rule-breaking market behavior.

All that is the work of the human hand, the whole world of culture, is distinguished from the natural world because it is a product of human imagination and creativity based on imagination. L.S. Vygotsky (as quoted in Smolucha 1992, p. 52)

Without wanting to degrade the many positive functions of culture, the sports cases have shown that the pursuit of a more "natural" rather than culturally accepted way can be a fruitful path to rule-breaking market behavior. Emphasizing different aspects each, this mainly derives from three of the underlying cases: swimming (Dolphin Kick), equestrian (Forward Seat), and basketball (Jump Shot). Two different potential catalysts of rule-breaking behavior have been identified: (1) consulting nature as a source of inspiration and (2) identifying dysfunctional cultural behaviors as a starting point for the development of more meaningful approaches.

The dolphin kick in swimming has been directly derived from the dolphin's movement, that is, nature served as a source of inspiration. From the perspective of human engineers, "nature's genius has been the common wisdom for almost 2500 years" (p. 10) and one may even argue that in several instances "nature is the ultimate designer, the gold standard" (Vogel 1999, p. 10). For instance, the chain saw is very much comparable to the mandibles of certain beetles, Velcro was inspired by the attachment mechanism found in burr seeds (Vogel 1999), micro robots that can walk on water mimic the locomotion of the basilisk lizard, the way a gecko's foot adheres to several surfaces has been used for the development of dry adhesives, and lotus leafs inspired the design of self-cleaning materials (the last three examples are taken from Vattam et al. 2009). Apart from these more technological specimens, also consider coffee as a concrete example. Coffee is a fruit, and the coffee bean is the seed of that fruit. When naturally brewed, coffee has a reddish color. When coffee is black, it means that the beans have been burnt to give us the roasted flavor we are used to. Thus, what most of the European coffee drinkers experience when sipping a brew is the taste of the roast and not of the naturally flavorful coffee bean. "Coffee definitely doesn't taste like 'coffee'. Coffee tastes like Bolivia or Natural or Burundi or Washed. It tastes like the country it comes from" (Linus Köster, owner of Törnqvist Hamburg, as quoted by Brose 2018, in section "Törnqvist's ethics of coffee"). The idea of being more faithful to the coffee bean, by, for instance, not burning it, provides a completely different and more natural customer experience that goes totally against the culturally imposed way of how coffee should look and taste like.

While, of course, not any novelty in the world of human artifacts can be based on natural models, "people still have much to learn from nature, simply because nature, for whatever its reasons, has gone about things differently" (Vogel 1999, p. 12). Ancient Greek philosopher Aristotle wrote, "If one way be better than another, that you may be sure is nature's way". And Albert Einstein suggested, "Look deep into nature, and then you will understand everything better." With this in mind, in the quest of discovering rule-breaking market behavior, it may be effective to think of what a more natural way could be[19] to solve customers' problems, both from a

---

[19]From a cognitive psychology perspective the idea of pursuing 'natural' approaches might seem paradox when considering that creativity itself is not assumed to be a natural process but rather goes against the original purpose of the brain, which is to establish and use routine patterns (De Bono 1995).

process and from a product perspective. Taking nature as an analogy, looking at nature's patterns and immersing in natural settings might be a helpful source of inspiration.

Closely related but yet different is the "cultural" lesson that can be learned from the Forward Seat. It has been shown that the classical way of riding a horse in equestrian was impairment to the animal's movement. After having studied how horses behave in freedom, the position of the rider changed from the culturally imposed way in which the rider was controlling the horse to the more natural Forward Seat where rider and horse "cooperate" more smoothly. In an organizational context, too, situations in which different parties are involved in the process of value creation are prevalent: Instead of a partnership between animal and human we can find manager-employee relationships, company-consumer interactions, buyer-seller relations, personality-type-A-colleague—personality-type-B-colleague cooperation, or man-machine interfaces to name but a few.

Each of those "value creation partnerships" can be characterized by dysfunctional asymmetries that may inhibit one of the collaborative partner's potential and, therefore, lead to less effective outcomes in consequence. With specific regard to innovation, this is discussed in the context of leadership style and coworker behaviors. Employees who receive supportive and non-controlling supervision, either by their colleagues or their responsible manager, are more likely to be intrinsically motivated, which is positively related to creativity (Zhou and Shalley 2011). Anther, non-innovation literature stream addressing a similar issue is the principal-agent theory (e.g. Eisenhardt 1989).

In consequence, it might be reasonable to analyze internal and external human relationships in the corporate context by observing the other parties' natural behavior. In case the collaboration is characterized by culturally imposed asymmetries, it could be assessed if this is functional with regard to the outcome (can creativity take place? are certain agents exploited at the expense of positive goal-related traits or behaviors?) and, for the sake of a more positive environment for the development of rule-breaking market behavior, be changed or refined accordingly.

A second occurrence of dysfunctional cultural behavior has been identified with the help of the Jump Shot case. From a current perspective, jumping in basketball seems a very obvious, natural movement for a ball game. Completely staying on the floor, however, without question occurs to be a barrier to the full exploitation of physical possibilities. This has most certainly not been the case in the early twentieth century, when the first basketballers started jumping and by that deviating from the cultural law that almost served like a commandment at that time. What shall be directed attention to is the origin of such behavioral standards. The question is, why do people, groups, institutions or societies behave the way they do. Without further elaborating on the literature explaining how traditions form over time, it seems reasonable to summarize that there are many ways and many reasons how and why behavioral conducts emerge in the first place. The origins do not necessarily have to be reasonable or meaningful (anymore) to still be entrenched in our everyday lives. Maybe just a legend, but yet a very illustrative example for the many roots of behavioral standards is provided by the history of Bolivian Aymara women's bowler hats. There are multiple versions about how the bowler hat arrived to Bolivia and became such a meaningful tradition. One of the most accepted stories tells that the bowler hat got to Bolivia from Europe and was originally intended for male English railway workers. Instead, since the hats were manufactured in the wrong size, it is said that the owner sold them to the *cholitas* by promising the hats would bring them fertility (Keefe 2016). Bowler hats or other kinds of traditional clothing typically do not do any harm, which is why there may not be an objective need to change the tradition. In a corporate context, however, there may be cultural behaviors that might not be meaningful (anymore). Therefore, despite culture being deeply ingrained with values, norms and artifacts oftentimes only slowly to be altered, behavioral standards should be identified and objectively re-evaluated from time to time.

Functional Cues

Proposition 1.8 Dysfunctional attributes of the current solution to a problem may trigger the process of rule-breaking market behavior.

Apparent negative parameters or dysfunctional characteristics of the current solution to a problem have been observed to be the starting point for the development of a different and better approach in some of the sports cases: poor wax and poor terrain in Cross-Country Skiing, a horse's pain in Equestrian, and having difficulties of getting clear in Basketball, caused some athletes to rethink, engage in the search for and apply a technique that may be better suited.

This is closely related to discussions on what has long been recognized as the fundamental construct in marketing and the basis for all marketing activity: the creation of customer value (Woodruff 1997). Basically, customer value is composed of two parameters: what customers "get" in relation to what they have to "give up" (Zeithaml 1988).

In order for a company to maximize the value, unresolved or badly solved customer problems have to be identified (problem finding) and addressed (problem solving). In the context of creativity, Amabile (1996) notes, "a product or response will be judged as creative to the extent that . . . it is both a novel and appropriate, useful, correct or valuable response to the task at hand" (p. 35). Thus, the greater the perceived novelty and appropriateness of the solution, the greater the potential value to the user (Lepak et al. 2007). If, however, the solution is not appropriate to create customer value, or has shortcomings in certain contexts, it is likely that the search for less flawed solutions going along with better customer value may be initiated.

This process is also referred to as identification of customer pain points. "Pain points reflect customer's core concerns, main interests and emergent needs for products" (p. 102), they are not physical but emotional, caused by customer's dissatisfaction because certain expectations or needs are not fulfilled by market offerings (Wang et al. 2016). The pains that annoy, frustrate or make customers uncomfortable usually result from deficiencies, shortcomings, problems, or defects of the market offering (ibid.). To "use" pain points as the starting point for the development of rule-breaking market behavior, several mechanisms can be applied: effective complaint management, monitoring customer feedback, market research (e.g. user observation, social media monitoring), and company-internal issue tracking, to name a few. In that context, Homburg and Fürst (2007) hint at the natural human tendency of playing blind, deaf, and dumb in order to avoid recognizing unpleasant aspects of reality by citing a story rooted in Japanese folklore, tracing back as far as the late Muromachi period (1333–1568): the tale of the three monkeys (saru) who clasp both hands over eyes, ears, or mouth, thus not seeing (mizaru), not hearing (kikazaru), or not speaking (iwazaru) evil.

In addition, what has been subsumed under "physics explanation" in the domain of sports may also be thought of as being related to discussions under value creation in business. Many novel techniques have been based on biomechanical logic even though the athletes may not have been aware of that by the time of their discovery. The center of gravity, for instance, played a role in the Fosbury Flop, Forward Seat and V-Style. Biomechanics in sports is the science concerned with the mechanics of human movement and incorporates a detailed analysis of sportive motions to reduce the risk of injury and improve sports performance (Knudson 2007). Important biomechanical principles are, for instance, forces and torques, Newton's Laws of Motion, momentum, center of gravity, and balance (Knudson 2007). A precise equivalent in business is not clear, but would, like physical principles in biological systems, always be naturally true when operating in a market. Yet, there are, for instance, basic underlying logic of how markets function and how value is created, which could be thought of as the business analogue. It shall be noted, that it is not intended to stretch the business-sports analogy too far. Clear physical boundaries as in sports simply do not exist in the context of business. However, it is considered worthwhile to ponder what the equivalent to basic laws of human movement in a company's market would be. Maybe there are fundamental assumptions and mechanisms that generally count and should not be deviated from, maybe this could even be interpreted as the interface to discussions regarding technological facets of innovation.

External Cues

Proposition 1.9 Changes in the external environment may trigger or enable the process of rule-breaking market behavior.

Although this work is explicitly focusing on the deviation from endogenous rules (see Sect. 2.1.2 for an explanation), the case analysis has shown that a strict exclusion of external or exogenous factors is not meaningful and will, therefore, be briefly addressed as a contrast and amendment to the other endogenous cues. While the development of the rule-breaking behavior in neither of the underlying cases was initially triggered by changes in the environment they nevertheless were an enabling factor, especially with the Fosbury Flop, in which the use of new technology (i.e. landing pits) had been incorporated in the formal set of rules and, therefore, enabled jumps, which required the athletes to land on their backs.

External changes, such as significant transformations in environmental, societal, geo-political, economic, technological, and regulatory conditions, are commonly considered driving forces of organizational innovation and change processes (e.g. Utterback 1994, on how companies can seize opportunities in the face of technological change). To give just three broad ranging examples, deregulation in the financial services and airline industries caused a line of mergers and failures in the process of firms reorienting themselves in the new competitive environment. Similarly, the advent of the European Union along with the emergence of stronger global competition has changed the basic foundations of competition in the auto-mobile and electronics industries (Tushman and O'Reilly 1996). Third, the digital transformation enabled new value creation for companies that had not been possible before. To quote Fagerberg (2006), "a central finding in the innovation literature is that a firm does not innovate in isolation, but depends on extensive interaction with its environment" (p. 20). On an individual level, too, external factors are combined with internal processes, such as with Lewin's (1935, p. 73) expression, $B = f(P, E)$, where behavior is a function of both person and environment.

While companies direct efforts at impacting external developments in various ways (e.g. regulatory issues are addressed by industry lobbying, campaign contributions or government membership on company boards; for reviews, see e.g. Hillman et al. 2004; Lawton et al. 2013; Wrona and Sinzig 2018), for the endogenous change of rules where external changes are the enabling factors (like it was with the Fosbury Flop) it is, as a first step, sufficiently helpful to be aware and informed of such changes, at best before they become effective.

3.1.4 Rule-Breaking Market Behavior Challenge 2: Overcoming Resistance

Proposition 2 The second challenge in the process of rule-breaking market behavior is to overcome resistance.

The second major challenge identified in the cases of rule-breaking sports innovations is the process of gaining acceptance for the novel behavior. With regard to that, the cases have been interpreted as having two primary forces operating at the same time: the power of the novel attempt (i.e. how forceful is the rule-breaking behavior), and the resistance to the novel attempt (i.e. how strongly is the rule-breaking behavior opposed). Figure 3.7 shows how this could be visually integrated into the schematic conceptualization that has been used at earlier stages of this work before.

For the sake of parsimony, the technological and combined options on the right side of the figure have again been left out. Like in Fig. 3.6, the focus lies on the "way" between the current options in a market (a_1) and the potential new behavioral options in a market (c). In addition to the innovative impulse (in form of arrows) that

Fig. 3.7 Schematic
conceptualization of the
focal perspective, variant
4 (source: author)

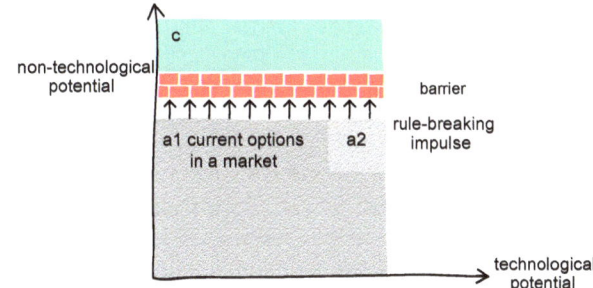

has been introduced before, a barrier, symbolizing the innovation resistance (red bricks), has been added.

Traditional studies in the field of diffusion of innovation have been criticized for mostly comprehending reasons for adoption and neglecting factors that lead to consumer resistance to innovations (Claudy et al. 2015; Ram and Sheth 1989; Sheth 1981). Reasons to resist innovation have been shown to differ qualitatively from motives to adopt innovation, thus, reasons for resisting innovations are not necessarily the opposite of reasons for adoption (Claudy et al. 2015). For instance, innovations may have clear competitive advantages over existing products, but they may still be rejected because they conflict with consumer beliefs or require large behavioral changes from a status quo that is perceived as satisfactory by the consumer (Garcia et al. 2007). Schein (1985) states that it is not the new product itself being resisted but rather the changes that it causes.

Only two out of eight underlying sports cases have not described major instances of innovation resistance in the collected and analyzed data: The Flip Turn and the O'Brien Shift. That does not mean that other athletes and coaches did not defy the new way, but it seems to have not been a prominent issue there. In the six other cases, the rule-breaking athletes reportedly faced high levels of different kinds of resistance from coaches and officials alike, less so from spectators. For example, the above outlined relation has been nicely illustrated by the V-Style: Even though jumping with skis in a V shape (and leaving all other parameters the same) has clearly been demonstrated to lead to substantially longer jumps, it still faced a strong degree of resistance (e.g. because it was perceived as unaesthetic by officials). That is, even though the innovative impulse can be considered to have been strong in that case, it did not lead to an immediate acceptance but had to face a rather thick barrier.

In general, studies on the diffusion of innovation can be broadly classified into works on innovation adoption and on consumer resistance to innovation (Claudy et al. 2015). As the barrier view has been more visible in the cases, neglected in the literature (referred to as pro-change bias, see e.g. Talke and Heidenreich 2014) and reasons against adoption have been proven to be almost twice as powerful as reasons for adoption, the following section is focusing on innovation resistance, reviewing relevant literature and discussing barriers that lead to the rejection of innovation.

3.1.4.1 Active and Passive Innovation Resistance

The evolution of novel ideas often involves a dynamic transition: when first proposed, the ideas are rejected because they are perceived as strange, inappropriate, impracticable, or too risky, but later, the identical ideas may be accepted as useful and breakthrough by the same social context (Mainemelis 2010). Akerlof's *The Market for Lemons* paper was rejected for being too trivial, but later won him the Nobel Prize in economics (Akerlof 1970). George Orwell's *Animal Farm* was rejected for animal stories being impossible to sell in the United States and became an American classic. Investors in Silicon Valley initially rejected Airbnb, Kodak rejected the digital camera, United Artists first rejected Star Wars (examples adapted from Mueller et al. 2018).

Unfavorable responses to change, or innovation resistance, are commonly acknowledged throughout the creativity and innovation literature (e.g. Ellen et al. 1991; Ram and Sheth 1989). It is asserted that most innovations fail due to rejection by consumers (Joachim et al. 2018). But even earlier, in the process of gaining acceptance for novel approaches, the rejection of creative ideas is one of the major challenges: Decision makers seem to routinely reject creative ideas, even when creativity is embraced as an important goal (Staw 1995). To better address this problem, there have been calls for a shift of the creativity field's current focus from "identifying how to generate more creative ideas to identifying how to help innovative institutions recognize and accept creativity" (Mueller et al. 2012, p. 17).

Innovations, especially behavioral innovations, demand changes, for example, in attitudes, intentions, and, of course, routine and habitual behaviors. Usually, people are inclined to resist such changes and instead prefer to maintain the status quo (Ford et al. 2008; Oreg 2003). As Schumpeter (1934) put it: "In the breast of one who wishes to do something new, the forces of habit raise up and bear witness against the embryonic project" (p. 86). At all levels of society, resistance to new ways is a threat to destroy novel initiatives (Fagerberg 2006). Helping employees contend with the change and uncertainty inherent in creative efforts is prominently highlighted in the creativity literature as one of the main challenges (Amabile 1996; Ford 1996; George 2007; Woodman et al. 1993).

To account for the lack of research attention that has been given to the conceptualization of innovation resistance, Talke and Heidenreich (2014) introduced a comprehensive typology of barriers to consumer adoption behavior. Based on conceptual literature regarding the innovation adoption process, they distinguish between two innovation resistance types: passive innovation resistance (resulting from a generic predisposition of consumers to resist innovations prior to new product evaluation) and active innovation resistance (stemming from an unfavorable new product evaluation) (Table 3.3).

Passive innovation resistance is understood as resistance to the changes that an innovation brings along (Talke and Heidenreich 2014). Thus, individuals resist innovations without having evaluated them. Passive innovation resistance is conceptualized to consist of two factors: adopter-specific factors, an individual's

Table 3.3 Sources of active and passive innovation resistance (adapted from Talke and Heidenreich 2014)

Type of resistance	Source of resistance	Factors
Passive innovation resistance	Inclination to resist change	Adopter-specific factors
	Status quo satisfaction	Situation-specific factors
Active innovation resistance	Functional barriers	Innovation-specific factors
	Psychological barriers	

personality-related inclination to resist change, and/or situation-specific-factors, an individual's status quo satisfaction regarding the current product in use or the dominant way of behaving (Talke and Heidenreich 2014). If, in the most extreme case, an individual is personally inclined to resist changes and very satisfied with the current solution, the innovation is likely be rejected without even having been evaluated (Talke and Heidenreich 2014).

There may be many reasons why individuals are personally inclined to change. The most prominent conceptualization of resistance to change from an individual differences perspective has been introduced by Oreg (2003). He summarizes six distinct elements related to innovation resistance: (1) *reluctance to lose control* refers to an individuals' tendency to resist change because they "feel that control over their life situation is taken away from them with changes that are imposed on them rather than being self-initiated" (p. 680); (2) *cognitive rigidity* relates to the trait of dogmatism, which means that such individuals are more rigid and close-minded and, therefore, "might be less willing and able to adjust to new situations" (p. 681); (3) *lack of psychological resilience* describes an individual's limited ability to cope with change as a stressor, for instance because one would "admit that past practices were faulty, and, therefore, change entails a loss of face" (p. 681); (4) *intolerance to the adjustment period involved in change* derives from the fact that change often involves more work in the short term because it requires learning and adjustment, and some people are said to be more reluctant to undergo this process of adjusting to new situations than others; (5) *preference for low levels of stimulation and novelty* refers to the fact that some individuals tend to generally perform better within a well-defined and familiar framework and others are better at finding novel solutions outside the given framework, that is, some individuals just seem to exhibit a weaker need for novelty and are, therefore, more reluctant to change in general; (6) *reluctance to give up old habits* refers to the argument that "familiarity breeds comfort" (p. 681), meaning that the encounter of new, unfamiliar stimuli produces stress because familiar responses may be incompatible with the situation. The results of Oreg's studies indicate a reliable four-facet structure resulting from the above-outlined elements: (a) routine seeking, (b) emotional reaction to the imposed change, (c) short-term focus, and (d) cognitive rigidity (Oreg 2003).

Active innovation resistance is conceptualized as a deliberate form of resistance that evolves from an unfavorable evaluation of innovation-specific factors (for an overview of the literature, see Talke and Heidenreich 2014). Active innovation resistance is further divided into nine functional and eight psychological barriers.

According to Talke and Heidenreich (2014), functional barriers arise "as soon as a consumer perceives any product attributes as dysfunctional or inadequate for his or her personal needs and usage expectations" (p. 899) and psychological barriers arise "as soon as the innovation conflicts with a consumer's social norms, values, or individual usage patterns, or if its usage is perceived as being too risky" (p. 899, for further information on the traditional conceptual background and first empirical evidence, see Joachim et al. 2018; Kleijnen et al. 2009). The potential sources of innovation resistance are summarized in Table 3.4 (for a list of references regarding each barrier, see also, Joachim et al. 2018). This approach is based on and extends

Table 3.4 Potential barriers of active innovation resistance (based on Joachim et al. 2018, Talke and Heidenreich 2014)

Type of resistance	Barrier type	Brief description
Functional barriers	Value barrier	Perceived lack of relative advantage
	Complexity barrier	Perceived as relatively difficult to understand or use
	Co-dependence barrier	Perceived as incompatible with other products in the range
	Trialability barrier	Perceived difficulties of testing the innovation prior to adoption
	Compatibility barrier	Perceived as being dependent on additional products to function
	Amenability barrier	Perceived difficulties of altering the innovation according to customer needs
	Realization barrier	Time span until realization of innovation is perceived as too long
	Visibility barrier	Perceived difficulties in observing others using the innovation
	Communicability barrier	Perceived ineffectiveness of describing innovation attributes to others
Psychological barriers	Functional risk barrier	Fear of improper functioning of the innovation
	Personal risk barrier	Innovation perceived as hazardous to a consumer's physical condition or property
	Economic risk barrier	Perceived as being too costly/a waste of financial resources
	Social risk barrier	Worries that the innovation prompts disapproval from social groups
	Information barrier	Perceived information asymmetries cause uncertainty of innovation
	Image barrier	Perceived associations of innovation (e.g. brand, country of origin) are unfavorable
	Norm barriers	Perceived violation of societal, group, and family values, social norms or entrenched traditions
	Usage barriers	Innovation is perceived to undesirably disrupt established usage patterns and routines

the traditional active innovation resistance typology from Ram and Sheth (1989) that comprises only five product-specific barriers, which have been empirically shown to negatively affect the intention to adopt innovation and ultimately leads to innovation rejection: usage, value, risk, tradition, and image barrier. First, the innovation may not be compatible with existing usage practices so that new skills need to be learned or long-ingrained routines have to be altered. Second, consumers may not understand the value of the innovation. Third, consumers may view the innovation as being too risky so that they postpone the adoption until the risk is mitigated (e.g. by acquiring new knowledge or by waiting how others experience the innovation). Fourth, the innovation may require a deviation from established social norms and tradition. Fifth, a negative image, whether deserved or undeserved, may be tied to the innovation.

To better illustrate the barriers in the context of this work, they are linked to what has been empirically observed in the underlying sports cases. This relates to 5 of the 21 criteria from the initial cross-case summary Table 2.5: coaches' reactance, officials' resistance, ridicule, harder to learn (risk of failure), and negative consequences. First of all, it can be stated that even though six of the historical sports cases have shown different types of innovation resistance, all of them have eventually been adopted as the, or one of several, dominant approach(es) in the respective sports domain. Thus, by analogy, if a novel way to behave in a market faces resistance, that does not necessarily imply that it ends up becoming one of the many innovation failures but simply that they are rather slow-diffusing. Slow-diffusing innovations that require consumers to change ingrained belief structures, accept unfamiliar routines or abandon deep-routed traditions are referred to as resistant innovations (Garcia et al. 2007). A typical example of a resistant (incremental) innovation in the context of business are screw cap wine closures, which solve the problem of "cork taint" that applies to an estimated 2–15% of all wine bottles using natural cork closures. Despite the relative advantage screw caps are providing, consumers have not historically accepted them for two main reasons: they are associated with cheap, high-alcohol wines (image barrier) and do not match the romanticism and tradition involved when opening a cork-bottled wine (tradition barrier) (Garcia et al. 2007).

Table 3.5 lists the innovation barriers that possibly played a role in the sports cases. The points have been set with different certainties based on the available case study data, which is not considered of crucial importance as the mapping is primarily intended to lead to a better understanding of the typology. Therefore, the table will be analyzed in a row-wise fashion below.

The first two rows in Table 3.5 contain passive innovation barriers. As there are many people involved at this stage in the sports cases, no statement can be made regarding the personal inclination towards change. Satisfaction with the status quo might have played a role in Ski Jumping, Basketball and Swimming Styles. In a more general fashion, it may be posited that the groups of traditionalists identified as being opposed to the development of the rule-breaking behavior are more likely to be characterized by passive innovation inclination than others.

Four of the nine functional barriers have been assessed to play a role. The Jump Shot is the only case in which the relative advantage of jump shots versus set shots was

Table 3.5 Mapping the cases according to innovation barriers

Barrier type	Fosbury Flop	Skate Skiing	Forward Seat	V-Style	Jump Shot	Dolphin Kick
Passive innovation barriers						
Inclination n.a.						
Status quo				•	•	•
Functional barriers						
Value				•		
Complexity		•		•	•	•
Co-dependence						
Trialability						
Compatibility	•	•				
Amenability						
Realization	•			•		
Visibility						
Communicability						
Psychological barriers						
Functional risk						
Personal risk	•	•	•			
Economic risk		•	•			
Social risk			•			•
Information						
Image			•			
Norm		•	•	•	•	•
Usage	•	•	•	•	•	•

Note: The points indicate which of the different innovation barriers presumably played a role in the athletic cases

not immediately certain, as jumping does not only increase the probability of getting clear but, especially when the basketballer is not well trained, also increases the risk of a flawed flight trajectory. Complexity basically refers to what has been summarized as harder to learn in the case study. The perceived difficulty to use the novel technique may have been a barrier in Skate skiing, where completely different motions (and muscles) are required; with the V-Style; with the Jump Shot, where jumping and precise throwing was perceived as a challenging combination; and with the Dolphin Kick, where the combination of arms and legs is hard to master. The Fosbury flop was dependent on landing pits and the Skate skiing technique on prepared tracks (compatibility barrier). The time span until athletes could master the novel style was perceived as rather long, especially with the Fosbury Flop and the V-Style.

Compared to the functional barriers, it has been assessed that the psychological barriers played an even greater role across the cases. There is no functional risk involved, as all styles have been demonstrated by the innovators to be clearly superior. Personal and economic risks have been subsumed under "negative consequences" in the cross-case analysis. The Fosbury Flop was first assumed to be detrimental to the jumper's back, Skate Skiing was suspected to cause ankle problems and destroy tracks, and the V-Style lead to alarming weight reductions with many jumpers and required costly adaptations in the sizes of the hills. Social risk may have been involved in the cases of the Forward Seat and the Dolphin Kick where there were worries that the innovation would prompt disapproval from influential stakeholders in favor of traditional techniques. Relinquishing control as a rider was perceived as unfavorable according to the cultural norms and traditions deeply entrenched in the history of Horsemanship. With the exception of the Fosbury Flop, norm barriers have also been reported in the other cases, and as norms are closely related to behavioral standards, this does not come as a surprise. The same is true for usage barriers, which have been observed in all cases. The deviation from dominant techniques inherently entails a disruption of established usage patterns and routines.

A further criterion, which also occurred in the diffusion stage of the sports cases, is ridicule. While ridicule could be subsumed under social risk in the above categorization of active psychological innovation barriers, here, it was more targeted at the innovative athletes instead of being characteristic of the adopters. More specifically, all other criteria outlined above refer to reactions of coaches and officials, which, in a business domain, would be the reactions to the rule-breaking behavior from the innovator's team, the responsible manager, company, or the consumer on the market ultimately. Ridicule, however, is targeted at the innovative agent, such as the athlete or the innovative pioneer introducing a novel approach on the market. Adopters do not usually have to fear as much ridicule anymore; therefore, ridicule is addressed separately and more extensive in the following.

> Whoever has overthrown an existing law of custom has hitherto always first been accounted a *bad man*: but when, as did happen, the law could not afterwards be reinstated and this fact was accepted, the predicate gradually changed;—history treats almost exclusively of these *bad men* who subsequently became *good men*! (from Nietzsche's *Daybreak*. 20, R.-J. Hollingdale trans., p. 18)

In several of the underlying sports historical cases, the athletes have reportedly been ridiculed or mocked after having demonstrated or competed with their newly developed style. Ridicule appeared either in the form of audience feedback during competitions ("everyone was laughing" when Dick Fosbury presented the Fosbury Flop; BBC World Service 2011, 3:58), the coach's and other team members' reactions, or was conveyed and spread through media reports. Despite varying degrees and forms of social embarrassment across the different cases, the overall level of ridicule experienced by the innovators appeared to be disproportionally and surprisingly strong.

In business, too, many now successful innovations endured plenty of public ridicule and scorn before becoming accepted by a particular market or society. In 1878, Thomas Edison's light bulb was mocked by a British Parliament Committee to be "good enough for our Transatlantic friends … but unworthy of the attention of practical or scientific men" (adapted from Clarke 1979, p. 18). Edison himself frequently mocked Nikola Tesla's model of alternating current as, "fooling around with alternating current (AC) is just a waste of time. Nobody will use it, ever" (as cited in Beckhard 2015, para. 7). In the early 1750s, when Jonas Hanway brought the umbrella, then known as a waterproof, lightweight version of the female parasol, to the British streets after a trip to France, he was highly jeered and insulted because of gendered associations (for more information, see Waters 2016). At the beginning of the twentieth century, the president of the Michigan Savings Bank told Ford's lawyer Horace Rackham, "the horse is here to stay but the automobile is only a novelty—a fad" (as cited in Beckhard 2015, para. 8).

In the social sciences literature, ridicule is considered a particular type of disparagement humor, which is "directed at an individual regarding some aspect of his or her behavior or appearance" (Janes and Olson 2000, p. 474). While group membership (e.g. swots, nerds, teens, particular races) is often the base for other types of disparagement humor, ridicule is more personal (Janes and Olson 2000). Ridicule has numerous effects, from rhetorical (communicate meaning to others) to psychological and emotional, and has been most studied as a corrective in the sense of being a "method of discipline or 'breaking in'" (Bergson 1911, p. 134). Billig (2005), in the only more recent book on the topic of ridicule *Laughter and Ridicule: Toward a Social Critique of Humour*, contends that, "laughter has its primary function in discouraging infractions of . . . codes and customs" and "functions conservatively to discourage the sort of social innovation that inevitably breaks rules" (p. 132). In other words, we are taught from an early age on (parents use "the laughter of ridicule to exert control and to impose the codes of social living" on children, p. 199) that if we comply to social codes, norms and rules, we avoid being laughed at (Billig 2005; also see Grewell 2013, for a thorough and more recent overview on the topic of ridicule). Ridicule is hurtful and in its strongest sense expressed by gelotophobia[20], the fear of being laughed at and appearing ridiculous to social partners (Ruch and Proyer René 2008). Ridicule as well as the mere observation of ridicule to others has particular behavioral effects, such as increasing conformity, increasing fear of failure and decreasing creativity (Janes and Olson 2000).

Consequently, rule-breakers encounter the conundrum that two strong goals are activated at the same time by (a) intending to develop and pursue a new, unconventional way of doing things they (b) automatically risk going against the deeply entrenched natural avoidance of undesirable and unpleasant humiliating situations resulting from the mere fact of behaving differently (prospect of ridicule and embarrassment).

To sum up, innovative attempts are facing a broad variety of barriers, either directly related to the novel offering (active resistance) or to the change that the innovative attempt causes (passive resistance). Several reasons for that have been outlined above, closely in line with existing research and explained on the examples of the underlying cases. Knowing reasons of *why* innovation is resisted is the first important step to reach market success with a rule-breaking behavior; knowing particular mechanisms of *how* to overcome such resistance is the second one. Thus, a number of existing techniques will be reviewed in the remainder of the chapter, all discussions again as closely aligned with the underlying cases as possible.

---

[20](Greek: gelos = laughter, phobos = fear).

3.1.4.2   Potential Mechanisms to Overcome Resistance

Turning Barriers into Questions

Proposition 2.1 Evaluating the innovative attempt regarding active and passive innovation diffusion barriers may prevent or overcome innovation resistance.

A good question is often the first step towards a solution. In innovation, too, asking the right questions is considered a powerful starting point for the generation of great ideas (VanGundy 2007). In the context of barriers to innovation diffusion, the above outlined active and passive barriers could be the starting point to prevent or overcome innovation resistance. In a first step, a question regarding each barrier could be posed. For instance: Could lack of relative advantage be a perceived functional barrier to the diffusion of the innovative behavior (value barrier)? Could personal inclination be perceived as a barrier to the diffusion of the innovative behavior (inclination to resist change, passive innovation resistance)? Could the innovative behavior be perceived as being too costly/a waste of financial resources (economic risk barrier)? In a second step then, the different questions need to be answered, for example by evaluating the barriers regarding their strength of innovation resistance. As the barriers are a matter of subjective perception, both the companies and the (different) consumer's perspectives should be considered. In a third step, potential strategies to overcome the barriers need to be developed. This involves an evaluation of the costs that go along with implementing such strategies. Eventually, a prioritization should take place considering both the effectiveness (strength of barrier) and the cost (implementation of potential strategy to overcome the barrier) regarding each barrier. Figure 3.8 displays one exemplified way of how to implement the steps.

In the first column of Fig. 3.8, some typical barriers to innovation (see Tables 3.3 and 3.4 for an overview) are phrased as questions. To decide about how many barriers should be addressed in which order, two parameters have to be taken into account: effectiveness (benefit) and cost. Here, the effectiveness is interpreted as the

Barrier as Question	Evaluation Perspective A (0 = no barrier, 6 = strong barrier)	Evaluation Perspective B (0 = no barrier, 6 = strong barrier)	Potential Strategy to Overcome the Barrier	Priority (see figure 31 for color code)
Could lack of relative advantage be perceived as a barrier?	0	1	highlight pain points in current solutions, focus on relevant market segment	✓
Could the novel behavior be perceived as relatively difficult to understand or use?	5	4 explanation: lorem ipsum	information campaign	!
Could it be perceived as difficult to test the innovation prior to adoption?	not relevant	0	---	¿
Could the novel way be perceived as a violation of societal, group, and family values, social norms or entrenched traditions?	6 explanation: lorem ipsum	6 explanation: lorem ipsum	reframing, debunking, calculate with long timeframe until commercial success	♩
.....				

Fig. 3.8 Evaluation of active and passive innovation diffusion barriers (source: author)

Fig. 3.9 2×2 Prioritization grid to overcome innovation barriers (source: author)

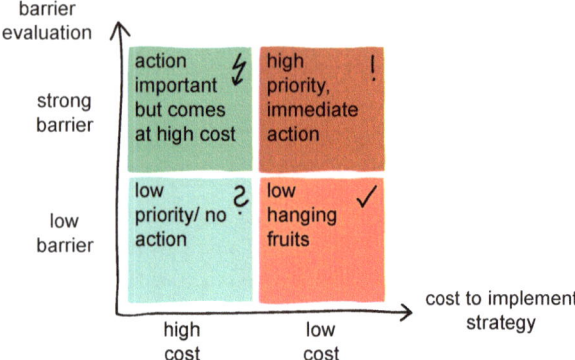

strength of the barrier. In column two and three of Fig. 3.8, the barrier strength is evaluated subjectively from two different perspectives, where 0 means that the barrier is subjectively irrelevant (no barrier) and 6 means that the barrier is highly relevant (strong barrier). To get more insight, an explanation of the individual assessment can be added (indicated by "lorem ipsum" as a place holder). Potential strategies to overcome the barrier have then been drafted in the fourth column of the table. Additionally, these strategies have to be assessed in terms of the cost incurring for the implementation. Based on all that information, the different barriers can be prioritized. Figure 3.9 integrates the two parameters of relevance in a simplified fashion, with the strength of the barrier plotted on the Y-axis and cost to implement the strategy on the X-axis. Based on the above explained prototypical evaluation procedure, each barrier can be assigned to one of the four fields accordingly.

The following sections "Reframing", "Debunking", "Brief Habits", and "Activation of a Procedural Mindset" will be focusing on the discussion of four potential strategies to overcome innovation barriers: reframing, debunking, brief habits and activation of a procedural mindset.

Reframing

Proposition 2.2.1 Inducing a shift in perspective or understanding of a situation can help overcome innovation resistance.

When an individual experiences a situation, the characteristics of that situation induce many interrelated assumptions and expectations, often unconsciously. This world of assumptions and expectations can be referred to as the frame (or scheme or script) of the situation (Gregson 2014). Frames function like filters or brackets that delimit our perception of reality. The act of deploying frames, or framing, means "to select some aspects of perceived reality and make them more salient" (Giorgi 2017, p. 713). Thus, basically, reframing refers to a shift in perspective or understanding of a situation. Watzlawick et al. (1974) describe what they term "the gentle art of reframing":

To reframe, then, means to change the conceptual and/or emotional setting or viewpoint in relation to which a situation is experienced and to place it in another frame which fits the "facts" of the same concrete situation equally well or even better, and thereby changing its entire meaning. (p. 95)

The literature has documented a variety of goals at which framing can be directed, such as shaping understandings, stimulating change, or appeasing fears (Giorgi 2017).

The theoretical construct of frame, or framing, according to Cornelissen and Durand (2014), originally traces back to Burke (1937) and Bateson (1972 [1955]) and has been popularized by Goffman (1974). In the social sciences, framing has been studied in a broad variety of scholarly traditions, such as linguistics and linguistic anthropology (e.g. Hymes 1974), sociology and social-movement research (e.g. Snow and Benford 1988), cognitive psychology and behavioral economics (e.g. Kahneman and Tversky 1979; Tversky and Kahneman 1981), journalism and mass-communication research (e.g. Scheufele 1999), and throughout the broad area of management and organization theory (Cornelissen and Werner 2014; Creed et al. 2002; Weick 1995).[21]

Framing is an essential part of how managers shape the meaning construction of others (Cornelissen and Werner 2014; Kaplan 2008). "Most of us passively accept decision problems as they are framed, and therefore rarely have an opportunity to discover the extent to which our preferences are *frame-bound* rather than *reality-bound*" (Kahneman 2011, p. 367). Small, sometimes even seemingly trivial changes in how situations are framed, e.g. (by the content of messages) have been shown to have substantial impact on social judgment and behavior (Vishwanath 2009).

Reframing as a cognitive technique is often used to turn a problem into an opportunity, similar to a cognitive counterpoint to rapid prototyping. Wedell-Wedellsborg (2017) presents an approach in the form of seven practices for successfully reframing problems that "frequently leads to creative solutions by unearthing radically different framings of familiar and persistent problems" (p. 79). Figure 3.10 displays a typical example of how to reframe a problem.

While the elevator illustration appears more like reframing as a creativity mechanism to be applied in the context of challenge one (Sect. 3.1.3), it is equally well suited as a tool in the quest of overcoming resistance. Consider, for example, ridicule as a potential barrier to innovation. As outlined above, the fear of being humiliated can prevent individuals from behaving against the norm. The default solution then would probably be to either not develop a novel technique, or in case the new style happened by accident, not to pursue it further. However, if one were to reframe the interpretation of what it means if others laugh about a new style, namely being a typical sign of something innovative and surprising they never encountered before, and, therefore, as a compliment, the social risk barrier may be reduced. Figure 3.11 applies the process of reframing a problem to the V-Style case. When Jan Boklöv encountered and demonstrated the novel technique in competition, he endured a lot

---

[21]See McNamee (2017) for an overview of the scholarly frames and framing history. Schoemaker and Russo (2001) explain how frames differ from mental models (less complete) and paradigms (less widely held).

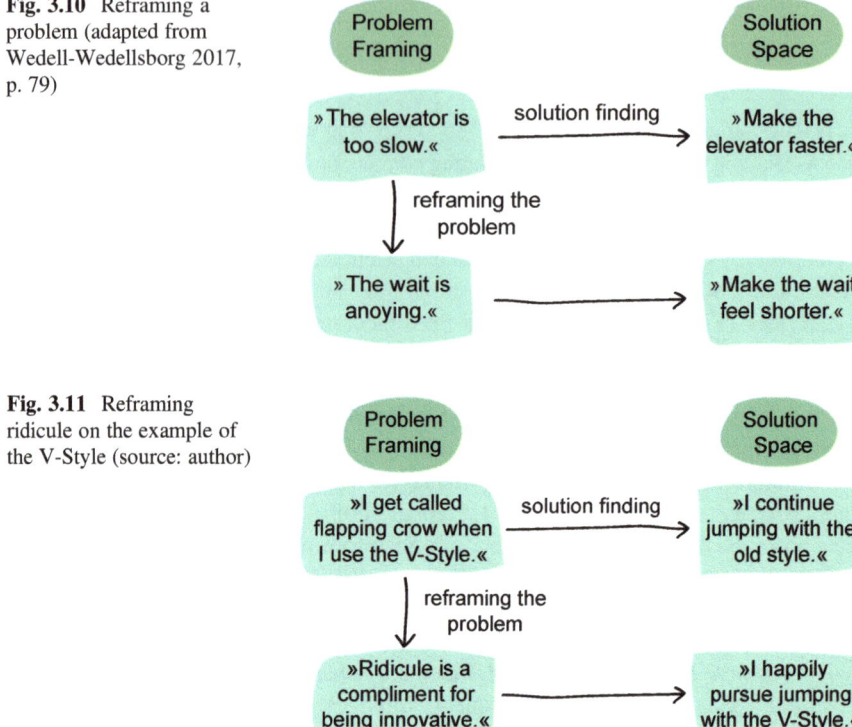

Fig. 3.10 Reframing a problem (adapted from Wedell-Wedellsborg 2017, p. 79)

Fig. 3.11 Reframing ridicule on the example of the V-Style (source: author)

of ridicule and humiliation such as being called a flapping crow, and the new jumping technique was referred to as frog style. Instead of being intimidated and continuing to jump the old style, he could for instance have reframed the ridicule as a compliment to be innovative (which he reportedly did in a similar way) and happily pursue and persist with his novel technique.

Regarding the effectiveness of framing attempts that are directed at others, Giorgi (2017) argues that it largely depends on the audiences' (i.e. the customers') resonance, defined as their experienced personal connection with a frame.

Two types of resonance are distinguished on the basis of their appeal to either cognition (cognitive resonance) or emotions (emotional resonance). Emotional resonance means that a frame "moves" its recipient, for example, by relieving from powerful emotions such as shame or fear by reducing "hot" reactions into "cool" ones, as in the V-Style ridicule example. Giorgi (2017) presents the US presidential campaign of 2016 as a further example, where a large percentage of voters identified with the Republican candidate and "did not 'care what he's saying, necessarily... It's emotion. It's a lot of emotion'" (p. 711). Identification is the main mechanism of emotional resonance (Giorgi 2017).

Cognitive resonance, on the other hand, means that frames need to align with interpretations, understandings, and beliefs that are salient or central to a particular audience. That is, not all plausible frames lead to cognitive resonance but, as Giorgi (2017) argues, it is effective when they are familiar to the intended audience. This idea is subsumed in a second proposition and further explicated below.

Proposition 2.2.2 Combining old and new when introducing novel ways can help overcome innovation resistance.

Think of a culinary business example of how to frame the new in a familiar way. The success of sushi in the US is attributed to the California roll, which consists of common ingredients such as rice, avocado and cucumber, and is, therefore, familiar to and aligned with consumers' existing tastes and understandings. This combination of familiar ingredients done differently (e.g. the ingredients are held together by a sliver of nori seaweed) is said to have provided the gateway to discover Japanese cuisine, with the opportunity of "converting" California roll lovers to sashimi and other more unfamiliar specialties later (Eyal 2015). Apple, too, is using established frames of reference to make users adopt a new behavior, as in making payment options in the Apple Wallet look like mini credit cards (Eyal 2015). Edison's electric lighting appealed to the general public because the design reminded users of gas, which was a familiar and trusted technology (Hargadon and Douglas 2001).

The combination of old and new in the context of framing is referred to as blending, namely building an analogical correlation of frames and concepts from different domains to create a separate "blended mental space" (Cornelissen and Durand 2012, p. 152). A similar idea, also related to familiarity as an important mechanism to help people deal with newness, is discussed in the context of anchoring innovation. Anchoring innovation is a research program in Classics about the way in which people deal with newness in all domains of society—not just technology but also politics, religion, arts or science, to name but a few. Anchoring is used as a label for the multifarious ways in which social groups connect what they perceive as new to what is already familiar to them (Sluiter 2017).

In sum, different kinds of framing attempts may help altering beliefs in the target audience so that potential barriers to the diffusion of innovation might be reduced or diminished. Changing beliefs is often seen as the key to successful innovation diffusion as they best predict the success or failure of an innovation (Rogers 2003).

Debunking

Proposition 2.3 Presenting a corrective message that establishes that the prior message was misinformation can help overcome innovation resistance.

> It may be insular, narrow-minded, prejudiced, and the rest of it, but I cannot believe that, generation after generation, jockeys have been sitting on the wrong part of a horse's back, that the best place for the saddle is not where it has always been, and that at the end of the nineteenth century the theory and practice of horsemanship as applied to racing is to be revolutionised.
>
> (as quoted in Dizikes 2000, pp. 59–60, with reference to "Notes," Badminton Magazine, January 1899, 26–27)

This reaction to the development of the more natural and effective Forward Seat is exemplary of a typical pragmatist account to novelties and closely related to research on misinformation (or false belief) persistence. The prevalence of misinformation is also a matter of concern in contemporary societies and business, such as some people's belief in an unfounded claim of a causal link between autism and the measles, mumps, and rubella vaccine, the rumor that genetically modified mosquitoes lead to the Zika virus outbreak in Brazil, or that Listerine helps prevent or reduce the severity of colds and sore throats.[22] The process of correcting such misinformation is complex and not yet completely understood (Chan et al. 2017; Lewandowsky et al. 2012, 2015; Schwarz et al. 2007). One technique to partially or completely correct such misinformation is referred to as debunking, which is defined as, "presenting a corrective message that establishes that the prior message was misinformation" (Chan et al. 2017, p. 1532). Lewandowsky et al. (2012) qualitatively reviewed the characteristics of effective debunking. According to the authors, the difficulties of correcting widespread belief in misinformation arise from two distinct factors. The first and more pragmatic reason is the ability to disseminate corrective information among the target audience. The second and more important reason is the cognitive persistence of erroneous beliefs within each person. While much could be said about the origins of misinformation (e.g. rumors and fiction, governments and politicians, vested interests, the media—see Lewandowsky et al. 2012, for further information) and possible underlying cognitive mechanisms leading to the persistence of misinformation (e.g. reactance; retrieval failure, viz. failure of controlled memory processes; preference of incorrect over incomplete mental models; fluency and familiarity of information—for further references and more thorough explanations, see Lewandowsky et al. 2012), the remainder of this section will focus on potential debunking strategies that might help to correct pervasive erroneous beliefs and thus help overcome innovation resistance due to fallacious assumptions.

Lewandowsky et al. (2012) condenses the complex debiasing literature with its many nuances and subtleties, which leads them to a set of concise managerial recommendations for reducing the impact of misinformation. In close accordance with their review, the key insights are briefly outlined below. The left part of each visualization shows a cognitive problem that is related to misinformation, the right part of Figs. 3.12, 3.13, 3.14 and 3.15 displays how these problems could possibly be solved.

First of all, numerous studies have found that retractions rarely, if ever, succeed at eliminating reliance on misinformation. As a consequence, Lewandowsky et al. (2012) suggest to identify and consider the gaps that have been created in people's mental models by debunking and filling them with the alternative explanation. Such retractions should be repeatedly used to strengthen the effect and reduce the influence of misinformation. It is suggested, however, that the original misinformation should not be mentioned in retractions because it would become more familiar and, therefore, more likely to persist.

Second, as already indicated above, repeating false information in the debiasing message increases familiarity and thus risks what Lewandowsky et al. (2012) term

---

[22]Examples are adapted from Chan et al. (2017) and Lewandowsky et al. (2012).

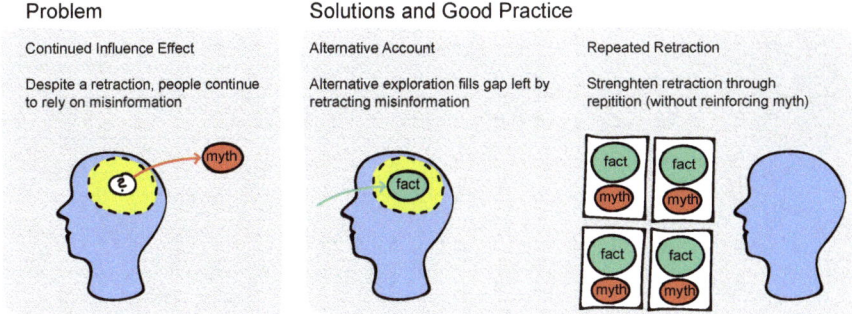

Fig. 3.12 Misinformation problem 1: continued influence effect (adapted from Lewandowsky et al. 2012)

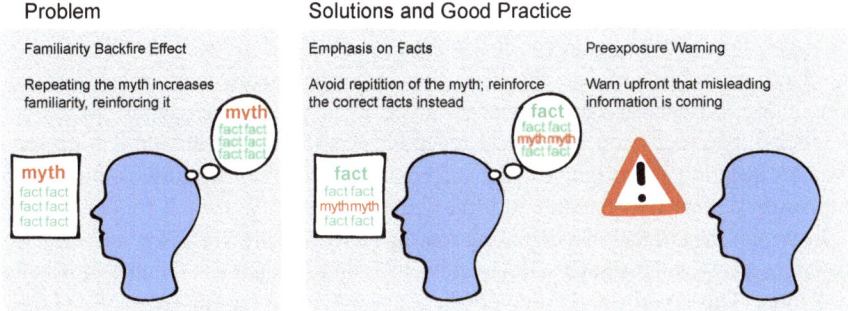

Fig. 3.13 Misinformation problem 2: familiarity backfire effect (adapted from Lewandowsky et al. 2012)

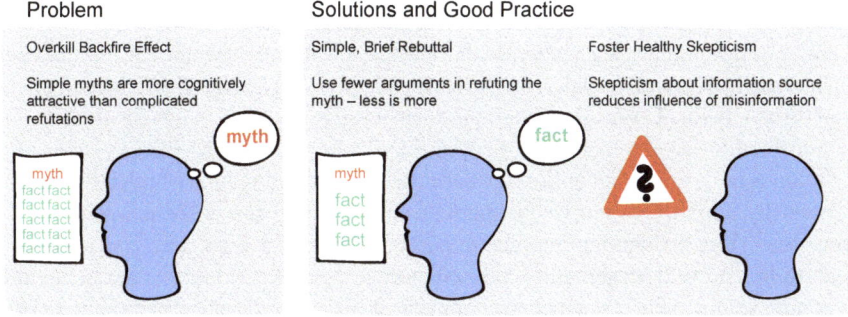

Fig. 3.14 Misinformation problem 3: overkill backfire effect (adapted from Lewandowsky et al. 2012)

familiarity backfire effect. That said, only the facts that want to be communicated should be emphasized in the message. Additionally, an explicit a priori warning before misleading information is presented is likely to induce a temporary state of skepticism ("being cognitively on guard"), which helps to discriminate between true and false information and may therefore mitigate misinformation effects.

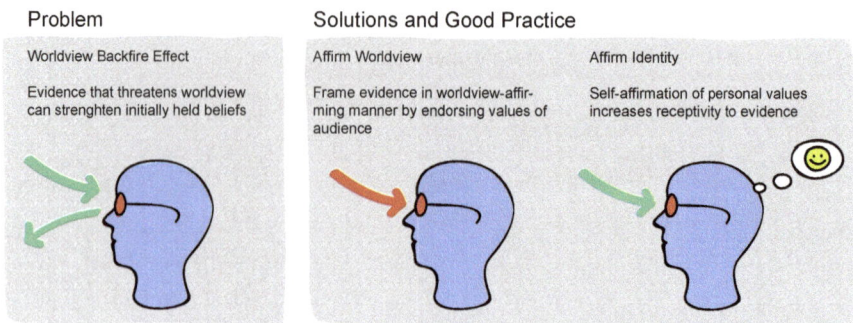

Fig. 3.15 Misinformation problem 4: worldview backfire effect (adapted from Lewandowsky et al. 2012)

Third, if the message is complicated and long, it will appear cognitively less attractive, thus entailing the risk of leading to a so-called overkill backfire effect. It is, therefore, suggested that the debiasing message should be simple, brief and compelling, with clear language and maybe even illustrative graphs. Moreover, skepticism can help reduce people's receptiveness to misinformation if it prompts them to question the origins of the information. Fostering healthy skepticism is, therefore, suggested as one key to increased accuracy.

Fourth, if the content of a debiasing message threatens the worldview and values of the target group, the message is likely to backfire and strengthen the initial (mis)belief even more. This is particularly problematic for people with very closed beliefs, whereas individuals with rather open worldviews on the topic are more receptive to the message. The authors suggest that the worldview backfire effect may be reduced if the evidence is presented in a way that affirms the audiences' worldview and endorses their values. For instance, there may be some elements in the rule-breaking attempt that go along with the audience's worldview or encourage their self-affirmation.

In essence, changing individual beliefs, or more specifically, rectifying misinformation in individuals, is a difficult endeavor, especially if erroneous beliefs are firmly held. Corrective attempts can easily backfire, causing beliefs in misinformation to entrench even further than to be reduced. Moreover, debiasing techniques raise important ethical concerns because the correction of misinformation is basically cognitively indistinguishable from replacing correct beliefs with incorrect ones. Thus, debunking attempts have to be executed with care, and messages need to be carefully designed to help encourage people to adapt certain behaviors over others. Obstinate resistance to change, as the one quoted at the beginning of this section, will certainly not disappear overnight after having given a corrective message. However, conversations that follow the above-mentioned techniques might be one step toward mobilizing individuals to gradually depart from persistent and dysfunctional beliefs to eventually accept the change of behavioral standards.[23]

---

[23]Opel's campaign "Umparken im Kopf" ("U-turn in your head") is an illustrative example of a communicative attempt to address prevailing misconceptions by encouraging people to have a rethink (see https://s-f.com/en/arbeiten/case/opel-umparken-im-kopf/).

Brief Habits

Proposition 2.4.1 The habit loop may help to change a habit to overcome innovation resistance.

Habit toward an existing practice or behavior is regarded as a fundamental construct in understanding the psychology of innovation resistance (Sheth 1981). As Glăveanu (2012, p. 80) quotes, in psychology and beyond, habits are basically considered "the most obvious barrier to creative thinking and innovation" and "any discussion of creativity or innovation necessarily introduces a general opposed concept of habit". Sheth (1981) states that habits are much more prevalent among people than innovativeness and hypothesizes them to even be the "single most powerful determinant in generating resistance to change", (p. 275). Even though habits have played a role in the barriers to innovation diffusion (see Sect. 3.1.4.1), it is meaningful to elaborate further on mechanisms to change habits, as habits are such an important facet in the context of innovation in general and rule-breaking market behavior in specific (for more information on habits hear Cantzen 2018).

Habits are generally regarded as hard to break and people tend to easily slip back into old habits despite favorable intentions (Labrecque et al. 2017). Even though the impeding role of habits on innovation diffusion has been conceptualized many years ago, Labrecque et al. (2017) offer one of the first empirical demonstrations of how existing habits impede consumers' adoption of new products. The authors suggest that it is important to assess the value of novel products, not only with standard consumer surveys and focus groups, but to incorporate the context of application into the study (i.e. to assess whether the offering does not only appear desirable in the abstract but also does not conflict with existing daily habits and, therefore, unlikely to be applied). Other works specify interventions to impede or alter unwanted regular daily practices (e.g. quitting smoking) or how to initiate a new behavior (e.g. regular workout), by controlling the cues that trigger performance, but they are less related to the notion of how to be creative or innovative (Wood and Rünger 2016; Wood et al. 2005).

One such example is a popular conceptualization of habits, based on research by MIT neuroscientists that has been introduced by Duhigg (2012). The neurological habit loop shows that a habit consists of three parts, a cue, a routine and a reward (see Fig. 3.16). The cue is the trigger that initiates a person to automatically carry out a habit; it could be an emotional state, a particular time of day, a sight, a location, or another person. The routine is the habitual action; the physical, mental or emotional behavior, following the cue. The reward is a positive stimulus that is delivered at the end of the routine; it could, for instance, be a feeling or a milestone or something tangible (e.g. a bonus at work). The craving develops when a habit is repeated many times, and ultimately it makes the habit become a pattern that will unfold automatically (Duhigg 2012).

In order to change a habit, Duhigg (2012) suggests identifying the components of the loop: recognize the routine (which behavior is supposed to be changed), discover and experiment with the reward (try to change the routine, the reward, or both), and

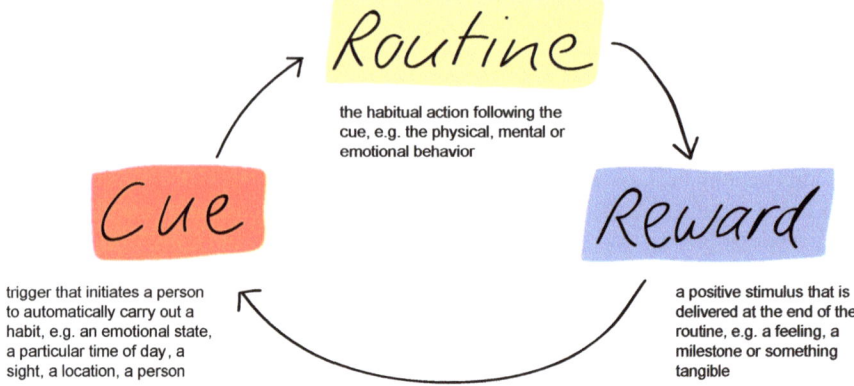

Fig. 3.16 Neurological habit loop (according to Duhigg 2012)

isolate the cue (identify the pattern that causes the craving, which often is not the most intuitive one). Once all three elements are identified, a plan consisting of all three elements can be set up to break the loop and change the habit by finding a better routine to perform. Related to the underlying topic, this procedure could, for instance, be applied if one would like to change one's habit of ridicule in the face of innovation. Maybe you have caught yourself laughing at people who deviate from typical behaviors and would like to change that. The routine here would clearly be "laughing about somebody who behaves differently". The obvious cue would probably be that you "see somebody who deviates from the norm", but the subtler one may rather be that you "see something you have never seen before and cannot figure out". Consequently, a plan could look like this: Whenever I see somebody behave differently and feel the urge to laugh or mock them, I will first think about whether I actually know what is going on and if I would rather show respect or interest instead of starting to laugh, which would make them feel uncomfortable. Usually, it will not work immediately but the mere action of setting up the plan is likely to start the process of habit change.

Proposition 2.4.2 Pursuing brief instead of enduring habits can help overcome innovation resistance.

A more general advice regarding habits, with origins outside the context of business, goes back to nineteenth century German philosopher Friedrich Wilhelm Nietzsche. He advocates the idea of brief habits rather than enduring habits (Nietzsche 1974 [1882]):

> I love brief habits and consider them an inestimable means for getting to know many things and states, down to the bottom of their sweetness and bitternesses ... I always believe that here is something that will give me lasting satisfaction—brief habits, too, have this faith of passion, this faith in eternity—and that I am to be envied for having found and recognized it ... But one day its time is up; the good things part from me, not as something that has come to nauseate me but peacefully and sated with me as I am with it ... Even then something new

is waiting at the door, along with my faith—this indestructible fool and sage!—that this new discovery will be just right, and that this will be the last time. That is what happens to me with dishes, ideas, human beings, cities, poems, music, doctrines, ways of arranging the day, and life styles. . . . Enduring habits I hate, and I feel as if a tyrant had come near me and as if the air I breathe had thickened when events take such a turn that it appears that they will inevitably give rise to enduring habits; for example, owing to an official position, constant association with the same people, a permanent domicile, or unique good health. (pp. 236–237)

It could be concluded that, for him, while some stability and temporary equilibrium are needed to allow for concentration of mental and emotional resources on the most important problems by not constantly questioning everything at once (perpetual improvisation), nothing should be granted permanent immunity (Nietzsche 1974 [1882], p. 237, as commented by Kaufmann in §295). Nietzsche's solution is to largely abandon long-lasting habits like permanently living in the same house and constantly meeting a similar group of people but to embrace a larger array of amenities the world has to offer.

Activation of a Procedural Mindset

Proposition 2.5 When a way of thinking is activated in one domain it is assumed to carry over across different domains and may, consequently, help overcome innovation resistance.

Last but not least, it is suggested that the cognitive technique of activating a procedural mindset can help in overcoming innovation resistance. A mindset denotes the factors at the forefront of the mind when assessing and choosing between options (Bhanji and Beer 2012). Mindsets are "characterized by the persistence of cognitive processes and judgmental criteria that are activated in the course of performing a task. Once activated, it generalizes to other situations, affecting responses in these situations as well" (Xu and Wyer 2007, pp. 556–557). In other words, a mindset is a way of thinking that can be activated in one situation and subsequently carries over to a following different situation (Gollwitzer 1990; Gollwitzer et al. 1990; Gollwitzer and Kinney 1989; Levav et al. 2012; Ma and Roese 2014; Xu and Wyer 2012). This understanding of mindset as a procedure has its origins in works on procedural priming, in which a momentary activation of sequential cognitive operations takes place and subsequently leads to a solution of problems or challenges (Förster and Liberman 2007; Schooler 2002; Smith 1990).[24] According to Xu and Wyer (2012), the idea of conceptualizing mindsets as a procedure traces back to

---

[24]This goes along with Janiszewski and Wyer (2014)'s categorization of procedural priming. They state that, "when cognitive behaviors are an associated sequence of cognitive acts (e.g. execute process one, then process two, then process three), knowledge of this sequence is called procedural knowledge (i.e. knowledge about how to do things) (Kolers and Roediger 1984). Procedural knowledge can be primed. This is not to be confused with 'cognitive process priming' in which the content of the two tasks have to be equivalent (Janiszewski and Wyer 2014).

theory and research on knowledge accessibility, arguing that if a cognitive procedure is used in one situation, it becomes more accessible and, therefore, more likely to be reactivated and applied in later situations. Generally, procedural priming (i.e. the activation of a procedural mindset) involves two stages (Ma and Roese 2014). First, a performance task within a specific domain is presented to the individual to activate a certain cognitive procedure or mindset. Second, another task in a different domain is given, whereby the performance on that task is expected to be impacted by the mere completion of the first task. This tendency has been demonstrated in several contexts. A classic demonstration is related to problem solving (Luchins 1942; Luchins and Luchins 1959), where participants had learned a complex rule for solving an initial series of problems, applied this rule to subsequent problems and were able to solve them more simply (Xu and Wyer 2012).

The idea of activating a mindset has been explored with regard to several different situations in consumer research as well: an improvisation mindset, a global mindset, a growth mindset, an entrepreneurial mindset (for a comprehensive description of prominent examples, see Ma and Roese 2014; Wyer and Xu 2010). For instance, work from Gollwitzer and colleagues stimulated the notion of mindsets in consumer research with the introduction of deliberative versus implemental mindsets (Gollwitzer 1990; Gollwitzer and Bayer 1999; Gollwitzer et al. 1990; Gollwitzer and Moskowitz 1996; Gollwitzer and Sheeran 2006). While people in a deliberative mindset focus on assessment and evaluation of goals prior to a decision, people in the implemental mindset are concerned with the post decisional execution of the goals. These two cognitive orientations are regarded as distinct and orthogonal. A further mindset is the counterfactual mindset (Galinsky and Kray 2004; Galinsky and Moskowitz 2000; Galinsky et al. 2000; Hirt et al. 2004; Kray and Galinsky 2003), which can be described as the tendency to consider alternatives about past outcomes. Counterfactual mindsets have been shown to impair performance on creative tasks but to increase performance on analytic tasks (Kray et al. 2006). Comparative mindsets promote choice and agentic action (Xu and Wyer 2007). Moreover, a maximizing mindset (the goal to get the best out of any situation and the tendency to compare and search for alternatives) has been investigated to impact affective and behavioral responses to decision outcomes (e.g. regret and dissatisfaction, likelihood of returning and switching products) (Levav et al. 2012; Ma and Roese 2014).

With regard to the underlying challenge of gaining acceptance for a novel behavior, the question is whether the activation of a particular mindset (e.g. "rule-breaking" or "change" mindset) in a different context would help decrease resistance to innovation across domains. Does, for example, positive experience with change in another situation have a cross-domain impact on rule-breaking behavior attempts by helping to accept or be in favor of novel behavior and thus reducing innovation resistance? Can individuals be trained to be less resistant to change? These, again, are empirical question that cannot be answered in the course of this work. First, it would need to be identified what kind of resistance hinders the innovation from being accepted. Second, regarding that specific kind of resistance, it needs to be assessed which goal or mindset would need to be activated, how a particular activation task could look, and which other domain would be suitable for the activation.

3.2   A Framework for Rule-Breaking Behavior in Business

3.2.1   Rationale and Design Principles for Visual Artifacts in Management

Literature in the field of innovation is overwhelmingly complex, yet practical guidance for managers is scarce (Keupp et al. 2012). The academic-practitioner divide has been contemplated for decades in the area of management science (Lilien 2011).

Based on the underlying research paradigm, it is an important objective of this work to provide guidance and advice for managers who would like to develop rule-breaking market behavior. It is suggested that the creation of competitive advantage generally benefits from templates or strategic tools, positing that structure-consistent ideas outperform random ideas regarding their creativeness.

Therefore, the process of rule-breaking market behavior is argued to require and be facilitated by giving structure and guidance to frame and focus thought. One way to provide structure and focus is to design artifacts in the form of frameworks or templates (Glaser 2017; Henderson 1991), such as the prominent example of the business model innovation canvas by Osterwalder and Pigneur (2010), which is an approach to map and visualize the structure of a business model.

Visual-spatial displays are omnipresent in human communication (Tversky 2011). Their origin can be traced back to prehistoric caveman drawings, evolving throughout history with perspective drawing in the Renaissance, mapping techniques during the age of exploration, drawing techniques in the industrial age, quantitative graphing techniques popularized by William Playfair, and the more recent development of dynamic and interactive displays (Hegarty 2011). Throughout different management domains, visualization techniques, such as sketches, visual metaphors, conceptual diagrams, and strategic thinking tools, have been used for a long time to support idea generation, decision-making processes, planning, learning, and knowledge sharing (Täuscher and Abdelkafi 2017).

Visual displays externalize thought (Tversky 2011). The reasons may be aesthetic (to arouse emotions or evoke pleasure), behavioral (to affect action or promote collaboration), communicative (to inform both self and others), or cognitive (to serve as reminders, to focus on thoughts, to reorganize and explore thoughts).[25] All of these reasons apply for the framework in this work, with the latter, the cognitive reason, being the most important. More specifically, Täuscher and Abdelkafi (2017, p. 161) summarize four potential benefits of how visualizations

---

[25]For detailed information on depictive expressions of thought see Tversky (2011).

as artifacts support cognitive managerial processes: they free working memory for other thinking processes by serving as external storage for information (Hegarty 2011), they enhance the representation of relationships by structuring and spatially grouping pieces of information (Larkin and Simon 1987), they help overcome cognitive overload by perceptual ("using vision to think") or haptic (physical process of visualizing) action (Card et al. 1999), and they provide multiple retrieval paths to access knowledge (O'Donnell et al. 2002). Moreover, visualization has positive effects on organizational communication and collaboration effectiveness (Eppler and Bresciani 2013).

Consequently, besides summarizing the key findings from this work, proposing a visual solution is intended to be a means for supporting the complex developmental process of rule-breaking market behavior to help managers in creating the conditions that allow for breakthrough innovation. The idea of working collaboratively on a simple visual representation is to enhance dialogue, structure and improve communication about the topic, trigger new ideas, and most importantly allow the capturing of the bigger picture at a glance. Normative recommendations on deliberate strategic actions, emanating from the case-based insight, that firms can take to help individual employees in the process of rule-breaking behavior will first be summarized and then visually consolidated in the "rule-breaking framework", which gives a precis of the complete work. In the framework, the findings are organized in temporal sequence. If some of the textual elements were exchanged with blank spaces, the framework would also serve as a canvas. Other than existing powerful but quite complex, thorough and time-consuming holistic frameworks such as Scrum, Six Sigma, and Design Thinking, the rule-breaking framework, instead, gives an overview of thinking directions, small effective strategies, and possible practices in overcoming significant challenges.

3.2.2 Mechanisms of Rule-Breaking Market Behavior at a Glance

Deriving from both the case insight and the successive transfer of the findings to relevant literature in creativity and innovation, nine creative cues and six barrier-reducing techniques intended to mobilize individual employees in the quest of developing rule-breaking market behavior have been presented in detail in the course of Sects. 3.1.3 and 3.1.4. Below, the most important findings will be summarized in tabular form. First, Table 3.6 gives the gist of mechanisms that are related to challenge one in the development of rule-breaking market behavior: how to cue the process of recognizing a new way. The catalogue of nine creative cues lists the key proposition and gives a brief description and representative implication each.

All in all, each of the creative cues that have been identified in the empirical case data could be linked to relevant discussions in the literature. The transfer process did not only help to assess whether the data-based findings qualify for generalizability

Table 3.6 Summary table: cueing rule-breaking market behavior

Cue type	Proposition	Brief description	Exemplary implications
Serendipitous cues	(Making sense of) A surprising encounter may trigger the process of rule-breaking market behavior	Accidental or unexpected discovery of something valuable (chance) + subsequent synthesis of the accident into insight (sagacity)	Systematic pursuit of accidental encounters: understand the importance of and recognize chance elements, fully harness positive side effects of seemingly random events instead of seeing them as detrimental, retrospectively streamline serendipitous discoveries to trace causes and look for principles behind observations
Incompatibility cues	A mismatch, e.g. between a person and his or her environment, may trigger the process of rule-breaking market behavior	While higher levels of person-environment fit are typically considered positive for both organization and individual, it can also lead to a lack of innovation; e.g. physical disabilities and diversity as potential triggers of rule-breaking behavior	Reframe misfit as not only being detrimental but potentially positive for organizational change; in times of dynamic organizations, the idea of fit does not hold anymore; embrace the idea of diversity, identify + observe "misfitting" lead users
Motivational cues	Failure, limited talent, rewards, and situational constraints may trigger the process of rule-breaking market behavior	Motivation is a commonly accepted factor with significant effects on creative and innovative performance; motivational factors can also be "negative", such as failure, lack of talent and resource constraints	Promote a high degree of psychological safety, tolerance for failure, "fail faster", identify the reasons of failure (systematic pursuit), handle competitive mechanisms (extrinsic) for innovation with care; use resource constraints to trigger improvisation (making a virtue of necessity)
Affective cues	Frustration or other negatively connoted emotion may trigger the process of rule-breaking market behavior	Different types of affect influence creativity and innovation positively or negatively; frustration may provoke incubation; empirical evidence on the relations between negatively valenced events and creativity is sparse	Frame negative emotions as potential sources of creativity, learning and renewal; catalyze dissent-related emotions: when do setbacks and negative feedback lead to persistence?, how can stages of frustration be overcome?
Cognitive cues	Both deep and/or broad knowledge search trajectories may indicate a way to rule-breaking market behavior	Knowledge is a crucial precondition for creativity, creation does not occur de novo but is a combination of previously available ideas: by recombining pieces of knowledge in novel ways; importance of historical knowledge	Recombine existing knowledge (set up deep search trajectories); balance both depth and breadth (renaissance man), consider antiquated routes as outlets for novel behavior; modify old styles; reactivate dormant approaches (historical knowledge); combine old and new

(continued)

Table 3.6 (continued)

Cue type	Proposition	Brief description	Exemplary implications
Experiential cues	Experience in another domain and/or distance to the problem space may help identifying a way to rule-breaking market behavior	Perspective shifting to distance from a task can inspire a rearrangement of prevalent concepts and lead to radically new ways to solve a problem (perspective is worth 50 IQ points); openness to experience fosters creativity; creative acts require a certain degree of independence (creative freedom)	Encourage broad search trajectories; access employees peripheral knowledge using analogical reasoning and abstraction; encourage mental and physical travelling, e.g. internship exchange between companies; set up experiential spaces; find a suitable balance between freedom and control; "take a fresh look at routines"; reverse onboarding
Cultural cues	Questioning dysfunctional culturally imposed behavioral standards may indicate a way to rule-breaking market behavior	Behavioral standards do not always have a meaningful origin; it can be functional to pursue a more natural instead of culturally imposed way of behaving; nature serves as an analogy	Identify and question dysfunctional cultural behaviors as a starting point for the development of a more purposeful approach (e.g. asymmetries in collaboration), have a list of routines and habits including where they come from and whether it would be functional to change them; consult natural patterns as a source of inspiration
Functional cues	Dysfunctional attributes of the current solution to a problem may trigger the process of rule-breaking market behavior	Customer value is composed of two parameters: what customers "get" (perceived benefits) in relation to what they have to "give up" (perceived costs or sacrifices), to increase the value, unresolved or badly solved customer problems have to be identified (problem finding) and addressed (problem solving)	Identify customer pain points, recognize corporate pain points, raise awareness and consideration of the value creation process
External cues	Changes in the external environment may trigger or enable the process of rule-breaking market behavior	E.g. significant transformations in societal, environmental, economic, geopolitical, regulatory and technological conditions can force companies to change their market behavior	Anticipate, know, change; track changes at an early stage; adapt strategies and offerings proactively

but also enriched the empirical results with additional insight above and beyond the domain of sports. It is noticeable that some of the cues that have been discovered by analyzing the cases appear to be the less obvious, maybe even counterintuitive variables with influence on the creativity and innovation process. For example, the positive effects of fit are much more thoroughly discussed than possible positive effects of misfit; the same being true for the effects of positive motivational and emotional triggers compared to "negative" ones, outlined here. Thus, they are both conceptually and empirically less understood or simply not as widely used in a corporate context. The representative implications have been built from the cases and go along with discussions in the literature.

Second, Table 3.7 gives a summary of particular techniques related to challenge two in the process of developing rule-breaking market behavior: how innovation resistance can be overcome to gain acceptance of the rule-breaking attempt.

Other than the creative cues, the mechanisms to overcome innovation resistance have not been developed explicitly in this work, but the existing concepts have been applied to address particular difficulties that were visible in the cases. Thus, all mechanisms are anchored in the empirical data (i.e. logically connected to and derived from discussions that occurred in the eight narratives on the Fosbury Flop, Forward Seat, Flip Turn, Jump Shot, Skating Technique, O'Brien Shift, V-Style and Dolphin Kick).

Based on all these findings, the rule-breaking framework in Fig. 3.17 summarizes how to trigger breakthrough ideas and overcome innovation resistance in the quest of developing rule-breaking market behavior.

3.2.3   Framework of Rule-Breaking Market Behavior

The rule-breaking framework in Fig. 3.17 visualizes this work's key findings in a temporal structure. It is suggested and displayed in the upper part of the rule-breaking framework that two major challenges have to be overcome in the quest of creating impactful ways to deviate from standard market behavior: First, the novel way needs to be recognized, and second, acceptance for the novel way needs to be gained. While recognition typically starts out at an individual (or very small group) level, acceptance means achieving mutual consent and use. It is further posited that the whole process necessarily includes at least one but often several systematic, evolutionary elements. This is graphically indicated by the grey bars in the "structure" part of the framework; breakthroughs do not arise in a single flash but continuously emerge over time. What may suddenly arise is the illumination, the idea for the novel approach or solution to the problem. However, this has been found to involve either a sense-making process before or after the illuminating event. Ad hoc acceptance, too, is asserted to be the exception rather than the norm.

The green part in the framework deals with possible techniques to help in recognizing new ways. Indicated by the Newton's cradle, the normal state of individuals (or companies in consequence) is being at rest, not meaning to imply

Table 3.7 Summary table: mechanisms to overcome innovation resistance

Mechanism	Proposition	Brief description	Exemplary implications
Turning barriers into questions	Evaluating the innovative attempt regarding active and passive innovation diffusion barriers may prevent or help to overcome innovation resistance	A good question is the first step to a solution; how to turn the barriers into action points	Identify, assess, and address the active and passive innovation diffusion barriers
Reframing	Inducing a shift in perspective or understanding of a situation can help to overcome innovation resistance	Reframing means to change the conceptual and/or emotional setting of how a situation is experienced and to place it in another frame that fits the "facts" of the same concrete situation equally well or even better	"Look at it another way": use framing as a cognitive technique to alter beliefs, turning a problem into an opportunity by shaping the meaning construction of others; e.g. reduce hot reactions into cool ones; shape the meaning construction of others toward a more rule-breaking oriented mindset
Blending/ anchoring	Combining old and new when introducing novel ways can help overcome innovation resistance	Building an analogical correlation of frames and concepts from different domains to create a separate "blended mental space"	Use established frames of reference to make people adopt a new behavior ("identify your California roll")
Debiasing	Presenting a corrective message that establishes that the prior message was mis-information can help overcome innovation resistance	Misinformation tends to persist cognitively; debunking is an attempt to present a corrective message in a way to establish that the prior belief was erroneous	Use repeated retractions; do not mention the original misinformation; present content in a world-view-affirming way; ensure that the message is simple and brief; use clear language and attractive graphs
Brief habits	The habit loop may help to change a habit to overcome innovation resistance; pursuing brief instead of enduring habits can help overcome innovation resistance	Habits are considered to be the single most powerful determinant in generating resistance to change	Turn some of the enduring habits into brief (er) ones; apply the habit cue
Activating a procedural mindset	When a way of thinking is activated in one domain, it is assumed to carry over across different domains and may, consequently, help overcome innovation resistance	When a cognitive procedure is used in one situation, it becomes more accessible and is more likely to be reactivated and applied in later situations	"Train" people in an un-related domain to adapt novel behaviors; e.g. tell stories about the long and hard but successful way of changing norms and traditions

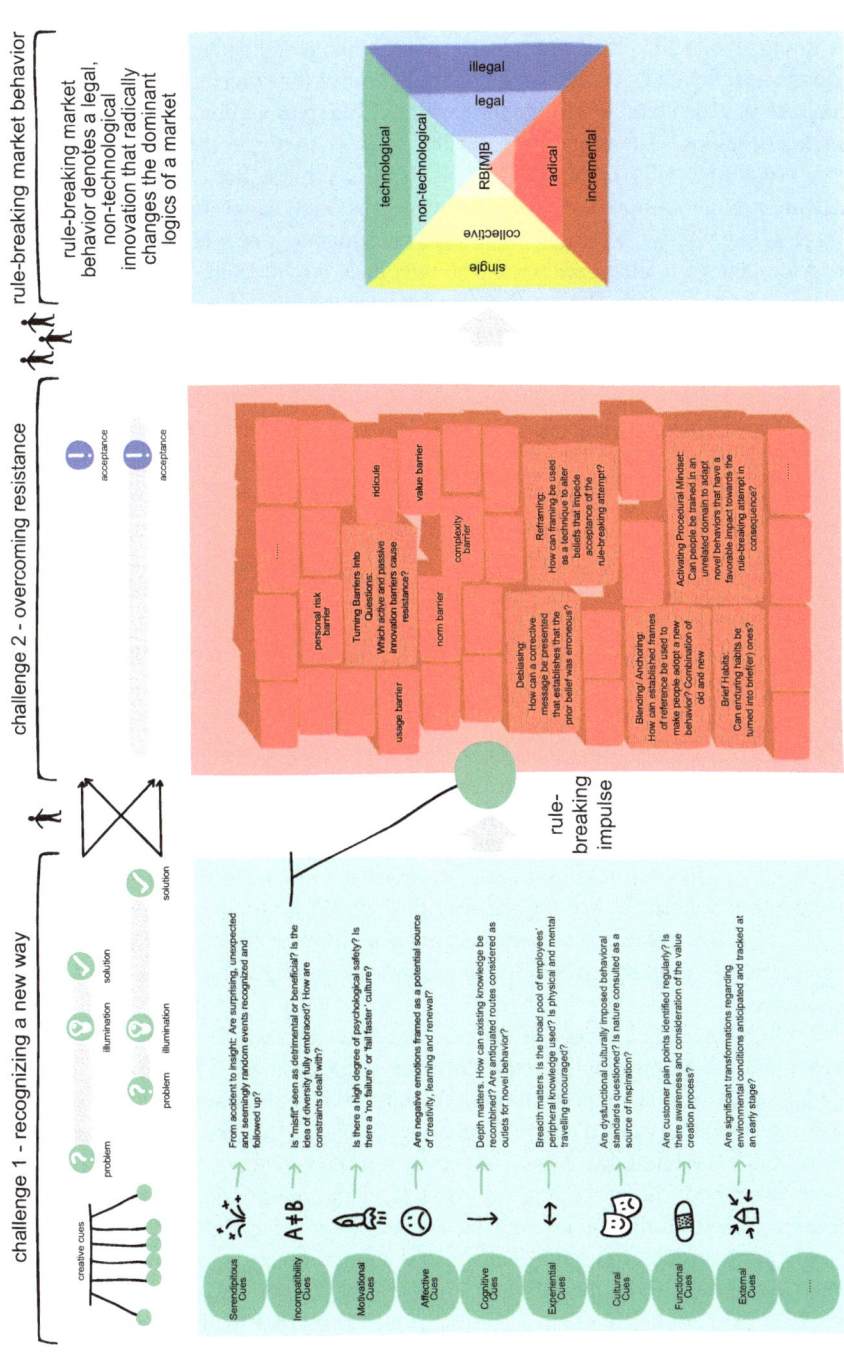

Fig. 3.17 Framework of rule-breaking market behavior (source: author)

that employees are lacking productivity but hinting at inertial tendencies in established processes, a lack of awareness when pursuing routine behavior, a default of doing things like they are usually done without deliberately thinking of new approaches. While this state can certainly be useful for efficiently attaining existing goals, it may also tend to impede the search for other, more functional and impactful market behaviors. Therefore, a "first ball" is needed to trigger the process. This work terms such first balls, creative cues, which means that either a signal for action or specific hint about how to behave is given. It is often suggested that very extreme triggers, like a crisis, environmental jolts, consultants or new leadership are needed for such change-related processes. The nine cues provided are less drastic than the above extreme triggers. Rather, they can basically be thought of as creative mindsets and techniques applicable to any employee above and beyond divisions of a firm that are primarily concerned with innovation and business development (e.g. R&D, chief innovation officers, the management, new business spin-offs, and other external or internal innovation laboratories) to solve existing problems in a novel and impactful way. The template includes visual icons and exemplary questions regarding each cue category (for more thorough explanations, see sections "Serendipitous Cues" and "Incompatibility Cues" and the summaries in Tables 3.6 and 3.7). The nine cue categories are not to be considered a complete list, they combine a number of different cues each, and more than one cue can be meaningfully combined in the process of rule-breaking market behavior.

Eventually, the (combination of several) cues supposedly lead(s) to a rule-breaking impulse, which can, for instance, be a very different product prototype, process or business model. This rule-breaking impulse on its way to turning into rule-breaking market behavior is likely to face resistance, presented in the form of a brick wall in the template (red part). As can be seen, there are tiny barrier-free routes in the wall for the rule-breaking impulse to come through and turn into rule-breaking market behavior without facing high degrees of resistance. Most paths are, however, blocked by different bricks. Similar to the creative cues, a number of mechanisms to overcome resistance by paving the way through the wall are listed in some of the bricks. Just like creative cues, the mechanisms to overcome innovation resistance can be expanded and purposefully combined, depending on the kind and degree of resistance.

To sum up, each element of the rule-breaking framework can be used (e.g. by managers) to systematically reflect on and implement the idea of rule-breaking market behavior as a strategic option. The questions in the framework are supposed to direct thought to guided action. These questions represent only the very essence of the action-related findings. Many other questions could come to mind when thinking about the broad variety of relevant aspects in the realm of rule-breaking market behavior: How would you assess your companies creative and innovative mindset? Would you consider you, your manager, or your company as rule-breaking? If not, what would need to happen in your company or for you to adopt a rule-breaking mindset? Is there an innovative culture at all? Does that apply to all departments alike? How could potential gaps be closed? Is there a program at your company that could raise awareness of rule-breaking market behavior as a fruitful way to create competitive advantage? Is innovation considered a top-management concern, does everybody feel involved and responsible? Are non-technological innovations actively addressed? Which examples can you think of? Is there awareness regarding the two major challenges? Which one do you consider more relevant for your work? Is there an overview of current problems that need to be solved and could any of the cues be helpful? Which of the cues are already part of your processes and strategies? Can you think of further cues? Do you have a list of important routines and habits, including where they come from? Would it be functional to change them? Have behavioral standards ever been questioned? Are they questioned at regular intervals? Are there particular barriers that often play a role in your particular company or industry? Is active or passive resistance more prevalent? Do you know how to deal with them? Which other mechanisms can you think of to address innovation resistance? Are there popular examples of rule-breaking market behavior in your industry? How can you sensitize your rule-breaking radar?

3.2.4   First Evaluation of the Frameworks' Value Creation Potential

In general, the rule-breaking framework is a conceptual structure developed with the intention to serve as a support or guide for managers and other corporate individuals who would like to understand better the process of developing rule-breaking market behavior and alter prevalent behaviors by taking action accordingly. Ultimately, the practice of purposeful, systematic rule-breaking market behavior is conceptualized to be an impactful way in the ever more challenging quest of successfully operating in the market.

The framework provides a clear and coherent overview of findings related to the development of rule-breaking market behavior. First of all, it is informative. Four things are displayed at a glance: (1) the four features that characterize rule-breaking market behavior, (2) two major challenges in the developmental process, (3) a number of mechanisms that help to master either of these two challenges (nine creative cues, six mechanisms to overcome resistance), and (4) the temporal sequence of the process. With that, the framework can be used to cognitively focus on particular aspects, helping to direct, structure, reorganize and explore thought. Furthermore, it is of collaborative character and can be applied to spark discussions and stimulate both individual and collective action. The latter is also supported by the questions provided. The visual elements (such as the dynamics of Newton's Cradle, the barrier character of the brick wall, and the three easily distinguishable colors) might facilitate ad hoc sense-making and serve as cognitive and communicative anchors.

Beyond question, the template does not serve as a solution to solve all problems and challenges in innovative processes. It is important to highlight that the mechanisms provided cannot be regarded as universal recipes which, when applied, are sure to lead to rule-breaking market behavior. Such causal relationships are not known to exist in innovative processes. Instead, many different paths can lead to success, and the framework displays some of these. Besides, only the very essence of rule-breaking market behavior's multifarious character could be pinpointed. For particular purposes, it may also be helpful to consider the associated in-depth textual discussions in this work.

From a scholarly perspective, the framework can be considered a very first, systematically derived, application-oriented contribution in the long endeavor of building a Theory of Rule-Breaking Market Behavior.

References

Abernathy WJ, Clark KB (1985) Innovation: mapping the winds of creative destruction. Res Policy 14(1):3–22. https://doi.org/10.1016/0048-7333(85)90021-6

Akerlof GA (1970) The market for "lemons": quality uncertainty and the market mechanism. Q J Econ 84(3):488–500

Alba JW (2012) In defense of bumbling. J Consum Res 38(6):981–987. https://doi.org/10.1086/661230

Amabile TM (1983) The social psychology of creativity: a componential conceptualization. J Pers Soc Psychol 45(2):357–376. https://doi.org/10.1037/0022-3514.45.2.357

Amabile TM (1988) A model of creativity and innovation in organizations. In: Staw BM, Cummings LL (eds) Research in organizational behavior, vol 10. JAI Press, Greenwich, CT, pp 123–167

Amabile TM (1996) Creativity in context. Westview Press, Boulder, CO

Amabile TM (2012) Componential theory of creativity. Working Paper 12-096. Harvard Business School, Boston, https://www.hbs.edu

Amabile TM, Mueller JS (2008) Studying creativity, its processes, and its antecedents: an exploration of the componential theory of creativity. In: Zhou J, Shalley CE (eds) Handbook of organizational creativity. Lawrence Erlbaum, New York, NY, pp 33–64

Amabile TM, Pratt MG (2016) The dynamic componential model of creativity and innovation in organizations: making progress, making meaning. Res Organ Behav 36:157–183. https://doi.org/10.1016/j.riob.2016.10.001

Amabile TM, Conti R, Coon H, Lazenby J, Herron M (1996) Assessing the work environment for creativity. Acad Manag J 39(5):1154–1184. https://doi.org/10.5465/256995

Anderson NR, West MA (1998) Measuring climate for work group innovation: development and validation of the team climate inventory. J Organ Behav 19(3):235–258. https://doi.org/10.1002/(SICI)1099-1379(199805)19:3<235::AID-JOB837>3.0.CO;2-C

Anderson N, Dreu CKWD, Nijstad BA (2004) The routinization of innovation research: a constructively critical review of the state-of-the-science. J Organ Behav 25(2):147–173. https://doi.org/10.1002/job.236

Anderson N, Potočnik K, Zhou J (2014) Innovation and creativity in organizations: a state-of-the-science review, prospective commentary, and guiding framework. J Manag 40(5):1297–1333. https://doi.org/10.1177/0149206314527128

Andriopoulos C (2001) Determinants of organisational creativity: a literature review. Manag Decis 39(10):834–841. https://doi.org/10.1108/00251740110402328

Andriopoulos C, Lewis MW (2010) Managing innovation paradoxes: ambidexterity lessons from leading product design companies. Long Range Plan 43(1):104–122. https://doi.org/10.1016/j.lrp.2009.08.003

Appelt KC, Milch KF, Handgraaf MJJ, Weber EU (2011) The decision making individual differences inventory and guidelines for the study of individual differences in judgment and decision-making research. Judgm Decis Mak 6(3):252–262

Ariely D, Gneezy U, Loewenstein G, Mazar N (2009) Large stakes and big mistakes. Rev Econ Stud 76(2):451–469. https://doi.org/10.1111/j.1467-937X.2009.00534.x

Armstrong SJ, Cools E, Sadler-Smith E (2012) Role of cognitive styles in business and management: reviewing 40 years of research. Int J Manag Rev 14(3):238–262. https://doi.org/10.1111/j.1468-2370.2011.00315.x

Ashton K (2015) How to fly a horse: the secret history of creation, invention, and discovery. Doubleday, New York, NY

Atuahene-Gima K (2005) Resolving the capability-rigidity paradox in new product innovation. J Mark 69(4):61–83. https://doi.org/10.1509/jmkg.2005.69.4.61

Baas M, De Dreu CKW, Nijstad BA (2008) A meta-analysis of 25 years of mood-creativity research: hedonic tone, activation, or regulatory focus? Psychol Bull 134(6):779–806. https://doi.org/10.1037/a0012815

Baer M (2012) Putting creativity to work: the implementation of creative ideas in organizations. Acad Manag J 55(5):1102–1119. https://doi.org/10.5465/amj.2009.0470

Baer M, Oldham GR (2006) The curvilinear relation between experienced creative time pressure and creativity: moderating effects of openness to experience and support for creativity. J Appl Psychol 91(4):963–970. https://doi.org/10.1037/0021-9010.91.4.963

Bateson G (1972 [1955]) Steps to an ecology of mind. Ballantine, New York, NY

BBC World Service (2011) The Fosbury Flop [audio podcast]. https://www.bbc.co.uk. Accessed 12 Oct 2017

Beckhard AJ (2015) 15 worst tech predictions of all time. Forbes, January 5, https://www.forbes.com

Bennett VM, Snyder J (2017) The empirics of learning from failure. Strateg Sci 2(1):1–12. https://doi.org/10.1287/stsc.2016.0020

Bergson H (1911) Laughter: an essay on the meaning of the comic (trans: Brereton CSH, Rothwell F). Macmillan, New York, NY

Bhanji JP, Beer JS (2012) Taking a different perspective: mindset influences neural regions that represent value and choice. Soc Cogn Affect Neurosci 7(7):782–793. https://doi.org/10.1093/scan/nsr062

Billig M (2005) Laughter and ridicule: towards a social critique of humour. Sage, Loughborough University, London

Bledow R, Frese M, Anderson N, Erez M, Farr J (2009a) A dialectic perspective on innovation: conflicting demands, multiple pathways, and ambidexterity. Ind Organ Psychol 2(3):305–337. https://doi.org/10.1111/j.1754-9434.2009.01154.x

Bledow R, Frese M, Anderson N, Erez M, Farr J (2009b) Extending and refining the dialectic perspective on innovation: there is nothing as practical as a good theory; nothing as theoretical as a good practice. Ind Organ Psychol 2(3):363–373. https://doi.org/10.1111/j.1754-9434.2009.01161.x

Blomberg A, Kallio T, Pohjanpää H (2017) Antecedents of organizational creativity: drivers, barriers or both. J Innovat Manag 5(1):78–104

Boh WF, Evaristo R, Ouderkirk A (2014) Balancing breadth and depth of expertise for innovation: a 3M story. Res Policy 43(2):349–366. https://doi.org/10.1016/j.respol.2013.10.009

Bowen DE, Ledford GE, Nathan BR (1991) Hiring for the organization, not the job. Executive 5 (4):35–51. https://doi.org/10.5465/ame.1991.4274747

Bradler C, Neckermann S, Warnke A (2016) Incentivizing creativity: a large-scale experiment with tournaments and gifts. Discussion Paper No. 16-040. ZEW – Zentrum für Europäische Wirtschaftsforschung [Center for European Economic Research], http://ftp.zew.de

Bretz RD, Ash RA, Dreher GF (1989) Do people make the place? An examination of the attraction-selection-attrition hypothesis. Pers Psychol 42(3):561–581. https://doi.org/10.1111/j.1744-6570.1989.tb00669.x

Brose A (2018) Törnqvist serving an enlightened coffee experience in Hamburg. https://www. europeancoffeetrip.com. Accessed 21 Jun 2018

Bunderson JS, Sutcliffe KM (2002) Comparing alternative conceptualizations of functional diversity in management teams: process and performance effects. Acad Manag J 45(5):875–893. https://doi.org/10.5465/3069319

Burke K (1937) Attitudes toward history. The New Republic, New York, NY

Büschgens T, Bausch A, Balkin DB (2013) Organizational culture and innovation: a meta-analytic review. J Prod Innov Manag 30(4):763–781. https://doi.org/10.1111/jpim.12021

Byron K, Khazanchi S (2012) Rewards and creative performance: a meta-analytic test of theoretically derived hypotheses. Psychol Bull 138(4):809–830. https://doi.org/10.1037/a0027652

Byron K, Khazanchi S, Nazarian D (2010) The relationship between stressors and creativity: a meta-analysis examining competing theoretical models. J Appl Psychol 95(1):201–212. https:// doi.org/10.1037/a0017868

Cable DM, Parsons CK (2001) Socialization tactics and person-organization fit. Pers Psychol 54 (1):1–23. https://doi.org/10.1111/j.1744-6570.2001.tb00083.x

CAIB (2003) Columbia accident investigation board report. U.S. Government Printing Office, Washington, DC. https://www.nasa.gov/columbia/home/CAIB_Vol1.html

Caldwell SD, Herold DM, Fedor DB (2004) Toward an understanding of the relationships among organizational change, individual differences, and changes in person-environment fit: a cross-level study. J Appl Psychol 89(5):868–882. https://doi.org/10.1037/0021-9010.89.5.868

Calhoun C (2004, Summer) "Accidental wisdom" [Review of the book The travels and adventures of serendipity, by R. Merton and E Barber] Book Forum 11(2)

Cameron KS (1984) The effectiveness of ineffectiveness. In: Staw BM, Cummings LL (eds) Research in organizational behavior, vol 6. JAI Press, Greenwich, CT, pp 235–285

Caniëls MCJ, De Stobbeleir K, De Clippeleer I (2014) The antecedents of creativity revisited: a process perspective. Creat Innov Manag 23(2):96–110. https://doi.org/10.1111/caim.12051

Cantzen R (2018) Immer dasselbe – Anmerkungen zur Gewohnheit [Always the same – notes on habits, audio podcast]. https://www.br.de/mediathek/podcast/radiowissen/immer-dasselbe-anmerkungen-zur-gewohnheit/33293. Accessed 23 Jun 2018

Card SK, Mackinlay JD, Shneiderman B (1999) Readings in information visualization: using vision to think. Morgan Kaufmann, San Francisco, CA

Cerasoli CP, Nicklin JM, Ford MT (2014) Intrinsic motivation and extrinsic incentives jointly predict performance: a 40-year meta-analysis. Psychol Bull 140(4):980–1008. https://doi.org/ 10.1037/a0035661

Chan D (1996) Cognitive misfit of problem-solving style at work: a facet of person-organization fit. Organ Behav Hum Decis Process 68(3):194–207. https://doi.org/10.1006/obhd.1996.0099

Chan M-pS, Jones CR, Jamieson KH, Albarracín D (2017) Debunking: a meta-analysis of the psychological efficacy of messages countering misinformation. Psychol Sci 28(11):1531–1546. https://doi.org/10.1177/0956797617714579

Chase WG, Simon HA (1973) Perception in chess. Cogn Psychol 4(1):55–81. https://doi.org/10. 1016/0010-0285(73)90004-2

Chatman JA (1989) Improving interactional organizational research: a model of person-organization fit. Acad Manag Rev 14(3):333–349. https://doi.org/10.5465/amr.1989.4279063

Chi MTH, Feltovich PJ, Glaser R (1981) Categorization and representation of physics problems by experts and novices. Cogn Sci 5(2):121–152. https://doi.org/10.1207/s15516709cog0502_2

Choi JN, Anderson TA, Veillette A (2009) Contextual inhibitors of employee creativity in organizations: the insulating role of creative ability. Group Org Manag 34(3):330–357. https://doi.org/ 10.1177/1059601108329811

Christgau J (1999) The origins of the jump shot: eight men who shook the world of basketball. University of Nebraska Press, Lincoln, NE

Churchland PM (1988) Perceptual plasticity and theoretical neutrality: a reply to Jerry Fodor. Philos Sci 55(2):167–187. https://doi.org/10.1086/289425

Clancy A, Vince R, Gabriel Y (2012) That unwanted feeling: a psychodynamic study of disappointment in organizations. Br J Manag 23(4):518–531. https://doi.org/10.1111/j.1467-8551.2011.00780.x

Clarke AC (1979) Hazards of prophecy. New Scientist Magazine – Seventies Scientist, 20/27 December, p 18

Claudy MC, Garcia R, O'Driscoll A (2015) Consumer resistance to innovation – a behavioral reasoning perspective. J Acad Mark Sci 43(4):528–544. https://doi.org/10.1007/s11747-014-0399-0

Cohendet PS, Simon LO (2016) Always playable: recombining routines for creative efficiency at Ubisoft Montreal's video game studio. Organ Sci 27(3):614–632. https://doi.org/10.1287/orsc.2016.1062

Conti R, Collins MA, Picariello ML (2001) The impact of competition on intrinsic motivation and creativity: considering gender, gender segregation and gender role orientation. Personal Individ Differ 31(8):1273–1289. https://doi.org/10.1016/S0191-8869(00)00217-8

Cornelissen JP, Durand R (2012) More than just novelty: conceptual blending and causality. Acad Manag Rev 37(1):152–154. https://doi.org/10.5465/amr.2011.0129

Cornelissen JP, Durand R (2014) Moving forward: developing theoretical contributions in management studies. J Manag Stud 51(6):995–1022. https://doi.org/10.1111/joms.12078

Cornelissen JP, Werner MD (2014) Putting framing in perspective: a review of framing and frame analysis across the management and organizational literature. Acad Manag Ann 8(1):181–235. https://doi.org/10.1080/19416520.2014.875669

Costa PT Jr, McCrae RR (2008) The revised neo personality inventory (neo-pi-r). In: Boyle GJ, Matthews G, Saklofske DH (eds) The Sage handbook of personality theory and assessment, vol 2. Personality measurement and testing. Sage, Thousand Oaks, CA, pp 179–198. https://doi.org/10.4135/9781849200479.n9

Crease RP (1989) Righting the antibiotic record. Science 246(4932):883–884

Creed WED, Langstraat JA, Scully MA (2002) A picture of the frame: frame analysis as technique and as politics. Organ Res Methods 5(1):34–55. https://doi.org/10.1177/1094428102051004

Crossan MM, Lane HW, White RE (1999) An organizational learning framework: from intuition to institution. Acad Manag Rev 24(3):522–537. https://doi.org/10.5465/amr.1999.2202135

Csikszentmihalyi M (1999) Implications of a systems perspective for the study of creativity. In: Sternberg RJ (ed) Handbook of creativity. Cambridge University Press, New York, NY, pp 313–335

Cue (n.d.) In Oxford English Dictionary. https://en.oxforddictionaries.com/definition/cue. Accessed 21 Jun 2018

Cyert RM, March JG (1963) A behavioral theory of the firm. Prentice-Hall, Englewood Cliffs, NJ

Daft RL, Weick KE (1984) Toward a model of organizations as interpretation systems. Acad Manag Rev 9(2):284–295. https://doi.org/10.5465/amr.1984.4277657

Damanpour F (1991) Organizational innovation: a meta-analysis of effects of determinants and moderators. Acad Manag J 34(3):555–590. https://doi.org/10.5465/256406

Damanpour F (2010) An integration of research findings of effects of firm size and market competition on product and process innovations. Br J Manag 21(4):996–1010. https://doi.org/10.1111/j.1467-8551.2009.00628.x

Damanpour F, Aravind D (2012) Managerial innovation: conceptions, processes, and antecedents. Manag Organ Rev 8(2):423–454. https://doi.org/10.1111/j.1740-8784.2011.00233.x

Dane E (2010) Reconsidering the trade-off between expertise and flexibility: a cognitive entrenchment perspective. Acad Manag Rev 35(4):579–603. https://doi.org/10.5465/amr.35.4.zok579

Davis MS (1971) That's interesting! Towards a phenomenology of sociology and a sociology of phenomenology. Philos Soc Sci 1(2):309–344. https://doi.org/10.1177/004839317100100211

Davis MA (2009) Understanding the relationship between mood and creativity: a meta-analysis. Organ Behav Hum Decis Process 108(1):25–38. https://doi.org/10.1016/j.obhdp.2008.04.001

Davis JP, Eisenhardt KM (2011) Rotating leadership and collaborative innovation: recombination processes in symbiotic relationships. Adm Sci Q 56(2):159–201. https://doi.org/10.1177/0001839211428131

Dawkins R (1998) Unweaving the rainbow: science, delusion and the appetite for wonder. Allen Lane, London

De Bono E (1995) Serious creativity. J Qual Particip 18(5):12–18

De Castro JO, Brigham KH (2003) Entrepreneurial fit: the role of cognitive misfit. In: Katz JA, Shepherd DA (eds) Cognitive approaches to entrepreneurship research, vol 6. Emerald Group, Bingley, pp 37–71. https://doi.org/10.1016/S1074-7540(03)06003-3

Dizikes J (2000) Yankee doodle dandy: the life and times of Tod Sloan. Yale University Press, New Haven, CT

Dosi G (1982) Technological paradigms and technological trajectories: a suggested interpretation of the determinants and directions of technical change. Res Policy 11(3):147–162. https://doi.org/10.1016/0048-7333(8290016-6

Drazin R, Glynn MA, Kazanjian RK (1999) Multilevel theorizing about creativity in organizations: a sensemaking perspective. Acad Manag Rev 24(2):286–307. https://doi.org/10.5465/amr.1999.1893937

Duhigg C (2012) The power of habit: Why we do what we do in life and business. Random House, New York, NY

Dusya V, Crossan M (2005) Improvisation and innovative performance in teams. Organ Sci 16(3):203–224. https://doi.org/10.1287/orsc.1050.0126

Edmondson AC (1999) Psychological safety and learning behavior in work teams. Adm Sci Q 44(2):350–383. https://doi.org/10.2307/2666999

Edmondson AC (2011) Strategies for learning from failure. Harv Bus Rev 89(4):48–55

Eisenberger R, Cameron J (1996) Detrimental effects of reward: reality or myth? Am Psychol 51(11):1153–1166. https://doi.org/10.1037/0003-066X.51.11.1153

Eisenhardt KM (1989) Agency theory: an assessment and review. Acad Manag Rev 14(1):57–74. https://doi.org/10.5465/amr.1989.4279003

Eisenhardt KM, Santos FM (2006) Knowledge-based view: a new theory of strategy? In: Pettigrew A, Thomas H, Whittington R (eds) Handbook of strategy and management. Sage, London, pp 139–164. https://doi.org/10.4135/9781848608313.n7

Ellen PS, Bearden WO, Sharma S (1991) Resistance to technological innovations: an examination of the role of self-efficacy and performance satisfaction. J Acad Mark Sci 19(4):297–307. https://doi.org/10.1177/009207039101900401

Eppler MJ, Bresciani S (2013) Visualization in management: from communication to collaboration. A response to Zhang. J Vis Lang Comput 24(2):146–149. https://doi.org/10.1016/j.jvlc.2012.11.003

Erat S, Gneezy U (2016) Incentives for creativity. Exp Econ 19(2):269–280. https://doi.org/10.1007/s10683-015-9440-5

Eyal N (2015) People don't want something truly new, they want the familiar done differently Entrepreneur, June 18, https://www.entrepreneur.com/article/247467

Fagerberg J (2006) Innovation: a guide to the literature. In: Fagerberg J, Mowery DC (eds) The Oxford handbook of innovation. Oxford University Press, Oxford, pp 1–26. https://doi.org/10.1093/oxfordhb/9780199286805.003.0001

Feist GJ (1998) A meta-analysis of personality in scientific and artistic creativity. Personal Soc Psychol Rev 2(4):290–309. https://doi.org/10.1207/s15327957pspr0204_5

Fine GA, Deegan JG (1996) Three principles of Serendip: insight, chance, and discovery in qualitative research. Int J Qual Stud Educ 9(4):434–447. https://doi.org/10.1080/0951839960090405

Fleming L (2001) Recombinant uncertainty in technological search. Manag Sci 47(1):117–132. https://doi.org/10.1287/mnsc.47.1.117.10671

Ford CM (1996) A theory of individual creative action in multiple social domains. Acad Manag Rev 21(4):1112–1142. https://doi.org/10.2307/259166

Ford JD, Ford LW, D'Amelio A (2008) Resistance to change: the rest of the story. Acad Manag Rev 33(2):362–377. https://doi.org/10.5465/amr.2008.31193235
Förster J, Liberman N (2007) Knowledge activation. In: Kruglanski A, Higgins ET (eds) Social psychology: handbook of basic principles. 2nd edn. Guilford, New York, NY, pp 201–231
Frijda NH (1993) Moods, emotion episodes, and emotions. In: Lewis M, Haviland JM (eds) Handbook of emotions. Guilford, New York, NY, pp 381–403
Fury S (2016) Rise and fire: the origins, science, and evolution of the jump shot – and how it transformed basketball forever. Macmillan, New York, NY
Galinsky AD, Kray LJ (2004) From thinking about what might have been to sharing what we know: the effects of counterfactual mind-sets on information sharing in groups. J Exp Soc Psychol 40 (5):606–618. https://doi.org/10.1016/j.jesp.2003.11.005
Galinsky AD, Moskowitz GB (2000) Counterfactuals as behavioral primes: priming the simulation heuristic and consideration of alternatives. J Exp Soc Psychol 36(4):384–409. https://doi.org/10.1006/jesp.1999.1409
Galinsky AD, Moskowitz GB, Skurnik I (2000) Counterfactuals as self-generated primes: the effect of prior counterfactual activation on person perception judgments. Soc Cogn 18(3):252–280. https://doi.org/10.1521/soco.2000.18.3.252
Garcia R, Bardhi F, Friedrich C (2007) Overcoming consumer resistance to innovation. MIT Sloan Manag Rev 48(4):82–88
Garfinkel H (1967) Study in ethnomethodology. Prentice-Hall, Englewood Cliffs, NJ
Genius (2018) In Encyclopædia Britannica. https://academic.eb.com. Accessed 20 Jun 2018
George JM (2007) Creativity in organizations. Acad Manag Ann 1(1):439–477. https://doi.org/10.1080/078559814
George JM, Zhou J (2007) Dual tuning in a supportive context: joint contributions of positive mood, negative mood, and supervisory behaviors to employee creativity. Acad Manag J 50 (3):605–622. https://doi.org/10.5465/amj.2007.25525934
Giorgi S (2017) The mind and heart of resonance: the role of cognition and emotions in frame effectiveness. J Manag Stud 54(5):711–738. https://doi.org/10.1111/joms.12278
Girma H (2017) Break down disability barriers to spur growth and innovation. Financial Times, September 13, https://www.ft.com
Glaser VL (2017) Design performances: how organizations inscribe artifacts to change routines. Acad Manag J 60(6):2126–2154. https://doi.org/10.5465/amj.2014.0842
Glăveanu VP (2012) Habitual creativity: revising habit, reconceptualizing creativity. Rev Gen Psychol 16(1):78–92. https://doi.org/10.1037/a0026611
Glăveanu VP (2017) Thinking through creativity and culture: toward an integrated model. Routledge, New York, NY
Goffman E (1974) Frame analysis: an essay on the organization of experience. Harvard University Press, Cambridge, MA
Goldenberg J, Lowengart O, Oreg S, Bar-Eli M, Epstein S, Fosbury RD (2004) Innovation: the case of the fosbury flop. Marketing Science Institute (MSI) Reports Working Papers Series, No 04-106. https://www.msi.org
Gollwitzer PM (1990) Action phases and mind-sets. In: Higgins ET, Sorrentino RM (eds) Handbook of motivation and cognition: foundations of social behavior, vol 2. Guilford, New York, NY, pp 53–92
Gollwitzer PM, Bayer U (1999) Deliberative versus implemental mindsets in the control of action. In: Chaiken S, Trope Y (eds) Dual-process theories in social psychology. Guilford, New York, NY, pp 403–422
Gollwitzer PM, Kinney RF (1989) Effects of deliberative and implemental mind-sets on illusion of control. J Pers Soc Psychol 56(4):531–542. https://doi.org/10.1037/0022-3514.56.4.531
Gollwitzer PM, Moskowitz GB (1996) Goal effects on action and cognition. In: Higgins ET, Kruglanski A (eds) Social psychology: handbook of basic principles. Guilford, New York, NY, pp 361–399

Gollwitzer PM, Sheeran P (2006) Implementation intentions and goal achievement: a meta-analysis of effects and processes. Adv Exp Soc Psychol 38:69–119. https://doi.org/10.1016/S0065-2601 (06)38002-1

Gollwitzer PM, Heckhausen H, Steller B (1990) Deliberative and implemental mind-sets: cognitive tuning toward congruous thoughts and information. J Pers Soc Psychol 59(6):1119–1127. https://doi.org/10.1037/0022-3514.59.6.1119

Grant RM (1996) Toward a knowledge-based theory of the firm. Strateg Manag J 17(S2):109–122. https://doi.org/10.1002/smj.4250171110

Gregson J (2014) Reframing. Encyclopedia of humor studies. Sage, Thousand Oaks, CA. https://doi.org/10.4135/9781483346175.n278

Grewell G (2013) Rhetoric of ridicule. Doctoral dissertation. University of Arizona. https://www.arizona.edu

Griffith BC, Mullins NC (1972) Coherent social groups in scientific change. Science 177 (4053):959–964

Gross DP (2016) Creativity under fire: the effects of competition on creative production. Working Paper 16-109. Harvard Business School, Boston. https://www.hbs.edu

Haas MR, Ham W (2015) Microfoundations of knowledge recombination: peripheral knowledge and breakthrough innovation in teams. In: Gavetti G, Ocasio W (eds) Cognition and strategy (Advances in strategic management, 32). Emerald, Bingley, pp 47–87. https://doi.org/10.1108/S0742-332220150000032002

Hambrick DC, Cho TS, Chen M-J (1996) The influence of top management team heterogeneity on firms' competitive moves. Adm Sci Q 41(4):659–684. https://doi.org/10.2307/2393871

Hamel G (1996) Strategy as revolution. Harv Bus Rev 74(4):69–82

Hammond MM, Neff NL, Farr JL, Schwall AR, Zhao X (2011) Predictors of individual-level innovation at work: a meta-analysis. Psychol Aesthet Creat Arts 5(1):90–105. https://doi.org/10.1037/a0018556

Hargadon AB, Douglas Y (2001) When innovations meet institutions: edison and the design of the electric light. Adm Sci Q 46(3):476–501. https://doi.org/10.2307/3094872

Harrison SH, Rouse ED (2014) Let's dance! Elastic coordination in creative group work: a qualitative study of modern dancers. Acad Manag J 57(5):1256–1283. https://doi.org/10.5465/amj.2012.0343

Hauser J, Tellis GJ, Griffin A (2006) Research on innovation: a review and agenda for marketing science. Mark Sci 25(6):687–717. https://doi.org/10.1287/mksc.1050.0144

Hegarty M (2011) The cognitive science of visual-spatial displays: implications for design. Top Cogn Sci 3(3):446–474. https://doi.org/10.1111/j.1756-8765.2011.01150.x

Henderson K (1991) Flexible sketches and inflexible data bases: visual communication, conscription devices, and boundary objects in design engineering. Sci Technol Hum Values 16 (4):448–473. https://doi.org/10.1177/016224399101600402

Hennessey BA, Amabile TM (2010) Creativity. Annu Rev Psychol 61(1):569–598. https://doi.org/10.1146/annurev.psych.093008.100416

Hillman AJ, Keim GD, Schuler D (2004) Corporate political activity: a review and research agenda. J Manag 30(6):837–857. https://doi.org/10.1016/j.jm.2004.06.003

Hirt ER, Kardes FR, Markman KD (2004) Activating a mental simulation mind-set through generation of alternatives: implications for debiasing in related and unrelated domains. J Exp Soc Psychol 40(3):374–383. https://doi.org/10.1016/j.jesp.2003.07.009

Homburg C, Fürst A (2007) See no evil, hear no evil, speak no evil: a study of defensive organizational behavior towards customer complaints. J Acad Mark Sci 35(4):523–536. https://doi.org/10.1007/s11747-006-0009-x

Huber GP (1991) Organizational learning: the contributing processes and the literatures. Organ Sci 2(1):88–115. https://doi.org/10.1287/orsc.2.1.88

Hülsheger UR, Anderson N, Salgado JF (2009) Team-level predictors of innovation at work: a comprehensive meta-analysis spanning three decades of research. J Appl Psychol 94 (5):1128–1145. https://doi.org/10.1037/a0015978

Hymes D (1974) Foundations in sociolinguistics: an ethnographic approach. University of Pennsylvania, Philadelphia, PA

Internet Hall of Fame (n.d.) Vint Cerf. https://internethalloffame.org/inductees/vint-cerf. Accessed 21 Jun 2018

Isaksen SG, Kaufmann AH, Bakken BT (2016) An examination of the personality constructs underlying dimensions of creative problem-solving style. J Creative Behav 50(4):268–281. https://doi.org/10.1002/jocb.75

Isen AM (1999a) On the relationship between affect and creative problem solving. In: Russ SW (ed) Affect, creative experience, and psychological adjustment. Brunner/Mazel, Philadelphia, PA, pp 3–17

Isen AM (1999b) Positive affect. In: Dalgleish T, Power MJ (eds) Handbook of cognition and emotion. Wiley, New York, NY, pp 521–539. https://doi.org/10.1002/0470013494.ch25

Isen AM, Johnson MM, Mertz E, Robinson GF (1985) The influence of positive affect on the unusualness of word associations. J Pers Soc Psychol 48(6):1413–1426. https://doi.org/10.1037/0022-3514.48.6.1413

Isen AM, Daubman KA, Nowicki GP (1987) Positive affect facilitates creative problem solving. J Pers Soc Psychol 52(6):1122–1131. https://doi.org/10.1037/0022-3514.52.6.1122

Janes LM, Olson JM (2000) Jeer pressure: the behavioral effects of observing ridicule of others. Personal Soc Psychol Bull 26(4):474–485. https://doi.org/10.1177/0146167200266006

Janiszewski C, Wyer RS (2014) Content and process priming: a review. J Consum Psychol 24 (1):96–118. https://doi.org/10.1016/j.jcps.2013.05.006

Joachim V, Spieth P, Heidenreich S (2018) Active innovation resistance: an empirical study on functional and psychological barriers to innovation adoption in different contexts. Ind Mark Manag 71:95–107. https://doi.org/10.1016/j.indmarman.2017.12.011

Kahneman D (2011) Thinking, fast and slow. Farrar, Straus and Giroux, New York, NY

Kahneman D, Tversky A (1979) Prospect theory: an analysis of decision under risk. Econometrica 47(2):263–292. https://doi.org/10.2307/1914185

Kaplan S (2008) Framing contests: strategy making under uncertainty. Organ Sci 19(5):729–752. https://doi.org/10.1287/orsc.1070.0340

Katila R, Ahuja G (2002) Something old, something new: a longitudinal study of search behavior and new product introduction. Acad Manag J 45(6):1183–1194. https://doi.org/10.5465/3069433

Kaufman SB, Kaufman JC (2007) Ten years to expertise, many more to greatness: an investigation of modern writers. J Creat Behav 41(2):114–124. https://doi.org/10.1002/j.2162-6057.2007.tb01284.x

Keefe A (2016) These women rock indigenous clothes to reclaim their history. https://www.nationalgeographic.com. Accessed 1 Jun 2018

Keupp MM, Gassmann O (2013) Resource constraints as triggers of radical innovation: longitudinal evidence from the manufacturing sector. Res Policy 42(8):1457–1468. https://doi.org/10.1016/j.respol.2013.04.006

Keupp MM, Palmié M, Gassmann O (2012) The strategic management of innovation: a systematic review and paths for future research. Int J Manag Rev 14(4):367–390. https://doi.org/10.1111/j.1468-2370.2011.00321.x

King AA, Baatartogtokh B (2015) How useful is the theory of disruptive innovation? MIT Sloan Manag Rev 57(1):77–90

Kirton M (1976) Adaptors and innovators: a description and measure. J Appl Psychol 61 (5):622–629. https://doi.org/10.1037/0021-9010.61.5.622

Kleijnen M, Lee N, Wetzels M (2009) An exploration of consumer resistance to innovation and its antecedents. J Econ Psychol 30(3):344–357. https://doi.org/10.1016/j.joep.2009.02.004

Knight E, Harvey W (2015) Managing exploration and exploitation paradoxes in creative organisations. Manag Decis 53(4):809–827. https://doi.org/10.1108/MD-03-2014-0124

Knudson D (2007) Introduction to biomechanics of human movement. In: Fundamentals of biomechanics, 2nd edn. Springer, Boston, MA, pp 3–22. https://doi.org/10.1007/978-0-387-49312-1_1

Kolers PA, Roediger HL (1984) Procedures of mind. J Verbal Learn Verbal Behav 23(4):425–449. https://doi.org/10.1016/S0022-5371(84)90282-2

Kray LJ, Galinsky AD (2003) The debiasing effect of counterfactual mind-sets: increasing the search for disconfirmatory information in group decisions. Organ Behav Hum Decis Process 91 (1):69–81. https://doi.org/10.1016/S0749-5978(02)00534-4

Kray LJ, Galinsky AD, Wong EM (2006) Thinking within the box: the relational processing style elicited by counterfactual mind-sets. J Pers Soc Psychol 91(1):33–48. https://doi.org/10.1037/0022-3514.91.1.33

Kristof AL (1996) Person-organization fit: an integrative review of its conceptualizations, measurement, and implications. Pers Psychol 49(1):1–49. https://doi.org/10.1111/j.1744-6570.1996.tb01790.x

Kristof-Brown AL, Guay RP (2011) Person–environment fit. In: Zedeck S (ed) APA handbook of industrial and organizational psychology, vol 3. American Psychological Association, Washington, DC, pp 3–50. https://doi.org/10.1037/12171-001

Kristof-Brown AL, Zimmerman RD, Johnson EC (2005) Consequences of individuals' fit at work: a meta-analysis of person-job, person-organization, person-group, and person-supervisor fit. Pers Psychol 58(2):281–342. https://doi.org/10.1111/j.1744-6570.2005.00672.x

Kukla A (2013) Observation. In: Curd M, Psillos S (eds) The Routledge companion to philosophy of science, 2nd edn. Routledge, New York, NY

Labrecque JS, Wood W, Neal DT, Harrington N (2017) Habit slips: when consumers unintentionally resist new products. J Acad Mark Sci 45(1):119–133. https://doi.org/10.1007/s11747-016-0482-9

Larkin JH, Simon HA (1987) Why a diagram is (sometimes) worth ten thousand words. Cogn Sci 11(1):65–100. https://doi.org/10.1016/S0364-0213(87)80026-5

Larkin JH, McDermott J, Simon DP, Simon HA (1980) Expert and novice performance in solving physics problems. Science 208(4450):1335–1342. https://doi.org/10.1126/science.208.4450.1335

Lawton T, McGuire S, Rajwani T (2013) Corporate political activity: a literature review and research agenda. Int J Manag Rev 15(1):86–105. https://doi.org/10.1111/j.1468-2370.2012.00337.x

Lepak DP, Smith KG, Taylor MS (2007) Value creation and value capture: a multilevel perspective. Acad Manag Rev 32(1):180–194. https://doi.org/10.5465/amr.2007.23464011

Leung AKY, Maddux WW, Galinsky AD, Chiu CY (2008) Multicultural experience enhances creativity: the when and how. Am Psychol 63(3):169–181. https://doi.org/10.1037/0003-066X.63.3.169

Levav J, Reinholtz N, Lin C (2012) The effect of ordering decisions by choice-set size on consumer search. J Consum Res 39(3):585–599. https://doi.org/10.1086/664498

Levinthal DA, March JG (1993) The myopia of learning. Strateg Manag J 14(S2):95–112. https://doi.org/10.1002/smj.4250141009

Lewandowsky S, Ecker UKH, Seifert CM, Schwarz N, Cook J (2012) Misinformation and its correction: continued influence and successful debiasing. Psychol Sci Public Interest 13 (3):106–131. https://doi.org/10.1177/1529100612451018

Lewandowsky S, Cook J, Oberauer K, Brophy S, Lloyd EA, Marriott M (2015) Recurrent fury: conspiratorial discourse in the blogosphere triggered by research on the role of conspiracist ideation in climate denial. J Soc Polit Psychol 3(1):142–178. https://doi.org/10.5964/jspp.v3i1.443

Lewin K (1935) A dynamic theory of personality: selected papers (trans: Adams DK, Zener KE). McGraw-Hill, New York, NY

Lilien GL (2011) Bridging the academic-practitioner divide in marketing decision models. J Mark 75(4):196–210. https://doi.org/10.1509/jmkg.75.4.196

Lubart TI (2001) Models of the creative process: past, present and future. Creat Res J 13 (3-4):295–308. https://doi.org/10.1207/S15326934CRJ1334_07

Luchins AS (1942) Mechanization in problem solving: the effect of Einstellung. Psychol Monogr 54(6):i-95. https://doi.org/10.1037/h0093502

Luchins AS, Luchins EH (1959) Rigidity of behavior: a variational approach to the effect of einstellung. University of Oregon Books, Eugene, OR

Ma J, Roese NJ (2014) The maximizing mind-set. J Consum Res 41(1):71–92. https://doi.org/10. 1086/674977

Madjar N, Oldham GR, Pratt MG (2002) There's no place like home? The contributions of work and nonwork creativity support to employees' creative performance. Acad Manag J 45 (4):757–767. https://doi.org/10.5465/3069309

Madsen PM, Desai V (2010) Failing to learn? The effects of failure and success on organizational learning in the global orbital launch vehicle industry. Acad Manag J 53(3):451–476. https://doi. org/10.5465/amj.2010.51467631

Mainemelis C (2010) Stealing fire: creative deviance in the evolution of new ideas. Acad Manag Rev 35(4):558–578. https://doi.org/10.5465/amr.35.4.zok558

March JG (1981) Footnotes to organizational change. Adm Sci Q 26(4):563–577. https://doi.org/ 10.2307/2392340

March JG, Simon HA (1958) Organizations. Wiley, New York, NY

Markman GD, Baron RA (2003) Person-entrepreneurship fit: why some people are more successful as entrepreneurs than others. Hum Resour Manag Rev 13(2):281–301. https://doi.org/10.1016/ S1053-4822(03)00018-4

Maule T (1960) The shotput explosion. Sports Illustrated, April 25, https://www.si.com

McCrae RR (1987) Creativity, divergent thinking, and openness to experience. J Pers Soc Psychol 52(6):1258–1265. https://doi.org/10.1037/0022-3514.52.6.1258

McCrae RR, Costa PT Jr (1997) Conceptions and correlates of openness to experience. In: Hogan R, Johnson J, Briggs S (eds) Handbook of personality psychology. Academic, New York, NY, pp 825–847. https://doi.org/10.1016/B978-012134645-4/50032-9

McGrath RG (1999) Falling forward: real options reasoning and entrepreneurial failure. Acad Manag Rev 24(1):13–30. https://doi.org/10.5465/amr.1999.1580438

McGrath RG (2011) Failing by design. Harv Bus Rev 89(4):76–83. 137

McIntyre MM, Graziano WG (2016) Seeing people, seeing things: individual differences in selective attention. Personal Soc Psychol Bull 42(9):1258–1271. https://doi.org/10.1177/ 0146167216653937

McNamee LG (2017) Frame/framing. The international encyclopedia of organizational communication. Wiley, New York, NY. https://doi.org/10.1002/9781118955567.wbieoc084

Melero E, Palomeras N (2015) The renaissance man is not dead! The role of generalists in teams of inventors. Res Policy 44(1):154–167. https://doi.org/10.1016/j.respol.2014.07.005

Merced WD (2017) How can we hear the stars? [video]. https://www.npr.org. Accessed 1 Jun 2018

Merton RK, Barber E (2004) The travels and adventures of serendipity. Princeton University Press, Princeton, NJ

Miron E, Erez M, Naveh E (2004) Do personal characteristics and cultural values that promote innovation, quality, and efficiency compete or complement each other? J Organ Behav 25 (2):175–199. https://doi.org/10.1002/job.237

Miron-Spektor E, Erez M, Naveh E (2011) The effect of conformist and attentive-to-detail members on team innovation: reconciling the innovation paradox. Acad Manag J 54(4):740–760. https:// doi.org/10.5465/amj.2011.64870100

Muchinsky PM, Monahan CJ (1987) What is person-environment congruence? Supplementary versus complementary models of fit. J Vocat Behav 31(3):268–277. https://doi.org/10.1016/ 0001-8791(87)90043-1

Mueller JS, Melwani S, Goncalo JA (2012) The bias against creativity: why people desire but reject creative ideas. Psychol Sci 23(1):13–17. https://doi.org/10.1177/0956797611421018

Mueller JS, Melwani S, Loewenstein J, Deal JJ (2018) Reframing the decision-makers' dilemma: towards a social context model of creative idea recognition. Acad Manag J 61(1):94–110. https://doi.org/10.5465/amj.2013.0887

Mumford MD, Gustafson SB (1988) Creativity syndrome: integration, application, and innovation. Psychol Bull 103(1):27–43. https://doi.org/10.1037/0033-2909.103.1.27

Mumford MD, Medeiros KE, Partlow PJ (2012) Creative thinking: processes, strategies, and knowledge. J Creat Behav 46(1):30–47. https://doi.org/10.1002/jocb.003

Murayama K, Nirei M, Shimizu H (2015) Management of science, serendipity, and research performance: evidence from a survey of scientists in Japan and the U.S. Res Policy 44 (4):862–873. https://doi.org/10.1016/j.respol.2015.01.018

Nedo J (2016) Der V-Stil im Skispringen: Jan Boklöv: Per Zufall zum Visionär [The v-style in ski jumping: Jan Boklöv: Visionary by chance]. Tagesspiegel, December 28, https://www.tagesspiegel.de

Nelson RR, Winter SG (1982) An evolutionary theory of economic change. Harvard University Press, Cambridge, MA

Newell AF, Gregor P (1999) Extra-ordinary human-machine interaction: What can be learned from people with disabilities? Cogn Tech Work 1(2):78–85. https://doi.org/10.1007/s101110050034

Nietzsche F (1974 [1882]) The gay science with a prelude of rhymes and an appendix of songs (trans: Kaufmann W). Vintage, New York, NY

O'Donnell AM, Dansereau DF, Hall RH (2002) Knowledge maps as scaffolds for cognitive processing. Educ Psychol Rev 14(1):71–86. https://doi.org/10.1023/a:1013132527007

O'Reilly CA, Tushman ML (2008) Ambidexterity as a dynamic capability: resolving the innovator's dilemma. Res Organ Behav 28:185–206. https://doi.org/10.1016/j.riob.2008.06.002

O'Reilly CA, Tushman ML (2013) Organizational ambidexterity: past, present, and future. Acad Manag Perspect 27(4):324–338. https://doi.org/10.5465/amp.2013.0025

O'Reilly CA, Chatman J, Caldwell DF (1991) People and organizational culture: a profile comparison approach to assessing person-organization fit. Acad Manag J 34(3):487–516. https://doi.org/10.5465/256404

Oreg S (2003) Resistance to change: developing an individual differences measure. J Appl Psychol 88(4):680–693. https://doi.org/10.1037/0021-9010.88.4.680

Osterwalder A, Pigneur Y (2010) Business model generation: a handbook for visionaries, game changers, and challengers. Wiley, Hoboken, NJ

Paulus P (2000) Groups, teams, and creativity: the creative potential of idea-generating groups. Appl Psychol 49(2):237–262. https://doi.org/10.1111/1464-0597.00013

Perra DB, Sidhu JS, Volberda HW (2017) How do established firms produce breakthrough innovations? Managerial identity-dissemination discourse and the creation of novel product-market solutions. J Prod Innov Manag 34(4):509–525. https://doi.org/10.1111/jpim.12390

Pettitt C (2015) Anthropology: one-man multidisciplinarian. Nature 525(7569):319–320. https://doi.org/10.1038/525319a

Poolton J, Ismail H (2000) New developments in innovation. J Manag Psychol 15(8):795–811. https://doi.org/10.1108/02683940010379350

Potočnik K, Anderson N (2016) A constructively critical review of change and innovation-related concepts: towards conceptual and operational clarity. Eur J Work Organ Psychol 25 (4):481–494. https://doi.org/10.1080/1359432X.2016.1176022

Raisch S, Birkinshaw J (2008) Organizational ambidexterity: antecedents, outcomes, and moderators. J Manag 34(3):375–409. https://doi.org/10.1177/0149206308316058

Raisch S, Birkinshaw J, Probst G, Tushman ML (2009) Organizational ambidexterity: balancing exploitation and exploration for sustained performance. Organ Sci 20(4):685–695. https://doi.org/10.1287/orsc.1090.0428

Ram S, Sheth JN (1989) Consumer resistance to innovations: the marketing problem and its solutions. J Consum Mark 6(2):5–14. https://doi.org/10.1108/EUM0000000002542

Ramos J, Anderson N, Peiró JM, Zijlstra F (2016) Studying innovation in organizations: a dialectic perspective-introduction to the special issue. Eur J Work Organ Psychol 25(4):477–480. https://doi.org/10.1080/1359432X.2016.1192364

Ritter SM, Dijksterhuis A (2014) Creativity – the unconscious foundations of the incubation period. Front Hum Neurosci 8(215):1–10. https://doi.org/10.3389/fnhum.2014.00215

Ritter SM, Rietzschel EF (2017) Lay theories of creativity. In: Zedelius CM, BCN M, Schooler JW (eds) The science of lay theories: how beliefs shape our cognition, behavior, and health. Springer, New York, NY, pp 95–126. https://doi.org/10.1007/978-3-319-57306-9_5

Rogers EM (2003) Diffusion of innovations, 5th edn. Free Press, New York, NY

Rose PM (1997) Creativity, freedom and the promise of knowledge: an historical overview. Doctoral dissertation, Queen's University Canada, ProQuest Dissertations & Theses Global Database

Rosing K, Frese M, Bausch A (2011) Explaining the heterogeneity of the leadership-innovation relationship: ambidextrous leadership. Leadersh Q 22(5):956–974. https://doi.org/10.1016/j.leaqua.2011.07.014

Ruch W, Proyer René T (2008) The fear of being laughed at: individual and group differences in gelotophobia. Humor Int J Humor Res 21(1):47–67. https://doi.org/10.1515/HUMOR.2008.002

Rynes S, Gerhart B (1990) Interviewer assessments of applicant "fit": an exploratory investigation. Pers Psychol 43(1):13–35. https://doi.org/10.1111/j.1744-6570.1990.tb02004.x

Samuel A, Albert D, Moshfique U, Ofori DJ (2016) Entrepreneurs' optimism, cognitive style and persistence. Int J Entrep Behav Res 22(1):84–108. https://doi.org/10.1108/IJEBR-07-2015-0158

Sapp DD (1992) The point of creative frustration and the creative process: a new look at an old model. J Creat Behav 26(1):21–28. https://doi.org/10.1002/j.2162-6057.1992.tb01153.x

Schein EH (1985) Organizational culture and leadership. Jossey-Bass, San Francisco, CA

Scheufele DA (1999) Framing as a theory of media effects. J Commun 49(1):103–122. https://doi.org/10.1111/j.1460-2466.1999.tb02784.x

Schneider B, Goldstein HW, Smith DB (1995) The ASA framework: an update. Pers Psychol 48(4):747–773. https://doi.org/10.1111/j.1744-6570.1995.tb01780.x

Schoemaker PJH, Russo JE (2001) Managing frames to make better decisions. In: Hoch SJ, Kunreuther HC (eds) Wharton on decision making. Wiley, New York, NY, pp 131–155

Schön DA (1983) The reflective practitioner. Basic Books, New York, NY

Schooler JW (2002) Verbalization produces a transfer inappropriate processing shift. Appl Cogn Psychol 16(8):989–997. https://doi.org/10.1002/acp.930

Schultz TW (1961) Investment in human capital. Am Econ Rev 51(1):1–17

Schumpeter JA (1934) The theory of economic development: an inquiry into profits, capital, credit, interest, and the business cycle. Harvard University Press, Cambridge, MA

Schwarz N, Sanna LJ, Skurnik I, Yoon C (2007) Metacognitive experiences and the intricacies of setting people straight: implications for debiasing and public information campaigns. In: Advances in experimental social psychology, vol 39. Academic, New York, NY, pp 127–161. https://doi.org/10.1016/S0065-2601(06)39003-X

Shalley CE, Perry-Smith JE (2001) Effects of social-psychological factors on creative performance: the role of informational and controlling expected evaluation and modeling experience. Organ Behav Hum Decis Process 84(1):1–22. https://doi.org/10.1006/obhd.2000.2918

Shalley CE, Zhou J (2008) Organizational creativity research: a historical overview. In: Shalley CE, Zhou J (eds) Handbook of organizational creativity. Lawrence Erlbaum, Mahwah, NJ, pp 3–31

Shalley CE, Zhou J, Oldham GR (2004) The effects of personal and contextual characteristics on creativity: where should we go from here? J Manag 30(6):933–958. https://doi.org/10.1016/j.jm.2004.06.007

Shanteau J (1992a) Competence in experts: the role of task characteristics. Organ Behav Hum Decis Process 53(2):252–266. https://doi.org/10.1016/0749-5978(92)90064-E

Shanteau J (1992b) How much information does an expert use? Is it relevant? Acta Psychol 81(1):75–86. https://doi.org/10.1016/0001-6918(92)90012-3

Sheth JN (1981) Psychology of innovation resistance: the less developed concept (ldc) in diffusion research. In: Sheth JN (ed) Research in marketing. JAI Press, Greenwich, CT, pp 273–282

Simonton DK (2003) Expertise, competence, and creative ability: the perplexing complexities. In: Sternberg RJ, Grigorenko EL (eds) The psychology of abilities, competencies, and expertise. Cambridge University Press, New York, NY, pp 213–238. https://doi.org/10.1017/CBO9780511615801.010

Sitkin SB (1992) Learning through failure: the strategy of small losses. In: Staw BM, Cummings LL (eds) Research in organizational behavior, vol 14. JAI Press, Greenwich, CT, pp 231–266

Sluiter I (2017) Anchoring innovation: a classical research agenda. Eur Rev 25(1):20–38. https://doi.org/10.1017/S1062798716000442

Smith ER (1990) Content and process specificity in the effects of prior experiences. In: Srull TK, Wyer RS (eds) Advances in social cognition, vol 3. Lawrence Erlbaum. Hilldale, NJ, pp 1–59

Smith DK, Paradice DB, Smith SM (2000) Prepare your mind for creativity. Commun ACM 43 (7):110–116. https://doi.org/10.1145/341852.341870

Smolucha F (1992) A reconstruction of Vygotsky's theory of creativity. Creat Res J 5(1):49–67. https://doi.org/10.1080/10400419209534422

Snow DA, Benford RD (1988) Ideology, frame resonance, and participant mobilization. Int Soc Mov Res 1(1):197–217

Spender JC (1996) Making knowledge the basis of a dynamic theory of the firm. Strateg Manag J 17 (S2):45–62. https://doi.org/10.1002/smj.4250171106

Stahl GK, Maznevski ML, Voigt A, Jonsen K (2010) Unraveling the effects of cultural diversity in teams: a meta-analysis of research on multicultural work groups. J Int Bus Stud 41(4):690–709. https://doi.org/10.1057/jibs.2009.85

Staw BM (1995) Why no one really wants creativity. In: Ford CM, Gioia DA (eds) Creative action in organizations: ivory tower visions and real world voices. Sage, Thousand Oaks, CA, pp 161–166. https://doi.org/10.4135/9781452243535.n21

Stebbins RA (2013) Serendipity. In: Kaldis B (ed) Encyclopedia of philosophy and the social sciences, vol 1. Sage, Thousand Oaks, CA, pp 863–863. https://doi.org/10.4135/9781452276052.n327

Stompff G, Smulders F, Henze L (2016) Surprises are the benefits: reframing in multidisciplinary design teams. Des Stud 47:187–214. https://doi.org/10.1016/j.destud.2016.09.004

Talke K, Heidenreich S (2014) How to overcome pro-change bias: incorporating passive and active innovation resistance in innovation decision models. J Prod Innov Manag 31(5):894–907. https://doi.org/10.1111/jpim.12130

Täuscher K, Abdelkafi N (2017) Visual tools for business model innovation: recommendations from a cognitive perspective. Creat Innov Manag 26(2):160–174. https://doi.org/10.1111/caim.12208

Tidd J (2006) A review of innovation models. Discussion Paper 1. Imperial College London, Tanaka Business School, http://citeseerx.ist.psu.edu

Tierney P, Farmer SM, Graen GB (1999) An examination of leadership and employee creativity: the relevance of traits and relationships. Pers Psychol 52(3):591–620. https://doi.org/10.1111/j.1744-6570.1999.tb00173.x

Titus PA (2018) Exploring creative marketing thought: divergent ideation processes and outcomes. Psychol Mark 35(3):237–248. https://doi.org/10.1002/mar.21083

Tomoki S (2007) A contingency perspective of the importance of PI fit and PO fit in employee selection. J Manag Psychol 22(2):118–131. https://doi.org/10.1108/02683940710726384

Tushman ML, O'Reilly CA (1996) Ambidextrous organizations: managing evolutionary and revolutionary change. Calif Manag Rev 38(4):8–30

Tversky B (2011) Visualizing thought. Top Cogn Sci 3(3):499–535. https://doi.org/10.1111/j.1756-8765.2010.01113.x

Tversky A, Kahneman D (1981) The framing of decisions and the psychology of choice. Science 211(4481):453–458. https://doi.org/10.1126/science.7455683

Utterback JM (1994) Mastering the dynamics of innovation: How companies can seize opportunities in the face of technological change. Harvard Business School Press, Cambridge, MA

Van Andel P (1992) Serendipity: "expect also the unexpected". Creat Innov Manag 1(1):20–32. https://doi.org/10.1111/j.1467-8691.1992.tb00018.x

Van de Ven AH (1986) Central problems in the management of innovation. Manag Sci 32 (5):590–607. https://doi.org/10.1287/mnsc.32.5.590

VanGundy AB (2007) Getting to innovation: how asking the right questions generates the great ideas your company needs. AMACOM, New York, NY

Vattam SS, Helms ME, Goel AK (2009) Nature of creative analogies in biologically inspired innovative design. Proceedings of the seventh ACM conference on creativity and cognition, pp 255–264. doi:https://doi.org/10.1145/1640233.1640273

Verhaeghen P, Trani AN, Aikman SN (2017) On being found: how habitual patterns of thought influence creative interest, behavior, and ability. Creat Res J 29(1):1–9. https://doi.org/10.1080/10400419.2017.1263504

Vishwanath A (2009) From belief-importance to intention: the impact of framing on technology adoption. Commun Monogr 76(2):177–206. https://doi.org/10.1080/03637750902828438

Vogel S (1999) Unnatural acts. The Sciences 39(4):10–12. https://doi.org/10.1002/j.2326-1951.1999.tb03697.x

Wallas G (1926) The art of thought. Harcourt, Brace and Company, New York, NY

Walsh JP, Ungson GR (1991) Organizational memory. Acad Manag Rev 16(1):57–91. https://doi.org/10.5465/amr.1991.4278992

Wang B, Miao Y, Zhao H, Jin J, Chen Y (2016) A biclustering-based method for market segmentation using customer pain points. Eng Appl Artif Intell 47:101–109. https://doi.org/10.1016/j.engappai.2015.06.005

Waters M (2016) The public shaming of England's first umbrella user. https://www.atlasobscura.com. Accessed 24 Jun 2018

Watzlawick P, Weakland JH, Fisch R (1974) Change: principles of problem formation and problem resolution. Norton, New York, NY

Wedell-Wedellsborg T (2017) Are you solving the right problems? Harv Bus Rev 95(1):76–83

Weick KE (1979) The social psychology of organizing. 2nd edn. Addison-Wesley, Reading, MA

Weick KE (1995) Sensemaking in organizations. Sage, Thousand Oaks, CA

Weick KE (1998) Introductory essay – improvisation as a mindset for organizational analysis. Organ Sci 9(5):543–555. https://doi.org/10.1287/orsc.9.5.543

Weisenfeld U (2009) Serendipity as a mechanism of change and its potential for explaining change processes. Manag Rev 20(2):138–148. https://doi.org/10.1688/1861-9908_mrev_2009_02_Weisenfeld

Weiss M, Hoegl M, Gibbert M (2011) Making virtue of necessity: the role of team climate for innovation in resource-constrained innovation projects. J Prod Innov Manag 28(S1):196–207. https://doi.org/10.1111/j.1540-5885.2011.00870.x

West MA (1990) The social psychology of innovation in groups. In: West MA, Farr J (eds) Innovation and creativity at work: psychological and organizational strategies. Wiley, Oxford, pp 309–333

West MA, Anderson NR (1996) Innovation in top management teams. J Appl Psychol 81 (6):680–693. https://doi.org/10.1037/0021-9010.81.6.680

White M (2000) Leonardo da Vinci: the first scientist. Little, Brown and Company, London

Widmann A, Messmann G, Mulder RH (2016) The impact of team learning behaviors on team innovative work behavior: a systematic review. Hum Resour Dev Rev 15(4):429–458. https://doi.org/10.1177/1534484316673713

Wood W, Rünger D (2016) Psychology of habit. Annu Rev Psychol 67(1):289–314. https://doi.org/10.1146/annurev-psych-122414-033417

Wood W, Tam L, Witt MG (2005) Changing circumstances, disrupting habits. J Pers Soc Psychol 88(6):918–933. https://doi.org/10.1037/0022-3514.88.6.918

Woodman RW, Sawyer JE, Griffin RW (1993) Toward a theory of organizational creativity. Acad Manag Rev 18(2):293–321. https://doi.org/10.5465/amr.1993.3997517

Woodruff RB (1997) Customer value: the next source for competitive advantage. J Acad Mark Sci 25(2):139. https://doi.org/10.1007/bf02894350

Wrona T, Sinzig C (2018) Nonmarket strategy research: systematic literature review and future directions. J Bus Econ 88(2):253–317. https://doi.org/10.1007/s11573-017-0875-3

Wyer RS, Xu AJ (2010) The role of behavioral mind-sets in goal-directed activity: conceptual underpinnings and empirical evidence. J Consum Psychol 20(2):107–125. https://doi.org/10.1016/j.jcps.2010.01.003

Xu AJ, Wyer RS (2007) The effect of mind-sets on consumer decision strategies. J Consum Res 34 (4):556–566. https://doi.org/10.1086/519293

Xu AJ, Wyer RS (2012) The role of bolstering and counterarguing mind-sets in persuasion. J Consum Res 38(5):920–932. https://doi.org/10.1086/661112

Yaqub O (2018) Serendipity: towards a taxonomy and a theory. Res Policy 47(1):169–179. https://doi.org/10.1016/j.respol.2017.10.007

Yuan F, Woodman RW (2010) Innovative behavior in the workplace: the role of performance and image outcome expectations. Acad Manag J 53(2):323–342. https://doi.org/10.5465/amj.2010.49388995

Zeithaml VA (1988) Consumer perceptions of price, quality, and value: a means-end model and synthesis of evidence. J Mark 52(3):2–22. https://doi.org/10.2307/1251446

Zhou J, Hoever IJ (2014) Research on workplace creativity: a review and redirection. Annu Rev Organ Psych Organ Behav 1(1):333–359. https://doi.org/10.1146/annurev-orgpsych-031413-091226

Zhou J, Shalley CE (2003) Research on employee creativity: a critical review and directions for future research. In: Martocchio J (ed) Research in personnel and human resources management, vol 22. Elsevier, Oxford, pp 165–217. https://doi.org/10.1016/S0742-7301(03)22004-1

Zhou J, Shalley CE (2011) Deepening our understanding of creativity in the workplace: a review of different approaches to creativity research. In: Zedeck S (ed) APA handbook of industrial and organizational psychology, vol 1. American Psychological Association, Washington, DC, pp 275–302. https://doi.org/10.1037/12169-009

Chapter 4
General Discussion

Abstract The phenomenon-focused analysis of the eight sports cases is concluded with a critical reflection of the research process including limitations and future directions.

4.1 Summary

In increasingly complex environments, companies are in a constant quest for sources of value that could translate into sustainable competitive advantages. Leaders are facing increasingly high pressures to develop ever more creative and innovative means to provide the continuing surety to their firm's success. While the corporate landscape in the second half of the twentieth century has predominantly been shaped by efficiency-related strategies like improvements in productivity, a more effectiveness-oriented kind of innovation seems to be the business imperative of this decade and beyond. Empirical observation reveals a plethora of examples in which companies reinterpreted or deviated from established behavioral market standards causing changes in particular segments, markets, and whole industries. IKEA, Motel One, and Red Bull are just three of the most popular examples. The investigation at hand is concerned with all those cases that denote a legal, non-technological innovation leading to a radical change in the dominant logic of a market: rule-breaking market behavior. It has been shown that this is not only an interesting but also highly impactful phenomenon.

Even though a significant amount of anecdotal evidence exists for instances where companies find highly impactful ways to deviate from behavioral standards, scientific evidence is scarce. While many different areas in the literature are concerned with change, innovation, and creativity, fundamental processes continue to be poorly understood, and numerous open questions remain. Therefore, to systematically explore motivations for and potential prerequisites of rule-breaking market behavior is highly relevant from both a scholarly and business perspective. A better understanding of the phenomenon's underlying scientific principles is crucial to help practitioners select and shape the processes and circumstances that

© Springer Nature Switzerland AG 2019 197
A.-K. Veenendaal, *Toward a Better Understanding of Rule-Breaking Market Behavior*, Contributions to Management Science, https://doi.org/10.1007/978-3-030-16107-1_4

stimulate the creation of rule-breaking market behavior in the long-term endeavor of creating a sustainable competitive advantage.

This work has sought to provide some tentative insight into the nature and process of rule-breaking market behavior. The methodological approach has been to inductively uncover characteristic principles in the process of rule-breaking market behavior by analyzing multiple historical athletic cases which, by analogy, have been transferred back to the managerial context. In doing so, the following contributions have been made.

Addressing the first research question related to the *what* of rule-breaking market behavior, an initial definition has been offered and contrasted with related constructs. In defining the construct, an emphasis has been laid on the non-technological and breakthrough character of the innovative behavior, distilling the following core operational definition: *rule-breaking market behavior denotes a legal, non-technological innovation that radically changes the dominant logic of a market.* The conceptual features of rule-breaking market behavior have been posed as questions in a Four-Way-Rule-Breaking Test so that relevant phenomena can easily be identified: Is It a Non-Technological Innovation? Does the Innovation Comply with the Formal Set of Rules? Is the Innovation Radical? Is the Innovation Collectively Accepted? The Four-Way-Rule-Breaking Test follows the idea of a decision tree and thus characterized by a high level of intelligibility. For each of the four features, an overview of key discussions in the literature has been provided. Having specified the nature of rule-breaking market behavior, the foundation for this work's main quest has been laid: aiming at getting a better understanding of the *how*, the process of rule-breaking market behavior.

Because bottom-up, case-based research is well suited for studying processes or *how* questions, this method aligned nicely with interest in understanding how rule-breaking market behavior comes into place. Here, empirical insight into the development of rule-breaking behavior has been presented based on the stories of eight historical behavioral breakthroughs in the context of sports: the Fosbury Flop in the High Jump, the Flip Turn in Backstroke Swimming, the O'Brien Shift in Shot Put, the Skate Skiing Technique in Cross-Country Skiing, the Forward Seat in Equestrian Jumping, the V-Style in Ski Jumping, the Jump Shot in Basketball, and the Dolphin Kick in Butterfly Swimming. Each of those techniques is in full accordance with the four conceptual features of rule-breaking behavior by being (a) a non-technological deviation from existing practices, (b) compliant to the formal rules of the sports domain, (c) fundamentally different to the prior style and substantially better in terms of performance, and eventually (d) adopted by a large portion of athletes. As some of these innovations go back to more than one innovator, a total of 18 single innovative paths were considered for the analysis. The case selection provides both certain similarities that aid comparisons and replication, yet sufficient heterogeneity to help assess potential generalizability. Sports has been chosen for the analysis as the single most promising domain over and above business and other domains for a variety of screening criteria. The strongest positive aspects were the availability of cases and data, assumed degree of insight, and transfer potential. Stepping back from the familiarities of the researcher's main discipline of business studies, and taking a fresh and broad view, has been productive. With the luxury of hindsight, the development of these eight historical breakthrough sports cases has been analyzed thoroughly from both a single and cross-case perspective. As a result, the lessons learned have been summarized in 8 distinct narratives and 21 characteristics that yielded success in the process of rule-breaking behavior. The eight cases build the heart of this work. Each of the eight sports examples showcases a remarkable blueprint of rule-breaking behavior. Any manager or company would be delighted if they, in an analogy, were ever to develop and execute even one of those eight highly impactful ideas. The results obtained in this empirical step outside the context of business can be considered results of the first kind.

Next, the case-based insight has been systematically transferred back from the analogy of sports to the managerial context. Results obtained at this stage of the analysis can be considered results of a second kind. In this step, the empirical insight was related to research in the context of creativity and innovation, including further aggregation and interpretation of the case-data from a business point of view. Each of the 21 cross-case insights was linked to comparable scholarly discussions, contrasting empirical findings, and existing work with regard to structure and content.

From a comprehensive analysis, two major, separable challenges in the process of rule-breaking behavior have been identified across all eight sports cases: (1) recognizing a new way and (2) overcoming innovation resistance. First of all, the rule-breaking approach needs to be discovered in the sense of literally seeing it as an opportunity and then to be pursued. Usually, this stage occurs at the individual level. Secondly, the new way needs to gain acceptance from others. This means that the novel approach moves from level to level to ultimately be broadly adopted, which is a necessary prerequisite for sustainable corporate performance (e.g. from individual to group to company to market to societal to world acceptance). The independence of the two stages is manifest regarding temporal, spatial and actor-related terms: What has been recognized as a new way by, for instance, one actor from one company in a particular year could be popularized by another actor from a different company at any other time in the future.

Concerning the first challenge, the case study provides critical insight into how the athletes have mastered the discovery of a new way. By discussing the origins of significant sports innovations, more is found out on the potential origins of rule-breaking behavior itself. In close alignment with discussions in the context of creativity, recognizing a new way requires a willingness to deviate from conventional wisdom and adopt new ways of thinking and doing, enact new patterns, and move away from the status quo so that novel and useful ideas can be developed. From a temporal sequence perspective, two different pathways have been identified in this first stage: a problem-induced and a solution-oriented one. In the former pathway, the process of discovering a novel behavioral approach is typically triggered by a pressing problem to be solved, thus deliberately engaging in a search procedure for new approaches. In the latter pathway, the discovery of the novel behavioral approach, a rule-breaking solution, occurs without the prior intention of solving an existing problem. It thus, for example, comes by surprise or is introduced by an outsider. In total, the historical sports cases have revealed a reasonably large set of key factors that triggered the development of either of the two pathways to rule-breaking behavior. These different impulses have been clustered into nine categories of creative cues: serendipitous, incompatibility, motivational, affective, external, functional, cognitive, experiential, and cultural cues. These triggers of the process of rule-breaking behavior have been termed creative cues because they either signal for action or specifically indicate how to behave. Either way, when processes in a company or human behavior, in general, are thought of as having inertial tendencies, the cues can be thought of as occurrences that shake the snow globe. Cues differ from facilitating factors as they are conceptualized to initiate the process of discovering a novel approach. For the following course of action, what has been helpful to make the snow globe shake may not necessarily be helpful in what is required afterward. As there is a vast array of research on different facilitating and inhibiting factors *in* the process of creativity and innovation, this work has focused on the very first drivers, or cues, *of* the process. Based on the case data, it is posited that at least one cue is needed as a trigger, but several cues can also operate together in a combined fashion, for example, with one cue being dominant. In terms of the level of abstraction, the cues can be considered a combination of abstract and concrete at the same time. To better illustrate: When one comes from the oftentimes made statement that such processes are triggered by external shocks or crises, the creative cues that have been developed are much more concrete. When one comes from the expectation of getting information as precise as, "go to the playground at eight in the morning, have no breakfast before, wear a green shirt, go on the swings and bring your dog—then you will find a rule-breaking way", one finds the creative cues are more abstract. In other words, more can be done than wait for something big to happen from the external, but there may not be a precise recipe for success. All in all, the cues are sufficiently concrete yet universally applicable instructions, each provided with recommendations for managerial action. They can be considered the centerpiece of this work as the case study provided essential insight here.

Regarding the second challenge, rule-breaking attempts (i.e. rule-breaking offerings that have been developed as a result from the cue) have been shown to face various degrees of resistance. Arthur Schopenhauer once said, "All truth passes through three stages. First, it is ridiculed. Second, it is violently opposed. Third, it is accepted as being self-evident." This has proven to be true for the cases of rule-breaking behavior in sports, too. Ad-hoc acceptance of novel behaviors appears to be rather the exception than the norm. The fact that strategic change faces obstacles is not a new revelation. In the course of transformation, employees often feel threatened, customers become confused, investors dislike the unproven strategies, and the risk of failure is typically high. Based on the empirical insight, this work, too, finds that when fundamentally different approaches to solutions are introduced, they are often objected, no matter how effective they are.

Nevertheless, even seemingly insurmountable resistance, like in the case of the jump shot, has eventually been overcome. Strong performance and a wait-and-see mentality ("eventually they will get used to it") are two of the typical approaches to deal with resistance. In addition to these more general heuristics, this work has presented a range of mechanisms to improve conditions for a more rapid acceptance. Basically, they, too, are based on the case-insight, but in this step, compared to what has been proposed in the context of the first challenge, the mechanisms to overcome resistance are much closer to existing concepts in the literature, as empirical evidence was less precise here. In a nutshell, six possible approaches have been presented and explained in close alignment with the empirical data: turning typical barriers to innovation acceptance into questions (how to identify and address active and passive innovation barriers), reframing (how to place a situation in another frame and thus have an impact on meaning), debiasing (how to present corrective messages if erroneous beliefs persist), blending (how to combine old and new, "do the familiar differently"), activating a procedural mindset (providing innovation acceptance training in a seemingly unrelated domain), and an insightful note on habit change and brief habits. To sum up, it seems that as the pace of innovation accelerates, human behavior rather than technological restraints will be the deciding factor of whether products are adopted or discarded. Thus, a better understanding of this stage is considered to be of ever more crucial importance.

Finally, the results have been integrated into a framework of rule-breaking market behavior. The conceptual structure is intended to display the most important findings at a glance and thus serve as useful guidance that is rich and detailed enough to support the development of rule-breaking market behavior. As a visual tool, it can spark conversations about and direct thought on the several facets of rule-breaking market behavior. Together with the case stories and some exemplary questions listed both in the framework and its textual description, the rule-breaking framework provides managers and other corporate individuals with a comprehensive toolbox to reflect on their creativity and innovation mindset and processes. Several normative recommendations for directions of thought and measures to take are provided. A catalog of sources of creativity and resistance has not just been provided but gone a step further by offering normative recommendations regarding each of the challenges in the process of rule-breaking market behavior. Overall, care was taken throughout the whole analytical process that the characteristics could be designed by companies (i.e. are not related to fixed parameters such as childhood experience or intelligence quotient). Indeed, as visible throughout this work, social processes and especially market processes are characterized by an undetermined, open-ended series of exchanges—innovation in general and rule-breaking market behavior, in particular, can take many forms. As apparent in the cases and throughout the literature, there are no universal recipes to rule-breaking market behavior, but many paths can turn out to be fruitful. The framework provides a number of systematically derived principles of rule-breaking market behavior including mechanisms that are more concrete than to wait for crises or external shocks, or new or young employees.

Providing a coherent picture of the most important lessons to be learned involves processes of inference that are characterized by loss of information and subjectivity. Therefore, it is highly recommended for any practitioner in the quest of developing breakthrough behavioral innovations to not only consider the interpreted and aggregated case insight but also to review the eight case stories and reflect on the particulars independently. The interpretive generalization in this work represents one possible way to make sense of the data, and information reduction in the course of the analysis has been massive. Even though the data analysis with its several steps of interpretation has been executed with high care according to prevalent scientific standards, it is impossible to rule out all possible alternative explanations, especially when it comes to creative and innovative processes that do not seem to be following a strict sequence of repeatable causal relationships. What had to remain unrecognized due to the limited scope of this work may, in an unfortunate case, be regarded as a key specificity from the perspective of a very particular company and their respective problem space.

All things considered, this work's particular take on how to create competitive advantage offers some substantive contributions continuing along with Corley and Gioia (2011) who suggest that the idea of contribution rests largely on the ability to provide original insight into a phenomenon by advancing knowledge in a way that is deemed to have utility or usefulness for some purpose. First of all, as rather broad investigations and bottom-up approaches to better understand the root mechanisms of problems are sparse, the approach to inductively unpack rule-breaking market behavior to provide a deeper and richer understanding of the developmental process can be evaluated as useful. This work has further shown that scholars can generate fresh insights by studying phenomena in contexts other than business. Following philosopher E.M. Cioran's statement, "We are enriched only by frequenting disciplines remote from our own", the study captures not only what could have been seen in the "known" context of managerial research but what the different yet comparable realm of sports can teach us. All in all, by providing a coherent picture of a fascinating, impactful and under-researched phenomenon, new dimensions could be added to the literature, especially where empirical evidence is sparse and findings are contradictory (e.g. as outlined by Anderson et al. 2014; Elsbach and Stigliani 2018; Zeng et al. 2011). Some of the insight, for instance regarding creative cues, runs counter to established corporate practice, maybe even counter to what is believed to be common sense. The distinct rule-breaking perspective on the challenges of creativity and innovation processes (and how they can be overcome) hopefully proves helpful for the solution of real-world challenges, as they persist in companies. Even though none of the single research propositions or findings has been entirely new, their unique combination and integration together with various normative recommendations are hoped to be valuable for both scholars and practitioners alike.

While it continues to be a challenge to thoroughly understand the creative energy that leads to rule-breaking scholarly, business, and artistic masterpieces, it is at least aimed at spurring individuals to become their best creative selves. This work offers a particular mindset and specific ways on how companies and employees can endogenously, without hiring experts or consultants, create competitive advantage and manage the difficult quest of human transformation above and beyond the imperative of technological innovation. Embracing the idea of and the above-presented mechanisms for rule-breaking market behavior should enable employees to be their own consultant when it comes to questions involving behavioral change. In times, when technological progress has become the norm, issues of human transformation, will as a matter of course, accompany us in the continued journey through the twenty-first century.

4.2   Limitations and Future Research Directions

It has been shown that the systematic inquiry of how non-technological break-through innovations emerged in the domain of sports made several contributions to both theoretical and practical problems alike. However, the study of the underlying mechanisms of rule-breaking market behavior is still far from being complete and thus invites future research. Furthermore, to evaluate the findings, it is important to reflect critically on potentially limiting aspects. The scope of the study has been comparatively broad. Contrary to mainstream top-down research endeavors that investigate particular hypothesized cause-effect-relationships, this examination focused on a bottom-up approach to broadly explore the developmental process of rule-breaking market behavior.

In consequence, this leads to a dilemmatic space between the search for findings that are as holistic as possible but at the same time sufficiently detailed. In this quest, a number of compromises had to be made, which will be made transparent and critically reflected on below with more insight about the scholarly process, that is, the researcher's journey, to trust her as a legitimate ambassador, translator, and interpreter of the setting under study. Reflexivity, as in the act of critical (self-) reflection on biases and preferences, is considered central to any (but even more so to a qualitative) inquiry and impactful research (Jonsen et al. 2018). There are two dimensions to scientific inquiries: content and method. Both will be briefly investigated in the conclusion of this work.

First, the phenomenon under study can be evaluated regarding the content-dimension. Generally, the change and innovation area is "a complex conglomeration of different but related constructs, that change management is therefore necessarily going to be a complex and multifaceted undertaking, and that practicing managers should treat popular texts that purport to offer quick and easy solutions with . . . a healthy degree of skepticism" (Potočnik and Anderson 2016, p. 492). This work can certainly be distinguished from what is referred to with "popular texts"; however, it is to be highlighted that rule-breaking market behavior is not considered a one-approach-fits-all solution but just one way to approach the quest of gaining a competitive advantage. Rule-breaking market behavior has considerable potential to support managers when thinking of innovation from a behavioral insight perspective; however, this work does by no means want to ignore the crucial role of conventions and repeated practices. Thus, the idea is not to turn any established practice upside down for the mere sake of being innovative but to expressly incorporate the idea into the creative corporate mindset, be more receptive of this rule-breaking perspective, and take the mechanisms into account, either regularly or when appropriate.

As much as the "never change a running system" statement may need to be critically reassessed, the "all creativity and innovation is good; and the more, the better" (Anderson et al. 2014, p. 1320) proposition needs to be thought about carefully, too. In this context, Anderson et al. (2014) caution against an "innovation maximization fallacy" (p. 1320), challenging the mostly prevailing assumption that innovative attempts are always functional by pointing out that creativity and innovation do not always benefit all actors involved and can be counterproductive to other aspects of individual or organizational performance. Thus, we should be careful about not ending up in a state where individuals and organizations continuously break the rules, coming up with ever-new ways of behaving but failing to routinize core organizational processes. For years, "To Break the Rules, You Must First Master Them", has been Audemars Piquet's trademark campaign, expressing the essence of their brand philosophy. With regard to the underlying cases, this is not a negligible thought.

Second, this work needs to be evaluated regarding the method-dimension. Ultimately, bottom-up empirical approaches in order to better understand a particular phenomenon are directed toward the development of theory. While it has been outlined that this would be a quest too presumptuous to be achieved in a doctoral dissertation, general criteria of how to assess bottom-up theory building approaches are incorporated into the discussion. Theoretical contributions try to account for accuracy, simplicity, and generality. While those three characteristics are desirable, it is generally considered difficult if not impossible for any theory to fully achieve all three (Weick 1979).

Here, a bottom-up, multiple-case study has been chosen as the research design. Findings emerging from multiple-case research are typically said to be more focused than overarching theories and more valid, better grounded and generalizable than those of single case studies (Davis et al. 2007; Eisenhardt and Graebner 2007). However, it is important to take a closer look at several issues related to data, translation, writing, and sufficiency and critically discuss all of them individually.

The findings are not evaluated in whether they are true, as "truthfulness of a proposition is of limited duration" (Tellis 2017, p. 1), but whether they are trustworthy.

Overall, prescribed methods and measures for the process of data collection and analysis that sought to increase the reliability and validity of the findings have been adopted. These included: (1) a prolonged engagement with the empirical cases to become enmeshed in the context and data, (2) several sources of data (whenever possible primary sources) and varied empirical evidence in multiple cases and paths to triangulate perspectives, (3) thick and stepwise descriptions to capture the rich context and to ensure the quality and validity of interpretations, (4) following basic guidelines regarding fundamental principles of qualitative empirical research (e.g. grounded theory), (5) a 6-month period of (mental and physical) travel delving into a completely different scholarly context to challenge existing knowledge and perspectives on the topic at hand, (6) a 2-month intense research boot camp to experience how daily behavioral standards change in a completely different spatial and cultural context and free the mind from premature interpretations, (7) external feedback on various empirical and conceptual milestones such as case selection, construct definition and analytic approach, and, most importantly, (8) two experienced senior researchers as regular sounding boards reviewing the emergent constructs and structures to probe ideas and to increase the reliability and validity of interpretation.

Retrospective cases are often subject to difficulties we face in knowing the ordinary past. In pretty much any case, there has been controversy about who should be credited for the invention. For example, in what became known as the Fosbury Flop, other jumpers are said to have developed the same technique independently of Dick Fosbury. In cases of doubt, and whenever allowed for by data availability, all stories have been taken into account and made transparent in the analysis. Therefore, not 8 but 18 paths were delineated.

For several reasons (e.g. research scope, resources, historical character of the cases), the analysis had to rely on secondary data. Thus, the researcher could not act as a neutral observer but relied on subjectively biased accounts of the innovators themselves or other contemporary witnesses' reports. For instance, Tod Sloan's recollection of how the Forward Seat has been invented was obviously self-interested. Two actions have been taken in respect of this: (1) pre-selected, reliable sources, such as Christgau's (1999) curated compilation of eight men who shook the world of basketball was used predominantly; (2) just the information that was characterized by a certain degree of objectivity was transferred. For instance, in the case of Myer "Whitey" Skoog, his ski jumping experience was considered (experiential cue), rather than trying to interpret the impact his Nordic roots may have had on his character and thus on his inclination (or aversion) to be innovative.

The process of deriving insights from the data required two separate translational steps: One related to the context of the application, the transfer from sports to business, and one related to the level of aggregation, from a single case to multiple cases to principles in the creativity and innovation literature. All steps brought different challenges along.

First, even though several screening criteria have been applied to choose a promising source domain, sports and business still hold different features, which may be argued to interdict an analogical transfer of insights gained in the one to the other. As each of the eight sports examples showcases a striking cyanotype of rule-breaking behavior, one might question whether sport as a domain could be more receptive of revolutions whereas management, on the other hand, might be more receptive of evolutionary improvements. Reasons for that could be different motivational factors (e.g. higher passion for sports than business related questions), lower risk (e.g. usually "just" one person is affected if the rule-breaking attempt fails), different support structures and shorter ways (e.g. personal coaches, quicker decisions), different logic of competition (e.g. companies are dependent on customers' choices, athletes performance lies in their own hands), and other resource structures (e.g. physical and mental fitness required in sports versus focus on cognitive conditions in a corporate context). Whether any of these or other characteristics are so specific for either one of the contexts that a transfer of discovered criteria in one domain would lead to entirely different results in the other remains a matter of empirical research. By mindfully comparing every single empirical finding from the sports cases to existing literature in business, potentially critical concerns have been paid attention to (e.g. that innovation contests in companies have to be executed with care). Due to the overall impression that has been gained in the course of the analysis, it is posited that even though the fundamental logic of the two domains are not identical, as the case insight could straightforwardly be linked to existing discussions because they offered sufficiently comparable structures, a transfer of the discovered principles from sports back to the context of business is considered feasible to the extent that it has been done in this work.

Second, as already indicated above, the analytical process in this work started out with a large pool of unstructured empirical data that has been successively reduced to just a few key contributions. This gradual process of interpretation and aggregation from a single statement to a universal principle has been characterized by both gains of focus and loss of data. Innumerable decisions had to be made, all of them at least triple checked, some reversed at later stages of the work, and others persistent until the end. While a certain degree of subjectivity cannot and should not be ruled out, it is concluded that the above-explained measures taken throughout the process to increase the reliability and validity of the findings meet the most fundamental expectations regarding rigorous work.

One of the challenges in outlining case study results is to provide enough data to permit readers to draw their own conclusions and yet provide interpretation. The idea is to account for both "honest subjectivity" and creative craftsmanship (Jonsen et al. 2018, p. 31). First, an attempt to address this has been through separating descriptive and normative elements in the course of outlining the eight cases. Second, information has been presented in several forms (e.g. tabular, textual, graphical) and with different degrees of aggregation (exemplary quotes, long and short single case stories, preliminary cross-case interpretations, and a final interpretation of aggregated criteria). Further, the reader has been explicitly encouraged to not only rely on the interpretations that have been proffered in the summarizing template but also to consider the individual case stories and to derive their own understandings accordingly. One-size-fits-all answers to every company's problem cannot be provided as the effective course of action will generally depend on particular specifics of each firm (Carlile and Christensen 2004). Thus, the insight provided here needs to be re-evaluated and refined accordingly.

Another challenge that occurred over and over in different parts of this work relates to the depth-breadth-tradeoff. While this has also been discussed as playing a role in the development of rule-breaking behavior (deep versus broad knowledge and experience), here, it relates to methodological issues. Three decisions are exemplary: selecting one domain versus several domains, analyzing one single case versus multiple cases, or focusing on just a few or a variety of cross-case criteria for the transfer to the business literature. In the first pro-breadth decision, when several cases were chosen over a single case, the depth of data analysis necessarily had to suffer. From a historian's perspective, the scope of the eight case narratives would probably be considered superficial. To give just one example, historians would study as many primary sources related to the period under discussion as possible in order to make sense of the context and to get into the minds of contemporaries to see the world as they did. Secondary sources would only be used as a way to frame contemporary evidence (for further insight into historical methodology in a marketing context, see Fullerton 2011). From a marketer's perspective, however, the chosen procedure is typical. In the second pro-breadth decision, when a variety of cross-case criteria were chosen over just a few selected ones, the depth of how these criteria could be discussed and further investigated necessarily had to suffer. If this work's goal had been to provide precise, empirically tested insight on underlying causal relationships of rule-breaking market behavior, one would assess the work as having utterly failed.

In summary, critics could blame the results as not coming up to scientific expectations, by neither being fish nor fowl. Framed differently, from the perspective of a marketer following a decision-oriented paradigm, painting a reasonably holistic and sufficiently grounded picture of an insufficiently understood, impactful phenomenon that consequently helps to provide relevant managerial implications, is considered the more productive approach. All in all, while there is certainly more potential regarding the level of sufficiency, a coherent framework including major principles and how to address them has not deemed a compromise resulting from a depth-breadth dilemma but under consideration of all parameters at hand, the most purposeful and balanced approach feasible. Whenever a proposition has been made, it is based on sound empirical evidence, has undergone a thorough process of scientific analysis, and been challenged by both intra- and inter-personal processes of cognitive reasoning alike.

In conclusion, there indeed can be several parameters thought of that would further enrich and even better ground the results. Therefore, beyond research suggestions arising from the limitations of the study, several potentially important areas for future research are offered. This is to show at one glance what has and has not been part of this work and to broaden the reader's perspective for additional directions to complete the understanding and unlock the potentials of rule-breaking market behavior. Figure 4.1 maps content and method related elements of this study in dark green, each supplemented by prospective research options in light green to facilitate systematic discussion. These designate avenues of future research will be addressed below.

1. Although an immense body of research on creativity and innovation exits, the literature has seen relatively little holistic, bottom-up empirical research directed toward a systematic inquiry of underlying procedural mechanisms. Probably the most popular method to do so has been applied in this work: an inductive multiple-case study approach with the data analysis based on historical secondary data. Further methodological approaches to learn more about complex processes and maybe account for more recent (instead of historical) data would be to collect primary data by, for example, observing certain groups who are likely to deviate from behavioral standards and come up with novel solutions (e.g. observation of children), or by engaging in ethnographic research (e.g. in a particularly innovative corporation). Due to a lack of resources, research partners, and

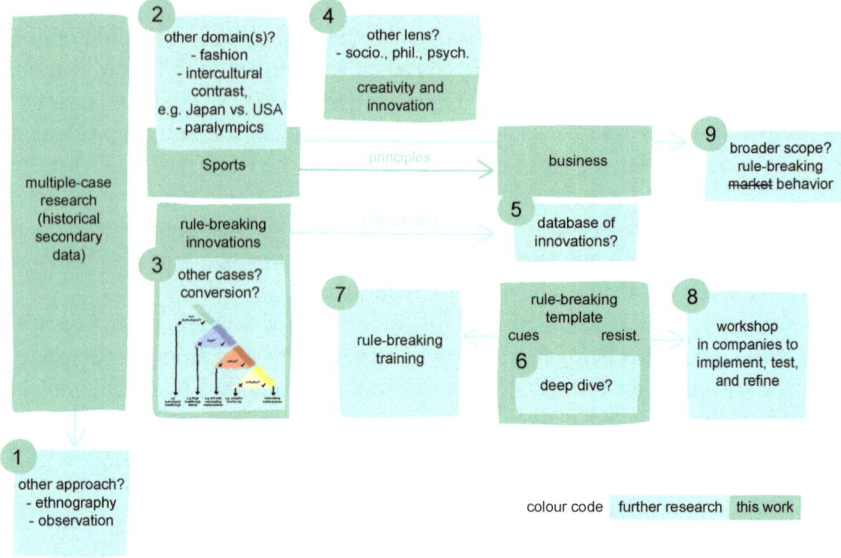

Fig. 4.1 Contrasting current research and future research (source: author)

methodological expertise, these approaches have not been pursued here but are deemed fruitful techniques to gain a further in-depth understanding of the processes leading to rule-breaking market behavior. Multiple-case research results are amenable to extension and validation with other methods (Davis et al. 2007).

2. Sports have been chosen as the single most promising domain to study cases of rule-breaking behavior. However, other contexts might be favorable as well, either to gain information on the whole process of rule-breaking behavior or just concerning particular aspects, like one of the major challenges that have been identified. For instance, the fashion industry is based on rather brief than enduring preference patterns as clothes typically change with every season. In many cases, fashion innovations are of the non-technological kind, too. Consequently, there may be interesting mechanisms that could be found to help better explain how creative ideas are rapidly developed and brought to market and how innovation resistance can be overcome. Moreover, the role of cultural differences in the development of rule-breaking market behavior could be focused on. It might, for instance, be assumed that rule-breaking behavior is supposedly even harder to achieve in more collectivistic cultures such as Japan than in individualistic cultures such as the United States or Germany. Also, instead of just focusing on Olympic disciplines in the domain of sports, Paralympics or Special Olympics might also provide insightful cases.

3. The sample of this work comprises eight cases of rule-breaking behavior in sports. They have been systematically selected from a larger pool of sports innovations and are distinctive by complying with all four features that have been defined to be characteristic of rule-breaking behavior. Besides these eight

cases, the database (see Table A.4 in the Appendix) entails other examples that could be beneficial to analyze. For instance, polar types or negative cases could be sampled in order to observe more easily contrasting patterns of data. Here, the conclusions can only be derived for a pure specimen of rule-breaking behavior. In addition to that, it would be interesting to reveal how the underlying processes differ from other classes such as second-order rule-breaking behavior, rule-breaking exceptions or technological breakthroughs (see Table 2.1). It could also be studied whether and how cases of second-order rule-breaking behavior or rule-breaking exceptions could be upgraded onto the next stage in the decision tree to turn ultimately into rule-breaking market behavior. Furthermore, a closer examination of the interplay between endogenous and exogenous rules have been identified as being of both scholarly and practical interest. Thus, how formal laws need to be designed in order to fuel creative behavior (and which effects replacements, changes, updates or eliminations of certain formal rules have) may be another area of future research.

4. The insights obtained by analyzing the sports cases have been transferred to and interpreted with the help of creativity and innovation research. In addition, further research can benefit from interpreting the data from a sociological, philosophical, and psychological perspective. Sociologists might, for instance, take a closer look at the topic from an institutional theory perspective, considering how far organizational structures (e.g. norms and routines) act as guidelines for social behavior (Tolbert et al. 2011). Philosophers, too, have been dealing with related themes such as the societal acceptance of change ever since and might have a lens that helps pinpoint aspects that have been neglected here.

5. This work has analyzed phenomena in a discipline different from business and, by analogy, transferred the principles back to the target domain. As outlined above, this transfer entails several possible sources of error that can only be revealed through empirical research. Therefore, it might be useful to also work backward from a database equivalent in management. Having a database of different kinds of innovations in business could be a valuable starting point to better analyze impactful creative endeavors in order to answer many of the questions that have remained open for decades. Uncovering patterns in data is best fulfilled by algorithms based on as many cases as possible. Setting up such a database from the vast array of unstructured empirical data, however, requires collaborative efforts preferably guided by a group of researchers or some independent scientific innovation society. The underlying study can only provide a starting point, developed within a single researcher's bounds of possibility, which can be extended, enlarged and used as a source of inspiration.

6. Despite the vast body of research already existing in the creativity and innovation literature, the transfer of case insights has uncovered a range of important questions that have not yet been answered satisfactorily. This concerns both the different creative cues and mechanisms to overcome innovation resistance. For instance, the literature has seen relatively little empirical research regarding the positive effects of negatively valenced emotions or events on creativity.

Innovation barriers, too, are lacking rigorous empirical investigation. Other open questions have been hinted at in the course of Sects. 3.1.3.2 and 3.1.4.2.

7. A particularly important additional question this study raises is how employees can be trained to become more rule-breaking. Even though the training idea has not been of focal interest here, it has been tried to not only uncover important challenges in the developmental process of rule-breaking market behavior but also to unravel specific means for corporate individuals to apply. The list of nine creative cues and five mechanisms to overcome resistance offer a number of possible practices that might fuel the development of rule-breaking market behavior; however, it is by no means exhaustive. Therefore, future research precisely directed at developing possible tools and training for individuals to become better at creating a rule-breaking competitive advantage is invited.

8. A typical process of developing theoretical contributions consists of two stages: discovery and justification (e.g. Hunt 2013). This work has focused on the first step, resulting in a number of propositions that have been summarized in a managerial template and enriched with managerial recommendations. However, propositions derived from exploratory research need to be tested in the next step. Apart from typical Y-centered experiential research approaches, which in the context of innovation are limited to a certain degree, for instance because of difficulties with manipulation and measurement, a workshop-based concept to involve practitioners in the research process as active, reflective and empowered participants to implement, test, and refine the ideas could be further pursued. Theorizing with managers has been suggested as one attempt to close the gap between practitioners and scholars and achieve both academically rigorous and practically relevant solutions to problems (for further insight on theorizing with managers, see European Journal of Marketing Volume 51, Issue 7/8; e.g. Nenonen et al. 2017).

9. Theoretical attempts are often valued according to their generality, as researchers desire to apply their insights to a wider set of phenomena or situations than where the theory was originally developed (Makadok et al. 2018). In fact, scientific research is increasingly expected to make an impact in the real world (e.g. http://www.emeraldgrouppublishing.com/realworldimpact.htm). For scholars in the realm of marketing and management, this can be interpreted as contributing to better industrial performance, and, more broadly, to economic growth and societal welfare.

   Correspondingly, it is suggested that additional research could extend this work's perspective and insights into a broader context beyond business: Rule-Breaking ~~Market~~ Behavior.

Thus, the endeavor to principally learn more about the process of rule-breaking behavior is much more far-reaching than to gain a competitive advantage. Knowing how to create and implement breakthrough non-technological innovations is likely to also help in creating better future societal concepts like infrastructure, urban planning, and educational and labor systems. One way of applying the underlying idea to an audience larger than academia and business would be to translate the topic to the political agenda. To name just two specific examples, some of the mechanisms (e.g. reframing ridicule, encouraging creativity and purposeful deviation from behavioral standards) could be included into curricular activities at all levels of education, and basic challenges of human transformation could be considered in discussions on labor policy planning (e.g. encouraging two jobs at the same time for individuals to become less likely to fall into inertial states and gain a better balance between depth and breadth of knowledge and experience). More broadly, a rule-breaking political party could help post-economized nations to refresh political discussions and being a small piece in the puzzle of paving the way for the populace to be better prepared for a future characterized of rapid technological innovations that probably requires a larger degree of willingness to habitual human re-thinking and transformation.

The final synopsis of selected research desiderata demonstrates that even though the present work could contribute to a better understanding of rule-breaking market behavior as a potentially impactful way of achieving competitive advantage, it can only be seen as a prelude to a holistic understanding of this subject. Hope remains that interest in further pursuing this corporate and societally relevant phenomenon is sparked.

References

Anderson N, Potočnik K, Zhou J (2014) Innovation and creativity in organizations: a state-of-the-science review, prospective commentary, and guiding framework. J Manag 40(5):1297–1333. https://doi.org/10.1177/0149206314527128

Carlile PR, Christensen CM (2004) The cycles of theory building in management research. Working Paper 05–057. Harvard Business School, Boston, https://www.hbs.edu

Christgau J (1999) The origins of the jump shot: eight men who shook the world of basketball. University of Nebraska Press, Lincoln, NE

Corley KG, Gioia DA (2011) Building theory about theory building: what constitutes a theoretical contribution? Acad Manag Rev 36(1):12–32. https://doi.org/10.5465/amr.2009.0486

Davis JP, Eisenhardt KM, Bingham CB (2007) Developing theory through simulation methods. Acad Manag Rev 32(2):480–499. https://doi.org/10.5465/amr.2007.24351453

Eisenhardt KM, Graebner ME (2007) Theory building from cases: opportunities and challenges. Acad Manag J 50(1):25–32. https://doi.org/10.5465/amj.2007.24160888

Elsbach KD, Stigliani I (2018) Design thinking and organizational culture: a review and framework for future research. J Manag 44(6):2274–2306. https://doi.org/10.1177/0149206317744252

Fullerton RA (2011) Historical methodology: the perspective of a professionally trained historian turned marketer. J Hist Res Mark 3(4):436–448. https://doi.org/10.1108/17557501111183608

Hunt SD (2013) The inductive realist model of theory generation: explaining the development of a theory of marketing ethics. AMS Rev 3(2):61–73. https://doi.org/10.1007/s13162-013-0040-2

Jonsen K, Fendt J, Point S (2018) Convincing qualitative research: what constitutes persuasive writing? Organ Res Methods 21(1):30–67. https://doi.org/10.1177/1094428117706533

Makadok R, Burton R, Barney J (2018) A practical guide for making theory contributions in strategic management. Strateg Manag J 39(6):1530–1545. https://doi.org/10.1002/smj.2789

Nenonen S, Brodie RJ, Storbacka K, Peters LD (2017) Theorizing with managers: how to achieve both academic rigor and practical relevance? Eur J Mark 51(7/8):1130–1152. https://doi.org/10.1108/EJM-03-2017-0171

Potočnik K, Anderson N (2016) A constructively critical review of change and innovation-related concepts: towards conceptual and operational clarity. Eur J Work Organ Psychol 25 (4):481–494. https://doi.org/10.1080/1359432X.2016.1176022

Tellis GJ (2017) Interesting and impactful research: on phenomena, theory, and writing. J Acad Mark Sci 45(1):1–6. https://doi.org/10.1007/s11747-016-0499-0

Tolbert PS, David RJ, Sine WD (2011) Studying choice and change: the intersection of institutional theory and entrepreneurship research. Organ Sci 22(5):1332–1344. https://doi.org/10.1287/orsc.1100.0601

Weick KE (1979) The social psychology of organizing, 2nd edn. Addison-Wesley, Reading, MA

Zeng L, Proctor RW, Salvendy G (2011) Can traditional divergent thinking tests be trusted in measuring and predicting real-world creativity? Creat Res J 23(1):24–37. https://doi.org/10.1080/10400419.2011.545713

Appendix

© Springer Nature Switzerland AG 2019   213
A.-K. Veenendaal, *Toward a Better Understanding of Rule-Breaking Market
Behavior*, Contributions to Management Science,
https://doi.org/10.1007/978-3-030-16107-1

A.1 Three Stages of the Data Analysis: Tabular Display

Table A.1 Stage 1

Fosbury Flop	Flip Turn	O'Brien Shift	Skate Skiing	Forward Seat		V-Style		Jump Shot	Dolphin Kick	
Dick Fosbury	Albert Vande Weghe	Parry O'Brien	Pauli Siitonen	Caprilli	Sloan	Graf	Boklöv	several players	Sieg/ Armbr.	Wilson
frustration (trying not to lose)	heavy legs	frustration (defeat)	poor wax, terrain	horses' pain	bolting horse	strained ankle	wind	it just happened	Corsan lay forgotten	dolphins in aquarium
no fit (too tall), could do the old better	diving	yoga, philosophy & other schools of thought	Lapp skiers, lay forgotten	horses in freedom	Native cans	center of gravity		getting clear		swimming as pastime
modified scissors	development together with coach	I save my best for competition	ski orienteering	center of gravity + less wind resistance		style point deductions, aesthetics		frustration		continuous vs. propelling force
evolution only at competition	development together with coach	the longer you apply pressure, the farther it goes	poor wax at competition, virtue of necessity	pragmatists: how could we have been wrong for so long? aesthetics		feels like somersault in the air, many fractures		being too small (4/8)	development with coach	
center of gravity	long and steady developmental process with coach	difficult to start from a position facing the opposite	ban/ restrictions	thorough study (psych +phys)	Native cans	hill size, weight reduction		jumping	development with coach	
support from coach after first success		persistence, tough and systematic preparation and training program	new style was smiled at		another jockey		semi-talented	leaping – ski jump, tree, fence (3/8), convention in lacrosse (1/8)	change breaststroke vs. new butterfly	
personal support		drive/ motivation, brains and brawn	different requirements		monkey seat	frog style, flapping crow		developed prior to career	hard to master (in combination with arms)	
skepticism, straddle was the ultimate			ankle problems, destroys tracks		perseverance, certainty		long process of trial + error	happened during meets or trainings	rule change, new stroke → butterfly	
laughter everywhere, laziest jumper in the world			long, gradual process of evolution (Siitonen-Koch-FIS)		extroverted?		outsider loner	strong disapproval, "benchings"	experiment	experiment
risky way of jumping, very different from other styles			prepared tracks					holy commandment: keep feet on the floor		
safety concerns (back)			personal motivation, training					awkward jump shot		
continuous slow evolution, exploration, imagination, persistence								shooting accuracy down, getting clear up		
landing pits								took a long time (e.g. long adaption period)		
meditates/ psyches himself, trained for the moment										

Table A.2 Stage 2

	Fosbury Flop	Flip Turn	O'Brien Shift	Skate Skiing	Forward Seat	V-Style	Jump Shot	Dolphin Kick
	Dick Fosbury	Albert Vande Weghe	Parry O'Brien	Pauli Siitonen	Caprilli Sloan / Graf	Boklöv	several players	Sieg/Armbr. / Wilson
Sudden change of external parameter					bolting horse	wind	it just happened	
Negative parameter of the sport				poor wax, terrain	horses' pain		getting clear	
Frustration	frustration (trying not to lose)		frustration (defeat)				frustration	
Dysfunctionality physical givens vs. style	no fit (too tall), could do the old better	heavy legs				strained ankle	being too small (4/8)	
Lack of talent					?	semi-talented		
Old style	modified scissors			Lapp skiers, lay forgotten	Native Americans			
Natural, instinctive (vs. cultural)					horses in freedom; Native Americans		jumping	dolphins in aquarium
Experienced in other area/ seen before w/o success		diving		ski orienteering	another jockey		leaping – ski jump, tree, fence (3/8), convention in lacrosse (1/8)	Corsan lay forgotten
Open mind			yoga, philosophy & other schools of thought					
Not main focus							developed prior to career	swimming as pastime
Competition as catalyst	evolution only at competition		I save my best for competition	poor wax at competition, virtue of necessity			happened during meets or trainings	
Physics explanation	center of gravity ?		the longer you apply pressure, the farther it goes	?	center of gravity + less wind resistance	center of gravity ?	?	continuous vs. propelling force
Coaches' reaction	support from coach after first success	development together with coach					strong disapproval, "benchings"	development with coach
Others/ help	personal support	development together with coach						development with coach
Officials' resistance	skepticism, straddle was the ultimate			ban/restrictions	pragmatists: how could we have been wrong for so long? aesthetics	style point deductions, aesthetics	holy commandment: keep feet on the floor	change breaststroke vs. new butterfly
Ridicule	laughter everywhere, laziest jumper in the world			new style was smiled at	monkey seat	? frog style, flapping crow	awkward jump shot	
Harder to learn	risky way of jumping, very different from other styles	?	difficult to start from a position facing the opposite	different requirements	?	feels like somersault in the air, many fractures	shooting accuracy down, getting clear up	hard to master (in combination with arms)
Negative consequence(s)	safety concerns (back)			ankle problems, destroys tracks		hill size, weight reduction		
Systematic, evolutionary process	continuous slow evolution, exploration, imagination, persistence	long and steady developmental process with coach	persistence, tough and systematic preparation and training program	long, gradual process of evolution (Siitonen-Koch-FIS)	thorough study (psych +phys); perseverance, certainty	long process of trial + error	took a long time (e.g. long adaption period)	experiment / experiment
Environmental change	landing pits			prepared tracks			journals, more freedom in shooting	rule change, new stroke → butterfly
Innovators characteristics	meditates/ psyches himself, trained for the moment	?	drive/ motivation, brains and brawn	personal motivation, training	extroverted? ?	outsider loner		? ?

Table A.3 Stage 3

	Fosbury Flop	Flip Turn	O'Brien Shift	Skate Skiing	Forward Seat		V-Style		Jump Shot	Dolphin Kick	
	Dick Fosbury	Albert Vande Weghe	Parry O'Brien	Pauli Siitonen	Caprilli	Sloan	Graf	Boklöv	several players	Sieg/Armbr.	Wilson
Serendipity					bolting horse			wind	it just happened		
Fit research, disabilities, diversity	no fit (too tall), could do the old better	heavy legs					strained ankle		being too small (4/8)		
Human capital							?	semi-talented			
Rewards, competition	evolution only at competition		I save my best for competition	poor wax at competition, virtue of necessity					happened during meets or trainings		
Negative affect, mood	frustration (trying not to lose)		frustration (defeat)						frustration		
Knowledge, deep search trajectory, historical knowledge	modified scissors			Lapp skiers, lay forgotten	Native Americans						
Peripheral and broad search, recombination		diving		ski orienteering	another jockey				leaping – ski jump, tree, fence (3/8), convention in lacrosse (1/8)	Corsan lay forgotten	
Perspective, openness, multicultural exposure			yoga, philosophy & other schools of thought								
Distance, creative freedom									developed prior to career		swimming as pastime
Nature as analogy, compatibility					horses in freedom	Native Americans			jumping		dolphins in aquarium
Customer value, problem finding				poor wax, terrain	horses' pain				getting clear		
Value creation	center of gravity	?	the longer you apply pressure, the farther it goes	?	center of gravity + less wind resistance		center of gravity		?	continuous vs. propelling force	
B = f(P, E), exogenous events	landing pits			prepared tracks					journals, more freedom in shooting	rule change, new stroke → butterfly	
Innovation resistance	support from coach after first success	development together with coach							strong disapproval, "benchings"	development with coach	
Innovation resistance	skepticism, straddle was the ultimate			ban/ restrictions	pragmatists: how could we have been wrong for so long? aesthetics		style point deductions, aesthetics		holy commandment: keep feet on the floor	change breaststroke vs. new butterfly	
Ridicule, gelotophobia	laughter everywhere, laziest jumper in the world			new style was smiled at		monkey seat	?	frog style, flapping crow	awkward jump shot		
Usage barrier	risky way of jumping, very different from other styles	?	difficult to start from a position facing the opposite	different requirements	?		feels like somersault in the air, many fractures		shooting accuracy down, getting clear up	hard to master (in combination with arms)	
Economic risk barrier, personal risk barrier	safety concerns (back)			ankle problems, destroys tracks			hill size, weight reduction				
Individual differences	meditates/ psyches himself, trained for the moment	?	drive/ motivation, brains and brawn	personal motivation, training			extroverted?	?	outsider loner	?	?
Social support	personal support	development together with coach								development with coach	
Creativity and innovation process models	continuous slow evolution, exploration, imagination, persistence	long and steady developmental process with coach	persistence, tough and systematic preparation and training program	long, gradual process of evolution (Siitonen-Koch-FIS)	thorough study (psych +phys)	perseverance, certainty	?		long process of trial + error, took a long time (e.g. long adaption period)	experiment	experiment

A.2 Database of Sports Innovations

Table A.4 Database of sports innovations

Category	Innovation	Year	Discipline	Brief description/insight	Non-techn.	Legal	Radical	Collective
1	Tennis racket	1970s	Tennis	Racket having thickened shaft portion		•	•	•
	Vilsbiburger racket	1970s	Tennis	Double-stringing ("spaghetti strings"), produced an incredible, erratic topspin and overnight enabled weak players to beat stronger players, invented by Bavarian Werner Fischer			•	•
	Rubber balls—celluloid balls	1890s	Table Tennis	Contributed to the success of the game at the very beginning of the twentieth century; James Gibb, an English engineer, found a celluloid ball in an American toy shop in 1890 and persuaded Jacques to introduce these revolutionary balls		•		•
	Built-up shoes	1950s	High Jump	Built up shoes were used by many top jumpers in 1956 and 1957, with soles of up to 5 cm. Yuriy Stepanov from the Soviet Union cleared what was then a world record height of 2.16 m in 1957 using such footwear but the IAAF banned these shoes the following year		•	•	•
	Boxing gloves/mufflers	1743	Boxing	Jack Broughton based the design for his mufflers on the ancient Greek 'cestus', a type of studded gauntlet sported by gladiators and used in hand-to-hand combat. It was not until October 1818 that Broughton's style of gloves was used		•	•	
	Leg grinding	2017	Sailing	This change requires a massive change in behavior, grinders used to grind with their hands/arms before, the bigger leg muscles will be able to produce more power for longer than arm-powered winch grinding	(•)	•	(•)	•
	Carving	1980s	Alpine Skiing	Shaped skis, also called parabolic skis, make carve turns possible at low speeds and with short turn radius		•	•	•
	Fiberglass poles	1950s	Pole Vaulting	Completely changed the nature of pole vaulting; pole vaulting with wood, bamboo or metal poles is a different sport than the one with fiberglass poles		•	•	•

(continued)

Table A.4 (continued)

Category	Innovation	Year	Discipline	Brief description/insight	Non-techn.	Legal	Radical	Collective
2	Doping		All	Use of banned athletic performance-enhancing drugs, see Anti-Doping Rules IOC	•			
	Goalkeeper as outfield player	2016	Handball	Alteration to the use of a goalkeeper as an outfield player; Substitution of a goalkeeper for a seventh outfield player during a suspension was already a widespread tactic, but prior to July 1, 2016, the player replacing the goalkeeper had to do on a shirt the same color as that of the goalkeeper jersey. Teams taking the high-risk approach therefore found it strenuous to change the outfield player replacing their goalkeeper	•	(•)		
	Forward pass	1906	American Football	The forward pass was having a dramatic effect on football; it had been attempted at least 30 years before the play was actually made legal	•	(•)		
	Bodyline	1932	Cricket	When Don Bradman dominated cricket, the English team came up with a tactic to try to counteract his brilliance. They bowled short-pitched balls on leg stump, then stacked the leg-side with fieldsmen. The rules were changed to outlaw Bodyline, by limiting the number of fieldsmen allowed behind square leg; rendered illegal because of sporting dominance	•			
	Gretzky-Rule	1980s	Hockey	When the Gretzky-era Oilers entered a four-on-four or three-on-three situation with an opponent, they frequently used the space on the ice to score one or more goals; in 1985 the NHL Board of Governors introduced offsetting penalties, where neither team lost a man when coincidental penalties were called; rendered illegal because of sporting dominance	•			
	Somersault long jump	1974	Long Jump	Doing a full forward somersault before landing; the style was rendered illegal due to safety concerns; the technique had been discussed before by Tom Ecker, a coach and authority on biomechanics who is the flip's No. 1 advocate, if not its modern-day originator. Ecker says he never heard of the flip before 1970, when he wrote his book. Since its publication in 1971, however, he has talked to a coach who says he saw it performed in 1947 and has heard from another reader who claims to have seen it in 1925	•			

	Javelin throwing by spinning it around like a discus	1956	Javelin Throw	A Spaniard named Felix Erausquin introduced his own technique for throwing the javelin where he would spin around on the spot and release the javelin, similar to a discus throw, this was dubbed the "Spanish Style" of javelin throwing and enabled the throwers to achieve incredible distances before it was banned almost immediately by the IAAF for being an incredibly dangerous method of throwing	•	
	Cartwheel shot put	2000s	Shot Put	Use of a cartwheel, such as a gymnast would use to generate horizontal velocity in tumbling; rendered illegal because of safety concerns	•	
	Korbut flip	1972	Gymnastics Artistic/High Bar	Soviet gymnast Olga Korbut demonstrated the move at the 1972 Olympics, where it was the first backward release move performed on uneven bars in international competition. Standing on the high bar was later declared illegal in accordance with the Code of Points, banning the Korbut Flip from Olympic competition because of the high level of risk involved	•	
	Nursery cannons	1910s	Billiard	Walter Lindrum was the supreme exponent of the 'nursery cannon', in which the cue ball travels along the cushion connecting with the two other balls on the table in a series of tiny point-scoring collisions. By 1932, the 'cushion crawlers' were accused of ruining the game for spectators, who were unable to see or appreciate the play. Accordingly, the Billiard Association and Control Council changed the rules of billiards so the ball had to cross the 'baulk line' of the table at set intervals.	•	
3	Dunking/slam dunk	1960s	Basketball	A type of basketball shot that is performed when a player jumps in the air, controls the ball above the horizontal plane of the rim, and scores by putting the ball directly through the basket with one or both hands; the dunk was outlawed in college basketball from 1967–1976, probably because Lew Alcindor (later known as Kareem Abdul-Jabbar) so dominated the court with it	•	(•) •

(continued)

Table A.4 (continued)

Category	Innovation	Year	Discipline	Brief description/insight	Non-techn.	Legal	Radical	Collective
	Triple loop	1952	Figure Skating	The loop jump is a figure skating jump that takes off from a back outside edge and lands on the same backwards outside edge. For a jump with counterclockwise rotation, this is the right back outside edge. It is named from its similarity to the loop compulsory figure. The invention is widely credited to Werner Rittberger, and the jump is also known as the "Rittberger" in Europe. However, evidence exists that it may have been first done as early as the 1880s.	•	•		•
	Quad loop	2016	Figure Skating	Advanced version of the triple loop (see above); first successful attempt in a competition by Yuzuru Hanyu (Japan)	•	•		•
	Death spiral	1948	Figure Skating	The man in the pivot position, his toe anchored into the ice, holding the woman by a single hand while she circles him on a deep edge with her body almost parallel to the ice; the death spiral had been performed before, but always with the pair holding on to each other with both hands, to use a single hand was revolutionary	•	•		•
	Button camel	1960s	Figure Skating	Dick Button was the first skater to land a double axel and a triple jump in competition and invented the flying camel spin (which was renamed the Button Camel). "[I] just always looked for more challenges within the framework of the sport," says Button. "That was why I kept doing more and more difficult jumps instead of being much more creative and working on differences in the creative side of the sports, which I didn't learn about until much later."	•	•		•
	Gienger salto I	1977	Gymnastics Artistic/High Bar	A backward giant swing into a backward somersault with a half turn to recatch the bar; Gienger had intended to perform the Deltschev salto but he didn't watch carefully enough and ended up with his own version	•	•		•
	Gienger salto II	2016	Gymnastics Artistic/High Bar	One-handed version of the Gienger salto	•	•		•

Name	Year	Sport	Description			
Tsukahara vault	1970s	Gymnastics	Mitsuo Tsukahara is a Japanese gymnast and Olympic Gold Medalist, who is well known for having invented a vaulting technique called the "Tsukahara vault," or "twist", which consists of a half turn off the springboard onto the vault table, then a push backwards, usually into a back salto or layout. His vault became universally recognized and used by both women and men; "this feat changed the future direction of vaulting forever"	•	•	•
Tkatchev reverse hecht	1970s	Gymnastics Artistic/High Bar	The name "Tkatchev" will likely live on for as long as gymnastics exists, for the skill that Alexandre Tkatchev developed in the 1970s has become a signature element of both men's and women's elite gymnastics. Alexandre Tkatchev first competed his reverse hecht, in which he flew backward over the horizontal bar and caught it again at the 1977 Riga Cup. His innovative element completely surprised the audience because he had not performed it during the warmups.	•	•	•
(full, half, quarter) Nelson		Wrestling	A grappling hold which is executed from behind the opponent, generally when both are on the mat face down with the opponent under the aggressor; one or both arms are used to encircle the opponent's arm under the armpit and secured at the opponent's neck. Several different Nelsons exist, they can be separated according to the positioning of the encircling arm(s).	•	•	•
Pokey shot		Beach Volleyball	A beach volleyball attack in which the ball is contacted with the attacking player's knuckles	•	•	•
Cobra shot/snakeshot		Beach Volleyball	The hand is folded over and the ball is moved with the fingertips over the net	•	•	•
Delayed (jump) shot	1970s	Handball	Invented by Hansi Schmidt, this shot is thrown in the sinking movement of the jump; it is reported that Schmidt discovered the style because of a dislocated shoulder	•	•	•
Kempa trick	1954	Handball	The Kempa trick is a combination throw, which became known due to the resulting spectacular and surprising goals. In this move, the thrower catches the passed ball during the jump, and finishes the shot for the goal whilst still in the air.	•	•	•

Table A.4 (continued)

Category	Innovation	Year	Discipline	Brief description/insight	Non-techn.	Legal	Radical	Collective
	Lochte turn	2016	Swimming	The flip-turn has seen no changes until now thanks to Ryan Lochte whose slightly altered method of flip-turning has shaved off almost a second from his lap time, a huge difference in competitive swimming.	•	•		(•)
	Crouching start	1880s	Running	A method of starting in sprint races in which the runner crouches down on all fours improving by 1/10th of a second.	•	•		•
	Suicide squeeze	1894	Baseball	A guaranteed way to score a runner from third base without the ball leaving the infield; is said to have been invented during a college game at Yale University by Dutch Carter and George B. Case	•	•		•
	Air pass/dry pass	1928	Water Polo	In 1928, Hungarian water polo coach Komjadi invented the "air pass," or "dry pass", a technique in which a player directly passes the ball through the air to another player, who receives it without the ball hitting the water. Previously, players would let the ball drop in the water first and then reach out for it, but the dry pass made the offensive game more dynamic and contributed to Hungarian dominance of water polo for 60 years.	•	•		•
	Filipino bomb	1916	Volleyball	It was after accepting the new set of rules created by the Americans regarding the "three-hit limit" when the Filipino volleyball players invented the "set and spike" maneuver. The new technique prompted American enthusiasts and participants in volleyball to call it the "Filipino bomb", because "spiking the ball" was like a "hit" or a form of "attack" that can squash or "kill" the opportunity of the opponent team to hit the ball back for a possible point or win. A more apt description of "hitting and spiking" is that it is "an offensive style of passing the ball in a high trajectory to be struck by another player."	•	•		
	Back row hit	1974	Volleyball	A back row attack in volleyball occurs when one of the three back row player attacks the ball and contacts it at the top of the net	•	•		•

Crossover dribble	1960s	Basketball	Maneuver in which a player dribbling the ball switches the ball rapidly from one hand to the other, to make a change in direction; has been used for many years in basketball, the first known person to use it on the national stage was Oscar Robertson but he reportedly took it from Rucker Park Legend Pee Wee Kirkland	•	•	•
Wildcat formation	1997	Football	The ball is snapped not to the quarterback but directly to a player of another position lined up at the quarterback position; while the Wildcat formation was invented by Billy Ford and Ryan Wilson, it was Kansas State coach Bill Synder who made it popular in the late 1990s as he utilized the many talents of quarterback Michael Bishop to confound opposing defenses	•	•	•
Wishbone offense	1950s	American Football	Offensive formation; the wishbone was the brainchild of Charles "Spud" Cason, who was a junior high football coach in Texas just trying to figure out how to make use of his slow fullback	•	•	•
Clean shooting	2017	Biathlon	Coaches have always stressed fast, accurate shooting, but the revolution that Fourcade spawned has reversed that trend a bit. Now it is more like accuracy first; speed second and make up the lost few seconds on the tracks.	•	•	(•)
Four corners offense	1941	Basketball	With no shot clock and looking for a way to stall, John McLendon would simply set one of his players up in each corner the offensive half court and let his point guard dribble around aimlessly.	•	•	(•)
The pistol formation	1999	American Football	A formation and strategy, invented by a guy playing in a softball league trying to come up with a way to hide his team's slow quarterback. Taylor shared his dilemma with a buddy (and softball teammate) who also happened to be a Division III coach named Tom Kaczkowski, and he suggested lining up the quarterback halfway between the traditional shotgun distance and directly under center.	•	•	(•)
Specialist relief pitchers	1980s	Baseball	Oakland A's manager Tony La Russa began to toy with the idea of matching up a relief pitcher with one specific hitter in the late 1980s. Righty vs. righty and lefty vs. lefty had not been a thing until that point, but now it has become one of the scourges of the modern game.	•	•	•

(continued)

Table A.4 (continued)

Category	Innovation	Year	Discipline	Brief description/insight	Non-techn.	Legal	Radical	Collective
	Hit and run	1892	Baseball	High risk, high reward offensive strategy: John McGraw was a player who came up with a tactical maneuver that would become a staple of all levels of baseball for the next century-plus. He devised the hit-and-run in part because at the time there was only one umpire, and it would be virtually impossible for him to make a close call on the basepaths while also watching the pitch coming in.	•	•		•
	The flying scotsman Graeme Obree	1993	Cycling Track	Graeme Obree, nicknamed The Flying Scotsman, is a Scottish racing cyclist who twice broke the world hour record, in July 1993 and April 1994, and was the individual pursuit world champion in 1993 and 1995. Obree has created some radical innovations in bicycle design and cycling position.	•	•		•
	Group sprint		Speed-Skating/ Cycling	A sprinter's team will target flat stages, creating a 'lead-out train' on the run into the finish or intermediate sprint. This train keeps the pace high and the leader tucks in at the back of the train, out of the wind. The lead-out men peel off one by one, getting faster and eventually leaving their rider at the front of the race, ideally with 250 m (820 ft) left to sprint to the line. The teams designated sprinter is supported by another sprinter who, they will follow in hectic final km's, their helper jostles for position and helps move the sprinter to the front of the pack.	•	•		•
	Drafting		Cycling/ Cross-Coun- try, etc.	Drafting or slipstreaming is a technique where two vehicles or other moving objects are caused to align in a close group reducing the overall effect of drag due to exploiting the lead object's slipstream. Especially when high speeds are involved, as in motor racing and cycling, drafting can significantly reduce the paceline's average energy expenditure required to maintain a certain speed and can also slightly reduce the energy expenditure of the lead vehicle or object.	•	•		•

4							
Severiano Ballesteros	1970s/80s	Golf	Was a Spanish professional golfer, a World No.1, who was one of the sport's leading figures from the mid-1970s to the mid-1990s; he is generally regarded as the greatest Continental European golfer of all time; Seve was the creator of several special shots	•	•	(•)
Becker hecht	1986	Tennis	Flying lunge, demonstrated by Boris Becker	•	•	(•)
Two handed forehand	1980s/90s	Tennis	Monica Seles two handed forehand ranks among the most effective—and unusual—shots in the annals of tennis; her brother played tennis, she asked father to teach her too, he read books on that, most importantly taught her to love it, and to hit it with two hands	•	•	(•)
Federer Forehand grip	2000s	Tennis	Roger Federer's hold on the racket is a modified Eastern grip version. Many tennis analysts and experts considered this to be more conservative, but his forehand is more adaptable and efficient compared to many tennis pros on tour today. With his amazing forehand, he is able to generate powerful passing shots, awesome topspin and an array of various shot selection in every game. Timothy Gallwey mentioned the grip in his influential 1974 book The Inner Game of Tennis	•	•	(•)
Biwott	1968	3000 m Steeple-Chase	Biwott would sprint off much faster than the rest of the field. He went over the hurdles with feet together and, perhaps most unusual of all, he would sometimes hop on to the steeplechase barrier—known as the hedge—and then hop off again, landing on the same foot and clearing the water as if he were a triple-jumper. On a couple of occasions, he seemed jumped over the entire hedge and water in one gigantic leap. He was the only person to finish either race with dry feet, having not once entered the water after the hedge.	•	•	•
Tampa 2 defense	1975	American Football	Defense strategy; the linebacker simply reads the play at the snap, and when he sees a pass he drops back into coverage; Tony Dungy has freely admitted that he lifted the strategy from his time playing under Chuck Noll and Bud Carson with the Pittsburgh Steelers in 1975.	•	•	(•)

(continued)

Table A.4 (continued)

Category	Innovation	Year	Discipline	Brief description/insight	Non-techn.	Legal	Radical	Collective
	Mike Tyson	1985–2005	Boxing	Tyson had techniques there, we could talk for hours about Tyson's double ups, the famous Tyson shift, or his work from the southpaw stance, but unarguably his best moments came as he bridged that distance, on the way in as his opponents panic jabbed at him. The pressure, the slip and the counter were the essence of Tyson.	•	•	•	
	Banana kick	1997	Football	On June 3, 1997, the former left-back Roberto Carlos scored the most famous goal of his career: a beautiful free kick for Brazil in a 1-1 tie against France in the opening game of the 1997 Tournoi de France (the ball was headed to the corner flag, then it curved back, glanced the edge of the post, and stopped only when it hit the net.). That goal was the catalyst for lots of studies and analysis about aerodynamics and the ball's curve (Magnus Effect).	•	•	(•)	
	From style to speed	1972	Badminton Doubles	Koh Chris, known as a remarkable playmaker along the baseline during his prime, believes that because badminton isn't a contact sport, height isn't a huge factor. Small players can compensate for their lack of height with agility. He used his gift of speed to transform the game of badminton. His revolution started at the 1972 All England championship. At the time, men's doubles were stylish and relatively slow, relying mostly on carefully placed shots. Realizing they were unable to directly compete with European players, Christian Hadinata and Ade Chandra decided to use speed to completely transform the way professional badminton was played. Small players can compensate for their lack of height with agility. Success formula: great talent + speed + instinct + broad variety of shots.	•	•	(•)	•
	Periodization	1950s	All	Periodization is the systematic planning of athletic or physical training. The aim is to reach the best possible performance in the most important competition of the year. It involves progressive cycling of various aspects of a training program during a specific period. Conditioning programs can use periodization to break up the training program into the off-season, preseason, inseason, and the postseason. Periodization divides the year-round condition program into phases of training which focus on different goals.	•	•	(•)	(•)

#	Innovation	Year	Sport	Description				
	Jogging—Arthur Lydiard	1950s/60s	Running	Inventor of jogging, system of training, based on long, steady running rather than the interval training favored by European and American coaches.	•	•	•	(•)
	Jogging—Ernst van Aaken	1960s+	Running	Ernst van Aaken was a German sports physician and athletics trainer. Van Aaken became known as the 'Running Doctor' and was the founder of the training method called the Waldnieler Dauerlauf (German: "Waldniel endurance run"). He is generally recognized as the founder of the long slow distance method of endurance training.	•	•	•	(•)
5	Telemark	1883	Ski Jumping	The landing requires the skiers to touch the ground in the Telemark landing style, named after the Norwegian county of Telemark. This involves the jumper landing with one foot in front of the other, mimicking the style of Telemark skiing. Failure to comply with this regulation leads to the deduction of style points, issued by the judges; subjective performance criterion	•	•	(•)	•
	Forearm pass/bump	1958	Volleyball	The bump, professionally known as a pass, is the most basic and most essential skill in volleyball. The bump is used to hit a ball that is below the head, or at your platform as most volleyball players would call it, and is typically used as the first touch to receive a serve or to receive a hard-driven hit; missing information regarding the development	•	•	•	•
	Possession soccer	1924	Football	Idea of possessing the ball with short passes rather than playing the direct, end-to-end style that was the British trademark. Largely dismissed in England, Jimmy Hogan's doctrine became a staple of the European game as his former players became the coaches that shaped future generations of players.	•	•	•	•
	Spin technique	1976	Shot Put	Shot put with a discus-style turn; no fewer than four coaches have been credited with its invention in the late 1950s and early 1960s: Toni Nett (Germany), Victor Alexeyev (USSR), Bob Ward (U.S.), and Klement Kerssen Brock (Czechoslovakia)	•	•	•	•

(continued)

Table **A.4** (continued)

Category	Innovation	Year	Discipline	Brief description/insight	Non-techn.	Legal	Radical	Collective
	Zonal marking	1990s	Soccer	Today, two major types of defense strategy are distinguished. The classic 'catenaccio' system is based on man-to-man marking, in which defenders are assigned a specific opposition player to mark, additionally employing a libero (free man behind the defensive line) as backup when needed. In zonal defending, however, defenders control specific areas instead of certain players. The underlying idea is completely different: "the man out of possession is just as important as the man in possession . . . football is not about eleven individuals but about the dynamic system made up by those individuals." In fact, a kind of zonal marking has been the first way defense was played. As it lacked organization (and therefore also referred to as 'chaos marking'), there is a vast difference to the modern zonal marking though.	•	•		•
	Fosbury Flop	1968	High Jump	Running in a curve and jumping backwards over the bar	•	•	•	•
	O'Brien Shift	1950s	Shot Put	Facing away from the direction of the throw, turning by 180°	•	•	•	•
	V-Style	1980s	Ski Jumping	Spreading the tips of the skis into a 'V' shape	•	•	•	•
	Jump Shot	1930s	Basketball	Shooting the basketball while jumping	•	•	•	•
	Forward Seat	1900s	Equestrian Jumping	Rider's weight is centered forward in the saddle over the horse's withers	•	•	•	•
	Flip Turn	1930s	Backstroke Swimming	Going under water when turning (tuck position)	•	•	•	•
	Dolphin Kick	1952	Butterfly Swimming	Beating the legs in unison, similar to a fish tail; what started out as seemingly unusual behavior by one swimmer is now a must do if you want to be successful (fastest form of swimming)	•	•	•	•
	Skate Skiing technique	1985	Cross Country Skiing	Pushing off the edges of the ski as in ice skating	•	•	•	•

A.3 Exemplary Illustration of Quotes Regarding Key Variables

Table A.5 Exemplary quotes Fosbury Flop

Category	Fosbury Flop, Dick Fosbury
Sudden change of external parameter	
Negative parameter of the sport	
Frustration	"... I was the worst high jumper on our team and in our league and I was very frustrated ..." (IOC 2014b, 00:11–00:14).
Dysfunctionality physical givens vs. style	"... his tall height (1.93 m) hampered his ability to maximize [*vic*] his potential using the prevailing straddle method ..." (IOC 2014a).
'Lack of talent'	
Old style	"Failing to master the straddle, Fosbury reverted to a scissors, then modified by going over the bar backward" (USATF Hall of Fame, "Dick Fosbury". n.d.).
Natural, instinctive (vs. cultural)	
Experienced in other area/seen before w/o success	
Open mind	
Not main focus	
Competition as catalyst	"An interesting point was that the entire evolutionary process took place solely at competitions." (Goldenberg et al. 2010, p. 41); "Competitors brought out the best in me" (Zarkos 2004, section "Best Day Ever", para. 3).
Physics explanation	"... by lowering his center of gravity by stretching out on his back he could actually jump higher" (Durso 1986, para. 5).
Others/help	"... the connection that I felt at the time was with my home town. The people that had supported me, even when it looked like I was failing. It was something that I'll never forget" (IOC 2014a, para. 3).
Coaches' reaction	"Fosbury continued to clear the bar at increasing heights, and his coaches no longer tried to stop him" (Fuqua 2014, para. 11).
Officials' resistance	"... skepticism [*vic*] from judges and coaches ..." (IOC, "Mexico 1968". n.d., textual video description); "Despite Fosbury's achievement, critics said the flop was dangerous, impractical and would not last" (Zarkos 2004, para. 3).
Ridicule	"... There was laughter everywhere, they couldn't believe what they were seeing ..." (BBC World Service 2011, 04:06–04:10).
Harder to learn	"Most of the early adopters came from secondary-level jumpers who could risk learning a new style ..." (Goldenberg et al. 2004, p. 154).
Negative consequence(s)	"His innovation was not immediately embraced, partly because of safety concerns" (Burnton 2012, para. 20).
Systematic, evolutionary process	"... involved a continuous slow evolution in the technique." (Goldenberg et al. 2010, p. 40).
Environmental change	"beginning in 1964 ... Fosbury's high school changed the landing pits by adding chunks of foam (cut up mattresses) under a net" (Goldenberg et al. 2010, p. 41).
Innovators characteristics	"Before he springs from the pad ... Dick Fosbury meditates, worries, psyches himself. Once he pondered four and a half minutes before approaching the bar" (Durso 1986, para. 2); "... showed an aptitude for science and mathematics at a very early age" (IOC 2014a, para. 1).

Table A.6 Exemplary quotes Jump Shot

Category	Jump Shot, Smawley, Sailors, Palmer, Minor, Skoog, Burton, Cooper
Sudden change of external parameter	"Cooper discovered the jump shot by accident" (Fury 2016, p. 16). Minor's "shot came from instinct, not deliberation" (Christgau 1999, p. 86).
Negative parameter of the sport	"... getting clear was the main thing on his mind as he walked ..." (Christgau 1999, p. 38, John Burton).
Frustration	"Meanwhile he had already suffered too many losses, already been knocked down too many times" (Christgau 1999, p. 195, Kenny Sailors).
Dysfunctionality physical givens vs. style	"... the taller men slapped the ball away effortlessly" (Christgau 1999, p. 38, John Burton).
'Lack of talent'	
Old style	
Natural, instinctive (vs. cultural)	Minor "... leaped for the shot with the same explosive spring that had carried him over the Froebel fence ..." (Christgau 1999, pp. 82–83); Smawley "... went into the same deep crouch he had used to explode off both feet when he jumped to touch higher and higher oak limbs" (Christgau 1999, p. 171).
Experienced in other area/seen before w/o success	"... explosive leaping ability he had developed on ski jumps" (Christgau 1999, p. 12, Skoog); Bud Palmer "... could remember playing lacrosse and disobeying one of its commandments ..." (Christgau 1999, p. 68).
Open mind	
Not main focus	"... he was too small and weak still to get a heavy basketball to the hoop without launching it with a leap" (Christgau 1999, p. 59, Bud Palmer was very young when he first jumped).
Competition as catalyst	"Myer took one long step that launched him into the air. None of the Bemidji fans would have seen the parallels" (Christgau 1999, p. 8).
Physics explanation	
Others/help	
Coaches' reaction	"His coach's disapproval was immediate. 'Skoog, you hot dog!' ... 'You're gonna sit down until you learn to shoot free throws correctly!'" (Christgau 1999, p. 11).
Officials' resistance	"... you never left the floor in basketball, *you never jumped*" (Christgau 1999, p. 194).
Ridicule	"Much later, Bud would laugh deeply and insist that his little brother's first awkward jump shot hadn't reached the backboard, or even hit the windmill" (Christgau 1999, p. 195, Kenny Sailors).
Harder to learn	Other "players tried secretly to learn the shot. ... 'Man, I don't know what the hell you're doin'.'" (Christgau 1999, p. 87, Minor).
Negative consequence(s)	"... first awkward jump shot ..." (Christgau 1999, p. 195, Kenny Sailors); "'I don't want you shootin' that shot!' ... 'No one shoot that damn shot!' ... 'Except Minor'" (Christgau 1999, p. 86, Dave Minor).
Systematic, evolutionary process	
Environmental change	In 1925 a basketball coach "argued for more freedom in shooting"; in 1933 another coach claims that it is "necessary for the sake of impetus that a player 'leave his feet' ..." (Christgau 1999, pp. 13–14).
Innovators characteristics	

Table A.7 Exemplary quotes Forward Seat

Category	Forward Seat, Tod Sloan	Forward Seat, Federico Caprilli
Sudden change of external parameter	"One day he and another jockey were galloping their horses together when his horse started to bolt; in trying to regain control Tod climbed up out of the saddle and onto the horse's neck" (Dizikes 2000, p. 58).	
Negative parameter of the sport		"… the horse is inflicted with aches and pains induced by the rider who mounts it, and thus learns to jump badly and to refuse …" (Caprilli 1901, in section "De Salto [Of the Jump]")
Frustration		
Dysfunctionality physical givens vs. style		
'Lack of talent'		
Old style	"Tod picked up hints of it from the white and African-American stable boys who exercised horses without proper equipment and with no previous training; and there was still older tradition of Native Americans riding bareback up on the necks of their horses" (Dizikes 2000, p. 62).	
Natural, instinctive (vs. cultural)		"Caprilli spent many years studying the natural movements of the horse …" (Self 1952, p. 8).
Experienced in other area/seen before w/o success		
Open mind		
Not main focus		
Competition as catalyst		
Physics explanation	"It significantly reduced wind resistance. It moved the rider's center of gravity forward and afforded him a better look ahead" (Dizikes 2000, p. 60).	
Others/help		
Coaches' reaction		
Officials' resistance	"… it was opposed by the 'pragmatists'. They believed, for example, that on descending from a jump the rider must lean backwards to save the horse from the jar of the rider's weight on landing, and to save it from a fall if it stumbled" (Fox and Mickley 1987, p. 97); "… I cannot believe that, generation after generation, jockeys have been sitting on the wrong part of a horse's back, that the best place for the saddle is not where it has always been …" (Dizikes 2000, pp. 59–60).	
Ridicule	"bring down on himself hoots of laughter from the audience" (Self 1952, p. 169); "crouch seat," or the "monkey mount" (Dizikes 2000, p. 59).	
Harder to learn		
Negative consequence(s)		
Systematic, evolutionary process	"… revealed itself gradually, as a continuous evolution, not as a single moment" (Dizikes 2000, p. 62).	
Environmental change		
Innovators characteristics	"But I was too cocksure to be discouraged. I was certain that I was on the right track. I persevered, and at last I began to win races!" (Dizikes 2000, p. 59).	

Table A.8 Exemplary quotes Flip Turn

Category	Flip Turn, Albert Vande Weghe
Sudden change of external parameter	
Negative parameter of the sport	
Frustration	
Dysfunctionality physical givens vs. style	"I always had trouble swinging my heavy legs around with the old turn, and while training with Mickey I started bringing them out of the water. This was so much easier and faster for me that I used it thereafter" (Wigo 2017a).
'Lack of talent'	
Old style	
Natural, instinctive (vs. cultural)	
Experienced in other area/seen before w/o success	"the 'tuck' position of the turn was no doubt influenced by his diving experience" (Wigo 2017a).
Open mind	
Not main focus	
Competition as catalyst	
Physics explanation	
Others/help	"Mickey Vogt and I developed it while practicing at the Newark AC late in 1933" (Wigo 2017a).
Coaches' reaction	
Officials' resistance	
Ridicule	
Harder to learn	
Negative consequence(s)	
Systematic, evolutionary process	"Mickey Vogt and I developed it while practicing at the Newark AC late in 1933" (Wigo 2017a).
Environmental change	
Innovators characteristics	

Table A.9 Exemplary quotes Dolphin Kick

Category	Dolphin Kick, Armbruster/Sieg	Dolphin Kick, Vilson Volney
Sudden change of external parameter		
Negative parameter of the sport		
Frustration		
Dysfunctionality physical givens vs. style		
'Lack of talent'		
Old style		
Natural, instinctive (vs. cultural)		"... he began to seriously think about the different ways that animals propelled themselves through water. At the aquarium, he noticed that fish moved their tails from side to side, while mammalian aquatic animals, such as whales and dolphins, moved their tails up and down" (Doezema 2016, para. 4).
Experienced in other area/seen before w/o success	"Armbruster's conversation with Corsan in 1911 regarding the fish-tail kick lay fallow for more than two decades in the inner sanctum of Armbruster's mind ..." (Barney and Barney 2008, p. 19).	
Open mind		
Not main focus		"Wilson, an idealistic young physicist ...", "As a student Wilson had analyzed the motions of swimming fish and invented the competition style known as the Dolphin ..." (Rhodes 2012, p. 422).
Competition as catalyst		
Physics explanation	"... in the Dolphin (fish-tail) kick, force is being exerted continuously, with no lost efficiency of effort or movement in relation to propelling force ..." (D. A. Armbruster and Sieg 1935, p. 25).	
Others/help	"... their work together ..." (Barney and Barney 2008, p. 19).	
Coaches' reaction		
Officials' resistance	"If Armbruster had couched the dolphin kick in language introducing the idea of an entirely new competitive stroke, instead of attaching it to the idea of altering, yet once again, the historically-oriented breaststroke, we might have seen the introduction of what we know today as the butterfly stroke by the mid-1930s instead of almost 20 years later" (Barney and Barney 2008, p. 20).	
Ridicule		
Harder to learn	"It's a tough kick to master ..." (Doezema 2016, para. 8).	
Negative consequence(s)		
Systematic, evolutionary process	"Sieg's progress under Armbruster's tutelage was steady and proved pro-missing" (Barney and Barney 2008, p. 19); "Experiment after experiment, photo session after photo session, time-trial after time-trial ..." (Barney and Barney 2008, p. 19).	"In the pool at the Chicago Athletic Club, he began to experiment with a new kind of leg movement for human swimmers: the dolphin kick ..." (Doezema 2016, para. 4).
Environmental change	"... more than half a century would pass before the dolphin kick would gain exclusivity as the only kick that the rules allowed when swimming butterfly" (Barney and Barney 2008, p. 19).	
Innovators characteristics		

Table A.10 Exemplary quotes Skate Skiing

Category	Skate Skiing, Pauli Siitonen	Skate Skiing, Bill Koch
Sudden change of external parameter		
Negative parameter of the sport		"after problems with his waxing" (Paal and Corradini 2007, p. 142); "For a long time cross-country ski racers skated in order to take advantage of terrain or to combat poor wax, although it was difficult to do over grooved tracks and in a narrow corridor" (Bengtsson n.d., para. 1); "... das Wachsen dabei das größte Problem" (Hottenrott and Urban 2004, p. 31).
Frustration		
Dysfunctionality physical givens vs. style		
'Lack of talent'		
Old style		"... skating has been with us for hundreds, if not thousands, of years ... was in regular use in the earlier part of the 20th Century, when the alpine disciplines were beginning to break away from the traditional Nordic events ... For decades the skating techniques lay forgotten or ignored by racers ..." (Paal and Corradini 2007, p. 142).
Natural, instinctive (vs. cultural)		
Experienced in other area/seen before w/o success	"During his time as a ski-orienteer, Siitonen had learned to ski using single-sided free technique whilst reading the map and navigating" (Paal and Corradini 2007, p. 142).	
Open mind		
Not main focus		
Competition as catalyst	"... Siitonen hatte sich 1972 bei einem Volkslauf, als er verwachst hatte, der einstmals nicht unüblichen Methode entsonnen" (Haffner 2004, in section "Erst verwachst, dann verehrt").	
Physics explanation	"Das effektive Zusammenspiel von Armen und Beinen ermöglicht in der Skatingtechnik optimale Kraftübertragungen" (Hottenrott and Urban 2004, p. 188).	
Others/help		
Coaches' reaction		
Officials' resistance		"... some officials tried to ban its use and others simply added so much vertical climb to courses that the technique was unusable. Some World Cup competition organizers tried to build up 'Snow Walls' along the classical tracks, but finally FIS, officials and organizers had to accept the evolution" (Paal and Corradini 2007, p. 142); "Officials ... were concerned that traditional cross-country racing was going to be corrupted. They wanted to ban skating entirely wherever prepared tracks existed. The ban did not happen, but at the 1983 FIS Congress the following rules were imposed ..." (Bengtsson, n.d., para. 7).
Ridicule		"Wieder wurde die neue Fortbewegungsart belächelt ..." (Haffner 2004, in section "Erst verwachst, dann verehrt").

(continued)

Table A.10 (continued)

Category	Skate Skiing, Pauli Siitonen	Skate Skiing, Bill Koch
Harder to learn	"Die Skatingtechniken haben auf Grund ihrer Dynamik einen hohen Aufforderungscharakter" (Hottenrott and Urban 2004, p. 32).	
Negative consequence(s)	"... auf einer akkurat gespurten klassischen Loipe verzichtet man darauf, um diese nicht zu zerstören" (Schlickenrieder and Elbern 2003, p. 101); "Anfängliche Einwände seitens einiger Sportmediziner hinsichtlich vorprogrammierter Belastungsschäden an den Gelenken (insbesondere am Sprung-, Knie- und Hüftgelenk) durch die Skatingbewegung haben sich nicht bestätigt" (Hottenrott and Urban 2004, p. 188).	
Systematic, evolutionary process	"... it has been a long and gradual process of evolution ..." (Paal and Corradini 2007, p. 143).	"He also began to experiment with a 'new' technique borrowed from speed skaters, holding his skis at an angle with the tips outward and pushing off the inside edge" (Paal and Corradini 2007, p. 142).
Environmental change	"... Veränderungen der Schneeunterlage durch den Einsatz von Präparierungsmaschinen" (Theiner and Karl 2002, p. 55); "Im Tiefschnee kann man nicht richtig skaten ..." (Schlickenrieder and Elbern 2003, p. 101).	
Innovators characteristics	"This technique, together with Siitonen's natural ability and training, brought him huge success" (Paal and Corradini 2007, p. 142).	

Table A.11 Exemplary quotes V-Style

Category	V-Style, Jan Boklöv	V-Style, Miroszlav Graf
Sudden change of external parameter	Im Training "blies der Wind stark von vorn, im Flug schob Boklöv den Oberkörper weiter nach vorn als sonst, plötzlich rissen die Ski weit auseinander und er flog fast 20 Meter weiter als vorher" (Nedo 2016, para. 3).	
Negative parameter of the sport		
Frustration		
Dysfunctionality physical givens vs. style		
'Lack of talent'	"Wäre der Schwede mit mehr Talent gesegnet gewesen ..." (Eiberle 2010, para. 2).	
Old style		
Natural, instinctive (vs. cultural)		
Experienced in other area/ seen before w/o success		
Open mind		
Not main focus		
Competition as catalyst		
Physics explanation	"... changed his center of gravity, leaned forward, and let his skis slide apart to form a V. This made his profile wider, which allowed him to control his speed and altitude for longer, lengthening the jump" (Svensson, n.d., para. 4).	
Others/help		
Coaches' reaction		
Officials' resistance	"some judges deducted points for reasons that his unconventional style looked neither safe nor attractive"; "traditionalists voicing concern that a sport of elegance and beauty could degenerate into a crude form of gymnastics" (both Ashburner 2003, p. 84); "... ski jump judges, tried to block the efforts of the 'crazy Swede' through the International Ski Federation ..." (Svensson, n.d., para. 3).	
Ridicule	"Boklöv was known as a 'flapping crow'" (Svensson, n.d.); "Er musste ja selbst über sich lachen. 'Es sah einfach zu komisch aus. Wie ein Witz', sagt Jan Boklöv. Und so störte es ihn auch nicht, dass die anderen Athleten über ihn lachten und er von den Stadionsprechern als 'der Froschspringer' angekündigt wurde"(Nedo 2016, para. 1).	
Harder to learn	"V-Stil ein sehr riskantes Element hat.", "Um früh in die günstige Ausgangsposition zu kommen, müssen die Springer einen Salto vorwärts provozieren, um dann eine stabile Fluglage einzunehmen" (Michalek 2017).	
Negative consequence(s)	"... led to a major revision of the sizes of hills used for major competitions" (Ashburner 2003, p. 83); "... problem of drastic weight reduction among the jumpers ..." (Ashburner 2003, p. 86).	
Systematic, evolutionary process	"Ich brauchte viel Zeit", sagt Boklöv. "Mal gelang mir ein guter Sprung, dann bin ich wieder gestürzt. Ich habe es einfach sehr oft probiert" (Nedo 2016, para. 5).	
Environmental change		
Innovators characteristics	"young, stuttering, religious, epileptic red-head" (Svensson, n. d., para. 1); "Zumal Boklöv immer schon als zurückhaltender, eigenbrötlerischer Typ galt" (Nedo 2016, para. 5).	

Table A.12 Exemplary quotes O'Brien Shift

Category	O'Brien Shift, Parry O'Brien
Sudden change of external parameter	
Negative parameter of the sport	
Frustration	"... after losing to Otis Chandler in the Fresno Relays, he returned home to Santa Monica, Calif. At 3 the next morning, by street lights on a vacant lot next door, he experimented with a 180-degree turn" (Litsky 2007, para, 4–5).
Dysfunctionality physical givens vs. style	
'Lack of talent'	
Old style	
Natural, instinctive (vs. cultural)	
Experienced in other area/seen before w/o success	
Open mind	"He searches for tricks that help him 'dig deep into what you might call an inner reserve of strength.' a search that has taken him into studies of physics and aerodynamics, through a canvass of religions and a long flirtation with the postural exercises and 'positive thought' notions of yoga" (*TIME Magazine* 1956, p. 38).
Not main focus	
Competition as catalyst	"I do not put well in practice," he said. "I save my best for competition. I am no pasture performer" (Maule 1960, para. 9).
Physics explanation	"It's an application of physics which says that the longer you apply pressure or force to an inanimate object, the farther it will go ..." (Elliott 2007, para. 11).
Others/help	
Coaches' reaction	
Officials' resistance	
Ridicule	
Harder to learn	"... very difficult task for throwers, especially younger throwers or combined event athletes" (Gemer 1990, p. 34).
Negative consequence(s)	
Systematic, evolutionary process	"... due to his unique and systematic preparation and well-designed strength training programme ..." (Gemer 1990, p. 33).
Environmental change	
Innovators characteristics	"... he is the epitome of the spirit of single-minded pursuit of perfection ..." (*TIME Magazine* 1956, p. 37).

References

Armbruster DA, Sieg JG (1935) The dolphin breast stroke. J Health Phys Educ 6(4):23–58

Ashburner T (2003) The history of ski jumping. Quiller Press, Shrewsbury

Barney DE, Barney RK (2008) A long night's journey into day: the odyssey of butterfly. J Olympic Hist 16(3):11–25

BBC World Service (2011) The Fosbury Flop [audio podcast]. https://www.bbc.co.uk. Accessed 12 Oct 2017

Bengtsson BE (n.d.) Cross-country skating: how it started. https://www.skiinghistory.org. Accessed 2 Mar 2018

Burnton S (2012) 50 stunning olympic moments no28: Dick Fosbury introduces the flop. The Guardian, May 8. https://www.theguardian.com

Caprilli F (1901) Per l' equitazione di campagna [For riding in the field]. Translation from the Italian by Dan Gilmore, Originally Published in Revista di Cavalleria, January–February. https://www.gilmorehorsemanship.com/caprillinaturalsystem.html

Christgau J (1999) The origins of the jump shot: eight men who shook the world of basketball. University of Nebraska Press, Lincoln, NE

Dizikes J (2000) Yankee doodle dandy: the life and times of Tod Sloan. Yale University Press, New Haven, CT

Doezema M (2016) The murky history of the butterfly stroke. The New Yorker, August 11. https://www.newyorker.com

Durso J (1986) Fearless Fosbury flops to glory. The New York Times, October 20. https://www.nytimes.com

Eiberle H (2010) Typen und Tüftler, Teil I – Wie ein Papierdrachen [Types and tinkerers, part I – like a paper kite]. Süddeutsche Zeitung, May 10. https://www.sueddeutsche.de

Elliott H (2007) Parry O'Brien, 75; Champion revolutionized shotput throw. Los Angeles Times, April 23. https://www.latimes.com

Fox MW, Mickley LD (1987) Advances in animal welfare science 1986/87, vol 3. Martinus Nijhoff, Dordrecht, Netherlands doi:https://doi.org/10.1007/978-94-009-3331-6

Fuqua B (2014) Fosbury takes track and field to new heights. The Corvallis Gazette-Times, March 29. https://www.gazettetimes.com

Fury S (2016) Rise and fire: the origins, science, and evolution of the jump shot – and how it transformed basketball forever. Macmillan, New York, NY

Gemer GV (1990) Overview of the shot put technique. IAAF New Stud Athl 5(1):31–34

Goldenberg J, Lowengart O, Oreg S, Bar-Eli M, Epstein S, Fosbury RD (2004) Innovation: the case of the fosbury flop. Marketing Science Institute (MSI) reports working papers series, no 04-106. https://www.msi.org

© Springer Nature Switzerland AG 2019

A.-K. Veenendaal, *Toward a Better Understanding of Rule-Breaking Market Behavior*, Contributions to Management Science, https://doi.org/10.1007/978-3-030-16107-1

Goldenberg J, Lowengart O, Oreg S, Bar-Eli M (2010) How do revolutions emerge? Int Stud Manag Organ 40(2):30–51. https://doi.org/10.2753/IMO0020-8825400202

Haffner S (2004) Tricks von gestern: revolutionen und Marotten [Tricks of yesteryear: revolutions and quirks]. Frankfurter Allgemeine Zeitung, January 10. https://www.faz.net

Hottenrott K, Urban V (2004) Das grosse Buch vom Skilanglauf [The big book of cross-country skiing]. Meyer & Meyer Verlag, Aachen

IOC (2014a) Leap of faith: Dick Fosbury on how a new jump style changed his sport forever. April 11. https://www.olympic.org

IOC (2014b) Leap of faith: Dick Fosbury on how a new jump style changed his sport forever [video interview]. April 11. https://www.olympic.org

IOC "Mexico 1968" (n.d.) Mexico 1968 athletics high jump men [video]. https://www.olympic.org. Accessed 17 Oct 2017

Litsky F (2007) Parry O'Brien, pioneer in shot-putting technique, dies at 75. The New York Times, April 23. https://www.nytimes.com

Maule T (1960) The shotput explosion. Sports Illustrated, April 25. https://www.si.com

Michalek G (2017) Die Geburtsstunde des V-stils [The birth of the v-style]. https://www.deutschlandfunk.de. Accessed 29 Sep 2017

Nedo J (2016) Der V-Stil im Skispringen: Jan Boklöv: Per Zufall zum Visionär [The v-style in ski jumping: Jan Boklöv: Visionary by chance]. Tagesspiegel, December 28. https://www.tagesspiegel.de

Paal E, Corradini A (2007) Worldloppet – 30 years of skiing around the world. Worldloppet International Ski Federation, Estonia. http://www.worldloppet.com/magazines/pdf/WL-anniversary-book-full.pdf

Rhodes R (2012) Making of the atomic bomb. Simon and Schuster, New York, NY

Schlickenrieder P, Elbern C (2003) Skilanglauf: Das Trainingsprogramm (Nordic walking) [Cross-country skiing: the training program (Nordic walking)]. Ehrenwirth, Bergisch Gladbach

Self MC (1952) Horsemastership: methods of training the horse and the rider. A. S. Barnes, New York, NY

Svensson H (n.d.) Evolution of skiing – ski jump. http://www.sporteventgellivare.com/en/evolution-of-skiing/evolution-of-skiing-ski-jump/. Accessed 25 Sep 2017

Theiner E, Karl C (2002) Skilanglauf: Geschichte, Kultur, Praxis [Cross-country skiing: History, culture, practice]. Die Werkstatt, Göttingen

TIME Magazine (1956) Faster, higher, farther. TIME Magazine, December 3, pp 36–41

USATF Hall of Fame "Dick Fosbury" (n.d.) Dick Fosbury. https://www.usatf.org. Accessed 12 Oct 2017

Wigo B (2017) History of the backstroke flip or somersault turn. [Information compiled by the ISHOF past president for the purpose of this work]. Taken from Letters in the ISHOF Archive. Copy in Possession of Author

Zarkos J (2004) Raising the bar: a man, the 'flop' and an Olympic gold medal. Sun Valley Guide. https://www.svguide.com

Printed by Printforce, the Netherlands